Economic Warfare and Sanctions Since 1688

How have economic warfare and sanctions been applied in modern history, with what success and with what unintended consequences? In this book, leading economic historians provide answers through case studies ranging from the eighteenth-century rivalry of Britain and France and the American Civil War to the two world wars and the Cold War. They show how countries faced with economic measures have responded by resisting, adapting to, or seeking to pre-empt the attack so that the effects of an economic attack could be delayed or temporarily neutralised. Behind the scenes, however, economic measures shaped the course of warfare: they moulded war plans, raised the adversary's costs of mobilisation, and tipped the balance of final outcomes. This book is the first to combine the study of economic warfare and sanctions, showing the deep similarities and continuities as well as the differences, in an integrated framework.

Stephen Broadberry is Professor of Economic History in the Department of Economics at the University of Oxford.

Mark Harrison is Emeritus Professor of Economics at the University of Warwick.

Economic Warfare and Sanctions Since 1688

Edited by

Stephen Broadberry
University of Oxford

Mark Harrison
University of Warwick

CAMBRIDGE
UNIVERSITY PRESS

Shaftesbury Road, Cambridge CB2 8EA, United Kingdom

One Liberty Plaza, 20th Floor, New York, NY 10006, USA

477 Williamstown Road, Port Melbourne, VIC 3207, Australia

314–321, 3rd Floor, Plot 3, Splendor Forum, Jasola District Centre, New Delhi – 110025, India

103 Penang Road, #05–06/07, Visioncrest Commercial, Singapore 238467

Cambridge University Press is part of Cambridge University Press & Assessment, a department of the University of Cambridge.

We share the University's mission to contribute to society through the pursuit of education, learning and research at the highest international levels of excellence.

www.cambridge.org
Information on this title: www.cambridge.org/9781009474894

DOI: 10.1017/9781009474887

© Cambridge University Press & Assessment 2026

This publication is in copyright. Subject to statutory exception and to the provisions of relevant collective licensing agreements, no reproduction of any part may take place without the written permission of Cambridge University Press & Assessment.

When citing this work, please include a reference to the DOI 10.1017/9781009474887

First published 2026

Cover image: WW II, naval warfare, U-Boat war: View through the periscope - a sinking enemy vessel hit by a U-boat torpedo.1942 from ullstein bild Dtl. / Contributor / Getty Images

A catalogue record for this publication is available from the British Library

Library of Congress Cataloging-in-Publication Data
Names: Broadberry, S. N. editor | Harrison, Mark, 1949- editor
Title: Economic warfare and sanctions since 1688 / edited by Stephen Broadberry, University of Oxford, Mark Harrison, University of Warwick.
Description: Cambridge, United Kingdom : Cambridge University Press, New York, NY, 2026. | Includes bibliographical references and index.
Identifiers: LCCN 2025025970 (print) | LCCN 2025025971 (ebook) | ISBN 9781009474894 hardback | ISBN 9781009474863 paperback | ISBN 9781009474887 epub
Subjects: LCSH: War–Economic aspects–History | Economic sanctions–History | International trade–Political aspects–History | Economics–Political aspects–History | Economic history
Classification: LCC HC79.D4 E265 2026 (print) | LCC HC79.D4 (ebook) | DDC 355.02/73–dc23/eng/20250815
LC record available at https://lccn.loc.gov/2025025970
LC ebook record available at https://lccn.loc.gov/2025025971

ISBN 978-1-009-47489-4 Hardback
ISBN 978-1-009-47486-3 Paperback

Cambridge University Press & Assessment has no responsibility for the persistence or accuracy of URLs for external or third-party internet websites referred to in this publication and does not guarantee that any content on such websites is, or will remain, accurate or appropriate.

For EU product safety concerns, contact us at Calle de José Abascal, 56, 1°, 28003 Madrid, Spain, or email eugpsr@cambridge.org

In memory
Nick Crafts (1949–2023)

Contents

List of Figures	*page* ix
List of Tables	xii
List of Contributors	xiv
Preface	xvii
Acknowledgements	xix

	Economic Warfare and Sanctions since 1688: An Overview STEPHEN BROADBERRY AND MARK HARRISON	1
1	The Second Hundred Years War: France vs Britain (1688–1815) LOÏC CHARLES AND GUILLAUME DAUDIN	28
2	Economic Warfare: The American Civil War W. WALKER HANLON, PAUL W. RHODE, AND HUGH ROCKOFF	56
3	Blockading Britain and Germany during World War I: Preparations, Conduct, and Consequences of Economic Warfare STEPHEN BROADBERRY AND TAMÁS VONYÓ	82
4	Can Economic Sanctions Work in a Smaller Conflict? The Italo-Ethiopian War of 1935–1936 MATTIA BERTAZZINI, JARI ELORANTA, AND ELINA KUORELAHTI	112
5	Economic Warfare against Japan, 1931–1945 TETSUJI OKAZAKI AND AKIRA OKUBO	142
6	War of Attrition: Economic Warfare between Britain and Germany in World War II MARK HARRISON AND HANS-JOACHIM VOTH	176

7 No Trading with the Enemy: COCOM Commemorated 216
VINCENT GELOSO AND ALBRECHT RITSCHL

8 From Condemnation to Action? United Nations
Sanctions on Rhodesia and South Africa 240
LEIGH A. GARDNER AND MARTINE MARIOTTI

Index 267

Figures

0.1 'Economic warfare' and 'economic sanctions': their frequency in printed books, 1860–2019	*page* 2
1.1 French and British income from predation, 1688–1815	35
1.2 French and British trade by value, 1688–1815	36
1.3 French and British naval budgets, 1688–1815	37
1.4. Evolution of naval supremacy during the Anglo-French wars, 1688–1815	39
1.5 Bullion at the Bank of England, 1796–1820	48
2.1 The US cotton trade with the UK, 1760–1860	58
2.2 Cotton prices in Liverpool and New York City, 1860–1875	59
2.3 The disposition of Southern cotton, 1861–1864	62
2.4 Quantity and price of cotton imported into the UK, 1855–1875	66
2.5 Poor Law relief expenditures in England and Wales, 1850–1870	68
2.6 UK wool and linen export values, 1856–1870	69
3.1 The Battle of the Atlantic, 1914–1918	86
3.2 UK net fixed capital formation, 1900–1920	89
3.3 UK nominal and real wheat prices, 1913–1938	106
4.1 Italy's import values by source, 1921–1940	121
4.2 Italy's imports of weapons by source, 1921–1940	122
4.3 Italy's imports of oil by source, 1921–1940	122
4.4 Italy's imports of coal by source, 1921–1940	123
4.5 Italy's export values by destination, 1921–1940	127
4.6 The burden of military expenditures on GDP of the Axis powers, 1920–1938	129
4.7 The share of defence in central government spending, 1920–1938	129
4.8 Depreciated tonnage of seventeen navies, 1923, 1928, 1933, and 1938	130
4.9 Modified national capability scores of four powers, 1920–1938	132

4.10	Military components of national capability scores of four powers, 1920–1938	132
4.11	Given names of newborn sons in Italy, 1920–1940	135
5.1	Japan's supply of crude oil, 1936–1944	155
5.2	Japan's merchant shipping: gains and losses, 1941–1945	159
5.3	Japanese shipbuilding: actual and counterfactual, 1942–1945	161
5.4	Pig iron and scrap iron in Japan's steel production, 1936–1944	162
5.5	Japan's iron and steel production, 1936–1944	164
5.6	Blockade, import substitution, and Japan's real GNP, 1930–1944	166
5.7	The government expenditure/private consumption trade-off: Japan, 1937–1944	167
5.8	Food consumption per capita: Japan, 1930–1945	168
5.9	Height for age of Japanese children born in 1924 and 1931	169
5.10	Naval shipbuilding by private and navy shipyards: Japan, 1931–1945	170
6.1	Germany's operational submarines and the sinking of Allied and neutral shipping, 1939–1945	182
6.2	Allied and neutral shipping tonnage sunk per U-boat lost, September 1939–May 1945	183
6.3	Allied bombing of economic targets in Axis Europe, 1940–1945	187
6.4	Bomb tonnage dropped by RAF Bomber Command per airplane lost, 1939–1945	188
6.5	Adult civilian male and female death rates at ages 45–75, UK, 1938–1945	192
6.6	Infant deaths and stillbirths, UK, 1936/38 (average)–1945	193
6.7	German war production, potential and actual, 1941–1944	201
6.8	Effects of Allied bombing on German railway wagon loadings across Reichsbahn Direktionen, 1944	202
6.9	War production and railway loadings, June 1944–March 1945	203
6.10	Mortality in Germany (including Bavaria), 1928–1945	207
6.11	Infant mortality in Germany (including Bavaria), 1928–1945	208
7.1	Car assembly lines at the Zwickau works, East Germany	227

7.2	Total factor productivity growth in four East European economies: effects of revising the growth of the capital stock, 1950s–1980s	229
7.3	Total factor productivity growth: effects of revising the growth of the capital stock, West versus East Germany, 1950s–1980s	230
8.1	GDP per capita of South Africa and Rhodesia, 1885–1960	245
8.2	GDP per capita of four African economies, 1960–1995	257
8.3	Rhodesia's tobacco exports and stocks under sanctions, 1965–1979	258
8.4	South Africa's gold exports, 1960–1995	260

Tables

0.1	Combat, economic warfare, and sanctions: how they work	*page* 6
0.2	Three centuries of economic warfare and sanctions: a subject map	9
0.3	The adversary's options under economic attack	14
1.1	Wars between France and Britain in Europe, 1688–1815	29
1.2	War and economic competition among the great powers	30
2.1	Timeline of the American Civil War, 1858 and 1861–1865	57
2.2	Southern attempts to run the Union blockade, 1861–1865	60
2.3	Production of important materials, 1860–1870	61
3.1	International grain price spreads, 1870–1913	83
3.2	Growth of cereal production, 1885–1913	84
3.3	Convoy sailings and losses	87
3.4	Net loss or gain in Allied and neutral shipping during 1918	87
3.5	British import value shares by region of origin	88
3.6	British agricultural output	91
3.7	Per 'man' calorie value of weekly quantities of food consumed in Britain	92
3.8	Share of Scandinavian and Dutch exports going to Germany	94
3.9	American exports to the Central Powers' neutral neighbours	95
3.10	German wartime rations compared with peacetime consumption	96
3.11	Female mortality in Germany and in England and Wales, 1913–1923	97
3.12	German foreign trade in current and constant prices	98
3.13	German agricultural output, 1913–1918	99
3.14	Contribution of the decline in imports to the reduction of food consumption in Germany between 1913 and 1918	100

List of Tables

4.1	World military exports: the shares of five great powers, 1925 and 1935	125
5.1	Outline of the 'Five-Year Plan of Important Industries'	153
5.2	Japan's import of petroleum, 1939–1943	156
5.3	Japan's supplies of scrap iron, 1936–1944	163
5.4	Japan's supplies of iron ore, 1936–1944	165
6.1	Bomb tonnage on the UK and on Axis Europe, 1940–1945	185
6.2	Food availability in the UK, 1939–1945	191
6.3	Real civilian outlays on consumer goods in Germany and the UK, 1938–1944	192
6.4	Notifiable infectious diseases per 10,000 residents, UK, 1939–1945	193
6.5.	Germany's gross national product and resources available, 1938–1943	195
6.6	German production, 1942–1945: Allied estimates of reduction attributed to Allied area bombing	200
6.7	Germany's war production shortfall and Allied bomb tonnage on economic targets in three periods, 1941–1945	204
6.8	Energy content of food rations for a German worker family member, 1939/40–1945/46	205
6.9	Feeding worker households in Germany in World War II	206
6.10	Notifiable infectious diseases per 10,000 residents in Germany in the two world wars	207
6.11	Bombing frequency and risk of resistance, Germany, 1943–1944	210
7.1	Real GDP per capita of four East European economies, 1950–1989	226
7.2	Assumed capital shares and implicit elasticity of capital/labour substitution of three East European economies and West Germany	230

Contributors

MATTIA C. BERTAZZINI, Assistant Professor, School of Economics, University of Nottingham, UK

STEPHEN BROADBERRY, Professor of Economic History, Department of Economics, University of Oxford, UK

LOÏC CHARLES, Professor, Department of Economics and Business Administration, Université Paris 8 Saint-Denis, France

GUILLAUME DAUDIN, Professeur des Université, Université Paris-Dauphine, Université-PSL, LEDA, CNRS, IRD, DIAL, Université Paris-Dauphine, France

JARI ELORANTA, Professor of Economic History, University of Helsinki, Finland

LEIGH A. GARDNER, Professor, Department of Economic History, London School of Economics, UK

VINCENT GELOSO, Assistant Professor of Economics, George Mason University, USA

W. WALKER HANLON, Associate Professor, Department of Economics, Northwestern University, USA

MARK HARRISON, Emeritus Professor of Economics, University of Warwick, UK

ELINA KUORELAHTI, University Lecturer, Center of European and Nordic Studies, University of Helsinki, Finland

MARTINE MARIOTTI, Professor of Economics, Research School of Economics, Australian National University, Australia

TETSUJI OKAZAKI, Professor, Faculty of Economics, Meiji Gakuin University, Japan

List of Contributors

AKIRA OKUBO, Associate Professor, Graduate School of Law, Nagoya University, Japan

PAUL W. RHODE, Professor, Department of Economics, University of Michigan, USA

ALBRECHT RITSCHL, Professor, Department of Economic History, London School of Economics, UK

HUGH ROCKOFF, Distinguished Professor of Economics, Rutgers University New Brunswick, USA

TAMÁS VONYÓ, Associate Professor of Economic History, Department of Social and Political Sciences, Bocconi University, Italy

HANS-JOACHIM VOTH, UBS Foundation Professor of Economics, Department of Economics, University of Zurich, Switzerland

Preface

This book was conceived in the summer of 2021. It seemed to us that the history of economic warfare and sanctions was ripe for further development.

We had previously collaborated on studies of the economics of the two world wars (Harrison 1998; Broadberry and Harrison 2005). Both books were made up of country studies; this framework did not allow for special attention to a thematic investigation of economic warfare. As a field of scholarship, economic warfare seemed to have been left in the 1960s. A re-evaluation of the evidence of two world wars was overdue. We knew of work on Germany in World War II that pointed in this direction (O'Brien 2015; Adena et al. 2020). We also knew that the field of inquiry ought to be much wider. Economic sanctions were by this time a major feature of the global economy, but their record was puzzlingly mixed. Among scholars of international relations there was disillusionment with both 'forever wars' and 'forever sanctions' (Drezner 2021). Finally, the histories of economic warfare and sanctions were clearly intertwined (Dehne 2019) – but what did this mean for how they worked and under what conditions they might have succeeded or failed?

We gathered a team of scholars – eighteen including ourselves – who were knowledgeable about the practices of economic warfare and sanctions over three centuries, and we commissioned the case studies that form the chapters of our book. We met once online, in November 2022, to discuss preliminary ideas and plan their further development; and a second time in person, in January 2024 in a Palazzo on Venice's Grand Canal, to discuss our draft chapters. In Venice our team was joined by Duncan Weldon and Richard Overy, who read our drafts and guided our discussions.

While we worked, we felt the influence of developments in scholarship and world events. New work (Mulder 2022) suggested that during the interwar period fear of sanctions might have had the unintended consequence of driving Germany, Italy, and Japan to pursue policies of autarky that led them to attack other countries in order to secure supplies of vital strategic resources. Was it possible, then, that economic warfare could be not only ineffective but actually counterproductive?

Growing concerns about the international conduct of Russia and China today renewed policy interest in Germany as a rising power in the late nineteenth century, the scope for containment by economic measures, and the risks of precipitating conflict.

In February 2022 these concerns boiled over with the Russian invasion of Ukraine. Western threats of unprecedented sanctions did not deter aggression beforehand. Imposed after the event, they did not stop it in its tracks. In the period that followed, it became apparent that economic warfare was again being waged across Europe on several fronts, raising increasingly existential questions. Could Ukraine survive the Russian attack on its civilian infrastructure? Could Western Europe survive without Russian energy exports? Could Russia survive Western sanctions?

We are economic historians, not forecasters. We did not set out to inform policy makers. But it has become apparent that everybody ought to know a little more about what happened in the history that this book describes.

References

Adena, Maja, Ruben Enikolopov, Maria Petrova, and Hans-Joachim Voth. 2020. 'Bombs, Broadcasts and Resistance: Allied Intervention and Domestic Opposition to the Nazi Regime during World War II.' CEPR Working Paper no. 15292. London: Centre for Economic Policy Research.

Broadberry, Stephen, and Mark Harrison, eds. 2005. *The Economics of World War I*. Cambridge: Cambridge University Press.

Dehne, Phillip A. 2019. *After the Great War: Economic Warfare and the Promise of Peace in Paris 1919*. London: Bloomsbury.

Drezner, Daniel W. 2021. 'The United States of Sanctions: The Use and Abuse of Economic Coercion', *Foreign Affairs* 100(5): 142–154.

Harrison, Mark, ed. 1998. *The Economics of World War II: Six Great Powers in International Comparison*. Cambridge: Cambridge University Press.

Mulder, Nicholas. 2022. *The Economic Weapon: The Rise of Sanctions as a Tool of Modern War*. New Haven, CT: Yale University Press.

O'Brien, Phillips P. 2015. *How the War Was Won: Air–Sea Power and Allied Victory in World War II*. Cambridge: Cambridge University Press.

Acknowledgements

We are grateful to many for assistance, advice, encouragement, and material support. Duncan Weldon and Richard Overy guided our thinking, placing their immense knowledge and experience at our disposal. The ESRC Centre for Advantage in the Global Economy (CAGE) research centre of the University of Warwick funded our Venice conference, and Jane Snape, Neil Rickatson, and Sarah Thomson coordinated our activities. At Cambridge University Press, Michael Watson channelled our enthusiasm and steered us to publication. Anonymous readers scrutinised our drafts and suggested improvements. Victoria Gierok prepared the Index to a very tight deadline. We thank them all.

Economic Warfare and Sanctions since 1688
An Overview

Stephen Broadberry and Mark Harrison

What results are to be expected when one country tries to damage another's trade or resources? Why have the results so often disappointed? What options are open to a country under external economic attack? What are the economic stratagems that can mitigate the attack on the economy? What processes can allow the attack to succeed, and on whose side is time? Must civilian lives and interests be the first casualties? Can economic measures be effective if unaccompanied by force or the threat of force? These are questions for which scholars of modern economics, history, and international relations appear to have few generally accepted answers.

Our book makes a team effort to look for clues in three centuries of global history. It provides a companion volume to our previous collections on the economics of the two world wars (Harrison 1998; Broadberry and Harrison 2005), supplemented recently by eBooks featuring research updates to mark the centennial of the end of World War I (Broadberry and Harrison 2018) and the 75th anniversary of the end of World War II (Broadberry and Harrison 2020).

Definitions

Our field is spanned by three ideas: warfare, economic warfare, and economic sanctions. In warfare, one country uses its fighting power to attack the fighting power of another with the purpose of weakening or destroying it. Violence is regulated only, if at all, by the laws of war.

For simplicity we distinguish two aspects of warfare. One is conventional war, when the armed forces of each side attack each other directly. There is a theatre of war in which battles are fought on land, at sea, or in the air. The other aspect is economic warfare, which we define as armed attack on the adversary's economy.

Economic sanctions also impose losses on the adversary's economy but in peacetime, using peaceful means.

Economic Warfare

The terms 'economic warfare' and 'economic sanctions' entered public discourse only in the twentieth century. Considering the frequency of the phrase in printed books in English, Figure 0.1 shows that economic warfare came first, spiking at the time of World War I. Economic sanctions, enshrined in the Covenant of the League of Nations followed quickly, spreading widely in the inter-war period. With World War II, economic warfare took back its first place in literary usage, especially because of the temporary establishment of a British government department, the Ministry of Economic Warfare. After 1945 the usage of economic warfare again declined, while the United Nations Charter once again put sanctions at the disposal of the international community, which turned to them more and more over the post-war decades.

In fact, both economic warfare and sanctions were in use long before the twentieth century. The fact that they were not yet named did not prevent their application.

Economic warfare is the attack on the adversary's economy. Its purpose is the same as of warfare generally: to impair the adversary's fighting power (Vickers 1943: 14; Medlicott 1952: 7). The essential difference is

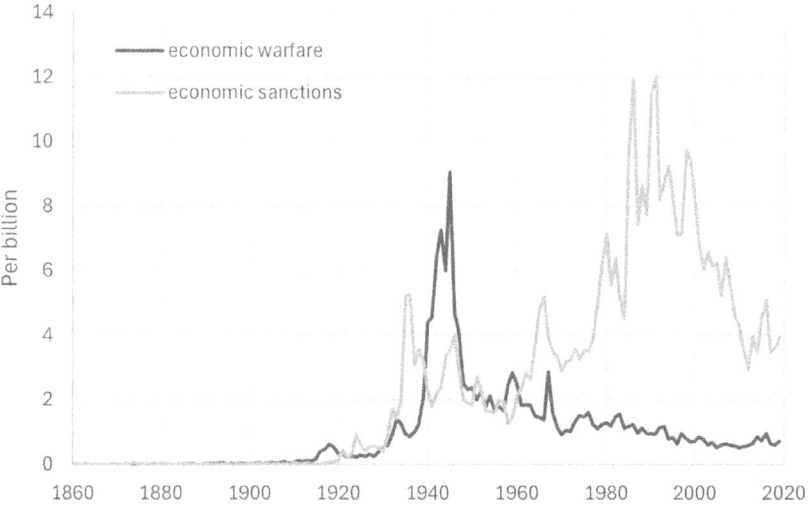

Figure 0.1 'Economic warfare' and 'economic sanctions': their frequency in printed books, 1860–2019 (per billion bigrams)
Source: A case-sensitive search for 'economic warfare', 1800–2019 (unsmoothed) on the Google Ngram viewer at https://books.google.com/ngrams/, using the English (2019) Google Books corpus. (A case-insensitive search is dominated by the existence of the UK Ministry of Economic Warfare, 1939–1945.)

that the adversary's fighting power is impaired not by direct attack but indirectly, by economic damage. In this sense, economic warfare is simply a specialized aspect of warfare generally.

The opportunity for economic warfare is created by the economic needs of fighting power. Fighting power must be financed by the government and supplied by the economy. This was always the case to some extent, but the industrialization of warfare has made it more so. The finance and supply of war have become the targets of economic warfare.

The finance and supply of war represent two sides of the production of fighting power. Historically this has provided economic warfare with two focal points. There is no established terminology to distinguish them; we call them 'demand-side focused' and 'supply-side focused'. In monetary economies, fighting power must be supplied and demanded. Demand-side-focused economic warfare started from the point at which the government pays for fighting power. To buy fighting services and equipment, the government must have means of payment, in other words gold (in the eighteenth century), sterling (in the nineteenth century), dollars (in the twentieth century), or credit. One way to get means of payment was by selling commodities or by borrowing in foreign markets. During the Napoleonic Wars, the purpose of naval blockades was usually to stop the adversary from getting gold by blocking their ships from export markets and by stealing their cargoes. Deprived of market access, the adversary could not earn gold and would become unable to finance its war.

This policy was justified, in part, by the prevailing economic doctrine of mercantilism which regarded access to export markets and the accumulation of gold as the means and measure of national power.

If fighting power must be supplied and demanded, supply-focused economic warfare started from the point of production and importation. The supply of fighting power was decided by domestic production and access to imports. By the time of the two world wars, the focus of blockade had switched from blocking the adversary's exports to blocking imports, which had the effect of reducing aggregate supply. The advent of long-range air power added a new capability, that of attacking domestic productive capacity directly.

This turn was soon harmonized with the then-new economics of national income accounting associated with J. M. Keynes. A country's national accounts made clear that the ultimate limit on the possible uses of resources was set by aggregate production capacity. If the supply side could be damaged by economic warfare, the adversary could continue to meet the extraordinary demands of military rearmament and war fighting only by imposing new sacrifices on the civilian sphere.

The particular effect of economic warfare is to weaken fighting power tomorrow, not today. Today's fighting power already exists, and it can only be attacked directly. But the production of fighting power takes time and resources. Today's fighting power will still be available tomorrow, only if civilian firms and households are given the time and the resources to make up today's losses. Attacking them makes fighting power less sustainable over time.

When does economic warfare make sense? In a war that can be won today, by direct attack alone, the attacker does not need to worry about the balance of fighting power tomorrow. Economic warfare is generally a feature of protracted conflicts. When today's fighting power is not enough to win a quick victory, and each side can only hold out while trying to wear the other down, targeting the adversary's future fighting power can become as important as fighting today's battles.

Economic warfare is primarily relevant, therefore, to wars of attrition. In a war of attrition, the winner is the side that turns out to have a superior capacity to bear losses. In the example of World War II (based on O'Brien 2015: 67–87), attrition was made up of the sum of losses at successive stages of the production of fighting power, of which the battlefield was only the final stage. Earlier stages involved losses in deployment, losses from stopped production, and losses in 'pre-production' (when production facilities were destroyed or never built). Economic warfare was aimed at the stages of production and preproduction: it contributed to losses by halting the production of equipment directly or by disrupting intermediate supplies, by dispersing the workforce, by destroying production facilities altogether, and by preventing the construction of new facilities.

Economic Sanctions

Like economic warfare, modern sanctions have a prehistory. From time to time in the nineteenth century the great powers practised a 'pacific blockade' or embargo of trade and exchange with a country that broke the international order; the intention was to coerce them by means short of war (Davis and Engerman 2006: 387–390). Later in the nineteenth century, the great powers imposed 'supersanctions' (a modern term, not used then) on smaller countries to enforce sovereign debt obligations when a default was threatened (Mitchener and Weidenmier 2010).

Economic sanctions were first given foundations in international law by the Covenant of the League of Nations after World War I. The experience of World War I suggested that Germany had suffered terribly from wartime blockade and had lost the war partly because of it. If blockade had helped to win the war for the Allies, perhaps the threat of blockade could help to keep the post-war peace (Dehne 2019, Mulder 2022). On similar arguments, sanctions were incorporated into the Charter of the United Nations after World War II and more recently in the European Union's Maastricht Treaty. Such sanctions were to be imposed by legislation and enforced in the courts by civil authorities and, if by armed force, then only in support of the civil power.

The manner of enforcement is a critical difference between economic sanctions and economic warfare. The *raison d'être* of sanctions has always been to resolve conflicts by legal means, without violence. This may seem to set sanctions and economic warfare far apart.

A closer look reveals deep similarities and connections. An obvious similarity is found in the attack on the adversary's economy. Economic sanctions and economic warfare both seek to make the adversary's power less sustainable, not directly, but indirectly by causing economic losses. Economic warfare threatens the adversary's military survival by reducing the resources available for future fighting power. Economic sanctions might undermine an aggressor's military survival in the same way, or they might threaten the adversary's political survival by reducing the resources available to the incumbent regime for co-option and repression. Either way, an incentive is created for the sanctioned regime to comply with the demands of the sanctioning authority.

Another similarity with economic warfare is that economic sanctions seem to have similar focal points, which we call demand (or finance) and supply. Discussing the period between the two world wars Mulder (2022: 203) contrasts the 'Treasury theory' of 'finance-based' or 'currency draining' measures (such as an embargo on the adversary's exports) with the more established 'Admiralty theory' of 'resource-based' or 'resource draining' measures that would throttle an aggressor's imports. Our own usage, and that of other authors in this book, will vary with the context. But the distinctions involved are roughly interchangeable with a focus on demand versus supply.[1]

Table 0.1 summarises our view of the similarities and differences of conventional warfare, economic warfare, and economic sanctions. Sanctions are applied in peacetime; war is the time for conventional warfare and economic warfare. In the first row, the similarities among

---

[1] Our distinction is foreign to the wider literature on sanctions (e.g. van Bergeijk 2021: 6–7; Jentleson 2022: 10), which typically distinguishes the main types as on trade (combining sanctions on exports with those on imports under one heading), on finance (combining lending with borrowing), and on various 'other' headings such as on non-state actors or on travel and so forth.

Table 0.1 *Combat, economic warfare, and sanctions: how they work*

	Wartime:		Peacetime:
	Conventional warfare	Economic warfare	Economic sanctions
Purpose:	Destroy or weaken power to resist	Destroy or weaken power to resist	Weaken power to resist
Means:	Campaigns and battles on land, at sea, and in the air	Commerce raiding, blockade, bombing, sabotage	Legal embargoes on foreign transactions
Transmission of effects:	Direct attack on armed forces	Indirect through finance and supply	Indirect through finance and supply

Source: See the text.

all three begin with purpose, which has always been to overcome an adversary's power to resist. A difference is that, while the goals of combat and economic warfare may be limited or unlimited, ranging from renegotiation to surrender, the goal of sanctions has generally been limited to shifting the balance rather than destroying it.

The table's next row shows the different means employed in each case. In conventional warfare, armed forces are directed against each other in combat. In economic warfare armed force is directed against the economy of the other side. The attack on the economy can take various forms from commerce raiding and blockade to bombing and sabotage. Conventional and economic warfare are both violent, regulated only by the laws of war, whereas economic sanctions take the form of legal embargoes appropriate to peacetime.

The final row of the table shows the transmission from cause to effect. In the case of conventional war, the transmission is direct: the adversary's power is impaired by losses in combat. In economic warfare and sanctions, the impairment is achieved indirectly by the damage caused to the adversary's finances or supplies.

This framework is simplified, not only because it omits such aspects of war as political or psychological warfare and nuclear war. It also ignores the many possible spillovers among the categories that we do consider. As discussed below, a sanction adopted as a step short of war on one side may look like an act of war on the other. The expectation of sanctions and economic warfare can decide which battles are fought, while the conduct of the attack on the economy can decide who wins them. Defending against the attack on the economy is an extension of conventional war. But the pace of conventional war can also be so rapid as to make economic warfare irrelevant. Unravelling such complexities in history has made our work both demanding and rewarding.

The simultaneous consideration of economic warfare with economic sanctions is a distinctive feature of our project. Our rationale is not only the similarities between economic sanctions and warfare, but also their historical connections, which are many and deep. As already noted, the modern idea of sanctions arose out of the great powers' experience of economic warfare against each other in the two world wars. Less well known is that in the American Civil War (Chapter 2) and both world wars (Chapters 3 and 6), while practising economic warfare against each other, the warring sides struggled simultaneously to monopolise access to the markets and supplies of the neutral powers by varying combinations of inducement and threat – in other words, by sanctions.

Most importantly, even if sanctions were always tried as a step short of war, this was not always how things turned out. When sanctions proved ineffective, and the sanctioning powers were too far committed to draw back, sanctions became a precursor of war (e.g. Lektzian and Sprecher 2007). Or the threat of sanctions could be too effective, posing an existential threat to which the sanctioned power responded by escalating violence. In that case, sanctions were a precipitant of war. 'These sanctions that are being imposed are akin to a declaration of war', Vladimir Putin said (on 5 March 2022) of the first Western responses to Russia's invasion of Ukraine.[2]

Therefore, we think it sensible to cover a wide range of adversarial uses of economic action, whether these were peacetime sanctions or acts of war.

Case Studies

In the field of economic warfare and sanctions, the bedrock of scholarship is made of case studies and historical narratives. For research on economic warfare there is no alternative method, because instances are too few and too varied to be studied in any other way than by the method of case studies.

Research on sanctions differs in that the number of cases available for study is now very large, with sanctions uses numbered in the hundreds in all decades from the 1970s. For that reason there are now several large-N sanctions datasets, coded numerically to enable quantitative analysis (van

---

[2] 'Putin says Western sanctions are akin to declaration of war', Reuters, 5 March 2022, available at www.reuters.com/world/europe/putin-says-western-sanctions-are-akin-declaration-war-2022-03-05/ (last accessed 23 August 2024).

Bergeleijk 2021: 1–2, 7). But while the number of cases is large, the problem of heterogeneity remains. The apparent clarity of numerical coding, for example, may be subverted by the wide range of roles available to the 'sender' (the sanctioning authority) and the even greater variety of adaptive responses of the 'target', which we discuss further below. As a result, scholars must continue to return to narratives and case studies because these may be the only way to capture the continuous interaction of sender and target and the rich array of choices available to both.

For that reason, in this introduction, we avoid the terminology of sender and target where possible. Depending on the context, we use the 'sanctioning power' (or 'authority') or the 'attacker' on one side and, on the other, the 'adversary' as the country that is under sanction or attack.

Similar considerations have made it a simple choice for us to base our project on case studies. Arranged chronologically, these form the chapters of our book. The chapters were selected to include well-known cases alongside others that are less well known. By this means we aimed to overcome a bias in the existing scholarship on economic warfare. The political scientist Paul Poast (2024) argues that the study of international security suffers from a 'Russia bias': it has drawn excessively on Russia's experiences of war over the twentieth century. In a similar spirit, we realised, the study of economic warfare has been characterised by a 'Germany bias': it is based largely on the experiences of a single country in the two world wars.[3]

To be sure, Germany's experiences are very important, and they are covered here in two of our eight chapters. But there should be more than Germany and more than two world wars, and we have included other cases to reflect this. Table 0.2 maps them chapter by chapter onto our field as we have described it above.

Chapter 1 ('The Second Hundred Years War: France vs Britain (1688–1815)', by Charles and Daudin) reviews a century of conflict in which two powers clashed repeatedly at sea, raiding each other's shipping

---

[3] Most of what we think we know about economic warfare can be traced back in some form to investigations conducted immediately after both world wars by the victorious powers as they tried to account for their victories over Germany: USSBS (1945), Medlicott (1952, 1959), Bell (1961, completed in 1937), and BBSU (1998, completed in 1946). These provided a foundation for later studies by historians and, more rarely, economists including Webster and Frankland (1961), Olson (1962, 1963), Milward (1977), Overy (1980, 1994, 2014), Hardach (1987), Mierzejewski (1988), Davis and Engerman (2006), Tooze (2006), Brauer and van Tuyll (2008), Kramer (2013), Biddle (2015), and Kramer et al. (2024).

Table 0.2 *Three centuries of economic warfare and sanctions: a subject map*

	Demand (market access) focus		Supply (capacity) focus	
Military actions:	Raiding trade and treasure	Chapters 1, 2	Naval blockade	Chapters 1, 2, 3, 5, 6
			Aerial bombing	Chapters 3, 5, 6
Economic sanctions:	Export embargo	Chapters 2, 4, 7, 8	Import embargo	Chapters 4, 7, 8

Source: see the text.

in order to seize cargoes and treasure. At stake was the market access of each side. The existence of neither side was threatened, and both could make concessions to the other if compelled, so each period of conflict typically ended in a new treaty that held for a while until the desire arose to renegotiate through renewed conflict. Towards the end of the period, however, both sides raised the stakes, having concluded that all-out war was a practical way to achieve their aims. Correspondingly the spasmodic raiding of trade and treasure gave way to a more comprehensive supply-focused blockade, which aimed to degrade the enemy's overall capacities.

Chapter 2 ('Economic Warfare: The American Civil War', by Hanlon, Rhode, and Rockoff) opens with an exercise in supply-focused sanctions. The Southern rebels sought to withhold cotton exports in the belief that the resulting shortage of cotton would create unemployment in the North and force the Union states to recognise the Confederacy. At the same time, the Confederate leaders hoped that the threat of a cotton famine would coerce Britain into neutrality or, better still, into favourable intervention on the Confederate side. In a curious parallel, the Union began the war with a demand-focused blockade of Southern exports, with the opposite expectation that this would undermine the war finances of the Confederacy. As the conflict dragged on and became a war of attrition, however, the Union switched the focus of blockade to supply, aiming to stop Confederate imports of munitions, ships, and other manufactured goods. It is not possible to identify the marginal contribution of the blockade to the defeat of the Confederacy; rather, the effects were merged with those arising from defeat on the battlefield. We will suggest below that this was typical of success in economic warfare.

The conflict described in Chapter 3 ('Blockading Britain and Germany during World War I: Preparations, Conduct, and Consequences of Economic Warfare', by Broadberry and Vonyo) became a war of attrition within weeks. Britain used its naval superiority to stop German shipping and maritime trade; Germany developed a powerful submarine fleet to do the same to Britain. The focus of both blockades was the adversary's supplies of imported food and war materials. The British economy, seemingly far more exposed to blockade, survived, drawing on a wide range of countermeasures to maintain shipping capacity, economise on the use of shipping, reduce consumption of importable goods, and boost agricultural production. The German economy eventually succumbed – but blockade was not the greatest of the pressures on supply. The single largest factor in the food shortage was the decline of supplies from domestic agriculture. This was a result of the excessive military mobilisation, which reallocated too many men and horses from Germany's farms into the military and diverted machinery and nitrate fertilisers into war industries.

Based on the experience of World War I, the victorious powers developed the idea of economic sanctions as a way of war prevention: an aggressor state could be deterred from going to war by the threat of economic isolation. Chapter 4 ('Can Economic Sanctions Work in a Smaller Conflict? The Italo-Ethiopian War of 1935–1936', by Bertazzini, Eloranta, and Kuorelahti) considers one of the notorious cases of the inter-war period when sanctions were tried and failed. In principle, the sanctions on Italy were far-reaching. Although this distinction was not made at the time, they were focused on both demand (embargoes on Italy's foreign exports and earnings, foreign credit, and borrowings) and supply (restrictions on Italy's imports of munitions and war materials). The problem, when Italy was threatened, was threefold. Mussolini's invasion of Ethiopia was part of a larger economic design to which he appeared to be committed and unwilling to concede. Fearing a wider conflict, the sanctioning powers were less than resolute; the prohibitions went largely unenforced and were quickly abandoned. And Italy retained other options, the most straightforward being closer commercial and military ties with Germany. Half-hearted sanctions were a double-edged sword, contributing to the increasing political alignment between the two countries from 1936.

The story of Chapter 5 ('Economic Warfare against Japan, 1931–1945', by Okazaki and Okubo) begins, like Chapter 4, with an aggressor state threatened by sanctions. In the 1930s, Japan, like Italy, became committed to a war of conquest, but against China. Germany's experience of Allied blockade in World War I had made Japanese leaders acutely aware of their dependence on imported supplies of war materials. They determined to secure a self-sufficient colonial empire in East Asia. Japanese aggression was met by talk of League sanctions against Japan's exports (of textiles, for example) and imports (of scrap iron, oil, and machinery). For fear of provoking a wider war, however, little was done until 1938. As talk turned to action, Japan widened its wars to attack the sanctioning powers. The Japanese attack on Pearl Harbor in December 1941 is a classic illustration of how sanctions can lead to a wider war. By 1942, Japan had roughly achieved its aim of a self-sufficient colonial sphere. The weak point was its dependence on maritime transport for economic integration. The United States now pivoted from sanctions to a submarine blockade. While disrupting the supply of Japan's war effort, the attack on coastal and inter-island shipping also increased its demands. As shipping losses rose, shipyards were converted to merchant shipbuilding while Japan's naval strength was diverted from battles in the Pacific to anti-submarine warfare. By means of production innovations and severe consumption sacrifices, Japan was able to postpone, but not avert, a progressive economic collapse.

A feature of Chapter 6 ('War of Attrition: Economic Warfare between Britain and Germany in World War II', by Harrison and Voth), shared with Chapters 4 and 5, is how the Axis powers anticipated the Allied blockade in their plans for conquest. This largely explains how a world war evolved from a series of border conflicts. Once the global war of attrition was in place, the blockades of World War II largely reprised those of World War I. A novel feature of economic warfare in the 1940s, however, was the rise of strategic air power. Both sides bombed each other's economy, but with different outcomes. While Germany lost patience with the indifferent outcomes of a relatively superficial assault on British industrial towns and ports, the Allies doubled down on a much larger air offensive that gradually hollowed out the German civilian economy. The process took much time and visible effects were long delayed. Nonetheless the rising intensity of Allied bombing and its increasing focus on overland transportation in occupied Europe together help to explain the collapse of the German war effort in 1944/45.

Chapter 7 ('No Trading with the Enemy: COCOM Commemorated', by Geloso and Ritschl) is set in the post-war period when, as between the wars, the great powers turned to economic sanctions for a peaceful means of conflict management that would avoid the cost of wars. In the late 1940s the United States, followed by Britain and other European partners, imposed an embargo on Western exports of munitions and dual-use equipment and materials to communist countries. The purpose was to weaken them militarily (by impeding the availability of munitions) and economically (by preventing their acquisition of leading-edge technologies – a novel consideration for the time). The chapter shows the difficulty of disentangling the effects on the adversary of two sources of economic friction – Western sanctions and the innately inefficient command economy. The chapter concludes that the economic effects of sanctions, although observable, were relatively small – and, in the case of Cuba, nearly non-existent. Consistently, the main Soviet-bloc countermeasure, industrial espionage, brought observable but small gains. The costs of the command economy were much greater than the costs of sanctions. Given that the communist leaders were willing to accept the costs, Western sanctions did not have any substantial political effects either.

Chapter 8 ('From Condemnation to Action? United Nations Sanctions on Rhodesia and South Africa', by Gardner and Mariotti) investigates the contribution of sanctions relative to other forces in ending the white-supremacist regimes of two countries of Southern Africa. The external sanctions were, on the face of it, coercive: they aimed to compel a peaceful handover of power to the majority. They were primarily demand focused, aiming to block the two countries' exports and access to international credit. Their dependence on imported oil was also targeted as a weak link in supply. In both countries, the white elites accepted a degree of economic isolation as the price of preserving minority rule. They were also able to redirect trade. Rhodesia had access to hydroelectric power, and South Africa was wealthy enough to develop its own synthetic oil industry (as Germany had done in the 1930s). Some white elites gained assets at discounted prices when foreign firms had to divest, or by association with state projects to replace imports. The costs of living under sanctions were substantially displaced onto African workers. The sanctions were in place for decades, were far from comprehensive, and were accompanied by internal resistance that did not shrink from armed insurgency. When apartheid was ended, sanctions were lifted, but the extensive government controls that had managed adaptation to sanctions did not disappear.

Key Themes

Preparations–Conduct–Consequences

We study economic warfare and sanctions in three phases: preparations, conduct, and consequences. The need to study preparations and consequences may seem obvious: we want to understand the spirit in which policy makers approached conflict and to evaluate the success or failure of their plans.

Comparing the preparations and consequences of economic warfare and sanctions raises many questions. Some questions are economic: how did those in charge of the design of economic warfare expect the adversary's economy to respond to attack? A fragile economy will be more immediately affected than a resilient one; how did they understand the sources of resilience and fragility? Other questions go beyond the economy. In peacetime, how were sanctions expected to work on the finance and supply of the target regime to restrain its behaviour? In wartime, how was economic warfare to be coordinated with combat to produce victory? Answers to these questions are required for us to trace the arrow of causation from preparations to outcomes.

If the need to study preparations and consequences is obvious, what links them is conduct. During the long peace since 1945, economic historians have paid little attention to the conduct of warfare, leaving it largely to military historians and international relations specialists. Conduct also matters, however, because conduct is the stage at which instruments prove themselves (or not) in action. It is also the stage at which the adversary takes a hand. And expectations of how the conduct stage will work out must also influence preparations.

Implementing such a framework throws up many difficulties. Until World War I, preparations to raid or block the adversary's trade relied more on the traditions and experiences that made sense out of them than on clearly articulated concepts and objectives. This was especially the case for British and French naval warfare from 1688 to 1918 (Chapters 1 and 3). There was also improvisation, such as Germany's unprecedented submarine blockade of World War I (also Chapter 3), which relied on vessels acquired to counter another contingency (the expected close blockade of German ports) that did not happen.

After World War I, all the powers engaged in focused study of the blockades (Chapters 3, 4, 5, and 6). They selected lessons that they found congenial and applied them while mobilising for the next war. World War II then gave economic warfare another novel dimension, that of strategic bombing, in which improvisation and learning by doing were key elements on both sides (Chapter 6).

A final difficulty is that in most cases that we discuss, the consequences of the attack on the economy remain hard to disentangle from the outcomes of a slow drip-feed or sudden avalanche of other measures that impede clear identification in retrospect. Rare exceptions are chiefly failures: the American Confederacy's failed attempt to sanction Britain by blocking its own exports of raw cotton (Chapter 2) and the failed sanctions on Italy and Japan (described in Chapters 4 and 5). We return to these issues below.

As a rule, our work suggests that the effects of economic sanctions and warfare have rarely been well anticipated. Believing in 'King Cotton', the Confederate leaders (Chapter 2) relied too much on predictions that a cotton export embargo would be devastating. Similarly, German naval leaders (Chapter 3) believed that six months of unrestricted submarine warfare could starve Britain into surrender. Conversely, the expectation that even restricted sanctions could ruin economic life led to over-caution as the British and French tried to manage Italian and Japanese aggression (Chapters 4 and 5). Only the study of conduct can suggest the reasons: were the preparations based on deficient economic understanding, or was the conduct of economic warfare thrown off-course by human weaknesses or by private agendas, or did the adversary have some hidden trump card that threw out the calculations?

The Moving Target

Who exercises agency in the conduct of economic warfare and sanctions? The language we use sets pitfalls for the unwary. The sanctions literature uses a shared terminology of 'sender' and 'target'. One trap is to think of the sender as active, leaving the target in a passive role. As van Bergeijk (2021: 11–12) suggests, these terms are inadequate. The sender is not the only active player. Once the game is in play, the target has as many choices and as much agency as the sender. Because of this, the empirical relationship between sender and target is not one way. Another trap is to think of sending the sanction as a single act. Rather, the sending of a sanction is often the start of a lengthy interaction that can go back and forth through many cycles.

To illustrate, our chapters show that, when the economy was attacked, the expectation of the attacker was often that the adversary had two choices, to fold (to cease resistance) or to suffer (to accept the intended damage). But folding or suffering were rarely chosen. Instead, the adversary could turn to a surprisingly long list of other options, listed below and summarised in Table 0.3:

Table 0.3 *The adversary's options under economic attack*

	Economic responses	Non-economic responses
Concurrent responses:	Drawing down stocks Economising and substitution Trade diversion and import substitution	Air defence Defence of shipping Conquest of suppliers and markets Escalate war
Anticipatory responses:	Stockpiling Economic autarky	New alliances Pre-emptive war

Source: See text.

- To retaliate with countersanctions or an economic counter-war: the mutual commerce raiding between Britain and France (Chapter 1); the Union blockade of the Confederacy (Chapter 2); Germany's submarine warfare against Britain in World War I (Chapter 3) and World War II (Chapter 6).
- To defend the economy by fighting off the attacker's ships and planes: Germany's attempt to break the Allied naval blockade in the Battle of Jutland in 1916 (Chapter 3); British anti-submarine warfare in World War I (Chapter 3) and World War II (Chapter 6); German air defence against Allied bombing (Chapter 6).
- To economise on domestic uses of blocked commodities; to create new domestic supplies through import substitution: Britain and Germany in World War I (Chapter 3) and World War II (Chapter 6); Italy in the inter-war period (Chapter 4) and Japan between the wars and in World War II (Chapter 5); Eastern Europe under Coordinating Committee for Multilateral Export Controls (COCOM) sanctions (Chapter 7); South Africa under anti-apartheid sanctions (Chapter 8).
- To re-route existing trade through third parties or otherwise conceal it from the attacker by smuggling commodities or technological secrets: Germany in the opening months of World War I (Chapter 3); Eastern Europe and Cuba in the Cold War (Chapter 7); Southern Rhodesia under UN sanctions (Chapter 8).
- To find new allies willing to provide markets or sources for the commodities that were sanctioned or blocked: Italy's inter-war partnership with Germany (Chapter 4); the Soviet Union's formation of an East European trading bloc and Cuba's alliance with the Soviet Union (Chapter 7).
- Or, if suitable allies could not be found, to conquer adjacent territory to provide the same: Italy's African empire (Chapter 4); Japan's Greater East-Asia Co-Prosperity Sphere (Chapter 5); Germany's *Drang nach Osten* (drive to the East) (Chapter 6).
- To escalate violence in such a way as to win the conflict quickly, with the fighting power on hand today, before the economic losses accumulate and so diminish fighting power tomorrow: Japan's attack on Pearl Harbor (Chapter 5) and Germany's attack on the Soviet Union (Chapter 6), both in 1941.

Finally, if economic measures were threatened, and if the threat was credible, the adversary could exercise foresight by responding in any or all of the ways listed above *in advance*. In that case, the effects of the attack on the economy would come before their cause.

For the attacker to underestimate the range of options available to the adversary, the efforts and ingenuity with which they might be pursued, and the possible timeline of their implementation looks to us like a typical bias in the historical practice of economic warfare and sanctions.

Impact Is Followed by Adaptation

At the end of the nineteenth century, influential observers believed that the industrialised world had arrived at a state of unparalleled fragility. Noting Britain's dependence on imported food, the Polish financier Jan Bloch (1899: lx) commented: 'A single cruiser let loose upon one of your great trade routes would send up the price of provisions enormously ... any interference with the stream of food products which are indispensable for the sustenance of your people, would endanger you far more than the loss of a pitched battle.' What would happen next could be imagined in different scenarios. Bloch expected that, cut off from imported food, civilians would quickly starve. Angell (1910) supposed that, deprived of imported materials and export markets, factories would close, forcing workers into unemployment and their families into poverty. Either way, the speedy collapse of economic life would bring down civil authority and end military resistance.

In the histories that we discuss, the speedy collapse did not materialise. Behind the scenes, the effects of external pressure were slowed and softened by economic adaptation. Somehow, life went on. It appeared that the attack on the economy might pass without serious repercussions.

The canonical studies of economic adaptation to economic warfare were conducted by Mançur Olson after World War II. Olson (1962) investigated the repercussions of the Allied bombing of Schweinfurt, home of Germany's ball-bearing factories, in 1943. Olson (1963) did the same for the blocking of Britain's food supplies by France in the Napoleonic Wars and by Germany in the two world wars.

Each of these cases saw a surprising outcome. The air attack on Schweinfurt was successful in destroying half of Germany's ball-bearing industry, yet there was no visible effect on war production (Chapter 6). Olson showed that, while ball-bearings were indeed 'essential' for some types of vital military equipment, there were plentiful stocks of them and many inessential uses. When new ball-bearings were suddenly scarce, it was not difficult to concentrate the reduced supply on the narrow range of truly essential requirements.

Similarly, Britain, of all countries the most reliant on food imports, survived their interruption without hunger (Chapters 3 and 6). Precisely because Britain was the richest, most industrialised, and least agricultural of the European powers, it was possible in emergency to return marginal land and marginal workers to home food production and get quick results. Again, in the two world wars, Britain's import capacity came under sustained attack. The shipping space available in peacetime was exceptionally large, however, and carried a large volume of commodities for uses that were not essential in wartime. When war came, therefore, by strict rationing and controls, it was possible for a substantially reduced wartime merchant fleet to continue to meet all essential needs.

The foregoing discussion is limited to adaptation after the event. When the impact was anticipated, it could also be pre-empted by adapting beforehand. All three Axis economies attempted this in the 1930s (Chapters 4, 5, and 6). Expecting to be blockaded in wartime, they sought to insulate their economies by the pursuit of autarky (economic self-sufficiency) before war broke out. They also directed the opening moves of their aggressive wars to bring sources of imported food and war materials under colonial control. In those circumstances, impact was *preceded* by adaptation.

Adaptation Is Costly

The fact that the first impact of economic attack could often be mitigated by adaptation often gave a false impression: that nothing had happened. The hopes pinned on economic warfare or sanctions were inflated because they failed to predict adaptation. When adaptation smoothed things over, the false hopes were replaced by disillusionment, as if the attack on the economy has been completely neutralised, so that the damage had been made to go away without trace. But the disillusionment, like the false hopes, was overdone.

The model of impact and adaptation has important implications. The adversary's adaptation was inevitable and predictable. But adaptation was costly and had to be paid for. The price of adaptation was expressed by the drive to economise at the margin, to search for alternative sources and substitutes, and to raid inventories.

Olson's ideas suggest a multi-period model of adaptation to economic attack. In the first period, the economy loses supply of a commodity – food, oil, or some material that is thought essential to war production or to another regime goal. Olson maintained that the idea of an essential good misses the importance of its marginal value. At the margin, all commodities have inessential uses, and this must be as true of 'essential' goods as of any other. Even though *some* of its uses may be essential, the good is no more essential at the margin than any other commodity. In the first period, therefore, the loss arising from economic attack can generally be made up by economising at the margin, finding alternative sources and substitutes, raiding inventories, and cutting back on inessential uses. There is little or no effect on resources available for essential uses.

Economising and substitution are costly, however. Entering the second period, therefore, the effect is to push up the marginal cost of all goods, including those thought of as 'essential'. In the second period, the economy has depleted reserves and reduced possibilities for further economising. If the economic attack continues, the defence of regime priorities will require further cycles of economising and substitution. This can continue only while worker households remain willing to exert increasing efforts and tighten belts. In other words, economic warfare works not through its immediate effects, which can generally be mitigated, but through the increasing costs of mitigation, which steadily hollow out the economy's reserves – the resources allocated to 'inessential' uses such as civilian consumption.

The rising costs of adaptation were a factor in peacetime just as much as in the middle of an existential war. Between the wars, as noted previously, anticipation of sanctions and blockade in a future war led the Axis powers to seek to reduce their dependence on foreign trade through import substitution. To varying degrees they succeeded. The elimination of imports that were inessential or could easily be produced at home left them with greatly reduced foreign trade shares even before war broke out. This seemed to make them stronger.

But the imports that they failed to eliminate consisted increasingly of those essential commodities that could not be supplied domestically at any price – oil for most of Europe, high-quality iron ore for Germany, coal and oil for Italy, and iron and oil for Japan. Although the value of trade was reduced in the aggregate, its value *at the margin* rose. Contrary to expectation, import-substitution policies generally *increased* the economy's vulnerability to the loss of one more unit of imports. Meanwhile, civilian consumption had already started to feel the squeeze arising from trade limitation, so that the wearing down of civilian resources was already under way when war broke out.

The expected costs of adaptation to blockade presented the Axis leaders with a harsh dilemma: whether to gamble on a short war. In a short war leading to certain victory, there would be no need to bear the costs of adaptation, whether during the war or beforehand. But victory could not be guaranteed. In 1914, the Central Powers had gambled on Germany's quick victory over France and had lost. 'Everyone's Armed Forces and Government must strive for a short war', Hitler remarked in May 1939. 'But the government must, however, also prepare for a war of from ten to fifteen years' duration. History shows that wars were always expected to be short' (quoted by Overy 1994: 190).

For Italy and Japan, as for Germany, bearing the costs of autarkic mobilisation beforehand provided a degree of self-insurance against the likelihood of getting bogged down in a drawn-out conflict.

The Displacement Effect

Who would bear the costs of adaptation? The attack on the economy could be indiscriminate or selective. Indiscriminate measures targeted trade or infrastructure. Selective measures were aimed more precisely (or 'smartly') at regime goods (such as imported war materials or domestic war industries) or regime incomes (such as export revenues). It was hoped that selective targeting of the activities that directly supported the adversary's goals would spare the lives and livelihoods of ordinary citizens.

As all our chapters show, however, economies were flexible under attack. Whether the attack was indiscriminate or smart, the regime would protect its priorities. Even if the immediate impact was successfully directed against regime goods or incomes, authoritarian rulers were generally able to displace the costs onto the ordinary citizens, and they encountered few scruples in doing so. Re-routing foreign trade or payments or investing in domestic capacities might be costly, but the government had enough fiscal and monetary means and coercive powers to compensate its servants and their enterprises by restricting the resources available to those outside the circle of power.

We call this shifting of the costs of adaptation the 'displacement effect'. The displacement effect ensured that, whatever was chosen as the target for economic warfare or sanctions, the burden ultimately fell on ordinary people who were left with no choice but to economise, find substitutes and workarounds, tighten belts, and carry on.

The displacement effect would work up to a limit – the point at which civilians would have nothing left to give up. The existence of a limit set up another gamble: the adversary had to gamble on achieving its goal before the limit became binding. The failure of such a gamble was at work in the defeat of both Germany and Japan in 1945, although differently expressed.

Where the limit was, and when it would bind, was always uncertain beforehand. It is easy to think of the limit as physical, measured by hunger, sickness, and exhaustion (Chapters 5 and 6). But the limit also had moral and political elements. The moral element is measured by the will to exert effort and make sacrifices. The political element is reflected in the rising anxieties of political leaders as they called on the citizens to draw on reserves that they feared might no longer exist.

All that was certain was that a limit existed and that a process subject to a limit could not be pursued indefinitely. When the limit was reached, citizens would withdraw their cooperation, and the process would stop. In this model the economy responded to economic warfare in the same way that Mike Campbell (Ernest Hemingway's character in his novel *The Sun Also Rises*) went bankrupt: 'Gradually, then suddenly.'

Cause and Effect

Our project describes five moments when resistance collapsed: France in 1814/15 (Chapter 1), the Confederate states in 1865 (Chapter 2), Germany in 1918 (Chapter 3) and 1945 (Chapter 6), and Japan in 1945 (Chapter 5). Each of these moments of defeat was an 'ultimate breakdown' (the words of Vickers 1943: 21–22) in which the 'effects of economic war' became 'completely merged with the phenomena of defeat'.

The problem this raises is to what extent the historian can look back on the moment of defeat and isolate the particular contribution of economic warfare. While those just mentioned were extreme cases, in fact the same problem arises in all the episodes we consider, including those involving peacetime sanctions.

It was always hard to identify the effects of the attack on the economy with any confidence. A variety of factors could be invoked to explain the difficulty of causal inference, such as the indirectness and delays of transmission and the difficulty of holding other things equal over the time required for economic warfare or sanctions to work. One factor rises above all others in explaining the difficulty: the effects were always mediated by the adversary's responses.

The story of the adversary's response begins as we have already discussed. In the first instance, the adversary, deprived of some existing source of an 'essential' commodity, looked for some other source or substitute. The displacement effect shifted the burden onto civilian supplies, so that the ultimate effects of the attack was found in the wearing down of the civilian sphere.

This was never a complete model, however. As discussed earlier, the adversary's response to the attack on its economy might not be limited to economic adaptation. Military options among those already listed could also be brought into play, and some could be realised much faster than others. Whether the adversary would consider any of these a better response would depend on all the circumstances of the moment.

If we limited the case to economic adaptation, then to trace the arrow of causation might seem straightforward. Another problem then intervened, however: the civilian sphere was always affected simultaneously by other factors, not only random exogenous shocks, but also the endogenous burden arising from pursuit of the priority that originally led the adversary into conflict.

An illustration is Germany, blockaded in World War I (Chapter 3). Before the war, Germany imported approximately 20 per cent of calories for human consumption. In the later stages of the war, the German population suffered hunger deaths, diseases, and stunting, and these continued after the war while the Allied blockade continued. At the time it seemed straightforward to attribute the civilian suffering to the blockade. The blockade was indeed partly responsible, because it drastically curtailed Germany's import capacity. But the blockade was not the only factor, or even the largest factor. Germany's home production of food also declined, and the loss of domestic supply was three to five times greater than the loss of imports. The cause of the decline of home production was Germany's own war mobilisation, which stripped German farms of young men and horses for the army and diverted supplies of machinery and nitrate fertilisers into the war industries.

German civilians starved not primarily because of the Allied blockade, but because Germany's own war effort imposed a large sacrifice on them – onto which the Allied blockade added a further, if smaller, burden. It was the combined effect that led to Germany's exhaustion and surrender.

Complementary Force

Could economic warfare take the place of conventional warfare? Could economic sanctions get results without the need to prepare for war? Our histories suggest not. The attack on the economy was effective only when accompanied by some complementary force or credible threat of force.

Economic warfare entered the picture when a conflict became protracted. While conventional war occupied and eroded the adversary's fighting power today, economic warfare did the same for it tomorrow. In that sense, conventional war and economic war were complements. At the same time as today's losses required the adversary to find the resources to replace them, economic warfare diverted or destroyed the resources available. This was how conventional warfare and economic warfare combined to wear down the adversary's powers of endurance.

We find no cases in which a protracted war could have been won by economic warfare on its own. The eighteenth-century competition of Britain and France (Chapter 1) was not settled by raiding each other's commerce from time to time. The rivalry was resolved only after the

British joined in conventional war on the continent. The American Civil War was settled on the battlefield, where the Union blockade helped by cutting back the forces the Confederacy could equip and deploy (Chapter 2). In World War I, Germany could have survived the Allied blockade alone with relative ease (Chapter 3). What Germany could not survive indefinitely was the complementary pressure created by the armies on several fronts, which forced Germany to strip resources from its farms, just when food imports were shut off by blockade.

In World War II, German rearmament and war plans anticipated another blockade (Chapter 6). By contrast the role assumed by strategic air power was largely unexpected. Early hopes that long-range bombing might bring about Germany's defeat without the need to struggle for territory proved unrealistic. What economic warfare did was to weaken resistance to the Soviet Army in the east and the Allied armies in the west and bring forward the point of Germany's collapse.

In the Pacific theatre, an American naval blockade did much more economic harm to the Japanese islands than the Allied blockade to Germany in both world wars (Chapter 5). Still, Japan could not have been defeated by blockade alone. In 1945, even after crushing military defeat, economic collapse, and the atomic destruction of two cities, a significant fraction of Japan's elite wished to fight on. Japan was defeated by everything – economic warfare and a range of complementary forces – not by any one force.

A related lesson applies to economic sanctions. The factor that too often made sanctions unproductive or counterproductive was the adversary's wide room for manoeuvre when threatened. Sanctions on their own could not be effective if the adversary remained free to find new allies, forge new trading partnerships, conquer new resources, or escalate violence to new levels. The effectiveness of sanctions required a complementary force to remove the room for manoeuvre.

In the rare cases when sanctions achieved quick results without violence, the adversary was small and lacked powerful allies. The would-be aggressor quickly drew back from a foreign adventure when credibly threatened by an overwhelming coalition (Mulder 2022: 151, 268). A great superiority of power was the complementary force that made those sanctions productive. By contrast, it was pointless for the Confederacy (Chapter 2) to sanction Britain by withholding an 'essential' import of which multiple sources were available when the Confederacy was a small power locked in its own conflict and Britain was a great power with a navy that dominated global sea routes.

In some circumstances, the force that could complement an effective sanction was war readiness, which could have closed the gate to further escalation. But the gateway stood open when the peace was challenged by an established or rising power and the sanctioning powers were visibly unprepared for conflict.

The absence of a complementary force could be obvious in the moment. The authors of the League sanctions on Japan and Italy in the early 1930s (Chapters 4 and 5) neutered them because they feared that more serious sanctions could trigger a wider uncontrolled conflict, for which they were unprepared. When Japan seized Manchuria in 1931, the League powers were already committed to disarmament. When Italy invaded Abyssinia in 1935. British and French rearmament had barely begun. Faced with limited economic sanctions, the revisionist powers brushed them off. At the same time, they correctly understood that those who sought to restrain them were militarily weak in the present but might become stronger in future: best to bring forward their own aggressive plans and preparations.

Credible war readiness was the complementary force missing from America's dealing with Japan in 1939 and 1940 (Chapter 5). US sanctions on Japan's supplies of oil and iron posed a serious threat to the Japanese economy and its war mobilisation. The forward movement of the US Pacific fleet to Hawaii, which was intended to deter Japan, provided Japanese commanders with their best target.

After World War II, the United States could sanction Cuba (Chapter 7). But the Cuban missile crisis ended with the superpowers' complementary forces stalemated. In that setting, the Soviet Union could not be deterred from supplying the economic assistance that sustained the island regime. Economic sanctions on the apartheid regimes of Southern Africa (Chapter 8) worked only in combination with complementary force: years of relentless armed insurgency and non-violent resistance.

To conclude, economic warfare and sanctions became effective in a context framed by complementary force. For economic warfare, the complementary force was provided by conventional fighting power, which ensured that any attempt to escalate or widen a conflict would simply bring forward the adversary's exhaustion and defeat. For sanctions, the role of complementary force was deterrent: only readiness for war could stop the adversary from exercising the many outside options.

Conclusions

We draw data from three centuries of economic warfare and sanctions across four continents (Europe, North America, Africa, and Asia). How did economic warfare and sanctions work and how well did they work?

To answer these questions requires us to isolate causes and effects from a complex, interactive process in a rapidly changing setting with many contingent intermediate choices and outcomes and long and variable time lags. The task is intrinsically difficult. It is only slightly easier for scholars with hindsight than it was for participants to learn from contemporaneous experience. With difficulty, therefore, and no doubt with the corresponding scope for error, we extract the following conclusions.

Surprising Adaptability

1. Our field is thickly populated by unintended consequences. Those who made policy often failed to expect the unexpected.
2. The sender/target paradigm, interpreted too literally, presents the sender of a sanction as active and the target as passive or lacking in agency. In practice, the country targeted by economic attack could exercise choice over many options – military as well as economic, beforehand as well as concurrently.
3. Economic adaptation always attenuated the impact of economic measures. Measures of economic adaptation included economising, trade diversion, technological and import substitution, and running down stocks.
4. Non-economic responses could also weaken the impact of economic attack. These ranged from self-defence to war escalation and the capture of external resources.
5. When economic attack was anticipated, it could be pre-empted by action beforehand. Measures of economic pre-emption included stockpiling and the pursuit of economic autarky. Measures of non-economic pre-emption included entering new alliances and starting pre-emptive wars.

The Gradual Accumulation of Costs

6. All the possible responses to economic attack were costly. Just because a sanction or trade disruption was manageable or survivable does not mean that nothing happened. Rather, the effect took the form of a gradual accumulation of costs.
7. Wealthier, more marketised, more diversified economies were more resilient in the sense that they were better able to afford these costs. For example, a richer economy generally had more inessential uses of 'essential' commodities, and this meant a greater capacity to economise in case of need.

8. The gradual accumulation of costs of economic warfare and sanctions took time to emerge. Rather than manifesting as a single act, it was normal for economic attack to develop into an interactive sequence of moves and countermoves. Consistently, immediate success was exceptional: it does not feature in any of our cases.
9. In other words, sanctions alone were a poor way to handle a crisis. Economic warfare alone could not produce a quick victory.

The Displacement Effect and the Fundamental Limit

10. In a flexible market economy, it was always possible for the regime under attack to make good its costs and losses by displacing the burdens of adaptation onto non-elites or non-combatants. The displacement effect would work as long as the civilian sector remained capable of bearing the burdens arising from conflict.
11. For the same reason, non-combatants or civilians were always the ultimate victims (and sometimes the first victims) of economic warfare and sanctions.
12. The fundamental limit that could end this process was the exhaustion of civilian reserves. 'Exhaustion' was in large part material, but there was necessarily a moral and political factor.

The Role of Complementary Force or Threats

13. For another reason already mentioned – the wide range of options open to a country subject to economic attack – success generally eluded measures of economic warfare and sanctions unless they were accompanied by some kind of complementary force, which acted as a deterrent or forcible constraint to close off the outside options.
14. In peacetime, in other words, sanctions and other kinds of pressure, such as investing in war readiness, were generally not alternatives; they were complements. In wartime, conventional war and economic warfare were also complements.

References

Angell, Norman. 1910. *The Great Illusion: A Study of the Relation of Military Power to National Advantage.* London: Heinemann.
BBSU (British Bombing Survey Unit). 1998. *The Strategic Air War against Germany, 1939–1945. Report of the British Bombing Survey Unit.* London: Frank Cass.

Bell, A. C. 1961. *A History of the Blockade of Germany and the Countries Associated with Her in the Great War, Austria-Hungary, Bulgaria, and Turkey, 1914–1918.* London: HMSO.
Bergeijk, Peter A. G. van. 2021. 'Introduction', in Peter A. G. van Bergeijk (ed.), *Research Handbook on Economic Sanctions*, pp. 1–24. Cheltenham: Edward Elgar.
Biddle, Tami Davis. 2015. 'Anglo-American Strategic Bombing, 1940–1945', in John Ferris and Evan Mawdsley (eds.), *The Cambridge History of the Second World War*, vol. 1, pp. 485–526. Cambridge: Cambridge University Press.
Bloch, Ivan. 1899. *Is War Now Impossible?* London: Grant Richards.
Brauer, Jurgen, and Hubert van Tuyll. 2008. *Castles, Battles, and Bombs: How Economics Explains Military History.* Chicago: University of Chicago Press.
Broadberry, Stephen, and Mark Harrison, eds. 2005. *The Economics of World War I.* Cambridge: Cambridge University Press.
   2018. *The Economics of the Great War: A Centennial Perspective.* A CEPR eBook.
   2020. *The Economics of the Second World War: Seventy-Five Years On.* A CEPR eBook.
Davis, Lance E., and Stanley L. Engerman. 2006. *Naval Blockades in Peace and War: An Economic History since 1750.* Cambridge: Cambridge University Press.
Dehne, Phillip A. 2019. *After the Great War: Economic Warfare and the Promise of Peace in Paris 1919.* London: Bloomsbury.
Hardach, Gerd. 1987. *The First World War, 1914–1918.* Harmondsworth: Penguin.
Harrison, Mark, ed. 1998. *The Economics of World War II: Six Great Powers in International Comparison.* Cambridge: Cambridge University Press.
Jentleson, Bruce W. 2022. *Sanctions: What Everyone Needs to Know.* Oxford: Oxford University Press.
Kramer, Alan. 2013. 'Blockade and Economic Warfare', in Jay Winter (ed.), *The Cambridge History of the First World War*, vol. 2, pp. 460–490. Cambridge: Cambridge University Press.
Kramer, Alan, Samuël Kruizinga, Elisabeth Piller, and Jonas Scherner. 2024. 'Introduction: The Blockade in the Era of the World Wars', *International History Review* 46(4): 383–392.
Lektzian, David J., and Christopher M. Sprecher. 2007. 'Sanctions, Signals, and Militarized Conflict', *American Journal of Political Science* 51(2): 415–431.
Medlicott, W. N. 1952, 1959. *The Economic Blockade* (History of the Second World War: United Kingdom Civil Series), vols. 1–2 (London: HMSO, vol. 1 1952, vol. 2 1959).
Mierzejewski, Alfred C. 1988. *The Collapse of the German War Economy, 1944–45.* Chapel Hill: University of North Carolina Press.
Milward, Alan S. 1977. *War, Economy, and Society, 1939–1945.* London: Allen Lane.
Mitchener, Kris James, and Marc D. Weidenmier. 2010. 'Supersanctions and Sovereign Debt Repayment', *Journal of International Money and Finance* 29(1): 19–36.
Mulder, Nicholas. 2022. *The Economic Weapon: The Rise of Sanctions as a Tool of Modern War.* New Haven, CT: Yale University Press.

O'Brien, Phillips P. 2015. *How the War Was Won: Air–Sea Power and Allied Victory in World War II*. Cambridge: Cambridge University Press.

Olson, Mançur. 1962. 'The Economics of Target Selection for the Combined Bomber Offensive', *Royal United Services Institution Journal* 107(628): 308–314.

1963. *The Economics of the Wartime Shortage: A History of British Food Supplies in the Napoleonic War and in World Wars I and II*. Durham, NC: Duke University Press.

Overy, Richard. 1980. *The Air War, 1939–1945*. London: Europa.

1994. *War and Economy in the Third Reich*. Oxford: Clarendon Press.

2014. *The Bombing War: Europe, 1939–1945*. London: Penguin.

Poast, Paul. 2024. *Man, Russia, and War: How Russia Shaped Our Understanding of International Security*. Unpublished manuscript.

Tooze, Adam. 2006. *The Wages of Destruction: The Making and the Breaking of the Nazi Economy*. London: Allen Lane.

USSBS (US Strategic Bombing Survey). 1945. *Summary Report (European War)*. Washington, DC: USSBS.

Vickers, C. G. 1943. 'Economic Warfare', *Royal United Services Institution Journal* 88(549): 14–22.

Webster, Charles, and Noble Frankland. 1961. *The Strategic Air Offensive against Germany, 1939–1945*, vols. 1–4. History of the Second World War: Military Series. London: HMSO.

1 The Second Hundred Years War
France vs Britain (1688–1815)

Loïc Charles and Guillaume Daudin

The long struggle between France and Britain[1] from 1688 to 1815 has been dubbed the 'Second Hundred Years War' (Buffinton [1929] 1975; Findlay and O'Rourke 2007: 247–262). The two countries were at war almost half of the time (see Table 1.1), and the periods of peace in between were characterised by fierce economic and commercial competition. We claim this period was crucial for the emergence of modern relations between violence and economic competition.

Economists and strategists routinely use the expression 'trade war' to describe acute, yet peaceful, economic competition between nations. They distinguish it from 'economic warfare', which implies violence (Oermann and Wolff 2022, chapter 2). This distinction did not exist during the mercantilist era, before 1815 (Heckscher 1922: 11–12). According to Colbert (Clément 1861, vol. 6: 266), 'Trade causes a perpetual struggle in peace and war between the nations of Europe over who can gain the best portion'. War and economic competition were then the same phenomenon: the struggle for power and dominance in the international arena (Viner 1948; Heckscher 1994: 13–52; Oermann and Wolff 2022: 3–5).

To explain how that distinction came about, it is useful to distinguish two types of economic warfare. 'Capacity-focused' economic warfare aims at achieving military outcomes through the disruption of the supply of war, which in the early modern era included, as we will argue, naval stores, sailors, and precious metals. Its oldest and simplest form was the siege blockade that aimed at forcing the surrender of a fortified locality through starvation and thirst.

A second type, 'market-focused' economic warfare, existed alongside 'capacity-focused' economic warfare. It aims at achieving economic outcomes, often the control of external markets. It assumes that the

---

[1] France's antagonist was England until 1707, Great Britain (adding Scotland) from then to 1801, and the United Kingdom (adding Ireland) thereafter. Where a term is required that encompasses the whole period from 1688 to 1815, we use 'Britain' and 'British'.

Table 1.1 *Wars between France and Britain in Europe, 1688–1815*

Period	Name	Main British allies	Main French allies	Outcome	Peace treaty
1688–1697	Nine Years War	United Provinces Spain Austria	None	English victory	Treaty of Ryswick (1697)
1702–1713	War of Spanish Succession	United Provinces Austria	Spain	Draw	Treaty of Utrecht (1713)
1744–1748	War of Austrian Succession	United Provinces Austria	Spain Prussia	French victory	Treaty of Aix-la-Chapelle (1748)
1756–1763	Seven Years War	Prussia	Austria Russia	British victory	Treaty of Paris (1763)
1778–1783	War of American Independence	None	Spain United Provinces 13 colonies	French victory	Treaty of Paris (1783)
1793–1802	French Revolutionary Wars	Austria Prussia Russia	None	French victory	Treaty of Amiens (1802)
1803–1814/1815	Napoleonic Wars	Austria Prussia Russia	None	British victory	Congress of Vienna (1815)

Table 1.2 *War and economic competition among the great powers*

	Trade war	Economic warfare	
		Market-focused	Capacity-focused
Means	Non-violent	Violent	Violent
Aim	To gain economic advantage	To gain economic advantage	To reduce adversary's fighting power
When	Before and after 1815	Mainly before 1815	Before and after 1815
Supporting ideas	Mercantilism	Mercantilism	Modern liberalism

economic spoils of war can make war a profitable enterprise. It was waged in Europe at least from the rivalry between Italian cities for Mediterranean markets in the late first millennium CE. In the seventeenth and eighteenth centuries, market-focused economic warfare was neither a strategic substitute nor a complement to military conflict; it was often the main motivation for war. The Second Hundred Years War is a direct illustration of this conception. It was first and foremost a series of events in which Britain and France aimed at gaining the upper hand in the global economic competition by either violent or peaceful means (Conybeare 1987: 129–159). When the slicing up of markets was decided, there was no need for further war. Thus, trade talks became a prominent aspect of peace settlements made by European countries and commercial treaties were a central feature of peace treaties from the seventeenth century on (Alimento and Stapelbroek 2017; Schnakenbourg 2017: 221). By contrast, the parcelling out of markets was not an aim of war between great powers after 1815 (Table 1.2). The French defeat and the Treaty of Vienna created a decisive break from the mercantilist era: the objectives of power and plenty were finally disentangled, and the modern liberal view came to dominance.

Our argument in this chapter is twofold. First, we show that the Second Hundred Years War was motivated by economic competition between France and Britain. Second, we show that the transition to the form of economic warfare compatible with modern liberalism that has prevailed until today was in large part a consequence of this long-standing conflict.[2]

---

[2] Thus, our argument goes against Shovlin's recent argument that trade and the emergence of capitalism played a major role in the setting of a more peaceful order (Shovlin 2021). We argue that the latter was a product of unchallenged British military and economic domination, which made mercantilist economic warfare irrelevant.

The practices of economic warfare during the Second Hundred Years War were diverse and evolving throughout the war. The British were by far the most consistent of the two protagonists. They clung aggressively to a strategy of market-focused economic warfare during the whole period (Baugh 1988; Oermann and Wolff 2022: 41–50). The French strategy went through a long, ultimately unsuccessful evolution. From 1713 on, market-focused economic warfare became less and less important as a strategy for the French. During peacetime, they gradually inclined to a less aggressive stance, arguing that French trade needed only liberty and protection. During wartime, rather than diverting their military resources by trying to launch a large-scale attack on British trade, they concentrated on maintaining their lines of communication and supply and, according to circumstances, to a limited recourse to capacity-focused economic warfare. After a period of indecisiveness following the French Revolution, the Continental system enforced by Napoleon implemented a capacity-focused economic warfare strategy with hitherto unknown intensity.[3]

Hence, we can divide our study on the Second Hundred Years War between France and Britain into three periods, each one dominated by a different French response to British market-focused economic warfare. In the opening period that was concluded by the Treaty of Utrecht, the French government confronted the British challenge head-on: Colbert and his successors built a large military fleet and had systematic recourse to privateering, a type of economic warfare that England had developed in its conflicts with Spain and the United Provinces. From 1713 to 1783, France switched to another strategy, employing both a convoy system and the large-scale use of neutral-flag shipping to supply its economy and preserve its markets during wartime. Britain reacted aggressively by applying a harsher policy against neutral ships and tried to use an economic blockade – a type of capacity-focused economic warfare – to cut off supply to the French colonies. During the last period, covering the Wars of the French Revolution and Napoleonic Wars, the conflict between the two nations and their allies reached a new level approaching total economic warfare, with both contenders using capacity-focused economic warfare on a larger scale, but with the British overall strategy still dominated by market-focused economic warfare. Their full victory in 1815 made this form of economic warfare redundant.

---

[3] For the argument that the Napoleonic Wars were the first total war, see Bell (2007).

The Heyday of Privateering, 1688–1713

The interconnections between war and the economy underwent large-scale transformations during the early modern period. On the one hand, the rising importance of heavy weaponry and the growing professionalisation of armed forces in Europe implied a huge growth in the cost of war (Roberts 1955; Parker 1988; Enciso 2016). Indeed, the 'military revolution' caused steeply rising costs of war for the French and British states (Brewer 2002; Chaline 2016: 173–191). On the other hand, the discovery of the Americas and the subsequent rise of Atlantic trade, especially in silver and gold, provided new opportunities for fiscal states. Hence, economic considerations linked to warfare became more important, even decisive, from the late seventeenth century for European statesmen and political writers.

During the early modern period, the conduct of war was very different whether it was fought at sea or on the ground. The contemporary theorist of military strategy and practitioners did not consider economic warfare as a significant weapon in the conduct of land war. Scorched-earth practices were common during the Thirty Years War, both to gather supplies and deny them to the enemy, but they had become rarer by the end of the seventeenth century. In continental Europe, where armies fought for only a limited period during the year (a campaign), roughly from April/May to November, the relative slowness of regular troops prevented raids to destroy lines of communication. War was seen by most officers on the ground as a discontinuous set of single events (individual battles) aimed at limited (tactical) objectives rather than a whole set of events united by a common objective – forcing the enemy nation to surrender. Although the period saw numerous battles fought with large-scale armies, early modern European wars were wars of attrition, and diplomacy played a key role in all the major conflicts of the period and especially those that constituted the Second Hundred Years War (Brewer 2002).

Sea warfare was different. It was absent from from all the continental military strategy manuals, which were interested exclusively in ground war. Also, economic warfare was routinely understood as being a major aspect of maritime conflict since maritime trade played a disproportionate role in the economy. Hence, there are countless statements from seventeenth- and eighteenth-century statesmen and political economists that equate military and economic power. As public credit was in its infancy, the limiting factor to war making was not what could be produced by the economy (the scale of military mobilisation compared to the economy was quite small), but what could be acquired by the state through taxation or importation of precious metals. In this context, market-focused economic warfare, because of the trade surplus and taxable income it could bring, became a central concern. Furthermore, the development of commercial elites increased the amounts of moveable funds the state could borrow. Britain was the first nation to react systematically to these new conditions by following a 'blue water policy' – that is, 'a form of technically advanced warfare emphasizing economic pressure' – that allowed Britain to balance its relative dearth in natural resources – in particular men – by greater access to foreign resources and a superiority in wealth, particularly monetary wealth (see Baugh 1988, cited by Brewer 2002: 257). Indeed, when the Spanish king died in 1700 without a direct heir, the War of the Spanish Succession (1702–1713) was triggered by England and United Provinces' shared belief that, if ever the kingdoms of France and Spain were to be united, the French merchants would exclude their merchants from the large and profitable market of the Spanish empire.

During the seventeenth century, privateering became a favoured military weapon to attack the lines of communication and to lessen the economic capacity of the enemy either temporarily or permanently.[4] England had been the first nation to use privateering, against the Spanish in the sixteenth century and later against the United Provinces and France. During the seventeenth century, as English trade had expanded and was now a major source of income for the English state, its enemies in turn made use of privateering against the English merchant fleet. While large-scale sea battles captured the imagination of military historians, privateering played a significant role in seventeenth-century conflict. The French decision to have recourse to privateering was not a choice by default. It went hand-in-hand with a huge increase of the French navy budget under Colbert, from 300,000 *livres tournois* in 1661 to an average of 10 million livres from 1662 to 1683, and a complete institutional reform of the navy (Villiers 1991: 58–59). Marshall Vauban – both a political economist and the major French military theoretician of the time – argued that privateering was the most efficient means of economic warfare. He identified wealth, in particular, as the main means of war for modern nations. England and the United Provinces were small countries with limited populations and natural resources. Their trade was their major asset and source of specie.

---

[4] Privateering is a predatory activity, by which an individual, provided with authorisation from the state of which that individual is a subject, obtains permission to seize on the open seas the commercial or fishing vessels of an enemy country. Part of the profits go to the privateer's state.

Thus, it was essential to attack trade to force these countries to end their war against France and privateering was the 'easiest, least expensive, least uncertain and least costly [means] for the state' to inflict significant casualties on the enemy's commercial empire (Vauban 1695: 158). Other French political economists went even further, arguing that the distinction between the commercial and military fleet was not pertinent as merchants were bringing more value, and ultimately power, to the state than soldiers.[5]

When the Nine Years War (1688–1697) broke out, France had a navy able to contest Anglo-Dutch supremacy during the first years of the war and a very well-defended base for its privateers in Dunkirk. Privateering was employed as a major weapon, especially after 1692 when the French fleet was no longer able to match that of the allies. During the whole war, the French privateers captured at least 6,000 enemy ships. During the War of the Spanish Succession (1702–1713), the French used the same means to the same result, capturing more than 6,500 merchant ships.[6] This was, indeed, the heyday of French privateering (see Figure 1.1) (Clark 1928: 263–264; Villiers 2006). The Royal Navy tried to blockade the French ports of the mainland and in the colonies, both Canada and the Caribbean, to no avail. The total value of British prizes was quite small. In Europe, the neutrals (Danish and Swedish flags) crucially helped French merchants to bypass the blockade (Schnakenbourg 2019). In Canada, the raids of French colonists, aided by their Indigenous allies and led by Frontenac, brought about heavy losses in the North American colonies, while in the West Indies a combination of neutral trade and attacks by the French privateers saved the French colonies from both starvation and an British invasion. The English obtained from the United Provinces in February 1703 an ambitious complete ban on all French and Spanish trade and access to the Amsterdam financial market for these two nations (Clark 1928: 271–273). Although the Dutch called it off after only one year as they found it too costly for their country, some of the difficulties that

---

[5] 'I don't even know if the State should make such a big difference between the action of an officer who, in war, defeats or causes to be defeated by his orders some of the enemy's troops, and the action of a merchant who, in war, has one or more ships built and armed at his own expense, which he sometimes mounts himself, or has mounted by captains he chooses, to run at the State's enemies, to seek them out in order to defeat them, at the risk of being defeated by a bloody and stubborn fight. If he is victorious, he brings his prize back to France, and often very richly loaded; the State profits, like this merchant. It seems to me that there is at least as much value on one side as on the other; they both weaken the enemies of the State; why then are honour and reward so different?' (Du Tot 1738, vol. 2: 318–319; see also Vincent de Gournay 2008: 225–231).

[6] Our figures are computed from Villiers (1991: 129, 142).

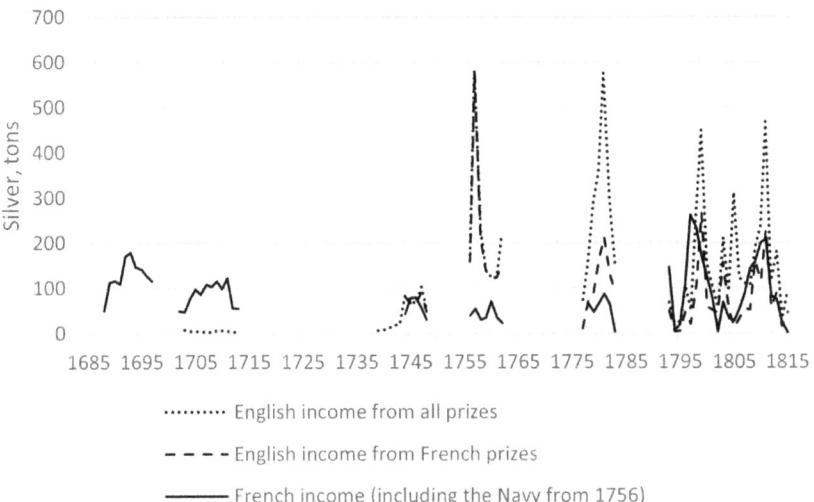

Figure 1.1 French and British income from predation, 1688–1815 (tons of silver)

Source: Calculated from Daudin and Tirindelli (2025) from several sources (for the French data, essentially the publications by Villiers listed in this article; for the British data, please refer to the article by Daudin and Tirindelli). We do not have data for English prizes during the Nine Years War. French income from mixed or state predation is excluded before 1756.

Louis XIV faced in financing the war can probably be ascribed to this scheme. The war continued until France and Britain opened discussions because of their growing financial difficulties. France, in particular, was in huge debt at the death of Louis XIV in 1715. Trade was the main focus of the peace talks in preparation of the Treaty of Utrecht, and as soon as an agreement was reached awarding the British the 'Asiento' (the contract for supplying slaves to the Spanish Empire) peace was settled, with Britain leaving its allies to fight France alone for another year (Bély 1990).

Economic Warfare versus Doux Commerce? 1713–1783

The commercial treaty agreed on at Utrecht was never signed by the English parliament. A majority of the members of parliament backed the interests of the English merchants and found that the conditions of the treaty were too good for French trade. Still, the Treaty of Utrecht marked a significant change in the relationships between the two countries and opened a long period of peace between 1713 and 1744. The French state, having survived the bankruptcy of Law's System in 1720 and brought down its debt, was in no mood to risk its financial health to build and maintain a sufficiently large fleet to compete with the Royal Navy. The British government, having reached its main strategic objectives at the end of the War of Spanish Succession, was likewise not willing to launch another major conflict, at least immediately.

Trade competition was still in motion, though, and the French economy seems to have been winning (see Figure 1.2). The rate of growth of its foreign trade in the 1720s and 1730s was very high and it outcompeted British products in some crucial markets such as the Ottoman Empire and Spain, where the Asiento proved much less profitable than expected. Moreover, France took over the re-export trade of colonial commodities (sugar, coffee, cocoa, indigo) to Europe, which had been dominated by England in the seventeenth century. These trends triggered growing anxieties in the British public and merchant community,

Figure 1.2 French and British trade by value, 1688–1815 (tons of silver)

Source: Daudin and Tirindelli (2025), from TOFLIT18 project and various sources (Deane and Cole 1969; Cuenca-Esteban 2001: 69–78, 2004: 65–66; Federico and Tena-Junguito 2016; Charles et al. 2022). Deane and Cole's figures for England (not corrected for official values) up to 1763, Cuenca-Esteban's figures are for Great Britain 1764–1822, and Federico and Tena-Junguito's figures are for the UK from 1823.

Note: The periods of maritime conflict between the powers (set out in Table 1.1) are indicated by a medium shade.

A darker shade marks the period of the Napoleonic blockade (1807–1815).

which in turn created tensions between the South Sea Company (which owned the Asiento contract), Spain, and the British government.

It is clear that the British actors saw the next two wars as the occasion to wage market-focused economic warfare in order to recover ground lost to France on the European markets (Wallerstein 1980; Tracy 1991; Davis and Engerman 2006b; Black 2007; Crouzet 2008). The British state, at the urging of mercantile interests, believed war was a good way to curtail French trade, despite the huge resources it required (see Figure 1.3) (Baugh 1965; Neal 1977; Brewer 2002). Building political coalitions around economic international competition was thus easy (Gülsunar 2021). The first result was the War of Jenkin's Ear (1739–1748), undertaken to improve British trading positions in the Spanish empire. Although France only formally joined the war in 1744 in the context of the disputed Austrian succession, it had been backing up the flagging Spanish since the beginning of the hostilities to protect its commercial interests. Even if the Spanish army and fleet were badly mauled, the British were forced to negotiate in view of the huge

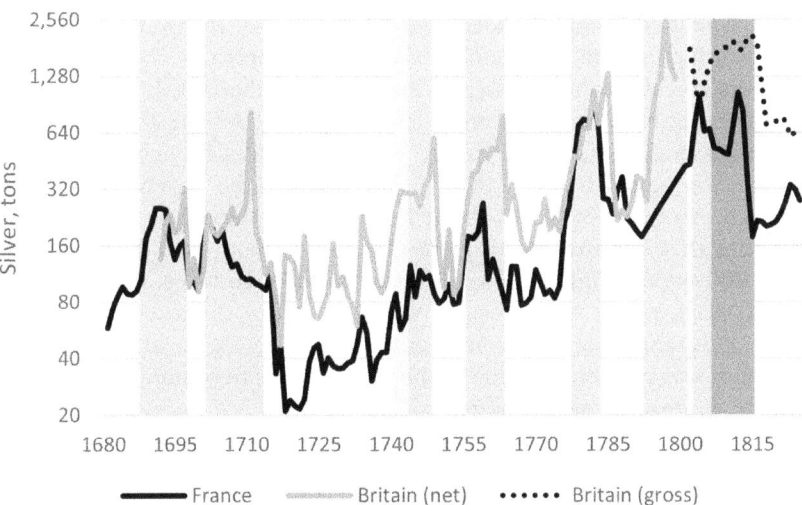

Figure 1.3 French and British naval budgets, 1688–1815 (tons of silver)

Source: Computations from Daudin and Tirindelli (2025) from several data sources. French data from 1793 to 1800 is extrapolated.

Note: The periods of maritime conflict between the powers (set out in Table 1.1) are indicated by a medium shade.

A darker shade marks the period of the Napoleonic blockade (1807–1815).

cost of war and the defeats of its continental allies (United Provinces and Austria). From 1744 to 1748, French use of neutral shipping as well as a system of convoy proved sufficiently efficient to carry on colonial trade and ship back part of the American silver (Villiers 2012). However, British merchants' and colonists' resentment did not abate and Britain entered the 1750s with the firm intention to make good their loss. Indeed, the American colonies and trade were the central motive to the Seven Years War (1756–1763).

During the whole period, the British clung to a market-focused economic war, pursuing economic competition using all means available to them, including violent conflict. Conversely, the French underwent a radical change of strategy. They applied a policy of avoiding direct armed conflict, and even used appeasement. This was illustrated by the alignment with British interests against the Spaniards after the end of the War of the Spanish Succession (including the War of the Quadruple Alliance, 1718–1720), the moderation of Louis XV's peace conditions in 1748, as well as the delay in the French declaration of war in 1756 despite the peacetime capture of French merchant ships by Boscawen (see below).

Accordingly, even during periods of direct conflict with Britain, the French relied less on privateering and predation of British trade than on policies focused on maintaining their own supply: the use of neutral carriers and the convoy system. Consequently, the British returns from privateering became much more important than for the French during the eighteenth century (see Figure 1.1). The role of French privateering became marginal from 1744 to 1783. During the Seven Years War, French privateers captured about 2,600 British ships, less than half the amount they captured during the Nine Years War, and they captured only 700 ships during the War of American Independence. From 1759 to 1763, privateering was a means of last resort for the merchants of the French Atlantic ports to continue some activity (since trade with the colonies was close to zero due to the British naval hegemony) rather than a state strategy to win the war.

In parallel, France implemented a policy of free trade and encouragement of neutral trade during war. This had roots in the Nine Years War when, faced with the coalition of two naval superpowers – England and United Provinces – France relied on the neutral Danes and Swedes. Accordingly, the French legislation on neutral trade evolved considerably from a very restrictive stance in the sixteenth and early seventeenth century to a very liberal one at the end of the eighteenth century (Schnakenbourg 2011: 95–96), especially from the 1740s onward. The War of Austrian Succession was a sharp break, for it was the first time that France suspended the stipulations of the 26th article of the regulation of April 1717 that prohibited foreign flags in the French colonies (Schnakenbourg 2015). France used neutral shipping on an unprecedented scale, even admitting Dutch merchants to its ports, despite the fact the United Provinces were allied with the British against France and its allies. The French further hoped that the neutrals would react to the aggressive British policy toward them (see below) by joining their side. Figure 1.4 vividly illustrates that, while the French fleet steadily weakened relative to the British fleet up until 1748, alliances increasingly favoured France, and neutral powers grew progressively stronger. France remained active at protecting the rights of neutral shipping up to the French Revolution (Schnakenbourg 2013: 129). In 1784, France gave the West Indies island of St Barthelemy to Sweden partly to encourage the continuation of French West Indies trade in wartime through neutral carriers (Schnakenbourg 2013: 326). This policy transformation went hand in hand with a growing preference for freer trade during peacetime.

Although historians have interpreted these transformations as the rise of the *doux commerce* ideology in France, it was in fact a policy aiming at undermining the British competition in the long run. The argument was roughly this: as France had more natural resources than Great Britain and Holland, it should concentrate on creating a political context in

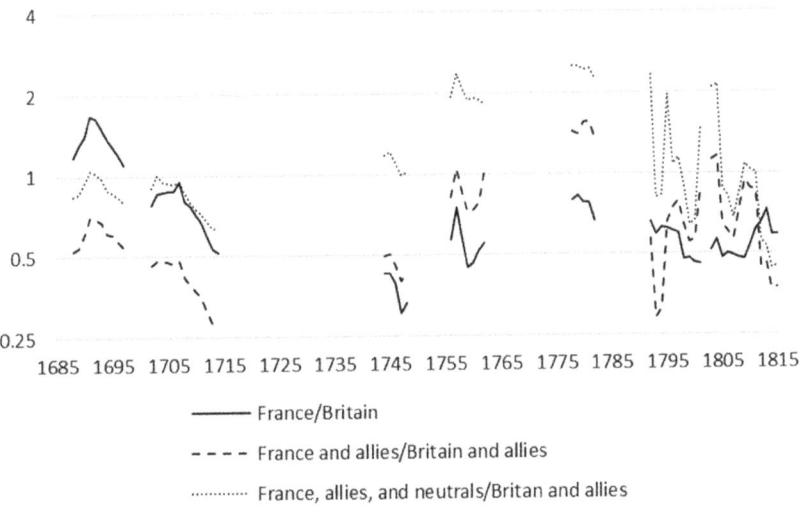

Figure 1.4 Evolution of naval supremacy during the Anglo-French wars, 1688–1815 (1 = parity)
Source: Computations from Daudin and Tirindelli (2025); data from Modelski and Thompson (1988).

which its natural superiority would be revealed, and a peaceful European order was the most efficient means to achieve this outcome. This objective was spelled out most clearly by the economist Du Tot in his influential *Political Reflections on Finance and Trade*: 'To make peace to obtain for ourselves all the advantages of a great trade is to make war on our enemies' (Du Tot 1738, vol. 2: 403).

Capacity-focused economic warfare was an important use of maritime power. The idea that wealth equates to power (political and military), which came to dominate in the seventeenth century, held full sway during the eighteenth century. Even a free-trade economist such as François Quesnay, the founder of physiocracy, was quite clear that wealth was the sole yardstick of a nation's military power.[7] His argument has a very modern flavour, since Quesnay argued that the bigger the net product created by the economy of one's nation, the more it will have for public service and in particular for the military (Quesnay 2005: 437).[8] In practice, as France had no central bank and did not use paper money, much of its capacity to mint currency and hence finance war was based on Spanish colonial silver gained through the French current account surplus with Spain (Morineau 1985: 465). Indeed, the return of the Spanish silver was one of France's main motives in supporting the Spanish Empire in the 1740s. Conversely, the Atlantic blockade of Spanish silver was a major war objective for the British. Although Britain failed in this endeavour during the 1740s, it succeeded in the early 1760s, pushing the French state to the brink of financial collapse.

Additionally, Britain made a systematic effort to deprive the French navy of sailors, notably through peacetime ship seizure and cessation of prisoner exchanges for sailors and lower-rank officers. This policy was particularly effective when in 1755, before the official beginning of the Seven Years War, Admiral Boscawen seized more than 300 merchant ships and captured 6,000 sailors (one-tenth of the French total). By the end of the war, slightly fewer than 60,000 sailors, civil and military, were rotting in British jails. This coup and the subsequent captures of sailors had a huge impact on the French capability to fight efficiently at sea or to continue Atlantic trade from 1759. Finally, although Britain did not try to impose a complete blockade on French trade, it was able to cut almost

---

[7] The complete *Tableau économique* was first published in 1759, at the beginning of the Seven Years War. It is therefore unsurprising that Quesnay evokes war in several instances (Quesnay 2005: 411, 418, 424, 436–437). For him: 'War on land and sea uses means other than the force of men, and requires much more considerable expenses than those of the soldiers' subsistence. So it is less men than riches which support the war' (p. 437).
[8] Compare this reasoning with the idea spelled out by Vickers (1943: 15) that war is fought with 'the surplus activities of men'.

completely the supply route to French Canada, which in turn enabled it to capture the whole territory in 1760 – something which it had been unable to achieve in previous conflicts with France.

To realise its strategic aims, Britain was increasingly hostile to neutrals. The British deemed all French-own cargoes to be liable to seizure. Yet the true nationality of the cargo was difficult to ascertain as neutral ships would not yield easily to inspection, especially when they were escorted by neutral warships. Neutrals claimed from the seventeenth century the 'right of convoys', that is 'immunity from search for neutral merchant vessels sailing under the convoy of a warship of the neutral' (Davis and Engerman 2006b: 17). This would allow French merchants to trade under a neutral flag. During the second half of the eighteenth century, Great Britain decided to undermine this possibility. During the Seven Years War, the British introduced the 'Rule of the War of 1756', including the doctrine of 'Continuous Voyage'. It stated that the very beginning of the journey and the very end determined the nationality of the cargo. The British also claimed and exercised the right to seize neutral shipping to look for contraband. Moreover, they forbade neutrals, in time of war, to conduct trade from which they were barred in time of peace. As the French colonies were under the *Exclusif* regime in time of peace (Tarrade 1972) – all their trade had to be conducted by French ships – the Rule of 1756 barred neutrals from trading with the French colonies in time of war. This had a considerable impact on French trade, which relied heavily on neutral ships during war.

However, the combination of growing British hostility and French liberal policy created great discontent among neutral countries. French policy was particularly vindicated when the Dutch not only refused to ally with Britain, but participated actively in the supply of the French colonial Atlantic empire during the Seven Years War and the American War of Independence. The Dutch would even join France in war against Britain in 1780. Likewise, on the eve of the American War of Independence, Russia, Denmark, and Sweden founded the League of Armed Neutrality to protect their interests against the threat of new losses by the Royal Navy and British privateers (Schnakenbourg 2013: 121–125). The experiment was put to an end in 1783 with the treaty of Paris (Griffiths 1971).

During the War of American Independence, the French navy had been largely reinforced and was on the offensive. Indeed, the British defeat at the Battle of Yorktown had similar causes to the French defeat in Canada twenty-one years earlier, as the French navy was able to successfully blockade all supplies to the British army. This accounted for a significant part of the Franco-American military-strategic success. Being able to match British military power at sea and benefiting from the help of the neutral fleets, French trade survived the war with minimal trade loss, while British trade was badly hit by the American ban on its products, effective from 1774 to 1783. Although the French did not win the dominance over the US market they had hoped, in the 1780s French international trade was nearly as great as British trade: a long century of British efforts had produced little abatement of French commercial competition, showing the futility of 'market-focused economic warfare' (Figure 1.2).

France still practised an appeasement policy. The free trade Treaty of Eden between France and Great Britain in 1787 satisfied British mercantile interests: for example, it did not give any market access in Britain to French silk products (Conybeare 1987: 138 and 154). For the British, it was the continuation of market-focused economic warfare that led to the Franco-Dutch trade treaties of 1678 and 1697 and the Asiento agreement in 1713. For the French, it should have contributed to the establishment of long-term peace that France thought was to its advantage. Actually, the short-term crisis it provoked in some French industrial regions fuelled hostility to the French *ancien régime* and played a role in starting the French Revolution. The cost of the War of American Independence, despite France's victory, put French finances on the brink of a major collapse. In 1788 the finance minister, Calonne, had to summon the Estates-General for the first time since 1615, which opened the door to a revolution in French political institutions.

The Paradoxical End of Mercantilist Economic Warfare, 1793–1815

In 1792 France declared war on Austria and Prussia, and in the following year on Great Britain and the United Provinces. The subsequent conflict lasted for nearly thirty years, with only two brief interruptions in 1802–1803 (Peace of Amiens) and in 1814–1815. In contrast with the rest of the Second Hundred Years War, the conflict between the French Republic and the various *ancien régimes* of Europe led by Britain had a fundamental ideological dimension (O'Rourke 2006). France stopped prioritising the defence against British market-focused warfare to conduct full-on, and ultimately unsuccessful, capacity-focused warfare.

The disproportion of forces between the British and French navies widened after 1792 (Figure 1.4) (O'Brien 2006). The former was both well-funded (see Figure 1.3) and had made significant technical and organisational progress. Conversely, the French navy suffered huge losses of experienced officers due to emigration and lacked experienced sailors because of the British policy of not releasing captured French sailors. However, the British strategy did not change as much. During the preceding wars, British capacity-focused economic warfare had been successful in peripheral theatres. British control of the sea cut off the French (and Dutch) colonies from support from Europe and greatly facilitated their capture. Tobago was taken in 1793, Martinique in 1794, Guadeloupe and French Guyana in 1810, Maurice, Réunion, and the French trading posts in India in 1811. In Egypt (1798–1801) as well as in Saint-Domingue (1801–1803), French overseas expeditions failed because the vastly superior Royal Navy broke the supply chain of the French troops. By contrast, capacity-focused economic warfare was never decisive in continental Europe, where France had access to the resources of most of the Continent. At the local level, however, the regular naval supply of specific locations contributed to the failure of French sieges (e.g. Cadiz, 1810–1812).

But most British efforts were directed towards market-focused economic warfare. Privateering resumed, but most of the predation on enemy trade was conducted by the Royal Navy (Hillmann and Gathmann 2011). As in previous wars, the British tried to blockade French ports, but the rising superiority of the Royal Navy in many dimensions made the blockade of French trade much more successful than during previous conflicts. There were two types of blockade (Corbett 2004), open (or distant) and close. For a distant blockade, the navy kept its ships in their home port, ready to sail as soon as the enemy fleet left its own harbour. This technique economised on ships and crews, but was less effective. A close blockade kept the enemy fleet bottled up in its harbour. The close blockade was more effective, but the cost of maintaining ships and men at sea off the enemy coast for a long time was a substantial burden. By the end of the eighteenth century, the British had implemented an effective system of resupply of the fleet at sea, enabling it to remain in position for long periods. Diets were improved to overcome scurvy, which, previously rife among seamen, accounted for only 2 per cent of British naval patients by 1795–1800 (Rodger 2005). Further, the British had started to coat their ships with copper; this reduced the damage done by barnacles and shipworms to the speed and the security of vessels. As a result, the British developed the capacity to obstruct French trade by maintaining a close blockade, while bearing the costs of doing so. One would expect that the number of ships captured declined as not many ships tried to run the close blockade, but that is not confirmed by data on prizes (Benjamin 2009).

As the British were highly successful in market-focused economic warfare, they were not eager to make peace. By 1808, Viscount Hamilton declared to the English parliament:

Great Britain at the present moment exhibited the astonishing spectacle of a country, which, at the end of 15 Years war with a most powerful antagonist, had gained everything, and lost nothing. Everywhere we had inflicted blows on our enemy; no where had we received a blow from him. Our commerce had flourished; our wealth had increased; our possessions had multiplied. Our navy, always formidable, had swept every hostile fleet from the face of the ocean. War, the curse of every other nation, had to Great Britain been a comparative blessing. Indeed, such was the extraordinary state of Europe, that he apprehended very much that war was the only mode by which the advantages which we had acquired, could be maintained. (Cited in Crouzet 1987: 280)

French trade was indeed recovering even in wartime, and the British could fear that peace would allow it to recover its dynamism, as happened after the eighteenth-century wars (see Figure 1.2).

That might have happened if only France had maintained its defensive eighteenth-century policies that favoured trade and the neutral powers. This was ruled out by the ideological conflict that made the destruction of Britain a more important objective than the economic health of France. Of course, France resumed privateering (see Figure 1.1). Based on Lloyd's List and Norman (1887), Mahan estimated 11,000 British merchant ships as captured or ransomed from 1793 to 1815, but that did not prevent the British merchant fleet increasing from 16,728 in 1795 to 23,703 in 1810 (Mahan 1892 and 1894, vol. 2: 223, 226). Privateering unsupported by a strong navy was not successful.

France also banned the import of all British goods. It initially encouraged neutral trade and gave neutral shipping access to its colonies. But very quickly French relations with neutrals soured. France found neutral shipping too compliant to British demands (e.g. the 1794 Jay Treaty was an important point of contention between France and the United States). Naturally, neutral countries wished to continue trade with both belligerent actors. France did not accept this and accused the United States of facilitating British trade, breaking with both neutrality and its alliance with France (Marzagalli 2015: 106–118). Tensions between France and the neutrals multiplied up to the climax of the undeclared naval war between France and the United States from 1798 to 1800. The rise of the United States as a new, powerful actor in international trade (Cuenca-Esteban 2014) was a considerable strategic upheaval. Given its size and economic dynamism, the USA could not be dismissed like other small neutral trading nations when peace returned. Furthermore, it was better able to fight back and keep its strategic autonomy. Recognising the situation, Bonaparte reconciled France with the USA and the other neutrals from 1800 on and encouraged the formation of the Second League of Armed Neutrality between Denmark, Sweden, Russia, and

Prussia. No later than 1801, though, the British blockaded these countries (with the exception of Prussia) and bombed Copenhagen. The League was terminated. Notwithstanding these difficulties, Bonaparte's neutral-favouring policy change had a positive effect and French trade recovered quickly during the short Peace of Amiens.

The Peace of Amiens of 1802 did not last. Neither France nor the United Kingdom fulfilled their peace commitments: France held on to the Low Countries and continued its conquests, Britain held Malta. No trade treaty was signed, and France continued its protectionist policy. A new war was started on 17 May 1803 by British peacetime seizure of French and Dutch merchant ships.

After the resumption of war, France again joined Britain in its hostility to neutral traders, including the emerging United States, in order to impede its enemy's trade. The decisive break from previous French policy came with the 1806 Berlin decree. It provided the basic structure of the Continental System. It stated that: (1) all trade with the British was prohibited; (2) all British subjects in French-occupied areas were prisoners of war and their property was 'fair prize'; (3) all trade in British goods was prohibited and all goods from Britain and its colonies were 'fair prize' (and one-half their value was to be used to indemnify French merchants for losses to the British); and (4) no ships coming from the ports of Britain or its colonies would be permitted to use any port on the Continent (Davis and Engerman 2006b). Britain responded to this policy with an Order-in-Council that required that neutral vessels call at a British port before proceeding to the Continent. The Napoleonic Milan Decree (1807) declared that all neutral shipping using British ports or paying British tariffs were to be regarded as British and seized. This clearly created an unsustainable situation where all neutral countries were barred from trading with both France and Britain.

The French policy was an unprecedented example of self-blockade. Historical economists have balanced between two interpretations of what objectives Napoleon might have pursued by implementing the Continental System. The classical interpretation is that of Eli Heckscher. For Hecksher, the Continental System was due to Napoleon's extreme mercantilist ideology and it was doomed to fail because, as classical trade theory teaches us, mercantilist policy is no match for liberal policy in terms of economic efficiency. Heckscher's interpretation has some points on its side. Certainly, Napoleon was a mercantilist, and his protectionist trade policy aimed at privileging the industrialisation of France in its 1789 borders. The blockade had concrete effects on French industrialisation (Juhász 2018), but these were only incidental. Moreover, if the aim of Napoleon's economic blockade was market-based economic warfare against the United Kingdom, it did not conduct it in a very coherent manner. As manufactures from Italy, Switzerland, and the Great-Duchy of Baden tended to be excluded from the French market and Italian exports of raw materials to France were encouraged, Napoleon was waging economic war not only upon Britain, but also upon France's own satellites, and even some French *départements* (Heckscher 1922: 259; Marzagalli 2022).

Crouzet (1987) challenged Heckscher's canonical interpretation of Napoleon's blockade. In a nutshell, his argument was that the Continental System was the result of the strategic bind that resulted from the battles of Trafalgar and Austerlitz. The coincidence of the great naval defeat and great land victory in the autumn of 1805 left the French struggling to find a way to actually hurt the United Kingdom. For France, which ruled on land but was completely outplayed on the sea, the only remaining possibility to significantly damage British trade was to block British industrial goods, even if carried by neutrals, from reaching their main outlet, the European continent. In the short term, this policy seemed relatively benign for France. Its colonial trade had been shattered by Saint-Domingue's declaration of independence and French producers had already re-oriented their trade towards continental markets. Neutrals did not need to be cajoled because their number and power were fast declining with the extension of the war to the whole of continental Europe. The Dutch came under French control early on. Denmark and Norway were thrown into French arms by a hostile British policy (with armed aggression in 1801 and 1807). Prussia, Sweden, and Russia had long been participants in anti-French coalitions (Russia and Prussia were part of the first coalition, Sweden part of the second one), despite spells of neutrality. The only sizeable neutral country remaining was the United States, and a major success of Napoleon was to kindle hostility between Britain and the USA. In late 1807, responding to renewed British and French hostility, the United States adopted an Embargo Act directed against trade with both France and the United Kingdom. This was effective at reducing British imports to the USA, but it was unpopular and did not change British policy. It was repealed in early 1809 and followed by the Non-Intercourse Act of 1809 and Macon's Bill Number 2 in 1810. The United States promised that if France or the United Kingdom lifted its restrictions on US trade, it would stop trading with the other power. Napoleon convinced the Americans he would lift the restrictions, and the USA stopped trading with the United Kingdom in late 1810. Tensions with the United Kingdom increased, and, despite a last-minute repeal of the Orders in Council in 1812, war finally broke out (1812–1814). Despite their size and newly gained role, however, the

Americans had no better luck than France in the war, which was ultimately won by the British. US commercial losses were substantial. In 1811, before the war, US net shipping earnings were $40 million; this plunged to almost zero in 1814. Part of the loss was temporary: shipping earnings bounced back in 1815 and the following years to around half the 1811 level. There was little hope of full recovery because earnings in 1811 had benefited from the temporary importance of the US as the last sizeable neutral carrier (North 1960: table A-4).

Returning to revisionist interpretation of the French policy, it was not market-focused, but rather aimed at hurting British capacity to fund war:

Chaptal and [Napoleon's] other advisers recognized (and Napoleon appreciated), the real (and perhaps the only) prospect for the Continental System resided in the economic impact that the more or less immediate oscillations and potentially significant reductions in British and colonial exports might exercise on three variables of direct and immediate concern to a state subsidizing and funding armies of British and foreign troops on the mainland, while maintaining command of the seas[:] the fiscal base for taxation, the capacity to borrow on London and European capital markets, and the supply of money and credit. (O'Brien 2006: 389)

This explains the well-known episodes of Napoleon agreeing to sell grain to Britain in 1809 and 1810, and his willingness to sell gin, though only in exchange for money (both discussed by Olson 1963: 61). Napoleon installed the Continental System out of the belief that cutting British exports would burden Britain with an unfavourable balance of payments and that loss of precious metals would leave the country unable to pay subsidies to its allies and bring the collapse of internal credit and, ultimately, a commercial crisis. The belief that bullion was still a central supply of war in the early nineteenth century was plausible. The military aid given by Britain to other members of the anti-French coalition was mainly in the form of money ('the Golden Cavalry of St George'), not war supplies.[9] Likewise, Napoleon did not extract war supplies from beaten foes and satellites, but indemnities in cash. For all these reasons, the aim of the Continental System can be best understood as being a form of capacity-focused warfare and not market-focused economic warfare.

Indeed, Napoleon's policy did create some difficulties for the British economy. The French Revolutionary Wars had not impeded British

---

[9] 'Napoleon's aim was to reduce Britain's specie supply (a goal he was successful in achieving in the years of the blockade, since bullion at the Bank of England fell from £6.9 million in 1808 to £2.2 million in 1814)' (Davis and Engerman 2006a: 359).

trade growth, but it did markedly decrease after 1802. According to Crouzet, the Continental System was successful in reducing British exports and creating an industrial crisis during two periods: in 1808 and 1810–1812. In both cases, this was because of the conjuncture of two things: the French armies were not fighting any major war and could impose the closure of northern Europe ports to British goods and the United States closed off British imports. The British stock of bullion was reduced (see Figure 1.5) and the Bank of England had to suspend the convertibility of the British pound from 1797 to 1821 despite pressure from the public and economists in the bullionist controversy. 'French hopes and anticipations went up and down with the fluctuations in the price of bonds on the London capital market', yet 'no correlation can be detected between monthly movements in the prices of government stocks and exports and re-exports recorded as shipped to market' and actually 'rates peaked during years of invasion scares (1797–98 and 1805)' (O'Brien 2006: 391–392). Yet the sophistication of the British financial system and its ability to function despite its reduced stocks of precious metals and the lack of convertibility of the pound sterling from 1797 to 1821 made French efforts ineffective in the long run.

It is not easy to assess quantitatively the success of the British and French economic policies. The period 1792–1815 was so tumultuous that it is difficult to distinguish the effects of warfare, let alone economic

Figure 1.5 Bullion at the Bank of England, 1796–1820 (£ thou.)
Source: Mitchell and Deane (1962: 442–443).

warfare, on either economy (Charles, Daudin, and Marzagalli 2021; O'Brien 2021). Numerous overseas markets for manufactures were lost to France (e.g. the Near East and the Spanish Empire) which redirected its textile trade to luxuries and continental Europe. That loss of markets contributed to the decline of several industries, in particular in the west of France, which became an industrial desert after 1815. Entrepot trade between the West Indies and continental Europe, which was the most dynamic part of eighteenth-century French trade, was destroyed and did not pick up after 1815. France was unable to recover its previous trading positions during the following peace. Economic warfare had a lasting impact on French trade: the share of trade in France's national income (total trade over gross domestic product) declined by half, from 20 per cent to 10 per cent between 1789 and 1820 (Charles, Daudin, and Marzagalli 2021: 62).

Based on the evolution of prices, O'Rourke estimates the loss of economic welfare for France at 3–4 per cent and for Britain at slightly less than 2 per cent (O'Rourke 2005: table 4, 2006). This is significant. Yet welfare losses for the population are not the same as military capacity losses, and military capacity losses due to the British blockade were probably limited (except in peripheral theatres). The British 'failure' can be easily explained because French resources for waging war did not depend on overseas trade.

Concerning the French failure, it is true that the Continental System was all the more difficult to implement since it was seen as a burden imposed by the French on the rest of Europe (Heckscher 1922: 159).[10] Smuggling was widespread (Marzagalli 1999). More fundamentally, the Continental System failed not because it was absurd, but for two reasons. First, it lacked time and consistency. It was only really enforced from mid-1807 to mid-1808 and from mid-1810 to mid-1812 (Crouzet 2006: 360). Second, it faced a historically very well-established system of public finance and monetary management (O'Brien 1989; Bordo and White 1991) that provided the United Kingdom with great resilience. One of the main consequence of the French wars – Britain's dominant position in terms of trade and service exports after 1815 – had little to do with the Continental System as it applied from 1808.[11] It was linked to the

---

[10] Note, however, that the idea that France invaded Russia to enforce the Continental System is probably wrong. Russian trade policy was actually quite hostile to the United Kingdom and Russia was not an important market for British goods in 1811 (Crouzet 1987: 654–656, 857 note 7, 858 note 9; Esdaile 2008: 456, 458).

[11] Between 1784–1792 and 1816–1820, Britain's re-exports tripled and its freight and insurance earnings more than doubled (Cuenca-Esteban 2001: table 1).

structural advantage the Royal Navy had gained over a weakened French navy even before the battle of Trafalgar in 1805.

Conclusion

The seventeenth and eighteenth centuries were a period when war and the economy were tied together. The transformation of the art of war, which necessitated ever growing financial means, made the control of international markets and trade a primary goal of nation states, to be achieved by all means necessary. Between 1688 and 1713, Great Britain and France aimed to achieve international dominance by conducting 'market-based economic warfare', using military means to obtain economic leadership. Our claim is that, convinced that its natural advantages and economic base made it the natural economic leader, *ancien régime* France gradually abandoned this form of economic warfare. Successive French governments favoured policies that disentangled economic competition from military conflict, in times of both peace and war. On the other hand, British policies were consistent throughout the period, favouring straightforward mercantilist market-focused economic warfare. The French Revolution and Napoleon's reign brought about fundamental changes in the relationship between economic rivalry and military conflict. Even if Napoleon was a mercantilist, the Continental System is best understood as a failed gamble on capacity-focused economic warfare rather than as a return to mercantilist market-focused economic warfare (Crouzet 1987, 2006; O'Brien 2006). Likewise, even if mercantilism and market-focused economic warfare still dominated British conceptions of the war against France, capacity-focused economic warfare became more important in the British conduct of war.

As the United Kingdom emerged as the uncontested military and economic victor and leader after the Congress of Vienna, market-focused economic warfare became irrelevant. New markets were still to be violently conquered outside Europe against lesser military powers, but the idea that war between great powers could pay economically through market-focused economic warfare receded, down to the arguments by Norman Angell and others that twentieth-century war had become too expensive ever to be economically justified. After 1815, the United Kingdom and France became long-term allies and proponents of a liberal international order in which economic competition and war became separate entities. Capacity-focused economic warfare became the only form of economic warfare practised between large states and economic competition between great powers took the form of non-violent trade wars that has persisted to the present day.

Bibliography

Alimento, A., and K. Stapelbroek. 2017. *The Politics of Commercial Treaties in the Eighteenth Century*. Cham: Springer International Publishing.

Baugh, D. A. 1965. *British Naval Administration in the Age of Walpole*. Princeton, NJ: Princeton University Press.

　1988. 'Great Britain's "Blue-Water" Policy, 1689–1815', *International History Review* 10(1): 33–58.

Bell, D. A. 2007. *The First Total War: Napoleon's Europe and the Birth of Warfare as We Know It*. New York: Houghton Mifflin.

Bély, L. 1990. *Espions et ambassadeurs au temps de Louis XIV*. Paris: Fayard.

Benjamin, D. K. 2009. 'Golden Harvest: The British Naval Prize System, 1793–1815'. Unpublished manuscript. www.academia.edu/14515791.

Black, J. 2007. *Trade, Empire and British Foreign Policy, 1689–1815: The Politics of a Commercial State*. London: Routledge.

Bordo, M. D., and E. N. White. 1991. 'A Tale of Two Currencies: British and French Finance during the Napoleonic Wars', *Journal of Economic History* 51(2): 303–316.

Brewer, J. 2002. *The Sinews of Power: War, Money and the English State 1688–1783*. London: Routledge. https://doi.org/10.4324/9780203193167.

Buffinton, A. H. [1929] 1975. *The Second Hundred Years War*. New York: Greenwood Press.

Chaline, O. 2016. *Les armées du Roi: Le grand chantier – XVIIe–XVIIIe siècle*. Paris: Armand Colin.

Charles, L., G. Daudin, and S. Marzagalli. 2021. 'In the Epicentre of the Storm? The Effects of the Revolution and Warfare on the French Economy, 1789–1815', in P. K. O'Brien (ed.), *The Crucible of Revolutionary Warfare and European Transitions to Modern Economic Growth*. Leiden: Brill.

Charles, L. et al. 2022. 'Exploring the Transformation of French Trade in the Long Eighteenth Century (1713–1823): The TOFLIT18 Project', *Historical Methods: A Journal of Quantitative and Interdisciplinary History* 55(4): 1–31.

Clark, G. N. 1928. 'War Trade and Trade War, 1701–1713', *Economic History Review* 1(2): 262–280.

Clément, P., ed. 1861. *Lettres, instructions et mémoires de Colbert (9 vols.)*. Paris: Editions impériales.

Conybeare, J. A. C. 1987. *Trade Wars: The Theory and Practice of International Commercial Rivalry*. New York: Columbia University Press.

Corbett, J. S. 2004. *Principles of Maritime Strategy (1911)*. Mineola, NY: Dover Corporation.

Crouzet, F. 1987. *L'Économie britannique et blocus continental*. Paris: Économica.

　2006. 'The Continental System after Eighty Years', in R. Findlay et al. (eds.), *Eli Heckscher, International Trade, and Economic History*, pp. 323–346. Cambridge, MA: MIT Press.

　2008. *La guerre économique franco-anglaise au xviiie siècle*. Paris: Fayard.

Cuenca-Esteban, J. 2001. 'The British Balance of Payments, 1772–1820: India Transfers and War Finance', *Economic History Review* 54(1): 58–86.

2004. 'Comparative Patterns of Colonial Trade: Britain and Its Rivals', in L. Prados de la Escosura (ed.), *Exceptionalism and Industrialisation: Britain and Its European Rivals*, pp. 1688–1815. Cambridge: Cambridge University Press.

2014. 'British "Ghost" Exports, American Middlemen, and the Trade to Spanish America, 1790–1819: A Speculative Reconstruction', *William & Mary Quarterly* 71(1): 63–98.

Daudin, G., and E. M. Tirindelli. 2025. 'Not "Easy to Win": The British War on French Trade, 1744–1815'. Working Paper.

Davis, L. E., and S. L. Engerman. 2006a. 'Eli Heckscher, Economic Warfare, Naval Blockades, and the Continental System', in R. Findlay et al. (eds.), *Eli Heckscher, International Trade, and Economic History*, pp. 347–371. Cambridge, MA: MIT Press.

2006b. *Naval Blockades in Peace and War: An Economic History since 1750*. Cambridge: Cambridge University Press.

Deane, P., and W. A. Cole. 1969. *British Economic Growth 1688–1959: Trends and Structure*. 2nd ed. Cambridge: Cambridge University Press.

Du Tot, N. 1738. *Réflexions politiques sur les finances et le commerce, où l'on examine quelles ont été sur les revenus, les denrées, le change étranger, les influences des augmentations et des diminutions des valeurs numéraires des monnoyes* (2 vols.). La Haye: Prévost. https://gallica.bnf.fr/ark:/12148/bpt6k10544005.

Enciso, A. G. 2016. *War, Power and the Economy: Mercantilism and State Formation in 18th-Century Europe* (1st ed.). London: Routledge.

Esdaile, C. 2008. *Napoleon's Wars: An International History, 1803–1815*. London: Penguin UK.

Federico, G., and A. Tena-Junguito. 2016. 'World Trade, 1800–1938: A New Data-Set', *European Historical Economics Society Working Papers* 93: 297.

Findlay, R., and K. H. O'Rourke. 2007. *Power and Plenty: Trade, War, and the World Economy in the Second Millennium*. Princeton, NJ: Princeton University Press.

Griffiths, D. M. 1971. 'An American Contribution to the Armed Neutrality of 1780', *The Russian Review* 30(2): 164–172.

Gülsunar, E. 2021. 'The State, Parliamentary Legislation and Economic Policy during the Structural Transformation of British Economy, 1700–1850'. PhD thesis. https://portal.research.lu.se/en/publications/the-state-parliamentary-legislation-and-economic-policy-during-th.

Heckscher, E. F. 1922. *The Continental System: An Economic Interpretation*. Oxford: Clarendon Press.

1994. *Mercantilism (1935)* (2 vols.). London: Routledge.

Hillmann, H., and C. Gathmann. 2011. 'Overseas Trade and the Decline of Privateering', *Journal of Economic History*, 71(3): 730–761. https://doi.org/10.1017/S0022050711001902.

Juhász, R. 2018. 'Temporary Protection and Technology Adoption: Evidence from the Napoleonic Blockade', *American Economic Review* 108(11): 3339–3376.

Mahan, A. T. 1892 and 1894. *The Influence of Sea Power upon the French Revolution & Empire in Two Volumes*. Boston: Sampson Low, Marston and Company.

Marzagalli, S. 1999. *Les Boulevards de la fraude: La négoce maritime et le Blocus continental 1806–1813*. Villeneuve d'Ascq: Presses Universitaire du Septentrion.
  2015. 'La navigation américaine pendant les French Wars (1793–1815): une simple reconfiguration des circuits commerciaux par neutres interposés?', in É. Schnakenbourg (ed.), *Neutres et neutralité dans l'espace atlantique durant le long XVIIIe siècle (1700–1820): une approche globale [Neutrals and Neutrality in the Atlantic World during the Long Eighteenth Century (1700–1820): A Global Approach]*, pp. 131–156. Bécherel: Les Perséides.
  2022. 'Napoleonic Wars and Economic Imperialism', in A. Forrest, M. Broers and P. Dwyer (eds.), *The Cambridge History of Napoleonic Wars. Vol. 1 Politics and Diplomacy*, pp. 232–252. Cambridge: Cambridge University Press.
Mitchell, B. R., and P. Deane. 1962. *Abstract of British Historical Statistics*. Cambridge: Cambridge University Press
Modelski, G., and W. R. Thompson. 1988. 'Seapower and Global Politics', in *Seapower in Global Politics, 1494–1993*, pp. 3–26. London: Macmillan Press.
Morineau, M. 1985. *Incroyables Gazettes et fabuleux métaux. Les retours des trésors américains dans les gazettes hollandaises XVIe–XVIIIe siècles*. Paris: Éditions de la Maison des Sciences de l'Homme.
Neal, L. 1977. 'Interpreting Power and Profit in Economic History: A Case Study of the Seven Years War', *Journal of Economic History* 37(1): 20–35.
Norman, C. B. 1887. *The Corsairs of France*. London: Sampson Low, Marston, Searle, & Rivington.
North, D. 1960. 'The United States Balance of Payments, 1790–1860', in *Trends in the American Economy in the Nineteenth Century*, pp. 573–628. Princeton, NJ: Princeton University Press.
O'Brien, P. K. 1989. 'Public Finance in the Wars with France 1793–1815', in H. T. Dickinson (ed.), *Britain and the French Revolution*, pp. 165–187. Basingstoke: Macmillan.
  2006. 'The Hanoverian State and the Defeat of the Continental System: A Conversation with Eli Heckscher', in R. Findlay et al. (eds.), *Eli Heckscher, International Trade, and Economic History*, pp. 373–406. Cambridge, MA: MIT Press.
  2021. 'Britain's Wars with France 1793–1815 and Their Contribution to the Consolidation of Its Industrial Revolution', in *The Crucible of Revolutionary and Napoleonic Warfare and European Transitions to Modern Economic Growth*, pp. 22–49. Leiden: Brill.
Oermann, N. O., and H.-J. Wolff. 2022. *Trade Wars, Past and Present*. Oxford: Oxford University Press.
Olson, M. J. 1963. *The Economics of Wartime Shortage: A History of British Food Supplies in the Napoleonic War and in World Wars I and II*. Durham, NC: Duke University Press.
O'Rourke, K. H. 2005. 'The Worldwide Economic Impact of the Revolutionary and Napoleonic Wars'. *NBER Working Papers* 11344. Cambridge, MA: National Bureau of Economic Research.
  2006. 'The Worldwide Economic Impact of the French Revolutionary and Napoleonic Wars, 1793–1815', *Journal of Global History* 1(1): 123–149.

Parker, G. 1988. *The Military Revolution: Military Innovation and the Rise of the West, 1500–1800.* Cambridge: Cambridge University Press.

Quesnay, F. 2005. *Oeuvres économiques complètes et autres textes [1759]* (2 vols.). Edited by C. Théré, L. Charles, and J.-C. Perrot. Paris: Institut national d'études démographiques (Classiques de l'économie et de la population).

Roberts, M. 1955. 'The Military Revolution 1560–1660', in C. J. Rogers (eds.), *The Military Revolution Debate: Readings in the Military Transformation of Early Modern Europe*, pp. 1–12. Boulder, CO: Westview.

Rodger, N. A. M. 2005. *The Command of the Ocean: A Naval History of Britain 1649–1815.* New York: W. W. Norton.

Schnakenbourg, E. 2011. 'From "Hostile Infection" to "Free Ship, Free Goods": Changes in French Neutral Trade Legislation (1689–1778)', in *Trade and War: The Neutrality of Commerce in the Inter-State System*, pp. 95–113. Helsinki: Helsinki Collegium for Advanced Studies (COLLeGIUM: Studies Across Disciplines in the Humanities and Social Sciences, 10).

Schnakenbourg, É. 2013. 'Entre la guerre et la paix', in *Neutralité et relations internationales, XVIIe–XVIIIe siècles.* Rennes: Presses Universitaires de Rennes.

ed. 2015. *Neutres et neutralité dans l'espace atlantique durant le long XVIIIe siècle (1700–1820): une approche globale [Neutrals and Neutrality in the Atlantic World during the Long Eighteenth Century (1700–1820): A Global Approach].* Bécherel: Les Perséides.

2017. 'The Conditions of Trade in Wartime: Treaties of Commerce and Maritime Law in the Eighteenth Century', in A. Alimento and K. Stapelbroek (eds.), *The Politics of Commercial Treaties in the Eighteenth Century*, pp. 217–242. Cham: Springer International. https://doi.org/10.1007/978-3-319-53574-6_8.

2019. 'Neutral Cover and Globalized Commerce in the Wars of the Eighteenth-Century', *Magallánica. Revista de Historia Moderna* 5(10): 55–77.

Shovlin, J. 2021. *Trading with the Enemy.* New Haven, CT: Yale University Press.

Tarrade, J. 1972. *Le commerce colonial de la France à la fin de l'Ancien Régime. L'évolution du système de l'Exclusif de 1763 à 1789* (2 vols.). Paris: Presses Universitaires de France.

Tracy, N. 1991. *Attack on Maritime Trade.* Basingstoke: Macmillan.

Vauban, S. L. P. 1695. 'Mémoire concernant la course', in *Oisivetés de Mr DE VAUBAN, ou ramas de plusieurs mémoires de sa façon sur différens sujets*, Manuscript at the Bibliothèque nationale de France, Département des manuscrits français, No. 9166.

Vickers, C. G. 1943. 'Economic Warfare', *Royal United Services Institution Journal* 88(549): 14–22. https://doi.org/10.1080/03071844309433858.

Villiers, P. 1991. *Marine royale, corsaires et trafic dans l'Atlantique de Louis XIV à Louis XVI* (2 vols.). Dunkerque: Société Dunkerquoise d'Histoire et d'Archélologie.

2006. 'Les ports de la côte d'Opale: Boulogne, Calais et Dunkerque face à la guerre sur mer sous Louis XIV', in S. Marzagalli and B. Marnot (eds.), *Guerre et économie dans l'espace atlantique du XVIe au XXe siècle*, pp. 223–236. Bordeaux: Presses Universitaires de Bordeaux.

2012. 'Les corsaires de Boulogne, Calais, Dunkerque et la Tamise (XVIIe–XVIIIe)', in *La traversée France-Angleterre du Moyen-Âge à nos jours*. Arras: Artois Presses Université. https://books.openedition.org/apu/493.

Vincent de Gournay, J. 2008. *Traités sur le commerce de Josiah Child suivis des Remarques de Jacques Vincent de Gournay*. Edited by S. Meyssonnier. Paris: L'Harmattan (Cahiers d'économie politique).

Viner, J. 1948. 'Power versus Plenty as Objectives of Foreign Policy in the Seventeenth and Eighteenth Centuries', *World Politics* 1(1): 1–29.

Wallerstein, I. 1980. *The Modern World System II: Mercantilism and the Consolidation of the European World Economy 1600–1750*. New York: Academic Press.

2 Economic Warfare
The American Civil War

W. Walker Hanlon, Paul W. Rhode, and Hugh Rockoff

The Failure of 'King Cotton'

The American Civil War was an unusual case in which both sides initially tried to block trade in a commodity they had been trading with each other. The South embarked, early in the war, on a policy of withholding cotton in the belief that the unemployment and decreased economic activity caused by the shortage of cotton would force the North to recognise the South, and even if it did not, would force Britain and other European nations reliant on Southern cotton to intervene on the South's behalf. Subsequently, the roles were reversed. The North tried to stop the South from selling cotton, believing that this would prevent the South from earning the funds it needed to purchase arms and ammunition and would impoverish Southern planters, undermining support for the war.

The Southern belief in the primacy of cotton was like the belief widely held, at least until recently, of the primacy of oil. The belief in the power of cotton was stated clearly in one of the most famous debates in American history that took place in the US Senate in March 1858. The Senator from New York William Seward, a leader of the anti-slavery Republican Party, spoke about ongoing legal and paramilitary conflicts in Kansas. He outlined what he would soon label the 'Irrepressible conflict' between the supporters of free labour and the defenders of slavery. See the timeline in Table 2.1 for a chronicle of subsequent events.

Senator James Henry Hammond from South Carolina rose to defend the South. Here is a key part of his speech. It speaks directly to the potential power of cotton as an economic weapon.

We thank Hoyt Bleakley, Stephen Broadberry, Mark Harrison, Josh Hausman, Naomi Lamoreaux, Alan Olmstead, Elyce Rotella, and participants at the University of Michigan Economic History Workshop and the 'Economic History in Modern Warfare' pre-conference for comments and helpful suggestions.

Table 2.1 *Timeline of the American Civil War, 1858 and 1861–1865*

Date	Event
1858	
4 March	Senator James Henry Hammond delivers his 'Cotton is King' speech
1861	
4 February	Delegates from seceded states meet to establish the Confederacy
9 February	Jefferson Davis elected provisional Confederate President
12 April	Civil War begins; Confederates fire on Fort Sumter
19 April	President Lincoln declares a naval blockade of the coast of South Carolina; 8 days later, he extends it to the coasts of North Carolina and Virginia
10 August	Revenue Act of 1861 creates the first US income tax
1862	
16 April	Slavery abolished in the District of Columbia
19 June	Slavery prohibited in western territories
30 August	Battle of Bull Run ends; decisive Confederate victory
22 September	Preliminary Emancipation Proclamation – slaves will be freed if you do not return to the Union
17 December	General Grant expels Jews from the territory he controls
1863	
1 January	Emancipation Proclamation
4 January	Lincoln countermands General Grant's order expelling Jews from the area he controlled
17 January	Issue of greenbacks approved
3 March	Lincoln signs the Conscription Act
24 April	Confederates passes a tax in-kind on one-tenth of all produce
6 May	Battle of Chancellorsville; Confederate victory
3 July	Battle of Gettysburg ends; Union victory
3 October	Lincoln proclaims a day of Thanksgiving
17October	Lincoln calls for 300,000 more volunteers
19 November	Lincoln delivers the Gettysburg Address
8 December	Lincoln issues Proclamation of Amnesty and Reconstruction
1864	
8 November	Lincoln re-elected
1865	
31 January	US House passes the 13th Amendment to abolish slavery
1 February	Sherman's march in 'full swing'
9 April	Lee surrenders to Grant at Appomattox Court House
15 April	Lincoln dies after he is shot at Ford's Theatre
23 June	President Andrew Johnson officially ends the blockade
6 December	The 13th Amendment is ratified by Georgia, abolishing slavery

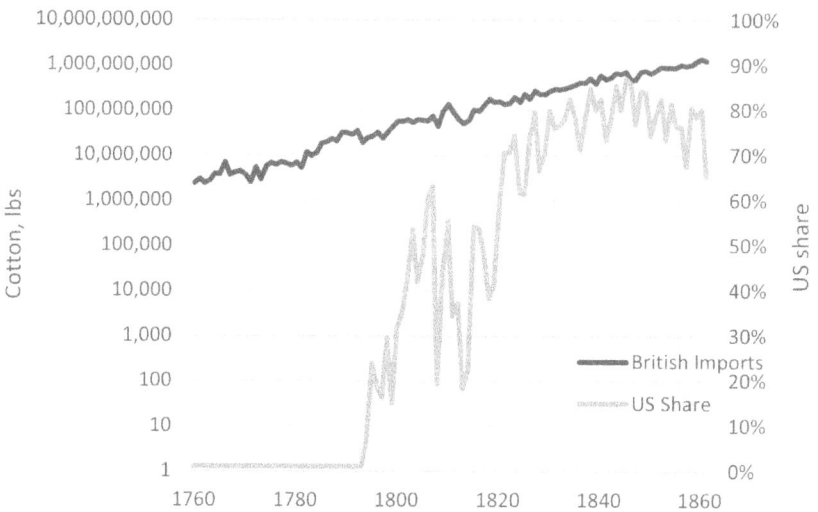

Figure 2.1 The US cotton trade with the UK, 1760–1860 (lbs weight and %)

Sources: Data for 1760–1800 are from Ellison (1886: 29); those for 1801–1814 are bales imported from the United States (from Ellison 1858, Appendix Table B) times pounds per bale for American cotton (from Holmes 1912: 6–7); 1815–1861 data are from Mann (1860, Table 17: 116) and Ellison (1886, Appendix Table 2).

Without firing a gun, without drawing a sword, should they make war on us, we could bring the whole world to our feet. What would happen if no cotton was furnished for three years? I will not stop to depict what every one can imagine, but this is certain: England would topple headlong and carry the whole civilized world with her, save the South. No, you dare not make war on cotton! No power on earth dares to make war upon it. Cotton is King.[1]

Hammond's King Cotton argument was founded upon three facts. First, cotton made up over one-half of the value of US commodity exports. Second, US-produced cotton had grown to account for 75–80 per cent of the British market, as shown in Figure 2.1. Its share of the trade of continental Europe and the northern United States was similar. Third, the cotton textile sector was highly important in Britain and other industrialised nations. For example. in terms of employment, the 1861 Census of Population shows 456,646 people in England and Wales worked in

---

[1] Speech of Hon. James H. Hammond, of South Carolina, on the Admission of Kansas, under the Lecompton Constitution. Delivered in the Senate of the United States, 4 March 1858. Library of Congress, available at www.loc.gov/item/11006808/.

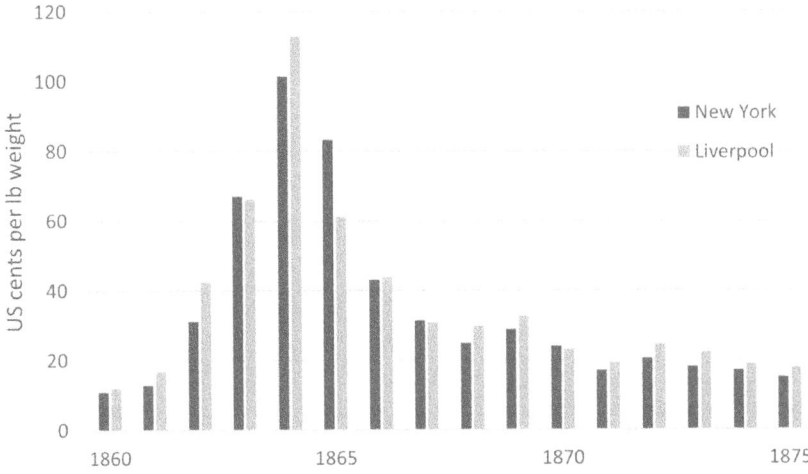

Figure 2.2 Cotton prices in Liverpool and New York City, 1860–1875 (US cents per lb weight)

cotton textile manufacturing, equal to nearly 10 per cent of manufacturing employment and more than 2 per cent of the total population (Hanlon 2015).

Hammond's prediction would soon be tested. When the Civil War began there were attempts in the South by planters to withhold cotton and by some state governments to prohibit sales. Then the North joined in. On 19 April 1861, President Lincoln issued an order creating a naval blockade of the South. This was the beginning of a successful blockade that would produce what was known in Britain as 'the cotton famine'.

The Union blockade was part of the Anaconda Plan. It was initially considered a paper measure, but it grew in effectiveness over time. The less formal Southern cotton embargo, ironically, contributed to the supply reductions in the early years. Cotton prices in Liverpool and New York soared, as illustrated in Figure 2.2.

The Supply Cut-Off in the South

The initial Southern effort to withhold cotton was led by planters and some state governments. It was not the policy of the newly established Confederate government. The Confederate government, however, did ban the cotton trade with the North and restrict shipments to the ports under its control. Its Produce Loan programme likely diverted resources from cotton to food production. And after 1862, Confederate forces

Table 2.2 *Southern attempts to run the Union blockade, 1861–1865*

Year	Attempts	Successful	Unsuccessful	Successful, percentage of total	Successful, percentage of successes in 1861
1861	3579	3,465	112	96.8	100.0
1862	858	568	290	66.2	16.4
1863	1003	731	272	72.9	21.1
1864	723	522	201	72.2	15.1
1865	153	103	50	67.3	3.0
Total	6,316	5,389	925	85.3	–
Of which, 1862–1865	2,737	1,924	813	42.3	–

Source: Surdam (2001, Table 1.1).

began to burn cotton intentionally to prevent it from falling into Union hands.

The South soon came to realise that withholding cotton was a mistake. The South needed the revenue produced by the cotton trade to buy arms, ammunition, and ships. For that reason, it turned to various measures to combat the blockade, including building and buying fast, hard-to-detect, blockade runners.

Table 2.2 shows how effective the Union naval embargo was. In 1861, there were 3,570 attempts to run the blockade and 3,465 (97 per cent) were successful. In 1865, when only specially built blockade runners had a good chance of getting through, there were only 153 attempts and only 103 were successful. The number of successful runs in 1865, because few attempts were made, was only 3 per cent of what it had been in 1861.

Surdam (2001) concluded that the Confederate armies lost no battles directly as a result of blockade-induced munitions shortages. Yet, after 1862, the Union naval effort had effects. The federal intervention cut off inter-coastal shipping, leading to the greater use of railroads for internal transport. The Southern railroad system had the 'wrong' orientation, going north–south rather than east–west, and connecting interior regions to ports rather than to each other. In the war effort, the railroad system became over-used and suffered from heavy depreciation of rails and equipment. And, due to the blockade, the worn-out rails and equipment could not easily be replaced. Disruption through this channel was not anticipated but proved important.

Table 2.3 details statistics on cotton production and exports from 1860 to 1870 in columns 1 and 2. The sharp reductions in the wartime

Table 2.3 *Production of important materials, 1860–1870*

Year	Raw cotton produced (thousand bales)	Raw cotton exported (thousand bales)	Raw cotton used in textiles (thousand bales)	Raw wool produced (thousand bales)	Anthracite coal (thousand short tons)	Pig iron shipped (thousand short tons)	Gold (kg)	Silver (metric tons)
	1	2	3	4	5	6	7	8
1860	3,841	3,615	845	49	10,984	821	75,874	4
1861	4,491	10	842	66	10,245	654	69,984	4
1862	1,597	23	369	91	10,186	704	69,207	51
1863	449	24	287	113	12,267	846	73,437	124
1864	299	18	220	157	13,027	1,014	76,734	243
1865	2,094	1,301	344	181	12,077	832	83,359	326
1866	2,097	1,402	615	177	15,784	1,205	86,967	319
1867	2,520	1,503	715	196	16,067	1,305	81,400	307
1868	2,366	1,300	844	237	17,708	1,431	74,495	351
1869	3,011	1,988	860	216	18,341	1,712	72,535	328
1870	4,352	2,922	797	185	19,958	1,665	73,748	324
								393

Sources: columns 1, 3, 5–8 Historical Statistics of the United States, Millennial Edition, series Da756, Dd844, M123, M217, Db94 and Db95, respectively. Column 2 from US Bureau of the Census, Cotton Production and Distribution, Bulletin No. 131 (1915) p. 82 in bales of 500 gross pounds, with a typo corrected for 1860. Column 4: Boston Board of Trade, Twentieth Annual Report, 1874 (Boston: James F. Cotter, 1874), p. 85.

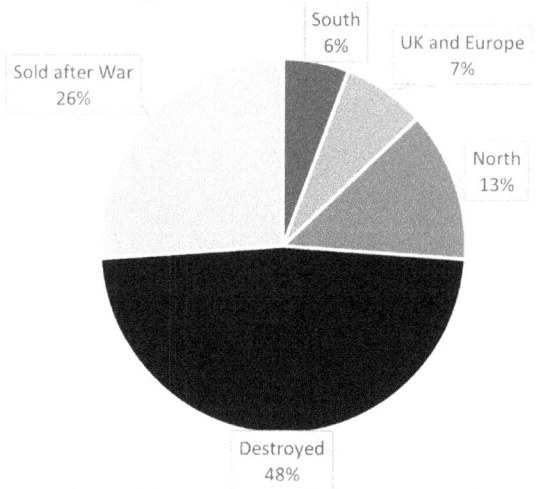

Figure 2.3 The disposition of Southern cotton, 1861–1864
(shares of total)
Source: Lebergott (1981).

years are evident. Figure 2.3 displays a pie chart of the disposition of Southern cotton output produced in the crop years 1861–1864, according to Stanley Lebergott (1981). He estimated that 6.8m bales were grown, of which almost half, 3.3m, were destroyed during the conflict. Somewhat more than a quarter remained in the South until after the war. So less than a quarter of the diminished supply was shipped out. All of these numbers contain large elements of statistical speculation and, in fact, were subject to intense financial speculation at the time.

Lebergott (1983) attributed the Confederacy's loss to the commercial-oriented, self-interested behaviour of its planter class. This group continued to direct extensive resources to cotton production and did not shift rapidly to food production or allow the release of their enslaved labour force into public activities defending their new state. Lebergott (1983: 64) reported scattered evidence showing the price of raw cotton in monetary terms at Confederate ports was roughly constant over the war years. He interpreted that stability of internal prices in the face of soaring external prices as a sign of the continued high devotion of resources to cotton production, arising from the commercial decisions of planters. The contrast between the movements of internal and external prices is even greater than Lebergott claimed. Price quotes collected more systematically from Southern newspapers shows the real price of cotton fell sharply within the Confederacy, especially after 1863 (Schwab 1901).

The South did not face a food crisis in the early years of the war. This is consistent with the findings of economic historians that the region was not overly dependent on food shipments from outside in the antebellum period (and counter to the recent resurrection of that claim by some writers in the New History of Capitalism literature). Food shortages did appear locally later in the conflict as the transportation system degraded, troops roamed through and fought on Southern soils, and adverse weather shocks hit the region (Hurt 2015). The food shortages helped undermine morale on the home front.

The Cotton Famine in the North

The US North coped with the shortage of cotton in a variety of ways. Many unemployed male factory workers joined the military. Others, including female workers, returned to family farms. In the North, trading with the South was restricted. Some cotton, however, did reach Northern mills (see Figure 2.3 and column 3 of Table 2.3). Some was obtained from slave states that remained loyal to the Union, some from territories conquered by Union forces, some was purchased legally through a licensing system, and some was purchased through black market channels.

Black market trading, incidentally, produced one of the most notorious orders issued during the Civil War: an order by General Grant in December 1862 expelling the Jews from the territories he controlled. This order was soon countermanded by Lincoln and Grant later apologised; however, the incident does perhaps illustrate the ubiquity of black-market trading and the ire that it created.

The effect of the attempt by the Lincoln administration to restrict trade with the Confederacy and early attempts by Southern planters and state governments to follow Hammond's plan and withhold cotton is shown in column 3 of Table 2.3. By 1864, consumption of cotton by the mills – the industry was concentrated in the North – had fallen to about a quarter of what it had been in 1860. As a result, many operatives in the Northern mills had been laid off.

However, things did not work out as Hammond and his followers expected. Wool was one of the closest substitutes for cotton. The US government supplied the Union troops with woollen uniforms and blankets. And, as might have been expected, production of woollens increased rapidly. The *Eleventh Annual Report* of the Boston Board of Trade (1865: 89) reported that 'No branch of our business has increased more rapidly than the domestic Wool trade'. Column 4 of Table 2.3 shows the amount of wool produced annually during the 1860s in thousands of bales. Between 1860 and 1864 the amount tripled.

Moreover, Edward Atkinson, in a report to the Boston Board of Trade included in the *Ninth Annual Report* (1863: 98) concluded that:

It is satisfactory to know that this large decrease in the operations of the Cotton Mills has not caused distress among the operatives; enlistments in the army and the demand for mechanics in the Government workshops, having given employment to men, while the activity of the manufacture of woolen goods, shoes and clothing has occupied the women, so that in Lowell, where the proportional stoppage has been the largest, from the mills being nearly all on heavy goods, the deposits in the Savings Banks have largely increased during the year.

Atkinson was not alone in concluding that the Northern war economy had coped well with the shortage of cotton. On 3 October 1863, Abraham Lincoln proclaimed a day of Thanksgiving, the beginning of the national holiday. What did Americans have to be thankful for? One thing, of course, was the success of Union arms. The Proclamation followed shortly after the great Union victory at Gettysburg. Two weeks after calling for a day of Thanksgiving, Lincoln would deliver the Gettysburg Address. However, it was not just success on the battlefield. Northerners should also be thankful, Lincoln wrote, for the success of the Northern economy. This part of the Proclamation read as follows:

Needful diversions of wealth and of strength from the fields of peaceful industry to the national defence, have not arrested the plough, the shuttle or the ship; the axe has enlarged the borders of our settlements, and the mines, as well of iron and coal as of the precious metals, have yielded even more abundantly than heretofore. Population has steadily increased, notwithstanding the waste that has been made in the camp, the siege and the battle-field; and the country, rejoicing in the consciousness of augmented strength and vigor, is permitted to expect continuance of years with large increase of freedom. No human counsel hath devised nor hath any mortal hand worked out these great things. They are the gracious gifts of the Most High God, who, while dealing with us in anger for our sins, hath nevertheless remembered mercy.[2]

Notice that Lincoln includes the shuttle, meaning production of cotton and woollen textiles.

Columns 5–8 of Table 2.3 show well-regarded modern estimates of the variables Lincoln referred to in his 1863 Thanksgiving Day Proclamation. As you can see, he was right. Between 1860 and 1864, production of coal and iron had each increased about 20 per cent. Production of gold had not changed very much but production of silver was up considerably.

---

[2] Proclamation 106 – Thanksgiving Day, 1863, available at www.presidency.ucsb.edu/documents/proclamation-106-thanksgiving-day-1863.

Lincoln again emphasised the booming Northern economy in his Thanksgiving Proclamation in 1864:[3] 'He has largely augmented our free population by emancipation and by immigration, while He has opened to us new sources of wealth and has crowned the labour of our workingmen in every department of industry with abundant rewards.' Not all went well for the Northern worker, however. Inflation was rapid in part because the money supply was increased through the issue of the greenbacks, a fiat paper money used to provide some of the money the government needed to prosecute the war. Wages did not rise as rapidly and so the real wages of workers fell during the war. This can still be seen in readily available modern data. On measuringworth.com (Officer and Willamson 2023) we find the real value of unskilled labour falling 37 per cent between 1860 and 1865 and the real value of production workers' hourly pay falling 32 per cent.

Wesley Clair Mitchell (1903) in his classic *History of the Greenbacks* argued that this was, for the most part, a straightforward case of prices rising rapidly while wages, due to a number of institutional factors, such as the need for workers to bargain with employers over wages, increased more slowly. This view was later challenged by Kessel and Alchian (1959), who did not deny that real wages had fallen, but argued that this was due to several real factors, such as the tax policy followed by the Union government, rather than a simple race between wages and prices. Subsequently, DeCanio and Mokyr (1977) concluded that Mitchell had got the story right.

The Emancipation Proclamation

We can consider the Emancipation Proclamation as a form of economic warfare, one related in part to the North's objectives with the blockade. The Proclamation did not promise freedom for all slaves.

The Emancipation Proclamation of 1 January 1863 read: 'all persons held as slaves within any State or designated part of a State, *the people whereof shall then be in rebellion* against the United States, shall be then, thenceforward, and forever free'.[4]

---

[3] Proclamation 118—Thanksgiving Day, 1864, available at www.presidency.ucsb.edu/documents/proclamation-118-thanksgiving-day-1864#:~:text=It%20has%20pleased%20Almighty%20God,is%20of%20our%20own%20household.

[4] Proclamation 95 – Regarding the Status of Slaves in States Engaged in Rebellion against the United States [Emancipation Proclamation], available at www.presidency.ucsb.edu/documents/proclamation-95-regarding-the-status-slaves-states-engaged-rebellion-against-the-united.

It left out those in four important loyal border states – Delaware, Maryland, Kentucky, and Missouri – and those in the parts of the Confederacy already conquered by the Union. The Proclamation created economic incentives in the border slave states to stick with the Union. Even if slaves in those areas were freed, slave owners might receive compensation, as proposed by Lincoln early in the war. On 6 March 1862, Lincoln's annual message proposed $400 per slave for loyal slave states. On 6 April 1862, the proposed compensated emancipation in the District of Columbia was $300 per slave. Compensation of $400 per enslaved person was equal to about half of the average market value at the time (see Carter et al. 2006: series Bb213). Based on the series in measuringworth.com, in today's money $400 is worth $12,700 using the CPI, $9,670 using the GDP deflator, and $93,300 using the unskilled wage series (Officer and Willamson 2023).

The Cotton Famine in Britain

Figure 2.4 shows cotton imports into Great Britain, from the United States and the total from all countries, annually from 1855 to 1875, and the price of cotton in Liverpool from 1860 to 1875. The attempts in the Confederacy early in the war to withhold cotton and the Northern blockade evidently had a dramatic impact. Imports from the United

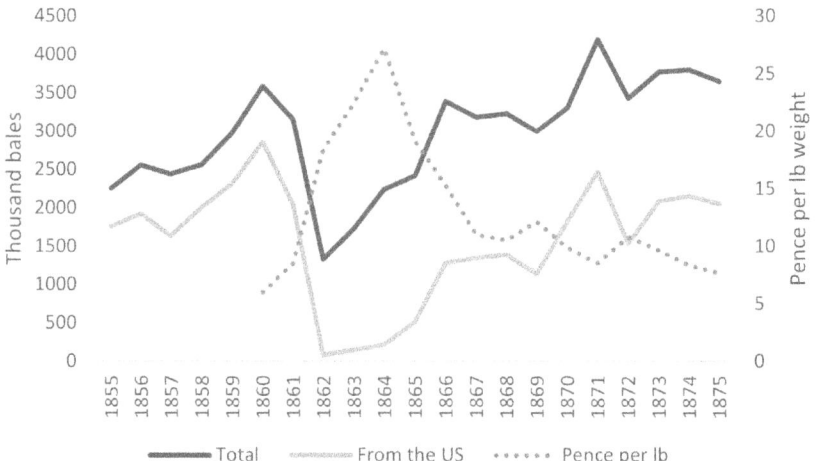

Figure 2.4 Quantity and price of cotton imported into the UK, 1855–1875 (bales and pence per lb weight)
Source: Carter et al. (2006: series EH98, EH99, and EH101).

States fell to very low levels from 1862 to 1865 and the price of cotton skyrocketed. Hence, the cotton famine.

However, several offsets allowed Britain to cope better with the shortage of American cotton than Southerners such as Hammond had expected. First, the bumper crop that arrived in 1860 allowed many cotton mills to build up their reserves of raw cotton and cotton yarn. It has been claimed, moreover, that it was the smaller mills that suffered the most from the cotton famine and that in some cases were forced into bankruptcy. The larger mills that had adequate reserves could then buy the equipment of the smaller mills at bargain prices. Thus, the most influential mills benefited to some extent from the cotton famine, and had less reason to push for a quick end to it.

It is also clear from the figures that increased imports from other producers – Egypt and India were especially important – helped to fill the gap. Total imports of cotton from the United States during 1862–1865 totalled just 952,000 bales, down 8,368,000 bales from the previous four years. However, imports from the rest of the world – the difference between the solid line and dashed line in the figure – were up by 3,502,000 bales, thus offsetting 45 per cent of the shortfall in American cotton. The increase, moreover, was mainly from producers within the British sphere of influence, rewarding some British citizens and providing the basis for a more autarkic empire.

The alternative suppliers could not increase production fast enough to offset the dearth of American cotton in the first years of the war. The supply disruptions caused economic hardship throughout European cotton production centres. In Lancashire, the largest of these, over 300,000 cotton textile workers were unemployed or working short-time during the height of the distress. Families reliant on the industry rapidly burned through their savings, and by the winter of 1862 large numbers were destitute and dependent on public assistance, through the Poor Law, or on private charity. This generated a massive increase in Poor Law relief expenditures in the cotton districts, as shown in Figure 2.5.

The relief efforts included publicly funded work projects, including the construction of new roads. These roads were collectively referred to as the 'Cotton Famine Roads'. By participating in these projects, unemployed cotton workers had a means to earn a living during the crisis. The construction of these roads also had a longer-term impact, improving infrastructure and connectivity in the regions where they were built. Many have since been incorporated into the modern road network.

Economic distress in the cotton districts did not precipitate a broader national recession. Outside of the cotton districts, the effects of the US

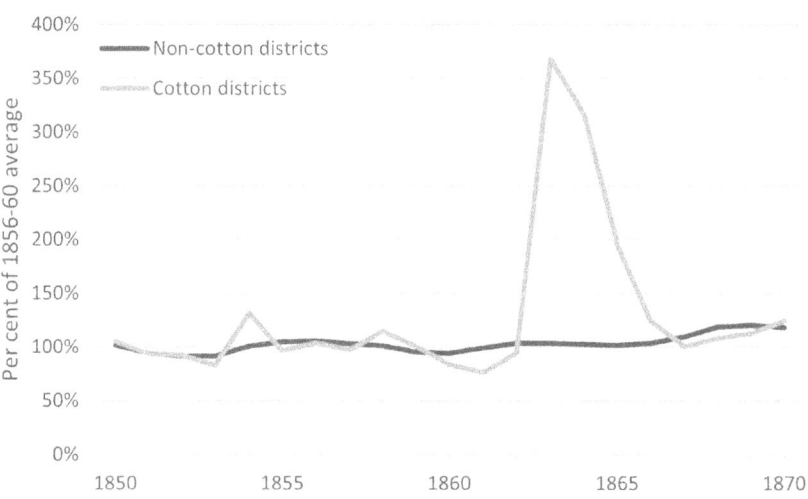

Figure 2.5 Poor Law relief expenditures in England and Wales, 1850–1870 (% of 1856/60 average)
Source: Southall, Gilbert, and Gregory (1998).

Civil War on the British economy were generally limited; as shown in Figure 2.5, Poor Law relief expenditures outside of the cotton districts were essentially unchanged. Some regions and sectors of the British economy benefited from the war. Producers of wool textiles, mainly located in Yorkshire, and the Irish linen industry grew as a result of reduced competition from cotton textiles. We can see this effect in the export values for these industries, shown in Figure 2.6. Exports of wool goods increased from £15 million to £25 million between 1861 and 1865, while the value of linen goods exports doubled from around £5 million to around £10 million over the same period.

Armaments manufacturers also benefited: firearms exports rose from £515,000 in 1861 to over £1.5 million in 1862.[5] Britain's position of neutrality and ban on direct arms sales to either side of the conflict limited somewhat the extent to which armaments manufacturers benefited from the conflict. However, there are well-known examples of sales that circumvented the ban, the most notable being the *CSS Alabama*, a commerce raider produced by a UK shipyard and supplied to the Confederacy. After the war, the UK eventually agreed to pay over $15 million to compensate the US for the damage that the ship caused.

---

[5] Data from the Annual Statement of the Trade and Navigation of the United Kingdom for 1865, available at www.escoe.ac.uk/research/historical-data/overseas-trade/.

Figure 2.6 UK wool and linen export values, 1856–1870 (£ million)
Source: Data on the declared real value of exports of UK manufactures collected from the *Annual Statement of the Trade and Navigation of the United Kingdom*, 1860 and 1865, available at https://onlinebooks.library.upenn.edu/.

Another sector of the British economy that profited from the war was the merchant marine. Prior to 1861, the US merchant marine was one of Britain's most important competitors. The disruptions caused by the war together with the increased risks that US-flagged vessels faced from Confederate commerce raiders shifted business away from US merchants. Reduced American competition benefited the British and other European merchant marines. Between 1861 and 1865, British merchant marine tonnage increased by just under 20 per cent.[6]

One other notable impact of the Civil War on the British economy was the effect on the financial system. As the shortage of American cotton drove up cotton prices and shifted purchases to alternative cotton suppliers such as India and Egypt, very large trade imbalances were created between the UK and these suppliers. This imbalance triggered large outflows of gold and silver from Britain to India and Egypt. Eventually, these outflows began to destabilise the British financial system, causing the Bank of England to respond by raising interest rates. While these imbalances would contribute to financial issues in the middle of the 1860s, the increase in interest rates did not spark a broader recession.

---

[6] Ibid.

The overall effects of the war on the British economy were therefore mixed; those districts where the economy was heavily dependent on the cotton textile industry experienced severe distress, but effects in the rest of the country were muted, and in some cases positive. Davis and Engerman (2006: 126–127) break down the overall effect:

Adversely affected sectors	Positively affected sectors
Cotton mills ~500k workers	Wool ~175k workers
Subsidiary textile ~400k	Linen ~95k
Indirect local employment in cotton textile regions ~150k	Merchant marine armaments

Clearly, the magnitude of the negative effects of the cotton shortage on affected sectors – a total of nearly a million workers unemployed out of a working population of around 10.5 million – dominated, but these were offset at least in part by gains in other areas.

At the same time, other parts of the Empire benefited from the war. In India, the largest pre-war cotton supplier outside of the US South, high cotton prices generated enormous profits as well as an increase in tax revenue that helped the Government of India pay off some of the debts incurred during the Indian Rebellion (1857/58). In Egypt, which was also within the British sphere of influence, cotton production boomed. Throughout the war, the Cotton Supply Association, a group that included many Lancashire manufacturers, promoted schemes to expand cotton production in other British colonies, including South Africa and Australia, though these were generally unsuccessful.

Economically, then, the forces that may have motivated Britain to intervene in the war were balanced by equally powerful counterforces. Politically, Britain was also divided over the question of whether to intervene in the conflict. While there was substantial sympathy for the South in some quarters, particularly among the aristocratic classes, in others there was strong opposition to intervening on behalf of the slave states (Foreman 2010).

The moral dimension of the war played a central role in the failure of 'King Cotton' to motivate British intervention. It was a war between those who favoured the continuation of slavery and those who opposed it. This was especially clear after Lincoln's Emancipation Proclamation went into effect. Thus, many in Britain who might have supported intervention on behalf of the South for economic reasons opposed it for moral reasons. This was especially important for the labour movement in Britain. Labourers were suffering as a result of the cotton famine, but they and their leaders did not want to see Britain engage in diplomatic or military actions that would promote the survival of slavery.

A particularly dramatic example of the impact of the moral issue was the 'Address of the Working-Men of Manchester to Abraham Lincoln'. Manchester was one of the leading centres of cotton production in Britain and was hit hard by the cotton famine. Understandably, there were supporters of the Confederacy in Manchester and there are reports of Confederate flags being flown. Yet at a meeting attended by many workers on the New Year's Eve before the Emancipation went into effect on 1 January 1863, those present drafted a letter to Abraham Lincoln endorsing his attempt to win the war and bring slavery to an end.

The address began as follows.

We, the working men of Manchester, assembled at the Free-Trade Hall, beg to present you with this address as a small token of our sincere respect and admiration for your public conduct during the terrible crisis through which you have successfully passed. We rejoice to know that the efforts which are now being made to reduce the great Republic of America to the condition of a broken and dishonored community of Slave States have been utterly defeated; and we think it our duty to express to you our deep sympathy with the cause which you represent, not so much from our abhorrence of slavery (deep as that feeling is), as from our profound conviction that the division of your great Republic into two hostile camps could only be productive of general calamity. (*Manchester Guardian*, 1 January 1863)

Lincoln responded with a letter recognising the suffering caused by the cotton famine and complimenting the workers on their courage in nevertheless supporting the North and abolition.

Geopolitical concerns also played an important role in the British decision not to intervene. As Lincoln's Secretary of State designee, William Seward, warned the British ambassador to Washington, recognition of the Confederacy would lead to war and could precipitate a US invasion of Canada (Boyko 2013: 64). Seward was not the only threat. James Gordon Bennett, the doughface editor of the widely circulated *New York Herald* (9 February 1861, p. 7), had advocated that the Union release the South and absorb Canada instead.

Contrary to Hammond's prediction, England did not 'topple headlong and carry the whole civilized world with her'. The cotton famine in Britain did not produce the intervention on the South's behalf that the Southerners had expected despite the effects on British employment. One reason for British inaction was the growth of production in the rest of the world, which undermined the hoped-for effect of the King Cotton strategy in several ways. Obviously, part of the story was that it suggested the problem would soon solve itself without a military intervention. That meant not going to war with a rich nation which was now beginning to show its military prowess.

The growth of cotton production in the rest of the world worked through other channels to reduce support in Britain for intervention. Much of the increased production occurred within the British sphere of influence. Production of flax for linen was stimulated in Ireland, production of wool in Britain, and production of cotton in India and Egypt. This meant that there were British interest groups that were benefiting from the high price of cotton and in no hurry to see American cotton back on the market. Moreover, British pundits and planners could see that producing cotton within the empire would be good insurance against a future war-related cut-off.

And where Britain led, the rest of Europe followed. France was home to a large textile industry, which began suffering from input shortages just as protective duties on British imports were being lowered. The continental power offered to mediate the American conflict with the aim of lifting the blockage. Napoleon III leaned towards the Confederacy but his advisors favoured neutrality, and the manoeuvres produced few results. Napoleon III instead used the distraction created by the American Civil War to pursue his ill-fated intervention into Mexico (Henderson 1933).

Overall, we can agree with Davis and Engerman's (2006: loc. 2825) conclusion about the effectiveness of the blockade. It did not 'garrot' the Confederacy, but it 'did play a significant role in the Union victory'. Its overall effects were 'less impressive than the South's initial attempt at suicide – a failed threat that had been designed to force England and France to recognize the Confederate succession'.

Taking the longer view, one interesting development revealed in Figure 2.4, on British imports, was the swift recovery of American cotton supplies. If some in the cotton trade had expected that the freeing of America's slaves would greatly reduce America's presence in the international cotton market, they were sadly disappointed. The sharecropping system that developed in the South after the Civil War, as vile as it was along many dimensions, produced a great deal of cotton. In the years 1870–1873, British imports of American cotton totalled 7,916,000 bales, about 86 per cent of what had been received from the United States in 1858–1861, years that included a bumper crop. The price of cotton in Liverpool, moreover, returned to the pre-war level despite the end of slave-based production of cotton in the United States.

The Erlanger Loan

The Confederates tried a clever way of evading the effects of the blockade, although one that in the end proved insufficient. The Confederate government issued bonds in Europe that were sold to European investors.

The most important were known as the Erlanger bonds because they were underwritten by Emile Erlanger & Company, a Paris-based investment banking firm. The bonds promised interest and principal in gold. But the key provision gave the holder the right to buy cotton at 6 pence per pound so that the bond holder stood to profit if cotton was selling at a higher price and a way could be found to bring the cotton to market. Cotton had been selling at 7 pence per pound in the British market during the first months of 1861, had risen to 12 and 13 pence per pound by the spring of 1862, and had reached nearly twice that by the end of the year (Schwab 1901: 30), Clearly, the purchase price in the bonds was attractive. The right to buy cotton would not expire until six months after the end of the war. So, bond holders could wait until the South won its independence and then profit from what would presumably be a high price for cotton prevailing after a long war in which the world was deprived of Southern cotton. Confederate defeat, of course, was a risk. But a speculator might hope that the treaty ending the war would include a provision for repaying foreign loans contracted by the South. This might be done to maintain the credit of the United States in the spirit, perhaps, of Hamilton's plan for paying the debts contracted by state governments after the establishment of the United States. The purpose of the loan, of course, was to use the funds received from European investors to purchase arms, including, importantly, naval vessels in Europe.

The bonds were issued in March 1863, when a Southern victory seemed highly likely. However, the tide of war soon turned with the Union victories at Gettysburg and Vicksburg in July 1863, and the market for the Erlanger bonds shrank accordingly. The Confederates might have done better if they had undertaken their external borrowing sooner. Grossman and Han (1996) explain that this may have seemed unnecessary to the Southerners because of the large volume of mobilisable resources with which the South began the war. The price of the Erlanger bonds did not, however, immediately fall to zero after the tide of war turned. Brown and Burdekin (2000) and Weidenmier (2000) analysed the price of the Erlanger bonds in London. They showed that, as might be expected, the price of the bonds responded to news about the war. But the news was not always to be interpreted negatively. Some rumours, for example that General Sherman's campaign was in trouble, or that General Mclelland might run for president on a peace platform, could send the price of Erlanger bonds back up. However, Weidenmier and Oosterlinck (2015) found a different pattern, a steady decline, when they examined the price of Confederate gold bonds sold in Amsterdam, reflecting the growing expectation that the South would be defeated, and the bonds would be repudiated.

There were no further bond issues and some of the first proceeds of the Erlanger loan were lost in a futile attempt to support the price of the bonds. But Gentry (1970) nevertheless described the Erlanger loan as a success for the Confederacy that raised a substantial sum and made it possible for the South to purchase arms in Europe in 1863 and 1864.

General Sherman and the Turn towards Total War

In the first phases of the Civil War, the assumption was that the war should be won on the battlefield. Civilians and the economy in which they worked were to be spared. Indeed, there were complaints that extensive 'trading with the enemy' was being permitted (Leigh 2014).

In the last phase of the war, however, the North turned to what is often referred to as 'total war'. The goals were to ease the path to victory by destroying the ability of the South to make and deploy arms and to undermine its willingness to continue the fight.

General William Tecumseh Sherman led the turn to total war. Sherman had revealed his willingness to wage total war in the campaigns for Vicksburg, Chattanooga, and Atlanta. Atlanta fell on 2 September 1864. It was an important victory for the North, where it was widely recognised that Atlanta was a key railroad hub and manufacturing centre. Indeed, the victory played an important role in the 1864 election. Abraham Lincoln was in a close race against former general George B. McClellan, who was running on a platform that called for a negotiated end to the war, one that might have permitted the continuation of slavery. Lincoln thought he would lose. The capture of Atlanta, however, electrified the North and helped Lincoln to a decisive victory.

Sherman wasn't done. His next idea was his famous 'March to the Sea'. In Atlanta he was supplied by rail. This would not be possible on a march across Georgia. But as he explained to General Grant, he believed he could, to some extent, live off the land: 'I would not hesitate to cross the State of Georgia with sixty thousand men, hauling some stores, and depending on the country for the balance. Where a million people find subsistence, my army won't starve' (Sherman 1876: 114–115). On 9 October 1864, he telegraphed Grant, reiterating that he could accomplish his march, and using a phrase (italics added) that has been quoted frequently.

By attempting to hold the roads, we will lose a thousand men each month, and will gain no result. I can make this march, and *make Georgia howl*! We have on hand over eight thousand head of cattle and three million rations of bread, but no corn, We can find plenty of forage in the interior of the State. (Sherman 1876: 152)

Economic Warfare: The American Civil War

The idea was not only to undermine Southern morale. There were mills, foundries, factories, machine-shops, cotton and cotton gins, telegraph lines, and railroads to destroy, all of which contributed to the Southern war effort.

Sherman's prediction that he could rely on foraging to furnish much of the needs of his soldiers and their mounts and pack animals proved correct. Historically, production of food had been high along the line of march, and high production appears to have been maintained during the war despite the drain of labour into the military. Possibly, decisions to plant food crops or use the land for fodder rather than cotton because foodstuffs from other areas, such as Northern corn, could not be obtained played a role.

The railroads were an important target because they were used to bring supplies from Atlantic ports to Southern armies. One method Sherman's army used to disable them was to heat rails until they became malleable and then bend them around telegraph poles or trees producing 'Sherman's neckties' or 'bowties'.

The March to the Sea ended with the capture of Savannah, an important Southern port, in December 1864. Sherman then turned North with the goals of inflicting more damage and ultimately of joining his army with Grant's.

The damage was done. One of the best-known cases occurred when Sherman's army entered Columbia, the capital of South Carolina, where the first ordinance of secession had been adopted. Sherman's army burned the city, although Sherman's exact role is controversial.

Sherman's army, however, never joined with Grant's. Lee surrendered to Grant at Appomattox Court House on 9 April 1865, effectively ending the war. The largest surrender took place on 26 April near Durham, North Carolina when General Joseph E. Johnston surrendered to Sherman.

Conclusions about the consequences of Sherman's marches, for example the effect on Southern morale, necessarily involve considerable speculation. We do know that the effects persisted long after the war. Southern bitterness about the treatment of plantations along the line of march was dramatised in Margaret Mitchell's *Gone with the Wind*, which struck a nerve in a nation traumatised by the Great Depression. The novel won the Pulitzer Prize in 1937 and the movie won the Academy Award for Best Picture in 1940.

There were also devastating and persistent effects on manufacturing and agriculture. Feigenbaum, Lee, and Mezzanotti (2022) compared counties through which Sherman marched with non-march counties and found that initially both manufacturing and agriculture took devastating hits. Manufacturing, they found, had largely recovered by 1880 but some of the effects on agriculture persisted as late as 1920. They attributed much of the slow pace of recovery to weaknesses in the financial system.

A phrase often associated with Sherman sums up America's experience in the Civil War: 'War is Hell.'

Commentary

The story of the Civil War cotton famine relates to two recent scholarly interventions. Mulder's highly publicised 2022 book, *The Economic Weapon*, treats 1919 as the birth of economic sanctions. This ignores the long story of 'peaceful coercion' as a weapon of choice in America's past. This history includes the non-importation agreements in the lead-up to the Revolutionary War, Jefferson's Embargo of 1807 and related measures in the Early National period, and the annexation of Texas in the mid-1840s with the explicit intention of maintaining the South's 'cotton monopoly'. The movement culminated in the King Cotton thinking prevalent in the late 1850s and early 1860s.

Regarding the 1845 Annexation of Texas, its leading proponent, President John Tyler, declared in 1850: 'The monopoly of the cotton plant was the great and important concern. That monopoly, now secured, places all other nations at our feet. An embargo of a single year would produce in Europe a greater amount of suffering than a fifty years' war' (Crapol 2006: 229). In 1861, when urging Virginia to join the secession movement, Tyler observed: 'Sir, you cannot do without the cotton States ... The foundation of all the exchanges of the world, the clothing of the world, the commerce of the world, proceeds chiefly from them' (Lebergott 1983: 59).

Woodrow Wilson, an advocate for the sanctions clause in the League of Nations negotiations, was well aware of this long and difficult history. Indeed, he personally lived through these events, growing up as a child in Georgia in the early 1860s.

Wilson wrote in his text *Division and Reunion* (1893: 222):

The story of the cotton famine relates to another important historical literature. Many recent accounts, drawing inspiration from the New History of Capitalism, paint the expansion of slave-produced cotton as the key driver for the rise of the United States to the status of a global economic superpower. They point to twin phenomena: 1. the position of the US South as the producer of 75–80 percent of the cotton sold in the Atlantic economy (Britian, continental Europe, and the northern United States); and 2. the role of cotton as the leading US export commodity, accounting over one-half of export revenues. The importance of US cotton in the world economy is most evident when supplies are cut off, in the cotton famine of the American Civil War period.

But the cotton-to-superpower story is oversimplified in many ways. Economists have long recognised that in the antebellum period the US would have generated more revenue if, on the margin, it produced less cotton (Wright 1978). The country was not exploiting its monopoly position, restricting output to improve its terms of trade. Indeed, in some instances, such as the annexation of Texas, the US undertook measures that increased cotton production, at the cost of its economic position, in order to maintain and expand its monopoly status for political purposes. The annexation of Texas also pushed the country into a war of conquest with Mexico and then exacerbated sectional conflict with the United States.

Finally, the South's monopoly position combined with booming demand in the late 1850s induced Southern white elites to entertain King Cotton thinking, as noted above. They took the gamble in 1860/61 that their dominance of the world cotton market would force Britain, France, and the Northerners in the United States to recognise their independence. It did not. Buying into their superpower status, the secessionists believed they could do what they could not. They failed, at great cost to themselves and the nation as a whole. Their steps led to the destruction of the slave system within five years, and the loss of their wealth and national political standing for the next fifty years, or more. The war itself took, by current estimates 800,000 to 1 million lives, and cost the equivalent of two years of GDP.

The New Historians of Capitalism, as Stanley Engerman (2017) observed, often replicate the thinking patterns of the 1850s confederates (see also Olmstead and Rhode 2018). In this case, they replicate the error of exaggerating the power of King Cotton in the global economy. When William Howard Russell of the *London Times* dined in Charleston, SC in April 1861, he was told: 'Why, sir, we have only to shut off your supply of cotton for a few weeks and we can create a revolution in Great Britain. ... No sir, we know that England must recognize us' (quoted in Powell 2021: 54). This was not to be. As Mancur Olson (1963) noted long ago, the economy's capability to adapt to supply disruptions, through substitution and innovation, should not be underestimated.

References

Boston Board of Trade. 1863. *Ninth Annual Report.* Boston: Alfred Mudge.
   1865. *Eleventh Annual Report.* Boston: T. F. Marvin.
   1874. *Twentieth Annual Report.* Boston: James F. Cotter.
Boyko, John. 2013. *Blood and Daring: How Canada Fought the American Civil War and Forged a Nation.* Toronto: Alfred A. Knopf Canada.

Brown, William O., and Richard C. K. Burdekin. 2000. 'Turning Points in the U.S. Civil War: A British Perspective', *Journal of Economic History* 60(1): 216–231.

Carter, Susan B., et al., eds. 2006. *Historical Statistics of the United States, Earliest Times to the Present: Millennial Edition.* New York: Cambridge University Press.

Crapol, Edward P. 2006. *John Tyler, the Accidental President.* Chapel Hill, NC: University of North Carolina Press.

Davis, Lance E., and Stanley L. Engerman. 2006. *Naval Blockades in Peace and War: An Economic History since 1750.* New York: Cambridge University Press. Kindle edition.

DeCanio, Stephen J., and Joel Mokyr. 1977. 'Inflation and the Wage Lag during the American Civil War', *Explorations in Economic History* 14(4): 311–336.

Ellison, Thomas. 1858. *Handbook of the Cotton Trade.* London: Longman Green. 1886. *The Cotton Trade of Great Britain.* London: E. Wilson.

Engerman, Stanley L. 2017. 'Review of *The Business of Slavery and the Rise of American Capitalism, 1815–1860* by Calvin Schermerhorn and *The Half Has Never Been Told: Slavery and the Making of American Capitalism* by Edward E. Baptist', *Journal of Economic Literature* 55(2): 637–643.

Feigenbaum J, J. Lee, and F. Mezzanotti. 2022. 'Capital Destruction and Economic Growth: The Effects of Sherman's March, 1850–1920', *American Economic Journal: Applied Economics* 14(4): 301–342.

Foreman, Amanda. 2010. *A World on Fire.* New York: Random House.

Gentry, Judith Fenner. 1970. 'A Confederate Success in Europe: The Erlanger Loan', *Journal of Southern History* 36(2): 157–188.

Grossman, Herschel I., and Taejoon Han. 1996. 'War Debt, Moral Hazard, and the Financing of the Confederacy', *Journal of Money, Credit and Banking* 28(2): 200–215.

Hanlon, W. Walker, 2015. 'Necessity Is the Mother of Invention: Input Supplies and Directed Technical Change', *Econometrica* 83(1): 67–100.

Henderson, W. O. 1933. 'The Cotton Famine on the Continent', *Economic History Review* 4(2): 195–207.

Holmes, George K. 1912. *Cotton Crop of the United States, 1790–1911.* US Department of Agriculture, Bureau of Statistics Circular 32. Washington, DC: GPO.

Hurt, R. Douglas. 2015. *Agriculture and the Confederacy: Policy, Productivity and Power in the Civil War South.* Chapel Hill: University of North Carolina Press.

Kessel, Reuben A., and Armen A. Alchian. 1959. 'Real Wages in the North during the Civil War: Mitchell's Data Reinterpreted', *Journal of Law & Economics* 2: 95–113.

Lebergott, Stanley. 1981. 'Through the Blockade: The Profitability and Extent of Cotton Smuggling, 1861–1865', *Journal of Economic History* 41(4): 867–888.

1983. 'Why the South Lost: The Commercial Purpose of the Confederacy, 1861–1865', *Journal of American History* 70(1): 58–74.

Leigh, Philip. 2014. *Trading with the Enemy: The Covert Economy during the American Civil War.* Yardley, PA: Westholme Publishing.

Mann, James. 1860. *Cotton Trade of Great Britain: Its Rise, Progress, and Present Extent*. London: Simpkin, Marshall.

Mitchell, Wesley C. 1903. *A History of the Greenbacks, with Special Reference to the Economic Consequences of Their Issue: 1862–65*. Chicago: University of Chicago Press.

Mulder, Nicholas. 2022. *The Economic Weapon: The Rise of Sanctions as a Tool in Modern War*. New Haven, CT: Yale University Press.

Officer, Lawrence H., and Samuel H. Williamson. 2023. Measuringworth. www.measuringworth.com.

Olmstead, Alan L., and Paul W. Rhode. 2018. 'Cotton, Slavery, and the New History of Capitalism', *Explorations in Economic History* 67(C): 1–17.

Olson, Mancur. 1963. *The Economics of Wartime Shortage: A History of the British Food Supplies in the Napoleonic War and in World Wars I and II*. Durham, NC: Duke University Press.

Powell, Jim. 2021. *Losing the Thread: Cotton, Liverpool and the American Civil War*. Liverpool: Liverpool University Press.

Schwab, John. 1901. *The Confederate States of America, 1861–1865: A Financial and Industrial History of the South during the Civil War*. New York: C. Scribner's Sons.

Sherman, William T. 1876. *Memoirs of General William T. Sherman*. New York: D. Appleton.

Southall, H. R, D. R. Gilbert, and I. Gregory. 1998. Great Britain Historical Database: Labour Markets Database, Poor Law Statistics, 1859–1939 [computer file]. UK Data Archive [distributor] SN: 3713.

Surdam, David G. 2001. *Northern Naval Superiority and the Economics of the American Civil War*. Columbia: University of South Carolina Press.

UK. 1854–1880. *Annual Statement of the Trade and Navigation of the United Kingdom*. London: HMSO.

US Bureau of the Census. 1915. *Cotton Production and Distribution*. Bulletin No. 131 Washington, DC: GPO.

Weidenmier, Marc D. 2000. 'The Market for Confederate Cotton Bonds', *Explorations in Economic History* 37(1): 76–97.

Weidenmier, Marc D., and Kim Oosterlinck. 2015. 'Victory or Repudiation? The Probability of the Southern Confederacy Winning the Civil War', NBER Working Paper No. 13567.

Wilson, Woodrow. 1893. *Division and Reunion, 1829–1889*. New York: Longsman,Green.

Wright, Gavin. 1978. *Political Economy of the Cotton South*. New York: W. W. Norton.

Further Reading

Arthi, Vellore, Brian Beach, and Hanlon W. Walker. 2022. 'Recessions, Mortality and Migration Bias: Evidence from the Lancashire Cotton Famine', *American Economic Journal: Applied Economics* 14(2): 228–255.

Beckert, Sven. 2004. 'Emancipation and Empire: Reconstructing the Worldwide Web of Cotton Production in the Age of the American Civil War', *American Historical Review* 109(5): 1405–1438.

2014. *Empire of Cotton: A Global History*. New York: Knopf.

Boyer, George R. 1997. 'Poor Relief, Informal Assistance, and Short Time during the Lancashire Cotton Famine', *Explorations in Economic History* 34(1): 56–76.

Campbell, Duncan A. 2003. *English Public Opinion and the American Civil War*. London: Boydell & Brewer.

Cochran, Thomas C. 1961. 'Did the Civil War Retard Industrialization?', *Mississippi Valley Historical Review* 68: 197–210.

Engerman, Stanley L. 1966. 'The Economic Impact of the Civil War', *Explorations in Entrepreneurial History* Second Series, III (Spring–Summer): 176–199.

Fite, Emerson David. 1910. *Social and Industrial Conditions in the North during the Civil War*. New York: MacMillian.

Goldin, Claudia. 1973. 'The Economics of Emancipation', *Journal of Economic History* 31(1): 66–85.

Goldin, Claudia, and Frank Lewis. 1975. 'The Economic Cost of the American Civil War: Estimates and Implications', *Journal of Economic History* 35(2): 299–326.

Hall, Nigel. 2021. 'The British Debate Concerning the Supply of Cotton during the American Civil War', *Journal of European Economic History* 50(2): 89–118.

Hanlon, W. Walker, 2017. 'Temporary Shocks and Persistent Effects in Urban Economies: Evidence from British Cities after the U.S. Civil War', *Review of Economics and Statistics* 99(1): 67–79.

Harnetty, Peter. 1965. 'The Imperialism of Free Trade: Lancashire and the Indian Cotton Duties, 1859–1862', *Economic History Review* 18(2): 333–349.

1966. 'The Imperialism of Free Trade: Lancashire, India, and the Cotton Supply Question, 1861–1865', *Journal of British Studies* 6(1): 70–96.

Henderson, W. O. 1931. 'The Public Works Act, 1863', *Economic History* 2(6): 312–321.

1969. *The Lancashire Cotton Famine, 1861–1865*. New York: Kelly.

Kiesling, L. Lynne. 1995. 'Collective Action and Assisting the Poor: The Political Economy of Income Assistance during the Lancashire Cotton Famine', *Journal of Economic History* 55(2): 380–383.

1997. 'The Long Road to Recovery: Postcrisis Coordination of Private Charity and Public Relief in Victorian Lancashire', *Social Science History* 21(2): 219–243.

Lerner, Eugene M. 1954. 'The Monetary and Fiscal Programs of the Confederate Government, 1861–65', *Journal of Political Economy* 62(6): 506–522.

1955. 'Money, Prices, and Wages in the Confederacy, 1861–65', *Journal of Political Economy* 63(1): 20–40.

1959. 'Southern Output and Agricultural Income, 1860–1880', *Agricultural History* 33(3): 117–125.

Nevins, Allan. 1959. *The War for the Union*. New York: Scribner.

Owsley, Frank L. 1931. *King Cotton Diplomacy: Foreign Relations of the Confederate States of America*. Tuscaloosa: University of Alabama Press.

Pecquet, Gary, George Davis, and Bryce Kanago. 2004. 'The Emancipation Proclamation, Confederate Expectations, and the Price of Southern Bank Notes', *Southern Economic Journal* 70(3): 616–630.

Ransom, Roger L. 2005. *The Confederate States of America: What Might Have Been*. New York: W. W. Norton.

1989. *Conflict and Compromise: The Political Economy of Slavery, Emancipation and the American Civil War*. New York: Cambridge University Press.

Scherer, James A. B. 1916. *Cotton as a World Power: A Study in the Economic Interpretation of History*. New York: Frederick A. Stokes.

Silver, Arthur W. 1966. *Manchester Men and Indian Cotton, 1847–1872*. Manchester: Manchester University Press.

Surdam, David G. 1998. 'King Cotton: Monarch or Pretender? The State of the Market for Raw Cotton on the Eve of the American Civil War', *Economic History Review* 51(1): 113–132.

Wilson, Mark. 2006. *The Business of Civil War: Military Mobilization and the State, 1861–1865*. Baltimore, MD: Johns Hopkins University Press.

Winks, Robin A., 1960. *Canada and the United States: The Civil War Years*. Baltimore, MD: Johns Hopkins University Press.

3 Blockading Britain and Germany during World War I
Preparations, Conduct, and Consequences of Economic Warfare

Stephen Broadberry and Tamás Vonyó

Introduction

Economic warfare was employed as a complement to military action during World War I by both the Allies and the Central Powers, as Britain tried to starve Germany through surface blockade while Germany tried to starve Britain through submarine blockade. The outcome of the blockades was very different from what many commentators had predicted before 1914 (Olson 1963: 38–42). Germany protected its agriculture and produced 80 per cent of its calorific requirements in the run-up to World War I, with the remaining calories supplied by imports that could largely be delivered overland. Britain, by contrast, allowed free trade in agricultural goods, and produced just 35 per cent of its requirements, leaving itself highly dependent on seaborne imports of food (Olson 1963: 74–75). In theory, then, Germany should not have suffered greatly from blockade, while Britain should have succumbed quickly to famine. And yet, in practice, Britain managed to feed its population adequately throughout the war, while Germans suffered grievously. In this chapter, we adopt a framework of preparations, conduct, and consequences to understand these outcomes.

Preparations: Agricultural and Food Policies before 1914

Policies towards agriculture and food differed sharply between Britain and Germany from the late nineteenth century to the start of World War I. Britain pursued a free trade policy from the 1840s, repealing the Corn Laws, the Navigation Acts, and phasing out restrictions on imported livestock (Afton and Turner 2000: 2106). Although Prussia and other Zollverein states had also pursued a low-tariff policy at this time, the situation changed following German unification in 1871.

During the 1850s and 1860s, German grain producers had initially opposed tariffs for industry, which they feared would lead to retaliatory tariffs against German grain exports, but by the late 1870s they were being undercut by American farmers as transport improvements drastically reduced price differentials between the United States and Europe (Gerschenkron 1943). In a 'marriage of rye and iron', Bismarck's tariffs of 1879 were imposed on both grain and manufactures, and in addition to further increases of these tariffs, livestock products were added in what Webb (1982: 309) called an 'empire of iron, pork and rye'. Although there was a vocal campaign for tariff reform in Britain during the early twentieth century, advocates of free trade successfully argued that British workers gained from cheap food imports, and Britain remained committed to free trade until World War I (Marrison 1996).

As a result of the different tariff policies pursued in Britain and Germany, the 'grain invasion' from the New World affected them very differently. In Britain, cereal producers were offered zero protection across the board, while in Germany tariffs had reached around 40 per cent by 1909–1913. Table 3.1 shows that the grain price spreads between Britain and the United Sates narrowed dramatically between 1870 and 1913, disappearing altogether for wheat, while the spreads between Bavaria and the United States narrowed marginally at best, and for barley and oats even widened. Accordingly, cereal production trends charted in Table 3.2 were also very different in the two countries. Whereas the output of all major crops increased substantially between 1885 and 1913 in Germany, in Britain their cultivation declined significantly or stayed constant. Whereas Britain became increasingly dependent on food imports, Germany continued to produce most of its food supply.

Table 3.1 *International grain price spreads, 1870–1913 (%)*

	Britain/USA, 1870	Britain/USA, 1913	Bavaria/USA, 1870	Bavaria/USA, 1913
Wheat	54.1	−0.8	44.0	37.1
Barley	45.9	10.9	5.4	43.6
Oats	138.1	28.1	82.6	106.3
Rye	n.a.	n.a.	66.5	48.5

Source: O'Rourke (1997: 782).

Table 3.2 *Growth of cereal production, 1885–1913 (% change)*

	Britain	Germany
Wheat	−28.2	+59.6
Barley	−25.9	+36.0
Oats	+3.2	+84.5
Rye	n.a.	+77.3

Sources and notes: Derived from Ministry of Agriculture, Fisheries and Food and Department of Agriculture and Fisheries for Scotland (1968: 108–112) and Hoffmann (1965: 292–293).

Conduct: Blockading Britain

Off to a Slow Start: Restricted Submarine Blockade, 1914–1916

The German submarine blockade got off to a slow start for two main reasons. First, when war broke out on 4 August, Germany had only a limited supply of thirty-three submarines, compared with Britain's seventy-four (Churchill 1923: 278). Second, submarine warfare was restricted by international law. Since the Hague Convention of 1899, the so-called prize rules compelled warships, including submarines, to warn merchant vessels of an impending attack, search the vessels, and move their crews into a place of safety.

For a brief period in 1915, the Germans did ignore the prize rules to counter the use of British ships with concealed deck guns and armed merchantmen. On 3 November 1914, London declared the entire North Sea, along with the waters around Iceland and southern Norway, a war zone to control maritime trade. In retaliation, on 4 February 1915, Germany declared the seas around the British Isles a war zone and, from 18 February, Allied ships in the area would be sunk without warning. However, neutral countries, particularly the United States, protested against the unrestricted attacks, which inevitably sank neutral as well as Allied ships. As a result, after the *Lusitania* was torpedoed on 7 May 1915, with many American passengers on board, Germany agreed to refrain from unrestricted submarine warfare until February 1917 (Hardach 1987: 37–41; Chickering 1998: 90). British shipping losses during this first phase of the German blockade of Britain averaged 83,000 gross tons per month, with the world total averaging 144,000 tons, significant but not yet sufficient to pose a serious threat to Britain's food supply (Beveridge 1928: 5–18, 26–27).

Unrestricted Submarine Blockade, 1917–1918

Throughout 1916, Chancellor Bethmann-Hollweg resisted calls from the German navy to return to unrestricted warfare on the grounds that it would bring the United States into the war (Olson 1963: 810). In addition, at the start of 1916, Germany clearly had insufficient U-boats to bring about a swift surrender of Britain (Churchill 1927: 220–221). By the end of the year, however, the German navy was confident that it could sink up to 600,000 tons of cargo per month, regarded as sufficient to starve Britain out of the war within six months. Unrestricted submarine warfare was declared in January 2017 and the campaign began on 1 February. Initially, German sinkings of Allied and neutral shipping increased dramatically, as can be seen clearly in panel (a) of Figure 3.1, peaking at over 850,000 tons in April 1917. Panel (a) also shows the number of U-boats in the German fleet, which doubled between mid-1916 and mid-1917. Although this expansion of capacity led initially to a sharp increase in the Allied and neutral shipping losses per U-boat, as can be seen in panel (b) of Figure 3.1, the German advantage was short-lived.

How were the British able to remain in the war and go on to achieve victory despite the initial success of the German unrestricted submarine campaign? Olson (1963: 86–113) points to a series of effective counter-measures. These can be divided into measures to maintain shipping capacity, economise on the use of shipping, reduce demand for importable goods, and boost home production to substitute for imports.

Counter-Measures to Maintain Shipping Capacity

The first important counter-measure was the development of the convoy system, which helped to reduce sinkings, since it was just as difficult for a U-boat to spot a convoy as a single ship in the vast expanse of the Atlantic and convoys could be escorted by destroyers and other patrol vessels capable of taking defensive counter-measures. The effectiveness of the convoy system is demonstrated by the statistics on convoy sailings and losses in Table 3.3. Of 16,693 ships sailing in convoys on both homewards and outwards voyages between 10 May 1917 and 23 November 1918, 99.08 per cent were escorted safely, with just 0.61 per cent torpedoed in convoy. The other 0.31 per cent of losses resulted either from marine perils or after leaving the convoy. This was more helpful than had been expected by British naval opinion, with a sceptical Admiralty being cajoled into experimenting with it by Prime Minister Lloyd George (Churchill 1927: 363–368). After reaching a peak of 881,000 tons in April 1917, world total sinkings fell back under 300,000 tons by September and fluctuated around this level for the rest of the war (Figure 3.1).

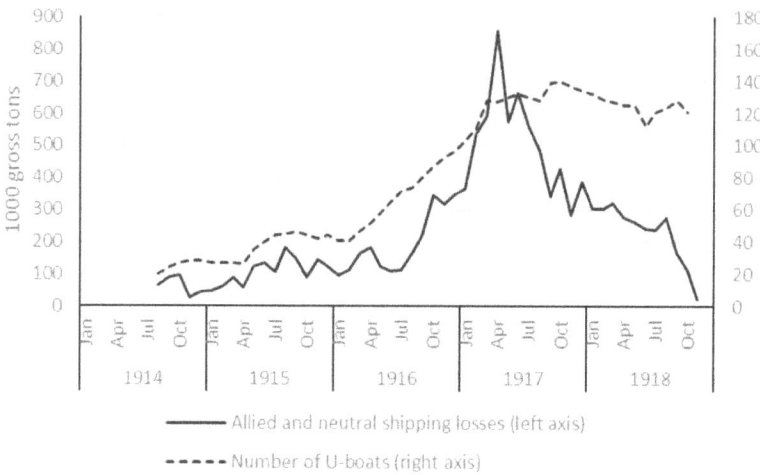

(a) Allied and neutral shipping losses and U-boats in the Germen fleet

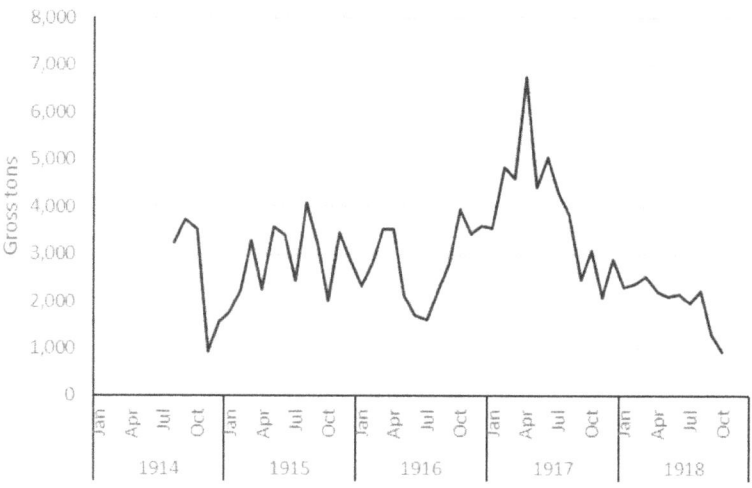

(b) Allied and neutral shipping losses per U-boat

Figure 3.1 The Battle of the Atlantic, 1914–1918
Source: Davis and Engerman (2006: 182–183).

Table 3.3 *Convoy sailings and losses*

	Ships	Gross tonnage	Ships, % of total	Tons, % of total
Escorted safely	16,539	86,373,725	99.08	99.04
Torpedoed in convoy	102	585,283	0.61	0.67
Lost in marine perils	16	82,359	0.09	0.09
Lost while not in convoy	36	172,052	0.22	0.20
Total sailings	16,693	87,213,419	100.00	100.00

Source: Fayle (1924: 473).

Table 3.4 *Net loss or gain in Allied and neutral shipping during 1918 (thousand deadweight tons)*

Month	Italy	France	UK	USA	Other Allies	Neutrals	Total
January	−21	−46	−212	88	8	−33	−216
February	−35	−10	−225	116	25	−45	−174
March	−56	−23	−56	158	5	−59	−31
April	6	−30	−186	164	−5	14	−37
May	−15	−24	−31	229	84	−20	223
June	12	−25	−47	252	72	5	269
July	−26	−20	−18	226	30	−18	174
August		−32	−17	275	62	−30	258
September	−3	−2	6	340	48	−3	386
October	−11	−13	106	385	46	−3	510
Total	−149	−225	−680	2,233	375	−192	1,362

Source: Salter (1921: 366–367).

Another way of offsetting the losses from sinkings was through building new ships. The United States made an enormous contribution to the maintenance of Allied shipping capacity through the devotion of resources to building cargo ships. By May 1918, the monthly gains through shipbuilding more than offset the losses through sinkings, and the Allies continued to record a net gain until the end of the war, as can be seen in Table 3.4.

Counter-Measures to Economise on the Use of Shipping

In addition to reducing sinkings and rebuilding capacity, however, it was important for the British to devise a series of counter-measures that

Table 3.5 *British import value shares by region of origin (%)*

	1914	1916	1918
Principal European trades cut off by war	10.8	0.2	0.0
Principal European allies	10.7	5.9	4.6
North European neutrals	10.3	8.7	4.5
Rest of Europe and Mediterranean	6.0	9.3	9.3
North America	24.6	37.2	48.7
Central America and West Indies	1.9	2.4	2.8
South America	9.0	9.3	8.8
West Africa	1.6	1.8	1.7
South and East Africa	2.5	1.9	1.8
Middle East	7.7	8.9	7.6
Far East	6.1	7.2	4.9
Australasia	8.8	7.2	5.3
Total	100.0	100.0	100.0

Source and notes: Fayle (1924: 480–483). Principal European trades cut off by war: Central Powers plus Belgium. Principal European Allies: France, Italy, Russia. North European neutrals: Norway, Sweden, Denmark plus Iceland and Greenland, Netherlands. North America: United States, Canada, Newfoundland, and Bermuda.

allowed them to get along without the merchant tonnage sunk by the German U-boats. The policy of Atlantic concentration was of critical importance. It meant that a much larger share of Britain's total imports was obtained from the United States and Canada, while shares from further afield declined. This shortened the average length of voyages, thus allowing more food to be carried to Britain with the same tonnage of ships. Table 3.5 shows a rising share of North America during the first two years of the war, which can be seen as offsetting the sharp decline in imports from the Central Powers and Belgium. From 1916, however, the further increase in the share of imports from North America largely reflects the policy of North Atlantic concentration, since there were no further gains to be had through the replacement of imports from the Central Powers. As a result, we see declining shares in British imports from Australasia, South America, the Far East, West Africa, South and East Africa, and the Middle East during the last two years of the war.

A further way of economising on scarce shipping was to reduce the amount of time spent by ships in port. This was aided by the formation of Transport Workers' Battalions to ensure the availability of more labour for the loading and unloading of ships (Fayle 1927: 171–172; Olson 1963: 93–95). They were widely used to speed up turnaround times at ports during the period of unrestricted submarine warfare, with the average number of men from the Battalions employed in daily work at the ports increasing from 2,131 in January 1917 to 5,760 in July of the same year (Fayle 1924: 166).

Counter-Measures to Reduce Consumption of Importable Goods

Another important British counter-measure to alleviate the shortage of shipping space caused by sinkings was a sharp reduction in investment, which can be seen clearly in Figure 3.2. Between 1900 and 1913, net fixed capital formation (NFCF) averaged £77 million per annum at 1900 prices but became negative during the war, reaching a trough of – £28 million in 1916. As Olson (1963: 93–94) notes, it is always possible during wartime to cut back on normal peacetime investment by continuing to use old capital stock. Since the largest element of the capital stock at the time of World War I was buildings in the form of dwellings, factories, and offices, cutting back on investment meant saving on bulky imports of materials such as wood and timber and iron and steel, thus freeing up valuable shipping space.

The demand for scarce shipping space was also reduced by limiting exports. Although not directly competing with imports since they were shipped on outgoing vessels, exports were produced using raw materials that had to be imported from abroad. Without the exports,

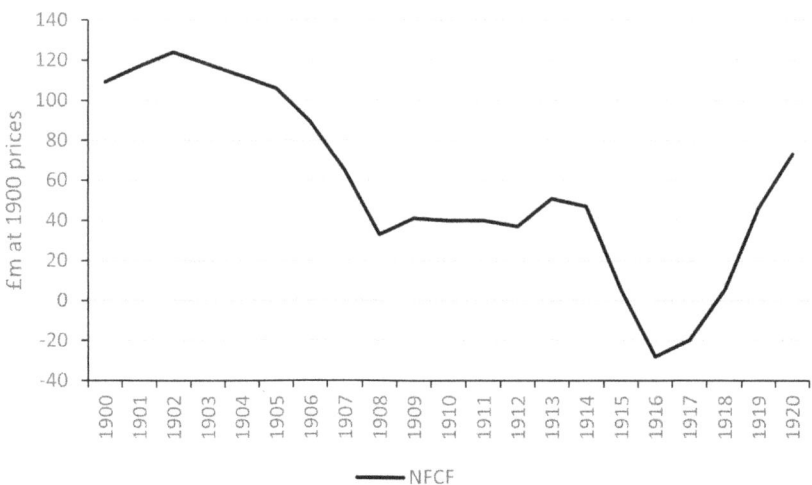

Figure 3.2 UK net fixed capital formation, 1900–1920 (£m at 1900 prices)
Source: Feinstein (1988: 442–443).

raw material imports could be reduced, so vital space on incoming ships was saved.

During the first two years of the war, the importation of non-essential items and the excessive consumption of essential food and war materials was limited to a large extent through the normal operation of the price mechanism. As shipping became scarcer, this raised the price of imported goods and deterred consumption. It was not quite 'business as usual', but the spread of government controls was generally slow (Broadberry and Howlett 2005: 222–224). The pace of change accelerated following the replacement of Asquith's government by Lloyd George's government in December 1916. With the start of unrestricted submarine warfare, it was clear that the volume of imports in 1917 would be significantly lower than in the previous year, so that direct government action would be needed to safeguard imports of essential food and war materials. In February 1917, the War Cabinet therefore approved a programme to both prevent the importation of non-essential items and to discourage the excessive consumption of essential imports (Fayle 1924: 57; Olson 1963: 94). The target of reducing imports by 500,000 tons per month was exceeded, with Board of Trade data showing that total imports declined from 44.3 million tons in 1916 to 37.3 million tons in 1917, a fall of 7 million tons between the two years, or a monthly saving of 583,333 tons (Fayle 1924: 477).

In another important move designed to reduce imports, whilst at the same time ensuring that the available food supply was distributed in a way that maximised its contribution to the health and energy of the nation, direct controls were extended over food supply to such an extent that the government bought and sold 85 per cent of the food consumed (Beveridge 1928: 56–57). A Wheat Commission was established at the end of 1916 with responsibility for the importation of cereals and control of home crops, making the most economic use of grains through policies such as increasing extraction rates and restrictions on brewing, and the introduction of a bread subsidy to keep down the price of bread to consumers (Beveridge 1928: 88–112). Other foods were the responsibility of the Ministry of Food under the direction of the Food Controller. Beginning in February 1917, the Food Controller appealed to the nation to place itself on voluntary rations with a prescribed maximum weekly allowance of bread, meat, and sugar (Beveridge 1928: 34–35). A formal rationing scheme was first approved in June 1917 for sugar but as queues built up for other foods, local rationing schemes were introduced, and in July 1918 formal national rationing was introduced, administered by autonomous local committees (Beveridge 1928: 188–217).

Counter-Measures to Boost Agricultural Production

One final important counter-measure against the German submarine blockade was the introduction of incentives for farmers to increase agricultural production and thus reduce dependence on food imports. Rowland Prothero, later Lord Ernle, became the President of the Board of Agriculture and Fisheries in Lloyd George's new coalition government in December 1916 and set up a new Food Production Department (Middleton 1923: 162–163). The new department moved quickly to develop a policy of ploughing up pasture land and converting it from grazing livestock to growing arable crops (Beveridge 1928: 105). This had the effect of increasing the supply of calories from a given acreage, as growing grain or potatoes on a given plot of land provided more calories than could be derived from meat and dairy produce derived from livestock raised on the same piece of land. This went against the trend of structural change away from arable towards livestock farming during the pre-1914 period, when British farmers found it increasingly difficult to compete against imports of cheap grain from the New World, and was therefore underpinned by the Corn Production Act of 1917, which guaranteed minimum prices for a five-year period (Whetham 1978: 94–95). Although there was a great deal of controversy surrounding the Corn Production Act, it provided the incentives for farmers to make the changes (Middleton 1923: 271–275). The effects can be seen in Table 3.6 in the bumper harvests of grains and potatoes in 1918, combined with a drop in home production of meat and dairy produce. The bumper harvests owed much to the high yields on the stored-up fertility

Table 3.6 *British agricultural output (thousand tons)*

	1913	1914	1915	1916	1917	1918
Wheat	1,541	1,706	1,961	1,559	1,634	2,428
Barley	1,408	1,367	986	1,110	1,189	1,299
Oats	1,986	2,033	2,168	2,100	2,730	2,965
Potatoes	3,865	4,031	3,830	3,036	4,451	5,360
Beef and veal	753	789	789	773	831	557
Mutton and lamb	322	283	282	304	318	218
Pork	224	194	227	228	134	65
Bacon and ham	125	120	130	136	108	71
Fresh milk and cream	4,510	4,630	4,565	4,190	3,825	3,325
Butter	126	126	126	125	114	103

Source: Beveridge (1928: 261).

of long-fallowed grassland, as well as to the increase in the acreage under crop (Middleton 1923: 247–256).

Assessing the Effects of the German Submarine Blockade

The success of the British counter-measures can be seen in Table 3.7, which shows the calorie value of weekly quantities of food consumed per 'man' in Britain prior to and during the war. Because food requirements of individuals vary by age, gender, size, amount of physical work performed, and other circumstances, they are all reduced to 'man equivalents' of an agreed average size and activity, requiring 3,300 calories a day. As Table 3.7 demonstrates, average food consumption barely declined during even the worst years of the war and always remained above the daily requirement of 3,300 calories per day.

Olson's (1963: 113) conclusion on Britain's ability to survive the submarine blockage is that '[i]t is the capacity for substitution that the German naval authorities must have failed to take into account when they advocated an unrestricted submarine campaign. It was the principle of substitution that accounted for the unexpected flexibility of the British economic system, and that deserves much of the credit for the campaign's failure'.

Table 3.7 *Per 'man' calorie value of weekly quantities of food consumed in Britain*

	1909–1913	1914	1915	1916	1917	1918
Flour	8,464	8,365	8,266	8,613	9,355	9,570
Butchers' meat	3,086	2,988	2,891	2,692	2,332	1,710
Bacon and ham	1,036	1,054	1,263	1,336	1,181	1,426
Butter	1,346	1,285	1,177	1,011	845	732
Margarine	458	574	854	1,036	1,022	945
Lard	520	512	608	540	412	708
Potatoes	1,408	1,638	1,715	1,574	1,488	2,029
Sugar	3,236	3,311	3,534	2,716	2,232	2,065
Fresh milk	1,642	1,654	1,654	1,530	1,402	1,219
Other foods	2,895	2,797	2,892	2,879	2,971	3,102
Total weekly calories	24,091	24,178	24,854	23,927	23,240	23,506
Calories per day	3,442	3,454	3,551	3,418	3,320	3,358

Sources and notes: Beveridge (1928: 313). Figures are quoted per 'man', based on a man of 15–16 stone weight doing average work during eight hours a day, requiring 3,300 calories a day.

Conduct: Blockading Germany

Restricted Blockade, 1914–1915

Just as the German submarine blockade of Britain began in a restricted manner out of concern over international law and the attitude of neutral countries, so too did the British blockade of Germany between August 1914 and March 1915 (Hardach 1987: 11–19). The London Declaration concerning the Laws of Naval War was signed in 1909 by the major powers of the day, including Britain and Germany, but was never ratified by any state. It nevertheless formed the basis of the initially restricted Allied blockade. The London Declaration permitted the maintenance of a patrol line off an enemy's ports and coasts but prohibited the blockading of neutral ports and littorals. It also stipulated that ships should not be sunk without warning and that the safety of the crews of sunk ships should be guaranteed (Hardach 1987: 12–13; Chickering 1998: 90). In addition, it also divided goods into three categories: absolute contraband, conditional contraband, and free list goods. Absolute contraband such as arms, munitions, and military equipment could be interdicted, even if en route to neutral countries, if there was good reason to believe that the ultimate destination was enemy territory. Conditional contraband consisted of non-military goods that could be used for warlike purposes, including foodstuffs, fuel, lubricants, and clothing. Free list goods included raw materials for industry and agriculture, such as ores, cotton, and fertiliser, and could not be declared as contraband (Hardach 1987: 13).

Initially, imports of contraband were stopped from reaching Germany, but free list imports were allowed and German exports in neutral ships were not indicted. However, as suspicions grew that contraband goods useful for the war effort were being re-exported to Germany via neutral northern countries, the contraband list was soon extended and more rigorous controls were imposed on the trade of neutral countries (Hardach 1987: 14–15). Davis and Engerman (2006: 207–208) provide data on the share of Scandinavian and Dutch exports and re-exports going to Germany consistent with these suspicions, shown here in Table 3.8. The share of Scandinavian exports going to Germany increased substantially at the start of the war, and it was some time before the blockade brought the shares back down close to pre-war levels, although the blockade appears to have been more effective in clamping down on Dutch exports to Germany from the start of the war. It was particularly concerning that Britain appeared to be becoming an entrepôt for overseas products reaching Germany via the northern neutrals, as the

Table 3.8 *Share of Scandinavian and Dutch exports going to Germany (%)*

	Denmark	Sweden	Norway	Netherlands
1911	29.8	20.2	17.1	49.7
1912	30.5	22.5	16.4	50.0
1913	28.1	21.9	17.0	47.9
Avg. 1911–13	29.5	21.5	17.0	49.2
1914	38.6	22.7	18.5	44.9
1915	49.7	36.9	28.5	40.8
1916	58.7	28.1	29.6	38.6
1917	50.5	26.1	19.0	38.6
1918	43.4	21.7	11.3	39.9
Avg. 1914–18	49.3	27.5	22.0	41.6

Source: Davis and Engerman (2006: 208).

share of northern neutrals in British exports doubled in the first six months of the war, while their share of British re-exports trebled (Hardach 1987: 18–19).

Unrestricted Blockade, 1915–1917

Following the announcement by the German government in February 1915 that they would treat the waters around Britain and northern France as a war zone and sink enemy merchant ships without warning, the Allies moved to unrestricted blockade from March 1915, announcing a more intensive policy of stopping all shipping movements to and from ports of the Central Powers and all goods entering or leaving those ports via neutral countries (Hardach 1987: 20). However, the British still had to be careful to avoid alienating neutral countries, particularly the United States, Scandinavia, and the Netherlands. This required the establishment of a trust system, whereby a neutral country's government and shipping companies undertook to restrict the import of all goods to the quantity required for internal consumption, based on prewar levels, in return for a relaxation of controls. Ultimately, this led to the navicert system, whereby an exporter could be given a certificate by a British consular officer after an inspection prior to dispatch. This ensured that the cargo would not be detained by a blockading ship (Hardach 1987: 20–26).

The unrestricted blockade was extended to the other Central Powers, Austria–Hungary, Bulgaria, and Turkey (Bell 1961). This involved the British navy controlling entry to the Mediterranean at Gibraltar and Suez and the French and Italian navies blockading the Mediterranean ports of the Central Powers (Hardach 1987: 26–27).

Blockade after the Entry of the United States into the War, 1917–1918

Germany's adoption of unrestricted submarine warfare in February 1917 inevitably led to a swift reduction in neutral shipping, thus to a decline of imports into the neutral countries and in turn to a fall in exports from the neutrals into Germany. The intensified U-boat offensive also brought the United States into the war on the Allied side in April (Hardach 1987: 27–28). The neutral countries now lost their most powerful advocate, as the US poacher turned gamekeeper and further strengthened the blockade. The Americans introduced a system of blacklists for companies that were caught violating the blockade rules, tight control of bunker coal and navicerts, and participated in schemes for rationing neutral imports, which were largely sourced from the United States. The effect of these measures on American exports to the neutral neighbours of the Central Powers can be seen in Table 3.9. The decline in American exports between the year June 1915 to June 1916 and the year June 1917 to June 1918 was 53 per cent for Norway and more than 90 per cent for Denmark, the Netherlands, and Sweden. Switzerland, which saw an increase of 165 per cent, received favourable treatment on the advice of the French, who thought it wise to respect the economic importance of Switzerland to the Allies.

Assessing the Effects of the Allied Blockade

Many contemporary and historical assessments have attributed the eventual German economic and military collapse to the effects of the British

Table 3.9 *American exports to the Central Powers' neutral neighbours ($m)*

Country	June 1915–June 1916	June 1917–June 1918
Denmark	55.9	5.0
Netherlands	97.5	6.4
Norway	53.6	25.2
Sweden	52.0	4.1
Switzerland	8.0	21.2

Source: Hardach (1987: 30).

blockade (Parmelee 1924; Skalweit 1927; Goebel 1930; Cox 2019). The legend of the starving out (*Aushungerung*) of Germany was born in the early days of the war. Even though the British blockade had barely made any impact on domestic food supplies by then, in their memorandum published in December 1914, the Eltzbacher Commission already spoke of a dangerous British plan to starve the German nation out of the war. Wartime propaganda built on this hyperbole. In a widely circulated pamphlet, von Bühlow (1917) placed the blockades in a historical context of British imperialism and accused British economic warfare of genocidal intent. A common approach to prove the legend was to highlight the decline in per capita food consumption and the increase in mortality.

Per capita wartime rations are compared with peacetime consumption in Table 3.10, taking the agricultural year as running from July to June. Although the consumption of sugar and potatoes held up reasonably well, the situation was far worse for most other items. Rations per head fell to just 1,344 calories by autumn 1916 and as low as 1,100 calories by summer 1917, which forced people to resort to the black market to survive (Davis and Engerman 2006: 204). However, the nutritional deprivation was not shared equally across all regions and classes (Roerkohl 1991). Using anthropometric data from World War II conscription records, Blum (2011) was able to confirm that while all social strata were affected by malnutrition and starvation, in the cohorts born

Table 3.10 *German wartime rations compared with peacetime consumption (peacetime consumption = 100)*

Commodity	July 1916–July 1917	July 1917–July 1918	July 1918–December 1918
Meat	31	20	12
Fish	51	–	5
Eggs	18	13	13
Lard	14	11	7
Butter	22	21	28
Cheese	3	4	15
Rice	4	–	–
Pulses	14	1	7
Sugar	49	56–67	80
Vegetable fats	39	41	17
Potatoes	71	94	94
Flour	53	47	48

Source: Hardach (1987: 119).

during the Great War, farmers, the urban poor, Catholics, and especially residents of the highly integrated food importing regions along the northern coastline and the Rhine suffered disproportionately. Cox (2019) has also used anthropometric data to provide evidence of nutritional deprivation, including weight, height, and body mass index of individuals from surveys carried out in Germany at the time.

As Offer (1989: 34) notes, to isolate the effects of living conditions on mortality, it is necessary to remove the effects of military casualties, and the easiest way to do this is to examine only female mortality. This is done in Table 3.11, which compares levels and trends of deaths per 1,000 females in Germany and in England and Wales. There was a moderate increase in German female mortality during the first two years of the war, but a severe crisis in 1917, rising further to a peak in 1918, when female mortality was more than 50 per cent higher than in 1913. Note how much worse German female mortality became relative to female mortality in England, which continued its pre-war downward trend.

However, simply documenting changes in per capita food consumption and mortality inevitably overstates the significance of the blockade, since it ignores the development of domestic food production. Olson (1963: 80–81) suggests that the major reason for the collapse of food consumption was Germany's inability to expand its farm output during the war, as Britain had done. Similarly, Hardach (1987: 34) conjectures that 'the tremendous economic decline of the Central Powers between

Table 3.11 *Female mortality in Germany and in England and Wales, 1913–1923 (deaths per 1,000 females)*

Year	Germany	England	Germany as a percentage of England
1913	14.3	12.2	117.2
1914	15.2	12.4	122.6
1915	15.3	13.2	115.9
1916	15.2	11.7	129.9
1917	17.6	11.4	154.4
1918	21.6	14.6	147.9
1919	16.7	11.9	140.3
1920	15.3	10.9	140.4
1921	13.6	10.2	133.3
1922	13.9	10.5	132.4
1923	13.6	9.3	146.2

Sources: Offer (1989: 36); Davis and Engerman (2006: 205).

Table 3.12 *German foreign trade in current and constant prices (billions of Marks)*

	Exports at current prices	Imports at current prices	Exports at 1913 prices	Imports at 1913 prices
1913	10.1	10.8	10.1	10.8
1914				
Jan.–July	6.0	6.4	6.0	6.4
Aug.–Dec.	1.4	2.1	1.5	2.1
Jan.–Dec.	7.4	8.5	7.5	8.5
1915	3.1	7.1	2.5	5.9
1916	3.8	8.4	2.9	6.4
1917	3.5	7.1	2.0	4.2
1918	4.7	7.1	2.8	4.2

Sources: Hardach (1987: 33). Data for 1913 from Hoffmann (1965: 817), data for 1914–1918 from Kleine-Natrop (1922: 11).

1914 and 1918 was caused less by the blockade than by the excessive demands made on their economies by the war'. Hardach's conjecture hinges on (1) the scale of the change in agricultural production, (2) the scale of the change in imports, and (3) the pre-war share of imports in food consumption.

Dealing first with the fall in imports, Hardach (1987: 33) constructs a table that compares Kleine-Natrop's (1922) series for imports and exports during 1914–1918 with Hoffmann's (1965) data for 1913, shown here in Table 3.12. We are interested in the scale of the fall in German imports at constant prices in the final column. Making a comparison with 1913, the last complete year before the outbreak of war, then imports had fallen by 61 per cent from their pre-war level by 1917. Note that annualising the monthly average for imports during the first seven months of 1914 rather than using 1913 as the pre-war benchmark level of imports does not significantly alter the scale of the decline. The monthly average for January to July was 0.91 billion Marks, which would imply a total for 1914 of 10.9 billion Marks in the absence of war, almost identical to the 1913 total, rather than the 8.5 billion Marks actually achieved. For exports the decline was substantially greater than for imports, with a peak fall in 1917 of 80 per cent measured against the 1913 level.

The second element in assessing Hardach's conjecture is the performance of German agriculture. In fact, the situation was worse than Olson had thought, since output did not merely fail to expand during the war, but decreased substantially (Starling 1920; Ritschl 2005: 46). Table 3.13

Table 3.13 *German agricultural output, 1913–1918 (% of 1913)*

Year	Rye	Wheat	Summer barley	Potatoes	Oats	Meadow hay	Total agriculture
1913	100	100	100	100	100	100	100
1914	85	86	86	85	93	100	89
1915	75	84	68	100	62	83	85
1916	73	68	77	47	73	99	65
1917	58	50	51	65	38	77	60
1918	66	56	58	56	49	76	60

Sources: Crops: Parmelee (1924: 212); Total agriculture: Ritschl (2005: 46).

sets out trends in the major crops and total agricultural output, including pastoral as well as arable production. Output of most crops declined throughout the war due to a serious loss of manpower and horses to the armed forces and a lack of fertiliser caused by the diversion of nitrates to the production of munitions. This shows up in a decline of harvest per hectare in metric tons. The situation was exacerbated by the priority given to war production, which limited the availability of manufactures that farmers might want to purchase. As food prices increased and the government introduced price controls, farmers began to retreat from the market into autarky rather than increase output, and to the extent that they did continue to produce more output than needed for their own consumption, farmers tried to sell as much as possible through the black market (Broadberry and Harrison 2005: 18–19).

The third element is the pre-war share of imports in food consumption, which is generally agreed to have met about 20 per cent of calorific needs. With these figures, Table 3.14 quantifies the relative contributions of the blockade and the excessive demands of the war economy to the reduction of food consumption in Germany. Column (1) shows the shares of domestic production and imports in food consumption before the outbreak of war, while column (2) shows the decline in production and imports between 1913 and 1918. Column (3) multiplies columns (1) and (2) together to obtain the weighted reduction of domestic production and imports, while column (4) reports the relative shares of domestic production and imports in the reduction of consumption. Imports accounted for 27.6 per cent of the decline in consumption, while domestic production accounted for the other 72.4 per cent. It is clear that the decline in agricultural production played a far more important role than the blockade-induced reduction of imports in the nutritional deprivation of the German people. Harrison (2025) reaches the same conclusion

Table 3.14 *Contribution of the decline in imports to the reduction of food consumption in Germany, 1913–1918*

	(1) 1913 shares of production and imports in food consumption (%)	(2) Reduction of production and imports, 1913–1918 (%)	(3) Weighted reduction of production and imports, 1913–1918 (%)	(4) Relative shares of production and imports in reduction of consumption (%)
Production	80	40	32.0	72.4
Imports	20	61	12.2	27.6
Consumption	100		44.2	100.0

Sources and notes: Food production and import shares of consumption in 1913: Olson (1963: 74). Reduction of agricultural production 1913–1918: Ritschl (2005: 46). Reduction of imports 1913–1918: Hardach (1987: 33). Column (3) = (1) x (2). Column (4) expresses the weighted reduction of production and imports from column (3) as shares of the reduction in consumption.

using data on trends in the energy content of home-produced and imported food between 1913 and 1917.

The excessive demands made by the war on the German economy weighed heavily on agriculture right from the start of the war, as farms were drained of manpower, horses, and fertiliser. These demands increased heavily after the launch of the Hindenburg Programme that planned a dramatic increase in munitions production from 1916 together with greater manpower mobilisation for the frontlines (Goebel 1930: 82–96). The first six months of the programme pushed the German economy to the brink of disaster. Increased mobilisation and the enhanced capacity needed to transport material to munitions factories stretched the railways to their limits. In the winter of 1916/17, the crisis in the transport sector resulted in an acute coal shortage in the economy. The rising costs of war financing and the resulting acceleration of resort to the monetary printing press led to a devaluation of the Reichsmark in international financial transactions. Germany could thus no longer attract imports from neutral partners by offering to pay high prices (Boldorf 2020: 503). It also became increasingly difficult for European neutrals to re-export to Germany after the American Export Prohibition Act of 16 June 1917 (Bell 1961: 622). Contemporary statistics highlight the drastic reduction in German food imports between 1916 and 1917. However, this cannot explain the deterioration of food supplies in Germany, which had more to do with the collapse of domestic food production. Whereas monthly imports of rye and wheat declined from 20,000 tons in 1916 to little more than 3,000 in 1917, much more consequential was the drop in domestic output from 985,000 tons to 703,000 tons per month between the two years (Skalweit 1927: 235–239).

It is worth emphasising that it took three years to reduce German imports by 61 per cent and that this had only a minor effect on overall food supply in Germany compared with the decline in domestic agricultural output. It is perhaps surprising, therefore, to find Lambert (2012) claiming that the British could have brought the war to a quick end if only they had implemented economic warfare according to aggressive plans drawn up by Admiral Sir John 'Jacky' Fisher and approved in 1912 by the Committee for Imperial Defence to collapse the international trading system. In contrast to the gradual implementation of the blockade that actually occurred at the start of the war, Fisher's plan envisaged the immediate and ruthless exploitation of Britain's control of the seas through the Royal Navy and the massive British merchant marine, combined with Britain's control of communications through the telegraph and telephone infrastructure of the empire and the City of London's leadership of the international financial system.

There are a number of serious problems with Lambert's interpretation. First, it seems likely that this more aggressive approach to economic warfare would have severely damaged the British economy and would also have alienated the most important neutral countries, particularly the United States, which would have been counter-productive. Second, however, as the war proceeded, economic warfare was indeed pursued more aggressively but without delivering the decisive blow that had been anticipated. The problem here is that Lambert has under-estimated the adaptability of the German economy and did not take into account the counter-measures that would be adopted. These measures included naval attempts to break the blockade, policies to reduce consumption of importable goods, and policies to boost availability of importable goods. Since Germany lost the war, it is tempting to dismiss these counter-measures as having failed miserably. However, we have seen that Germany was only dependent on imports for a small share of its food requirements before the war, so that the fall in agricultural production was what really mattered. A more nuanced approach to the evaluation of counter-measures is therefore needed. Things could have been a lot worse for the German people if at least some of these measures had not met with some success.

Naval Counter-Measures to Break the Blockade

Within a week of the outbreak of war, the German merchant fleet had been effectively banished from the oceans, following a strategic retreat by the German High Seas Fleet in the face of the Royal Navy's substantial numerical superiority. Of the roughly 1,500 German merchant ships of at least 100 gross registered tons, 245 had been captured, 1,059 were locked up in neutral ports, and 221 were confined to operating in the Baltic (Lambert 2012: 212; Boldorf 2020: 485). This dramatic reduction in Germany's capacity for overseas transport was further aggravated by the British policy to limit Germany's access to transcontinental telegraph cables, which made it more difficult for German companies to arrange trade with international partners and neutral shipping companies (Kramer 2014: 465).

Pre-war German naval policy had been based on systematically challenging British surface naval superiority. However, at the start of the war the High Seas Fleet was trapped in port by the British blockade, where it remained for the duration of the war apart from an indecisive skirmish with part of the British Grand Fleet at the Battle of Jutland in May 1916, after which the German ships returned to port while the British ships went back to blockade duty, so that effectively the 'prisoners had attacked their jailer … but in the end they were safely back in jail' (Chickering 1998: 91–92).

German naval counter-measures can thus reasonably be judged to have failed. By failing to break out from the blockade, the High Seas Fleet abandoned the German merchant fleet, which was effectively banished from the oceans. Despite the fact that submarine warfare had only held a subordinate place in German strategic planning before the war, Jutland left the German navy with intensifying the submarine blockade as its only realistic option, a risky move that brought the United States into the war on the Allied side.

Counter-Measures to Reduce Consumption of Importable Goods

Counter-measures to reduce consumption of importable goods included regulation and rationing, which played an important role in reducing demand from the early stages of the war. However, the system did not work well. Offer (1989: 65–66) suggests that the German tradition of political economy predisposed the authorities to a regulatory approach favouring organisation and compulsion rather than price incentives. As the supply of food fell and prices increased in the summer and autumn of 1914, state regulation initially tended to exacerbate the situation. Capping the prices of individual products led farmers to switch to producing more unregulated products, so that the regulated products became ever scarcer (Chickering 1998: 42). In early 1915, an Imperial Grain Corporation was introduced to implement grain rationing and was used as a model for rationing other products. By 1916, there was even a War Corporation for Sauerkraut (Chickering 1998: 43–44). However, the situation continued to worsen until the end of the war. A popular joke in Berlin later in the war after a heavy fall of snow was that the best way to clear snow from the streets would be to establish an Imperial Snow Corporation (Chickering 1998: 44).

One of the low points of the German administrative response to food shortages was the implementation of a *Schweinemord* (pig massacre) on the grounds that pigs were competing with humans for scarce grain (Kramer 2014: 475). This followed the recommendations of the Eltzbacher Commission of academic experts and officials that reported in December 1914 and resulted in the killing of 9 million pigs by mid-April 1915 (Offer 1989: 25–26). However, it soon became clear that pigs were producers of fertiliser as well as consumers of fodder, so that the measure had a negative rather than positive effect on long-run food supply (Chickering 1998: 42). So, regulation and rationing may have reduced consumption of importable goods, but it also contributed significantly to the decline in agricultural output.

Counter-Measures to Boost Availability of Importable Goods

One way in which Germany could boost the availability of importable goods during the blockade was through the exploitation of occupied Europe. In the west, occupied France offered rich reserves of iron ore while in Belgium the principal resource was coal (Scherner 2020: 79–81). In addition, a programme of forced deportations to Germany was introduced to boost the German labour force (Chickering 1998: 84). In the east, Germany was able to extract relatively few resources from Poland, although 600,000 Polish workers had been enticed or forced to work on German farms by the summer of 1917 (Chickering 1998: 85; Lehnstaedt 2020: 586–588). Romania remained neutral until August 1916, then joined the war on the Allied side before being occupied by the Central Powers between December 1917 and May 1918, which gave Germany an opportunity to gain control of Romania's substantial oil wells. However, this was largely frustrated by the actions of a group of British engineers in late 1917, who delayed German access to this important resource through sabotage (Kramer 2014: 477). Thus, even though the creation of a safe reservoir of raw materials for the German economy and 'extended economic space' in central and south-eastern Europe became an obsession of German leaders and policy makers in the 1930s in preparation for World War II, the German experience in World War I offered little justification for this strategy.

The development of *ersatz* (substitute) goods was another way to boost the availability of importable goods. The policy of using artificial substitutes to replace scarce imported natural products is particularly associated with Germany during World War II, but also played a role in World War I. The prime example is the development of the Haber–Bosch process just before the start of the war, which was crucial for the production of both fertiliser and explosives in Germany during World War I (Kramer 2014: 479). The Germans had more limited success in substituting mineral-oil imports with by-products of coke, especially benzene. Fuel shortages therefore remained critical, particularly since, although pre-war Germany had been a major exporter of coal, growing demand, transportation bottlenecks, and declining domestic mining due to shortages of labour and materials led to coal shortages during the war (Roelevink and Ziegler 2020: 126–134).

Germany devoted much attention to boosting the availability of metals through increased domestic mining, with state financial support for exploration and the development of new mines. These measures led to an increased production of key metals such as nickel, tin, and tungsten, while recycling campaigns for the collection of everyday objects, known as *Metallmobilmachung* (metal mobilisation), were more important for other metals such as copper, brass, and bronze (Scherner 2020: 72–78).

Germany succeeded in boosting the availability of importable goods with the exploitation of industrial raw materials from western Europe, but was less successful in the extraction of resources from eastern Europe. There were also notable successes in the production of *ersatz* goods, particularly those arising from the synthesis of ammonia using the Haber–Bosch process, while metal shortages were alleviated through state support for new mines and recycling campaigns.

Consequences: Agricultural and Food Policies after 1918

British Policy after World War I

It might have been expected that the British would maintain the incentives used to boost grain production during the war, to avoid dependence on vulnerable agricultural imports in any future war. The Corn Production Act of 1917 guaranteed minimum prices for the next six years, until 1922, and envisaged the payment of deficiency payments to farmers based on average yields per acre if market prices fell below the guaranteed minimum. During the war, however, market prices remained substantially above the guaranteed minimum price, so that the support given to farmers was purely hypothetical (Whetham 1978: 95). As the government began to wrestle with how to adjust the guaranteed prices to changing costs and the long-run position of agriculture, the problem was referred to a Royal Commission, which produced an interim report in 1919, recommending new minimum prices for wheat, barley, and oats, although barley was excluded from the resulting legislation to satisfy the temperance lobby (Whetham 1978: 120–121). The resulting Agriculture Act of December 1920 envisaged the new price guarantees coming into force from August 1921. Within a few months, however, prices stopped rising and began a precipitous fall, as shown in Figure 3.3. Once it became clear that the guaranteed prices would probably mean deficiency payments of £30 million a year at a time when government spending was being cut back drastically in most areas, the government repealed the guarantees. The Corn Production Acts (Repeal) Act of August 1921 effected what became known by farmers as the 'Great Betrayal' (Whetham 1978: 141).

Subsequent support for agriculture was kept low between the wars and generally took the form of subsidies and marketing schemes rather than tariffs, because of imperial preference (Pollard 1969: 134–145). If Britain were to obtain access to imperial markets for industrial exports, farmers in the empire had to have access to the British market for agricultural produce. Thus, short-run pressures on government continued to hinder long-term plans for food security during the 1930s, just as they had in the 1920s. Figure 3.3 shows how the real price of wheat continued to fall faster than the GDP deflator, so that by the 1930s, the real price of grain was barely half of its 1913 level. The share of agriculture in economic activity and agricultural employment continued to decline in Britain during the inter-war period, and Britain would enter World War II once again highly dependent on imported grain and vulnerable to German submarine blockade (Olson 1963: 117–119). Again, however, Britain used its flexibility to survive (see Chapter 6). Agricultural support was strengthened during World War II, again with promises of continued post-war incentives. This time, unlike after World War I, the incentives were retained in the 1947 Agriculture Act and Britain's reliance on imported food was greatly reduced (Bowers 1985).

German Policy after World War I

Mulder (2022) suggests that the German pursuit of autarky policies during the inter-war period may have been driven by an exaggerated belief in the power of blockade and fear of sanctions. We have already seen that the reduction of food consumption in Germany owed far less to the contribution of the blockade-induced decline in imports than to the

Figure 3.3 UK nominal and real wheat prices, 1913–1938 (1913 = 100)
Sources. Ministry of Agriculture, Fisheries and Food and Department of Agriculture and Fisheries for Scotland (1968: 82); Feinstein (1972: T132–T133).

decline in agricultural production caused by the disruptive effects of mobilisation. However, while the link between the blockade and a reduction in food imports was easy for people to grasp, the link between the spill-overs from mobilisation and shortages of food was more indirect and harder to perceive. Furthermore, the effects of the blockade were still visible for a further eight months after the end of the war, as the Allies kept it in place until Germany submitted to the terms of the Treaty of Versailles (Cox 2019: 53). Blaming the blockade was also encouraged by the way that Ludendorff acted during the final stages of the war to shape public opinion. After the failure of the Ludendorff Offensive of spring 1918 and as the Allied counter-offensive gathered momentum over the summer, military leadership realised that the war was lost and on 29 September handed over responsibility for negotiating an armistice to the civilian government (Chickering 1998: 178–189). As a result, during the run-up to the armistice on 11 November, civilians rather than soldiers shouldered the responsibility of suing for peace, while the military leadership spread the myth of the *Dolchstoss*, or 'stab in the back', blaming the home front for the failure of the Ludendorff Offensive through the withholding of adequate supplies and reserves. The soldiers in the field could then be portrayed as remaining valiant and in good order until the autumn of 1918, when subversive agitation by 'pacifists, socialists, slackers and Jews' could be blamed for bringing about the final collapse of morale on the home front after years of struggle against the blockade-induced shortages (Chickering 1998: 190).

As Germans formed an exaggerated belief in the power of blockade during and after the war, it was natural that this should spill over into a fear of sanctions, the peacetime application of the economic weapon. Thus, the blockade myth had a profound effect on German strategic thinking during the inter-war period, leading to an interest in the idea of *Mitteleuropa*, a German-led central European economic zone (Mulder 2022: 59–60). This led to sharp changes in the direction of Germany's trade during the 1930s as autarkic policies were actively pursued via bilateral trade and exchange clearing agreements. The share of southern and eastern Europe in German imports increased from 9.8 to 18.7 per cent between 1929 and 1938, while for exports the share increased from 11.2 to 20.8 per cent over the same period (Feinstein et al. 1997: 164). It highlights the strategic motive behind this shift that Germany was willing to pay between 20 and 40 per cent above world market prices for essential raw materials, including farm staples, from its 'extended economic sphere' (Abelshauser 1999: 519–520).

Conclusions

This chapter has compared the German blockade of Britain and the British blockade of Germany during World War I, using a framework of preparations, conduct, and consequences. We began by examining how domestic agriculture came to produce just 35 per cent of Britain's calorific requirements before the war, leaving the country highly dependent on seaborne imports of food, while Germany produced 80 per cent of its food requirements domestically. Trade policy is the answer to these divergent paths, with Britain pursuing a policy of free trade in food after the repeal of the Corn Laws while Germany continued to protect its farmers, with tariffs reaching about 40 per cent by the outbreak of the war.

We then explained how Germany came to face food shortages while Britain managed to feed itself adequately throughout the war despite the pre-war preparations apparently favouring Germany. How did the country that produced most of its food at home suffer greatly from the blockade while the country that imported most of its food manage to survive the blockade without any significant deterioration in the calorific value of the diet? The answer here is that Britain successfully adopted a range of counter-measures to maintain shipping capacity (the convoy system and shipbuilding), to economise on the use of shipping (Atlantic concentration, speeding up turnaround times at ports), to reduce consumption of importable goods (cutting back investment, limiting exports, controlling the importation of non-essential imports while discouraging excessive consumption of essential imports, and eventually introducing rationing) and also to boost agricultural production (introducing incentives for farmers to increase agricultural production). In essence, the British exhibited a capacity for substitution, allowing the economy to be flexible enough to survive the German submarine blockade.

By contrast, Germany suffered a substantial deterioration in the calorific value of its food supply. The main cause of this was the excessive demands made on the economy by mobilisation. Robbed of labour, horses, and fertiliser, and facing weak incentives to produce for the market as consumer goods disappeared, German farmers reduced output. We must be careful, therefore, not to follow much of the literature and overstate the role of the blockade in the relatively poor performance of the German economy during the war. Some simple calculations suggest that the blockade accounted for between 17.5 and 27.6 per cent of the decline in food consumption between 1913 and 1918, with the vast bulk of the decline in food consumption due to a 40 per cent collapse in domestic production.

Given the much greater importance of the fall in domestic production of food than the decline in imports, it is important to take a nuanced approach to the evaluation of German counter-measures to the blockade, rather than jumping to the conclusion that they all must have failed badly. Naval counter-measures were clearly unsuccessful as the German High Seas Fleet remained locked in port throughout the war apart from a couple of indecisive skirmishes, thus accepting the banishment of the German merchant fleet from the oceans. Counter-measures to reduce consumption of importable goods included regulation and rationing, but these were implemented in a less flexible way than in Britain, with the authorities favouring organisation and compulsion rather than price incentives. Counter-measures to boost availability of importable goods included the exploitation of occupied Europe. These met with some success in the west, but were limited in the east by the economic backwardness of the territories occupied. The most successful counter-measures to boost availability were the development of *ersatz* goods and policies to boost the availability of metals through subsidised development of new mines and recycling campaigns.

Finally, we consider the consequences of the war for agricultural and food policies after 1918. Perhaps surprisingly, the British government quickly reneged on the price guarantees offered into the future, resulting in a rapid reversal of the wartime increase in the production of grain, so that Britain entered World War II once again highly dependent on imported grain and vulnerable to German submarine blockade. Germany, by contrast, with an exaggerated belief in the power of blockade and a fear of sanctions, drew the conclusion that it needed to pursue autarkic policies and used bilateral trade and exchange clearing agreements to increase its trade with southern and eastern Europe.

References

Abeslhauser, W. 1999. 'Kriegswirtschaft und Wirtschaftswunder: Deutschlands wirtschaftliche Mobilisierung für den Zweiten Weltkrieg und die Folgen für die Nachkriegszeit', *Vierteljahrshefte für Zeitgeschichte* 47: 503–538.

Afton, B., and M. Turner. 2000. 'The Statistical Base of Agricultural Performance in England and Wales, 1850–1914', in E. J. T. Collins (ed.), *The Agrarian History of England and Wales, 1850–1914, Part II*, pp. 1757–2140. Cambridge: Cambridge University Press.

Bell, A. C. 1961. *A History of the Blockade of Germany and the Countries Associated with Her in the Great War, Austria–Hungary, Bulgaria, and Turkey, 1914–1918*. London: Her Majesty's Stationery Office.

Beveridge, W. H. 1928. *British Food Control*. Oxford: Oxford University Press.

Blum, M. 2011. 'Government Decisions before and during the First World War and the Living Standards in Germany during a Drastic Natural Experiment', *Explorations in Economic History* 48(4): 556–567.

Boldorf, M. 2020. 'Außenhandel und Blockade', in M. Boldorf (ed.), *Deutsche Wirtschaft im Ersten Weltkrieg*, pp. 479–520. Berlin: De Gruyter Oldenbourg.

Bowers, J. K. 1985. 'British Agricultural Policy since the Second World War', *Agricultural History Review* 33: 66–76.

Breemer, J. S. 2010. *Defeating the U-Boat: Inventing Antisubmarine Warfare*, Newport Papers No. 36. Newport, RI: Naval War College Press.

Broadberry, S., and M. Harrison. 2005. 'The Economics of World War I: An Overview', in S. Broadberry and M. Harrison (eds.), *The Economics of World War I*, pp. 3–40. Cambridge: Cambridge University Press.

Broadberry, S., and P. Howlett. 2005. 'The United Kingdom during World War I: Business as Usual', in S. Broadberry and M. Harrison (eds.), *The Economics of World War I*, pp. 206–234. Cambridge: Cambridge University Press.

Bühlow, H. Von. 1917. *Deutschlands Aushungerung?* Dresden: Globus.

Chickering, R. 1998. *Imperial Germany and the Great War, 1914–1918*. Cambridge: Cambridge University Press.

Churchill, W. S. 1923. *The World Crisis: 1915*. London: Thornton Butterworth. 1927. *The World Crisis: 1916–1918, Part II*. London: Thornton Butterworth.

Cox, M. 2019. *Hunger in War and Peace: Women and Children in Germany, 1914–1924*. Oxford: Oxford University Press.

Davis, L. E., and S. L. Engerman. 2006. *Naval Blockades in Peace and War. An Economic History Since 1750*. Cambridge: Cambridge University Press.

Fayle, C. E. 1924. *Seaborne Trade, Volume III: The Period of Unrestricted Submarine Warfare, with a Map and Statistical Diagrams*. London: Murray.

1927. *The War and the Shipping Industry*. Oxford: Oxford University Press.

Feinstein, C. H. 1972. *National Income, Expenditure and Output of the United Kingdom, 1855–1965*. Cambridge: Cambridge University Press.

1988. 'National Statistics, 1760–1920: Sources and Methods of Estimation for Domestic Reproducible Fixed Assets, Stocks and Works in Progress, Overseas Assets, and Land', in C. H. Feinstein and S. Pollard (eds.), *Studies in Capital Formation in the United Kingdom, 1750–1920*, pp. 257–471. Oxford: Oxford University Press.

Feinstein, C. H., P. Temin, and G. Toniolo. 1997. *The European Economy Between the Wars*. Oxford: Oxford University Press.

Gerschenkron, A. 1943. *Bread and Democracy in Germany*. Berkeley: University of California Press.

Goebel, O. 1930. *Deutsche Rohstoffwirtschaft im Weltkrieg: einschliesslich des Hindenburg-Programms*. Stuttgart: Deutsche Verlags-Anstalt.

Hardach, G. 1987. *The First World War, 1914–1918*. Harmondsworth: Penguin.

Harrison, M. 2025. 'Economic Warfare: Lessons from the Two World Wars', in J. Eloranta, P. Fishback, E. Kuorelahti, and J. Land (eds.), *The Routledge Economic History of War*, pp. 187–200. Abingdon: Routledge.

Hoffmann, W. G. 1965. *Das Wachstum der deutschen Wirtschaft seit der Mitte des 19. Jahrhunderts*. Berlin: Springer.

Kleine-Natrop, H. 1922. *Devisenpolitik (Valutapolitik) in Deutschland vor dem Kriege und in der Kriegs- und Nachkriegszeit*. Berlin: Preiss.

Kramer, A. 2014. 'Blockade and Economic Warfare', in J. Winter (ed.), *The Cambridge History of the First World War, Vol. 2: The State*, pp. 460–489. New York: Cambridge University Press.

Lambert, N. 2012. *Planning Armageddon: British Economic Warfare and the First World War*. Cambridge, MA: Harvard University Press.

Lehnstaedt, S. 2020. 'Bezatzungswirtschaft in Generalgouvernement Warschau und in Osteuropa', in M. Boldorf (ed.), *Deutsche Wirtschaft im Ersten Weltkrieg*, pp. 575–600. Berlin: De Gruyter Oldenbourg.

Marrison, A. 1996. *British Business and Protection 1903–1932*. Oxford: Clarendon.

Middleton, T. H. 1923. *Food Production in War*. Oxford: Oxford University Press.

Ministry of Agriculture, Fisheries and Food and Department of Agriculture and Fisheries for Scotland. 1968. *A Century of Agricultural Statistics: Great Britain 1866–1966*. London: HMSO.

Mulder, N. 2022. *The Economic Weapon: The Rise of Sanctions as a Tool of Modern War*. New Haven, CT: Yale University Press.

O'Rourke, K. H. (1997), 'The European Grain Invasion, 1870–1913', *Journal of Economic History* 57: 775–801.

Offer, A. 1989. *The First World War: An Agrarian Interpretation*. Oxford: Oxford University Press.

Olson, M. 1963. *The Economics of the Wartime Shortage: A History of British Food Supplies in the Napoleonic War and in World Wars I and II*. Durham, NC: Duke University Press.

Parmelee, M. 1924. *Blockade and Sea Power*. New York: Thomas Y. Crowell Company.
Pollard, S. 1969. *The Development of the British Economy, 1914–1967* (2nd ed.). London: Arnold.
Ritschl, A. 2005. 'The Pity of Peace', in S. Broadberry and M. Harrison (eds.), *The Economics of World War I*, pp. 41–76. Cambridge: Cambridge University Press.
Roelevink, E.-M., and D. Ziegler. 2020. 'Rohstoffwirtschaft: die bergbaulichen Rohstoffe', in M. Boldorf (ed.), *Deutsche Wirtschaft im Ersten Weltkrieg*, pp. 125–156. Berlin: De Gruyter Oldenbourg.
Roerkohl, A. 1991. *Hungerblockade und Heimatfront: Die kommunale Lebensmittelversorgung in Westfalen während des Ersten Weltkrieges*. Stuttgart: Steiner.
Salter, J. A. 1921. *Allied Shipping Control*. Oxford: Oxford University Press.
Scherner, J. 2020. 'Metallbewirtschaftung', in M. Boldorf (ed.), *Deutsche Wirtschaft im Ersten Weltkrieg*, pp. 67–88. Berlin: De Gruyter Oldenbourg.
Skalweit, A. 1927. *Die deutsche Kriegsernährungswirtschaft*. Stuttgart: Deutsche Verlags-Anstalt.
Starling, E. H. 1920. 'The Food Supply of Germany during the War', *Journal of the Royal Society* 83: 225–254.
Webb, S. B. 1982. 'Agricultural Protection in Wilhelminian Germany: Forging an Empire with Pork and Rye', *Journal of Economic History* 42: 309–326.
Whetham, E. 1978. *The Agrarian History of England and Wales, 1914–39*. Cambridge: Cambridge University Press.

4 Can Economic Sanctions Work in a Smaller Conflict?
The Italo-Ethiopian War of 1935–1936

Mattia Bertazzini, Jari Eloranta, and Elina Kuorelahti

It [the Italo-Ethiopian conflict] is a study in Public Opinion, that is to say, in the reaction of the civilised peoples to a flagrant and unashamed resort to force by a leading European Power in defiance of the recognised principles of civilisation. It is a study in World Unity, that is to say, in the degree of common feeling and public spirit that can be mobilised for a common sacrifice, or at least a common discipline, on behalf of those principles. It is a study in sanctions, that is to say, in the comparative efficacy of the various methods adopted in common against the outlaw State. (Zimmern 1935: 752)

Introduction

The Russian invasion of Ukraine in February 2022 has sparked new interest in the historical lessons of warfare and particularly the history of total war, especially the world wars. The EU and the West responded to Russia's attack by offering economic, humanitarian, and military support to Ukraine, yet also by imposing significant economic sanctions on Russia. The most recent round of sanctions applied by the EU, the fourteenth by the end of September 2024, extended them further. After over two years of war and sanctions, there is relatively little discussion of how to measure the success of the sanctions or the performance of the Russian economy. As such, blockades and economic sanctions come with a cost for those who impose them as well, which has raised questions concerning the effectiveness of economic sanctions as a soft form of policy intervention contrary to outright warfare. Can economic sanctions end wars? Are economic sanctions an effective means to pressure the aggressor to cease the attack? These are broad questions that have been addressed by scholars over the last 100 years or so, yet the perspectives and the popularity of sanctions as a policy tool has waxed and waned over time.

What is the track record of economic sanctions – that is, have they worked previously in history? Undoubtedly, that is a difficult question to answer comprehensively, given the breadth of conflicts and crises. Weaponising the economy and limiting access to resources is as old as war itself, but as an internationally codified measure of response to warfare it emerged with the birth of the first intergovernmental institution, the League of Nations in 1920. Under Article 16 of the Covenant, the member countries promised to join in a common action against any country instigating a military attack on a member state. Economic sanctions were the primary form of coercive action. The Article also indicated that the League of Nations could 'recommend' that the members should make a military intervention in case the economic sanctions did not yield results, and it could offer material help to the victim of the aggression – yet both of these ideas ended up a dead letter.[1] Subsequently, economic sanctions to maintain international peace lived on in the United Nations Charter under Article 41, which was reinforced with more developed and practical policy tools concerning economic aid for the victim of attack. Obviously, sanctions imposed by a single state are not going to be very effective, unless it maintains a stranglehold on a particular, vital resource or controls the access of the other state to the world economy. Yet international organisations face the difficulty of acting as a common body, with unanimous consent – for example, while some member states wanted the League of Nations to be a military alliance, others did not, leading to disfunction in its actions (Eloranta 2011).

There are ample reasons, in general, why economic sanctions are not very effective or why they might fail entirely. They include the inability to impact the target group in the opposing country, the nature and size of the conflict, types of economies involved, reciprocal impacts, the length of time involved, whether they are accompanied by actual warfare, and so on. The interdisciplinary literature on this is quite large, with scholars illustrating various theoretical and empirical reasons for the limited impact of sanctions (see e.g. Pape 1997; Jones 2015; Pala 2021). Of course, there is plenty of scholarship suggesting that sanctions *can* work in certain settings and when applied correctly. As Peksen (2019) has suggested, multilateral sanctions are more effective, especially when backed by a broad international consensus. Moreover, the targeting mechanisms and realism regarding the expected outcomes are also important. Sanctions aimed at trade and investments have a higher chance of success, yet negative externalities and unanticipated outcomes are to be expected in most cases of implementation. Furthermore, the success rate, however defined, is

---

[1] UN Archive; League of Nations: S128/78/20 'Provisional Economic and Financial Committee – The Economic Weapon of the League of Nations – Memorandum by Mr. Salter', 1919.

typically higher for sanctions as a threat, prior to actual implementation. Expectations and perceptions change following the implementation of sanctions, and actual conflict (Hovi, Huseby, and Sprinz 2005; see also Özdamar and Shahin 2021; on the failure of 2014 and Crimea, see Alexseev and Hale 2020; Bělín and Hanousek 2021).

One of the most extensive efforts to analyse sanctions centres around the construction of the Global Sanctions Data Base (GSDB), which covers all the various types of sanctions in the period 1950–2016. It also provides data to evaluate the effectiveness of the sanctions, for example trade flows. Analysis of the data involved highlights the way sanctions have evolved during and after the Cold War, with sanctions being increasingly targeted towards financial sphere and travel, with human rights becoming more important over time. Furthermore, the success of sanctions increased until 1995, and has declined since then (Felbermayr et al. 2020).

The case of the League of Nations offers us a lens through which to evaluate the impact sanctions have, and how they can erode the legitimacy of the organisation due to perceived failures. In fact, the League was originally viewed as an effective vehicle for deployment of the 'economic weapon', with some limited successes in the 1920s and 1930s, for example on disarmament (Mulder 2022). While the inability of this multinational organisation to contain Italy's aggression is usually considered a classic failure, Mulder (2022: 11–12) has recently pointed out that despite this apparent failure, the international economic coercion bringing together three-quarters of the world's states against Italy showed the force of a weaponised global economy, and the willingness of the broad international community to use it in defending peace and the liberal world order. For fascist and autarkic regimes like Germany and Japan, this fuelled national economic policies underlining the primacy of retaining material and strategic self-sufficiency.

Sanctions were somewhat rehabilitated with the World War II blockades and later Cold War actions. Blockades like the one imposed on Cuba and other failures in the 1970s and 1980s again weakened the reputation of sanctions as a policy tool, with the post-Cold War period displaying again greater appreciation for softer policy tools instead of outright military action (Hufbauer, Schott, and Elliott 1990). Next, we will take a closer look at the League, the context of the war, and the international global political environment.

The International Context of the Conflict

The Italo-Ethiopian (or Abyssinian) conflict, also known as the Second Italo-Ethiopian War, was an escalating war that occurred between Italy and Ethiopia from 1935 to 1936. The conflict arose from Italy's imperialist ambitions and desire to colonise Ethiopia, which remained one of the few African nations to maintain its independence during the era of European colonialism, which was even expanding in the 1930s (for context, see Gardner and Eloranta 2021).

Italy, under the leadership of dictator Benito Mussolini, sought to expand its influence and territories in Africa. This choice was in line with the long-standing Italian ambition of occupying Ethiopia, to connect the coastal territories of Somalia and Eritrea. This plan had come to an abrupt end in 1896, when the Italian army was obliterated at the battle of Adwa. By the end of the 1930s, revanchist sentiment and old colonial ambitions were combined with the economic plans of the fascist regime. Through the acquisition of colonial territories, Mussolini aimed to expand export markets and the supply of raw materials while finding a destination for surplus agricultural labour, in the context of autarkic economic policy (see next section, and Bertazzini 2020).

Using the pretext of an Ethiopian attack on an Italian border post, Italy launched a full-scale invasion of Ethiopia in October 1935. The Italian forces, equipped with modern weapons and superior technology, quickly gained the upper hand against the Ethiopian military, which relied on outdated weaponry and tactics. Despite its efforts to resist the Italian occupation, the conflict resulted in a devastating defeat for Ethiopia. Mussolini's forces carried out brutal and indiscriminate attacks on Ethiopian civilians, leading to the deaths of tens of thousands of people. The Italian forces also deployed chemical weapons, such as asphyxiating and tear gas, and other illegal weapons (such as dumdum bullets) (Sbacchi 2005; Grip and Hart 2009; on later use, see Endaylalu 2018).

The international response to the Italo-Ethiopian conflict was divided. The League of Nations, the predecessor to the United Nations, condemned Italy's aggression but failed to take effective measures to prevent the invasion. Economic sanctions imposed on Italy are often considered largely ineffective, as countries like the United Kingdom and France continued to trade with Italy (Tosi 2017). Moreover, one of the key issues preventing a more unified, multilateral application of sanctions concerned the requirement of consensus in League decision making. Another possible source of failure concerned the short duration of the conflict, which is typical for most applications of sanctions (Baer 1973). Moreover, the League was dominated by European imperial thinking when it came to newer states and their sovereignty, thus making it more difficult to mobilise support for a non-European newer state (Donaldson 2020). The global outrage over Italy's actions, and especially the war crimes, was more widespread than the sterile League of Nations committee reports imply (Wemlinger 2015). Ultimately, Italy achieved its objective of annexing Ethiopia in May 1936, establishing Italian East Africa. The conflict had significant implications for the global balance of power, contributing to growing tensions in the lead-up to World War II. It also emphasised the weaknesses of the League of Nations and its inability to prevent acts of aggression by its member states. To be fair, the process had already started with Japan's aggression in Manchuria in 1931, and it was reinforced by Germany's actions in the 1930s.

One of the key issues, beyond the inability to act collectively through consent to utilise the 'economic weapon', was the long bureaucratic effort to achieve disarmament. The League was an imperfect instrument for disarmament, lacking the necessary mechanisms and enforcement capabilities. Moreover, domestic political elites within member countries that were hostile to disarmament posed significant challenges. The Disarmament Conference was convened too late and under hostile conditions, reducing its chances of success once the Depression had begun. In addition, the confrontation between France and Germany at the Disarmament Conference further complicated the negotiations. Finally, the ambitious aims of disarmament and the practical problems involved in reducing armaments presented significant obstacles, prolonging the negotiations (Housden 2014; Ikonomou 2021). Most successes in disarmament in the inter-war period were achieved outside the League apparatus in the 1920s, which was due to the participation of non-League members enhancing the credibility of the negotiations. Many smaller nations had high hopes for the disarmament process, only to be disappointed by the outcome (Eloranta 2011; Gram-Skjoldager 2020).

Another key issue that the League tried to assess and contain credibly was the international trade in armaments. World War I, with one of the narratives blaming the conflict on the 'merchants of death', changed the impetus for limiting future arms races. The League of Nations took on this task in 1925, with a draft agreement that eventually was not ratified, despite support from many non-member states. In this case, the smaller states saw it as imperative to maintain their sovereignty through external arms imports, if necessary, and this doomed the agreement. This process once again highlighted the difficulties of governing international policy processes via consensus, leading to a merely moral stance by the League (Stone 2000; Eloranta 2002; on inter-war arms trade, see also Mehrl and Thurner 2023).

In this chapter, we will explore whether the sanctions had any impact on the Italian economy, and on trade patterns in particular. While the sanctions certainly did not end the war, or force Mussolini to retrench or even reconsider his imperial ambitions, there is no comprehensive evaluation on the impact of the sanctions. However, there has been some work done already to answer the counterfactual question of what could have made the sanctions effective. One of those avenues concerns an embargo on coal and oil. As pointed out by Strang (2008), British policy makers analysed the issue carefully when the negotiations over the sanctions were taking place and concluded that an embargo would not work, due to other nations stepping in to provide alternative markets, as we have seen in the case of Russia in 2022–2024. They also were worried that an embargo would lead to an alliance between Italy and Germany. Thus, publicly they supported the idea of an embargo, but worked actively against it behind the scenes. Ristuccia's (2000) analysis implies that Italy would not have been negatively impacted by an embargo on coal, since Germany likely would have stepped in as a supplier. An oil embargo would have been more effective. But, as we later saw in the case of Japan, an oil embargo, which could grind a modern military machine to a halt, can lead to war (Davis and Engerman 2006; Higgs 2011). In order to better understand the context and the challenges faced by the League in relation to the Italo-Abyssinian war, we delve deeper into its history and functioning in the next section.

The League of Nations and the Sanctions against Italy

When the League of Nations was established it lacked credibility as the keeper of international, collective security, as Arthur Saltier wrote in 1919: 'One of the most serious weaknesses of the League at present is perhaps that so many people think that it is founded more upon good intentions than upon a cool consideration of the stern realities of international trouble.'[2] The economic weapon as a collective action against a member that waged war or violated the principles of the Covenant, formulated in Article 16, came to fill this credibility deficiency. It did not differentiate between the League members and against whom coercion could be applied, but in practice sanctions were planned against peripheral European countries or non-European countries. Using it against one of the founding members of the League of Nations, Italy, was not in view during and after World War I[3] (Mulder 2022: 7–8).

Economic sanctions and blockades might today suffer from credibility deficiency, but after World War I they certainly did not. Like aerial bombing and gas warfare, they were considered new weapons of mass destruction and very effective as such. Compared with air power and gas

---

[2] Ibid.   [3] Ibid.

warfare, economic blockades had been the deadliest anti-civilian weapon in World War I, claiming 300,000–400,000 victims in central Europe and half a million more in the Ottoman provinces. Many believed that had economic sanctions existed and been used against Austria–Hungary and Serbia in 1914, the outbreak of World War I could have been avoided (Mulder 2022: 1–10). Great expectations were attached to the power of the 'economic weapon' as the guarantor of collective security. As Woodrow Wilson famously remarked in 1919, their sole existence could prevent wars: 'A nation that is boycotted is a nation that is in sight of surrender. Apply this economic, peaceful, silent, deadly remedy and there will be no need for force' (quoted in Gordon 2019: 3).

In the 1920s, the economic weapon was indeed effective; it worked just as planned – that is, in resolving the small, peripheral country conflicts in the Wilsonian spirit of preventing military escalation. The threat of activating Article 16 de-escalated crises such as the Yugoslav–Albanian case in 1921, the Greek–Bulgarian dispute, and the Paraguay–Bolivian crisis in 1928 (Zimmern 1935: 757). Paradoxically, when the economic weapon was actually applied against Italy it turned out to be not only ineffective in ending the aggressions but also destructive for the League's credibility as well as for European security by bringing together the fascist powers, Italy and Germany (Mulder 2022: 227–228).

The decision of the Council and the Assembly of the League of Nations on economic sanctions towards Italy came into force on 18 November 1935. Fifty countries agreed to suspend bilateral clearing agreements, impose a ban on arms trade and financial transactions between League members and Italy, stop import trade from Italy to League member countries (except gold or silver bullion and coin) as well as stop export of war materials to Italy. Strategic raw materials, such as coal, oil, pig iron, and steel were discussed during the embargo, but not included in it. Particularly the absence of oil from the embargo list has been raised in research as a major flaw as Italian warfare in Abyssinia relied on planes, tanks, and mechanical transport. Then again, even if oil had been on the embargo list, the effectiveness of energy isolation is debatable given that the United States was not a League member and therefore free to trade with Italy (Walters 1952, vol. 2: 667–668; Ristuccia 2000).

Why were oil and coal not included in the list of embargoed commodities? Starving Italy of energy supplies would have undoubtedly been an effective measure; 'oil governs the world', as the Peruvian member of the Technical Committee on Economic Sanctions said in early 1936.[4] That

---

[4] UN archive: LoN: R3681-1-22392-22392, 12 February 1936, quote Jochamowitz, p. 6.

Can Economic Sanctions Work in a Smaller Conflict? 119

is also the reason why these commodities were not embargoed: oil and coal were too crucial for the global economy. Denying them to a nation through sanctions was considered a declaration of war against Italy, particularly by Britain and France, rather than a way of checking its aggression in Ethiopia (Renwick 1981: 14–15). By trying to force peace through an energy embargo, the members of the League of Nations might in fact wage war. Secondly, the discussions of the Technical Committee in 1936 reveal that it was commonly accepted knowledge that oil embargo would not hold, Italy would find a way to get oil, and firms would find a way to supply it indirectly.[5] The key players in the international oil and coal trade were not members of the League of Nations in 1936. The Covenant and Articles on sanctions did not apply to Germany and the US, which were major supplies of oil and coal. In discussing oil, the British member of the Technical Committee underlined that there was no mechanism anywhere in the multilateral system of the 1930s, no actual economic weapon, to starve Italy of [6]oil and coal: 'In previous sanctions, the production of the commodities in question had been controlled almost entirely by the Members of the League. In the case of petroleum the question assumed a different aspect in view of the fact that some important producers were not Members of the League.' Imposing an oil or coal embargo without the USA and Germany would have led to 'considerable sacrifices' for British and French commercial interests while the actual goal, to force peace in the Abyssinian peninsula through sanctions, would not have been achieved.[7]

Mulder (2022: 202–203) has recently argued that discussing what was *not* created (energy embargo) begs the question what *was* created. What was the sanction model that the League of Nations believed in? Created on the desks of British and French politicians, economic coercion focused more on finance than strategic materials or energy. Sanctions were designed not by war experts but by economists who believed that turning the screw on foreign exchange reserves, which in Italy after the Great Depression were low to begin with, was the best method of coercion. The Treasury theory looked at foreign exchange reserves as a key commodity. The intention of sanctions was to tighten the budgetary constraints of warfare as well as to restrict Italian *exports* rather than deprive the country of European imports. Finance-focused sanctions, besides the undeniable logic of the Treasury theory, was in many ways easier for the sanctioning countries. The problem with the chosen path

---

[5] UN archive: LoN: R3681–1-22392-22392.
[6] Ibid., 7 March 1936, quote Starling, p. 4.   [7] Ibid., 7 March 1936, quote Brown, p. 6.

was the pace: coercion through balance of payments took effect very slowly compared with the pace of military developments on the Abyssinian front.

Given this international context, in order to make progress on question of the impact of the sanctions we first need to take a closer, and brief, look at the Italian economy under fascism, which we do in the following section.

The Italian Economy under Fascism

As described by Toniolo (1980) in his seminal work, by the time the Italian economy was hit by sanctions at the end of 1935, it had already experienced a long period of transformation owing to the peculiar economic doctrine championed by Mussolini, the so-called autarky (*autarchia*). In fact, the increased emphasis on colonial expansion and development that led to the invasion of Ethiopia can in itself be considered as an expression of this doctrine (Bertazzini 2020, 2022). Such economic context should be kept in mind when evaluating the impact and shortcomings of the sanctions.

The fascist economic doctrine in the 1930s can be broadly summarised as a combination of reducing dependence on foreign imports to decrease the balance of payments deficit – including strategic commodities (mostly coal, oil steel and iron, food crops) – while expanding the economy by strengthening the productive capacity of the primary and secondary sectors. To make up for the loss of foreign export markets and the import of cheap raw materials in this framework, Italy should have embarked on an expansionary and militaristic foreign policy. This was partly implemented in the 1930s with the expansion of colonial possessions in Somalia and Libya, as well as the occupation of Ethiopia and Albania. The participation of Italy in World War II with clear hopes of easy territorial gains could be interpreted as a continuation of this economic policy.

Autarky, however, was never coherently theorised and implemented by the regime. Rather, it was a collection of economic initiatives and propaganda moves that often diverged significantly. Policies such as the 'battle for grain' targeted at boosting Italian production of cereals, the draining of swampy areas, the foundation of new towns (see Carillo 2021, 2022), and colonial expansionism were coupled with currency manipulation such as 'Quota Novanta'. Implemented in 1927, this policy was aimed at artificially appreciating the Italian lira against the dollar and the pound. By making imports cheaper and reducing the competitiveness of Italian exports, this measure had the unintended consequence of slowing down

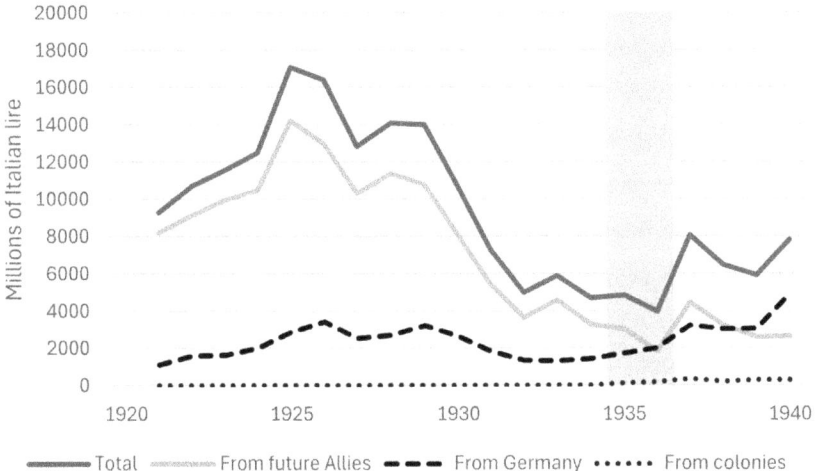

Figure 4.1 Italy's import values by source, 1921–1940 (Italian lire and millions)
Source: Federico et al. (2011).

import substitution and harming the industrial sector that the regime had intended to expand so as to achieve independence on the production of key intermediate goods and weapons (see Toniolo 1980).

Moreover, the switch from a relatively open market economy to the autarkic regime should not be thought of as a sudden shock imposed on the economy. Rather, it was a slow adjustment that followed an early period (at least spanning between 1922 and 1927) which saw the implementation of more mainstream conservative policies of financial austerity to curb inflation under Minister Volpi. Autarkic policies accelerated thereafter, partially as a consequence of the aggregate demand shock caused by the 1929 financial crisis and the Great Depression that followed. With all its contradictions, autarky had somewhat transformed the Italian economy in the first half of the 1930s, most notably by leading – together with the generalised break-down of international trade (Albers 2021) – to a significant reduction in imports, shown in Figure 4.1 (all goods), Figure 4.2 (weapons), and Figure 4.3 (oil), and a simultaneous drop in exports, shown in Figure 4.4.

The Economic Impact of Sanctions: Trade

Sanctions against Italy were only imposed for a short period of time, namely between November 1935 and June 1936. As discussed earlier,

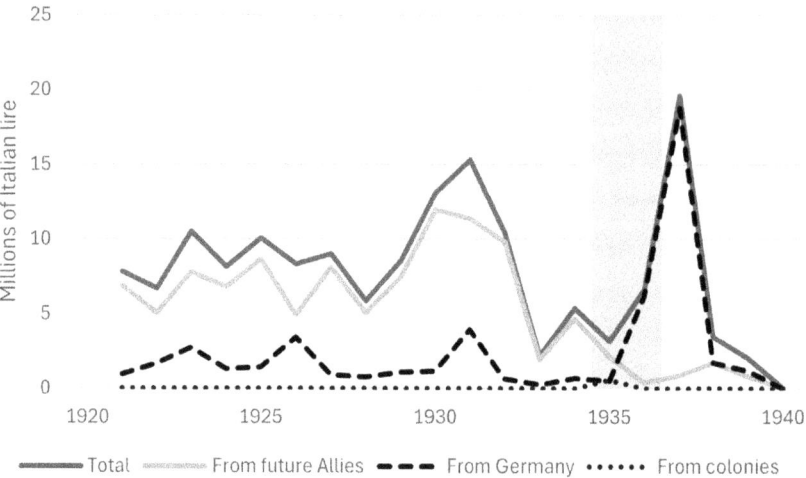

Figure 4.2 Italy's imports of weapons by source, 1921–1940 (millions of Italian lire)
Source: Federico et al. (2011).

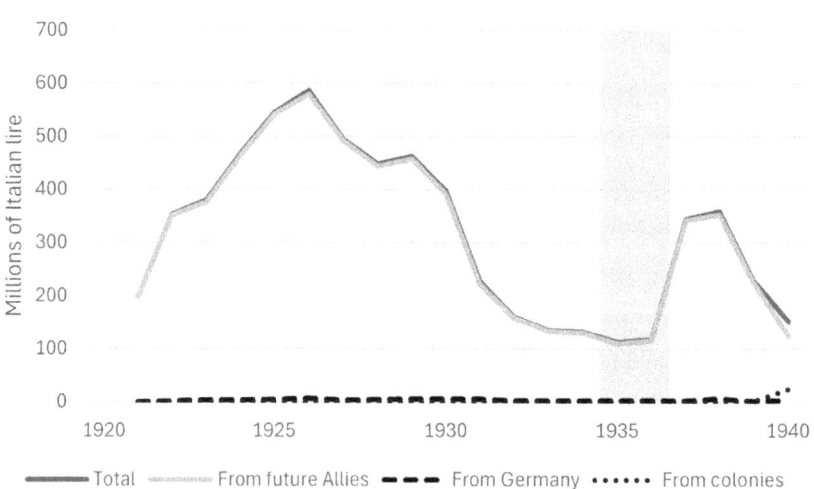

Figure 4.3 Italy's imports of oil by source, 1921–1940 (millions of Italian lire)
Source: Federico et al. (2011).

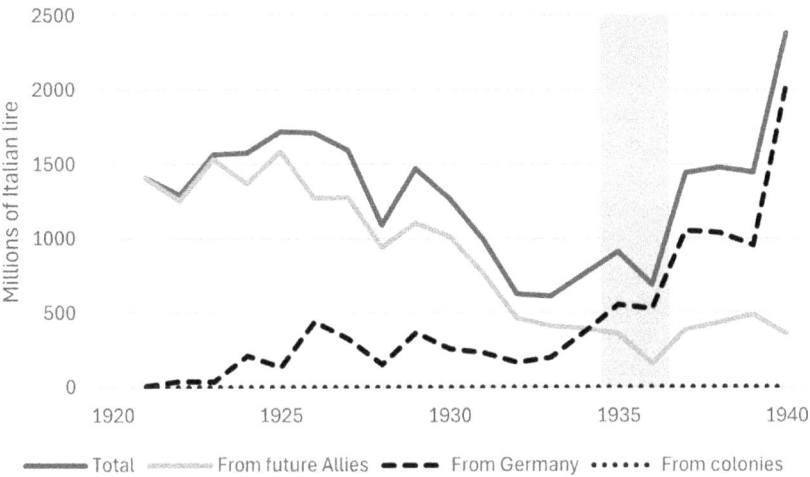

Figure 4.4 Italy's imports of coal by source, 1921–1940 (millions of Italian lire)
Source: Federico et al. (2011).

the sanctions imposed by the League of Nations had many shortfalls. Beside their short duration and failure to involve major Italian trading partners, most notably the United States and Germany, they also failed to target key commodities for the Italian economy, as we have already discussed. Based on Ristuccia's (2000) analysis, a full embargo on oil imports would have had a severe impact on Italian manufacturing capacity, and thus on the war effort. Yet even in this counterfactual scenario, the sanctions would likely have failed to target other key strategic goods vital for the military, such as pig iron and steel. Ultimately, only imports of weapons were actually embargoed.

Attempting to quantify the overall impact of sanctions on Italy at the macro level with some precision is a difficult task. First, given the shortfalls described, these are likely to have had a small effect on imports, exports, and other macroeconomic indicators, which could be difficult to quantify. Second, the sanctions came into play in a context of massive public spending to support the various initiatives of the fascist regime, not just the Ethiopian war, but also a general increase in spending for colonial development (Bertazzini 2022, 2023). So high was the spending that it acted as an 'expansionary' fiscal policy allowed the Italian economy to finally escape the stagnant growth of the Great Depression (Toniolo 1980). This fact is confirmed by GDP reconstructions, such as Baffigi (2011),[8] that show an overall recovery in coincidence with rearmament and the Ethiopian campaign. Third, the sanctions and the campaign occurred at the tipping point in a long-standing project of the regime to increase economic self-sufficiency. All these factors present a challenge when attempting to study the impact of the sanctions on macro-indicators and trade flows.

With these caveats in mind, we take a descriptive analytical approach using disaggregated trade data to shed some light on the economic impact of the sanctions. We use a large dataset assembled by Federico and co-authors (2011). This commodity-level (Standard International Trade Classification level 4) dataset covers all major trade partners of Italy and includes trade with Italian colonial possessions,[9] thus allowing us to observe a good approximation of total trade flows, both values and quantities, while also differentiating between classes of products. In Figure 4.1, we report total value of imports, which we further decompose into three groups, namely Italian colonies, Germany (including Austria), and 'Allies' – a broad category that includes France, United Kingdom and United States, Russia, Belgium, Netherlands, and Argentina. These represent the major trade partners of Italy during the period covered in the dataset.

Observationally, the first feature to emerge from the picture is the clear downward trend in total imports between 1929 and 1934, in line with the discussed isolationist Italian policies and the collapse of international trade. Interestingly, in the two years impacted by the sanctions – 1935 (two months) and 1936 (six months) – total imports declined, with the larger drop in 1936. This further decline is largely due to a reduction in imports from the Allies, which was only partly compensated by an uptick in imports from Germany. While both the upward (Germany) and the downward (Allies) trends pre-dated the sanctions, it is interesting to note how the total value of imports from Germany and the Allies fully converged in 1936 for the first time. Given the context, it is thus reasonable to hypothesise that sanctions played a role in triggering a further substitution in trade imports at this juncture, which then persisted all the way to 1940 (and beyond). An indirect validation of the notion of economic sanctions having a perhaps small but significant impact in the short term also emerges from the 1937 data point, which shows Allies' imports bouncing back to pre-1934 levels before dropping lower again from 1938. From these patterns, the notion that sanctions

---

[8] See Bertazzini (2020) for a visualisation of GDP patterns in relation to colonial expenditures from Federico (1998).
[9] These include Italian Aegean Islands, Eritrea, Ethiopia, Libya, Somalia, and Albania.

failed due to coalition-building problems and substitution of trade partners is confirmed.

Germany's increased importance as a trade partner – as shown in the data – certainly played a role in fostering a tighter political alliance between Hitler and Mussolini. This could then be considered as a first unintended consequence of the sanctions on international politics. In fact, while it is unclear whether, in a counterfactual world with no sanctions, Italy would have not allied itself with Germany anyway, the impact of sanctions on trade patterns certainly facilitated a political alignment between Italy and Germany, which did not happen until 1936 (Baer 1973; Knox 2000: 141–142).

While a small effect of sanctions on imports seems plausible, it is unclear what particular goods were driving it. To shed some light on the mechanics behind the described aggregate drop, we first look at those items that were fully embargoed by the League of Nations, namely weapons. In Figure 4.2, we report import values of weapons by source between 1920 and 1940. The range of items covered is broad, in order to capture all possible types of war materials. Among others, the chart reports values of rifles and pistols, but also gunpowder of different varieties, ammunition, and sabres of various kinds. As one would expect, the value of imported weapons from Allied countries, which stood above 5 million Italian lire in 1934, dropped to zero by 1936. Total imports, however, remained high and even rose by 1936, thanks to increased imports from Germany. This fact underlines the limited efficacy of sanctions even for items that were sanctioned due to coalition-building issues and important trade partners operating outside the League's perimeter. Even Italy's military exports, as seen in Table 4.1, did not drop to zero in 1935. However, whereas for many nations arms exports had been almost halved due to the Great Depression, Italy's

Table 4.1 *World military exports: the shares of five great powers, 1925 and 1935 (%)*

Country	1925	1935
France	15.2	15.3
Germany	11.0	5.7
Italy	4.3	1.6
UK	35.5	20.9
USA	22.2	13.1
Others	11.7	43.3

Source: Eloranta (2002).

exports had a dip of almost two-thirds. In fact, many of the smaller nations took over market share in small and medium-sized armaments in the 1930s, even selling these weapons to their eventual conquerors in World War II (Eloranta 2002).

An interesting picture then emerges from Figures 4.3 and 4.4, which show values of imports by source for oil and coal respectively. These energy commodities were discussed as potential targets for a full embargo by the League, but this proposal was eventually scraped. With respect to oil imports, Figure 4.3 shows how Italy was fully dependent on imports from the Allies. Although quantities were relatively small, Italy would have not been able to easily substitute forgone oil imports had sanctions been imposed (and had the US joined the blockade). Thus, we can speculate, in line with the cited literature (see Ristuccia 2000), that sanctions on oil might indeed have had a stronger impact on the Italian economy, and consequently the war effort in Ethiopia.

The picture that emerges from the coal imports data in Figure 4.4 is starkly different. In fact, the value of imported coal did drop significantly between 1935 and 1936, falling from a total of roughly 920 million to less than 700 million Italian lire, with Germany unable to compensate for the decline in the short term, and helps to explain the aggregate drop in imports. This finding is in line with Ristuccia (2000), who emphasises how the Italian economy reacted to the prospect of sanctions in key energy commodities by boosting internal production, and emphasises another unexpected consequence of the indecisive approach of the League: namely that it not only failed to bring the Ethiopian war to an end, but even accelerated the process of reduction of Italian energy dependence on the Allies in the short term, while increasing the economic influence of Germany in the medium term. In fact, while until 1933 Italy had progressively reduced imports without increasingly relying on Germany, after the implementation of the sanctions it fully embraced energy dependence on Germany, as visible from 1937. This shift in trade patterns went hand-in-hand with the process of political and military alignment of Italy with Germany and Japan that culminated in the Pact of Steel of 1939. The contemporary views recognised the role that economic sanctions played in reordering international relations:

Up until about three years ago [1935], Great Britain, France, and Italy were cooperating very comfortably in European international politics. ... The only real result [of failed sanctions] was to break very definitely the previous concert of action and to drive Italy willy-nilly into the arms of Germany, whose sympathetic support of Italy during her hour of trial was crowned by the formation of that understanding between the two countries which has come to be known as the Berlin–Rome axis. Germany and Japan had already formulated certain plans for

Can Economic Sanctions Work in a Smaller Conflict? 127

joint action against Russia whenever the time for it might appear ripe. A three-power pact between the world's great aggressor nations thus sprang into being. (European Realignment 1938: 189)

Thus, the trade data certainly suggest a role of the Ethiopian war and sanctions in fostering increasing cooperation between Italy and Germany for the trade of key commodities and international politics.

Finally, another article of the League of Nation's Resolution against Italy prohibited all imports (except gold) from Italy and its colonial possessions to member states. To examine whether this particular part of the Resolution had any impact on Italian trade patterns, in Figure 4.5 we report export values by destination between 1920 and 1940. Also, in this respect, we observe a mild reduction of exports to member states, which roughly declined from 2,000 million Italian lire to less than 1,500, a 25 per cent decrease. Total Italian exports, however, increased as a whole, with total value climbing from less than 4,000 million Italian lire to roughly 5,500 million, due to a boom in exports to the colonies and a moderate increase to Germany. While this result should be treated with caution, as most of the exports to the colonies were driven by direct transfers from Rome (Labanca 2002) and therefore were 'artificial', we can conclude that the League's sanctions failed to have a significant

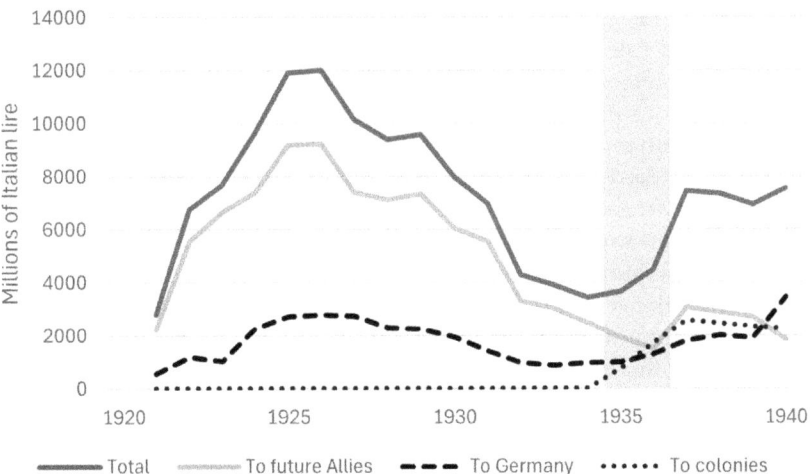

Figure 4.5 Italy's export values by destination, 1921–1940 (millions of Italian lire)Allies, and Germany.
This chart shows export values in total and disaggregated by regions of destination – Italy's colonies, the future Allies, and Germany.
Source: Federico et al. (2011).

impact on total Italian exports as well. Interestingly, with respect to exports, we do not observe a persistent switch in terms of trade partners, with the Allies bouncing back to again absorb the largest share of Italian exports by 1937, although now with a much smaller gap relative to Germany.

Overall, the analysis of the trade data suggests that sanctions failed to impact Italian trade significantly. They did, however, have one stark unintended consequence, namely accelerating the process of import (and to a lesser extent export) substitution from 'Allied' countries in favour of Germany. The analysis thus confirms how poorly implemented sanctions might have played a significant role in further destabilising the world order by facilitating the political alignment between Italy and Germany.

Impact on Military Capacity

In this section, we complement the wider assessment of the economic impact of the sanctions by looking at Italy's military capacity in the late 1930s through various indicators. We begin with an overview of Italy's military spending patterns. The military burdens (measured by military spending as a percentage of GDP) of authoritarian states such as Italy grew faster compared to those of, for example, France and the United Kingdom from 1933 onwards. The overall levels of countries under authoritarian rule were generally higher than those of most democratic states in the inter-war period. However, Mussolini's Italy seems to have been unable to match the militaristic drive of Japan (under a military regime), Germany, and perhaps even the Soviet Union, in the late 1930s. Hitler's Germany, for instance, increased its military burden from 1.6 per cent in 1933 to 18.9 per cent in 1938, while Italy was less successful in this respect, with a military burden of only 4–5 per cent in the 1930s. As seen in Figure 4.6, the Japanese rearmament drive was the most extensive, relative to its economic base, with a military burden as high as 22.7 per cent in 1938 (Eloranta 2017).

How did the defence shares (measured by military spending as a percentage of central government spending defence share) compare? The rearmament drive of the democratic nations was, first and foremost, quite modest, which could also be deduced from the development of their mean military burden. If we compare the French, German, Italian, and British defence shares (Figure 4.7), it seems clear that the German case was quite exceptional from the moment of Hitler's ascendancy to power. For example, the Italian and French defence shares were very similar. Thus, it would be difficult to characterise the Italian case as part

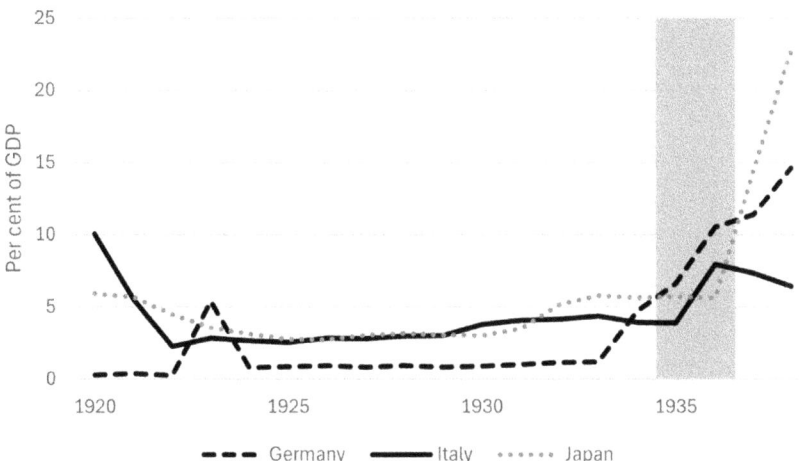

Figure 4.6 Military expenditures of the Axis powers, 1920–1938 (% of GDP)
Source: Eloranta (2011).

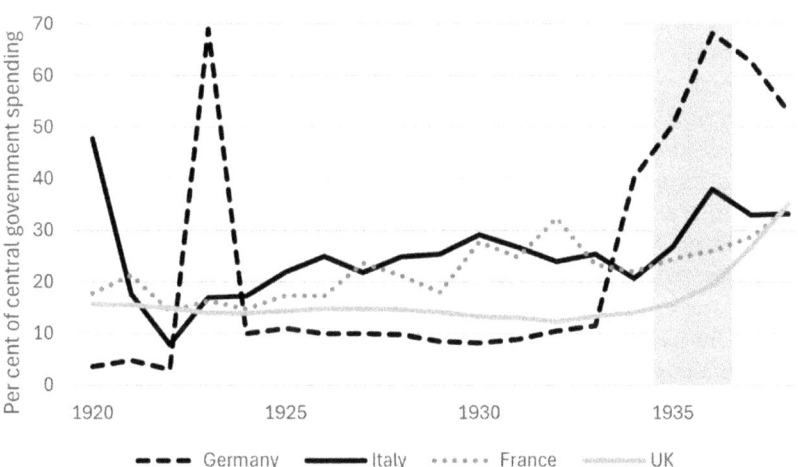

Figure 4.7 The share of defence in central government spending, 1920–1938 (%)
Source: Eloranta (2017).

of the totalitarian camp on the basis of its military spending alone. The 1935/36 war seems to have increased the Italian fiscal appetite for military spending, representing a strengthening of the rearmament trend. However, it did not make Italy move towards an actual war economy at

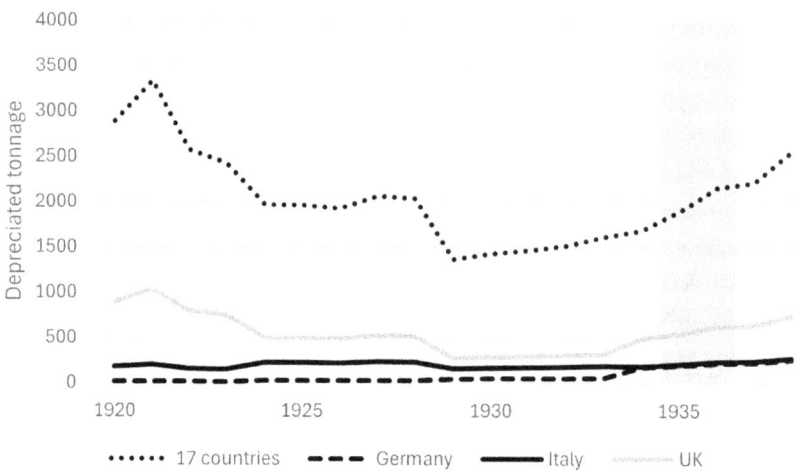

Figure 4.8 Depreciated tonnage of seventeen navies, 1923, 1928, 1933, and 1938
Source: Eloranta (2009).

this juncture, when perhaps Germany and Japan had already made the transition.

What about actual military capacity? Can we see any impact from the short period of sanctions on Italy? There are different ways to evaluate this, of course, with data limiting the analysis. We will first examine the navy (in terms of total tonnage), then overall military capacity. Here we have constructed figures on the total tonnages, allowing for their depreciation by age, of the navies of seventeen states (see Eloranta 2009 on the countries chosen), using the guidelines of the League of Nations on the depreciation periods of different kinds of ships. As this procedure is extremely labour-intensive, the depreciated tonnages were constructed only for the years 1923, 1928, 1933, and 1938 (Figure 4.8). The totals were then interpolated using the indices explained in Eloranta (2009). These figures should provide a better estimation of the 'true' naval stock of these nations, especially in terms of naval competition, because: (1) battleships represent perhaps merely the offensive capabilities of states, or the ability to maintain 'leadership'; and (2) outdated materials were indeed deemed to be useless in battle, as shown by the British estimates that during World War I an older standard German battleship would last no more than five minutes against a modern British Dreadnought.

Based on these comparisons, Italy's depreciated naval tonnage remained almost completely static throughout the period. It is also notable that while most countries increased their effective naval stock in the late 1930s, Italy did not. The economic sanctions may have hindered the rearmament drive in this regard, or at least delayed it. In comparison, while British rearmament programmes, often in connection with Depression-related employment efforts, produced a significant increase in the 1930s (with the US effort somewhat less), French naval stock declined, due to both lack of funding and the ageing of the ships. The German fleet, practically non-existent before the 1930s, was built up quite fast – at least enough to pose a significant threat to the French. Yet the naval lead of the United Kingdom and the United States remained clear (Eloranta 2009).

There are diverse ways of assessing military capacity. One commonly used measure in the political science literature is the CINC (Composite Index of National Capabilities), an annual measure of each country's share of the total of resources in the international system, provided by the Correlates of War Project.[10] Each country's CINC is calculated as an arithmetic average of six series: the country's share of military personnel, the military expenditure share, the energy consumption share, the iron and steel production share, the total population share, and the urban population share (Singer 1988; for more recent discussion on the measure, see e.g. Kadera and Sorokin 2004; Rauch 2017; Souva 2023). Following Eloranta (2017), here we have replaced the energy consumption share, which may be a poor proxy for economic stature in a system, with the real GDP share. Thus, the *military resource share* (MILCINC) of a country is calculated as an average of only the military components in the CINC (the military personnel share and the real military expenditure share) (see Eloranta 2017). Both measures are displayed for comparison in Figures 4.9 and 4.10.

The takeaway from these measures of national power, or capacity, is that Italy's relative material capacity was declining in the late 1930s, and substantially so. It was already below its competitors France and the UK during the entire period, and Italy's overall national capacity declined in a similar fashion to those two nations. Italy was closer to them in terms of military capacity alone (Figure 4.10), but that also declined in the late 1930s. The year 1936 was the only exception, but most likely that was due to war spending rather than any substantial increase in military capacity. Overall, we can assert that Italy's military spending, naval tonnage, and military capacity all indicate that it was not able to keep up with its competitors. Given the decline in total material capacity, sanctions targeting its coal and oil imports would have had a moderate

---

[10] https://correlatesofwar.org/.

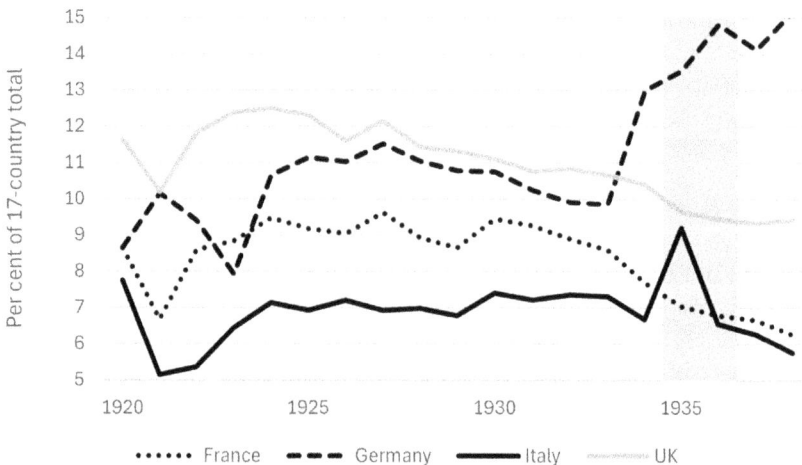

Figure 4.9 Modified national capability scores of four powers, 1920–1938 (% of total for seventeen powers)
Source: Eloranta (2017).

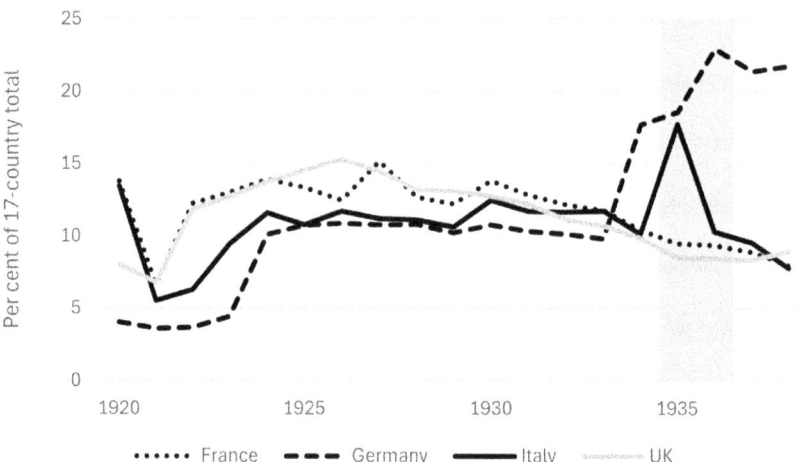

Figure 4.10 Military components of national capability scores of four powers, 1920–1938 (% of total for seventeen powers)
Source: Eloranta (2017).

impact. Additionally, unlike Japan in 1940, Italy was not yet on a war footing, meaning such sanctions would have had an even more significant impact. A war economy can, through greater government control and external military efforts, extract resources more effectively, albeit only for a short period. However, not everything can be measured in terms of macroeconomic indicators – for example, the patriotic boost a dictator might get from a successful, albeit brutal, conflict. We examine this political aspect next.

Sanctions and Support for the Fascist Regime

Among the many political consequences that sanctions had, at both the national and international level, one of the most intriguing hypotheses the literature has suggested is that they increased support for Mussolini's fascist regime. In his seminal work, De Felice (1974) highlighted the way the fascist regime exploited the sanctions imposed by the League of Nations, which in the words of Mussolini was an 'iniquitous war against the civil population of Italy', to stir up additional support for the regime (Dunham 1936: 367). To achieve this goal, the fascist party mobilised heavily in order to create a sense of 'encirclement', thus fostering 'rally-to-flag' feelings and nationalistic behaviours (see also Gurlev and Treisman 2020).

The most famous initiatives, beyond the mass rallies featuring famous speeches by Mussolini in Rome and elsewhere, was probably the so-called *oro per la patria* (gold for the nation), which proved to be a significant propagandist success. Within this particular initiative, all Italians – and women in particular – were pushed to donate their gold possessions (often jewellery and even wedding rings) to support the war effort. According to official propaganda, this measure was made directly necessary by the economic sanctions imposed by the League of Nations and, in particular, by the drop in trade with France and Britain, which was supposed to have created a shortage of bullion. While the actual role of the sanctions in creating a shortage of precious metals is debatable, the Italian government was spending more than it could afford for its Ethiopian adventure, which probably justified the effort in the eyes of policy makers. The gold collected was a non-negligible quantity, but it was dwarfed by colonial expenditures, which boomed to more than 30 per cent of total expenditures by 1936 (Federico 1998). The initiative benefited from illustrious sponsors, including the Queen of Italy, who donated her own wedding ring in a dramatic ceremony in Rome. Tangentially, the main target of fascist propaganda during the sanctions were Britain and France, accused of hypocrisy in applying economic sanctions against Italy to prevent it obtaining a colonial empire (theatrically referred to as '*un posto al sole*' – 'a place in the sun'), while ruling over large colonial possessions.

While the party staged public ceremonies and rallies that were broadcast in films and on radio (on the impact of radio for populists, see e.g.

Widener and Eloranta 2020), local party branches also constantly worked according to the central party's directives to stir up support for the war and the regime using economic sanctions as a propaganda tool. In an interesting case study on Venice, Ferris (2006) shows how the entire apparatus of the party was committed to this task, using local newspapers, authorities, and organisations to convey the powerful message of the international community trying to impoverish Italy through the sanctions.

While the propaganda activities of the party are well documented, the effective results of this strategy are only known through anecdotal evidence. This is largely due to the fact that democracy had been completely abolished by the fascist regime by 1935 and all information on newspapers and radio relating to public support were carefully created, or at least censored, by the party's apparatus. We take a first step towards a more systematic measurement of support for the regime in relation to economic sanctions by looking at first names, a new methodology increasingly employed in the literature (Jurajda and Kovač 2021; Carillo 2022; on the use of surnames, see e.g. Clark 2021).

To do so, we rely on the database Ancestry.com,[11] a massive effort to reconstruct family trees through combining existing datasets and allowing for user-based contributions. The dataset provides a wealth of information on each individual entry, including date of birth, death, name of spouse, parents and children, as well as place of birth. For our purpose we only focus on individuals born in Italy between 1920 and 1940. There are obvious selection concerns about these data. First and foremost, there is selection on user-based contributions. Many entries are for migrants, who were born in Italy and then migrated elsewhere, with interesting family stories that plausibly pushed heirs to research their history. This translates into a somewhat normal distribution of entries with respect to time, with a central tendency in the second half of the nineteenth century and fewer entries towards the tails. In our period of analysis, the number of entries ranges between roughly 13,000 and 60,000 (with the earlier years being better covered) entries of people born in Italy per year, compared to earlier years featuring hundreds of thousands. This is probably a feature of both declining migration rates from Italy and people born in later years still living or recently passed. With this caveat in mind, and based on the assumption that selection of entries did not change significantly over time, we can use time series of names to trace changes in people's beliefs as captured by the first names

---

[11] Last accessed 12 December 2023.

they decided to give to children born in Italy between 1920 and 1940. Our assumption is made more plausible by the short timespan we cover.

The analysis we perform on the data is very simple. We count the number of male children born in every calendar year between 1920 and 1940 and who were given the name of either 'Benito', Mussolini's first name, or 'Vittorio', the King of Italy's first name at the time. We then compute the share of these two names over the total number of entries for each year. The choice of the names is very simple. Naming your child 'Benito' between 1922 and 1940 was a somewhat strong sign of support for the regime. This is the central focus of our analysis. We like to compare the frequency of this particular name with 'Vittorio' over time to try and differentiate between general patriotic behaviour (the king's name) and specific support for the regime.

The results of this exercise are reported in Figure 4.11. Patriotic behaviour as measured by the frequency of 'Vittorio' is stable until 1934, with the share of names around 0.5 per cent of the total. In this period, support for the regime as measured by the frequency of the name 'Benito' grows slowly but significantly, moving from zero before Mussolini's coup in 1922 to 0.25 per cent in 1934. Both shares climb dramatically from 1934 in coincidence with preparations and then the start of the Ethiopian offensive in 1935. While both were gaining, suggesting a general increase in patriotic sentiment during the period, the 'Benito' share grew faster, reaching 0.75 per cent of the sample's names

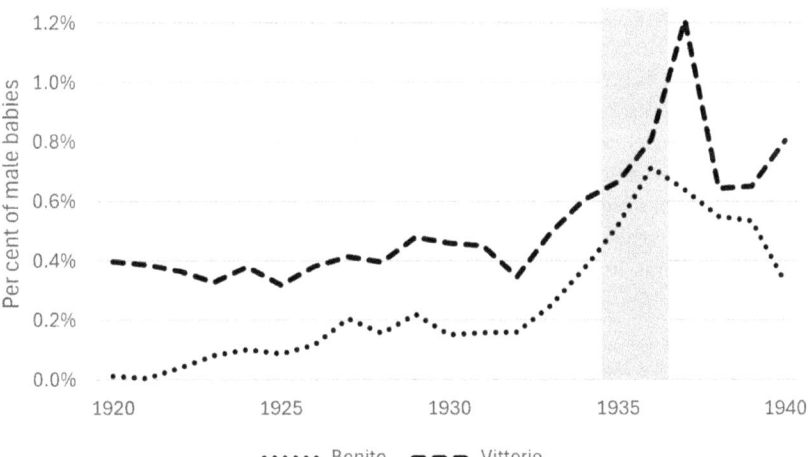

Figure 4.11 Given names of newborn sons in Italy, 1920–1940 (shares of male babies, %)
Source: Data from Ancestry.com. See the text for further details.

in 1936 and almost catching up with 'Vittorio'. This striking pattern is consistent with various historical evidence on the regime's popularity peaking with the invasion of Ethiopia (see De Felice 1974).

What is particularly interesting with respect to economic sanctions is the timing of the increase. The peak of support for the regime seems to have coincided with the sanctions, with the greater increase taking place between 1934 and 1936. The 'Benito' share drops in 1937 and starts a downward trend thereafter. 'Vittorio', by contrast, peaks in 1937 after the full occupation of Ethiopia. In this sense, while the evidence should only be taken as suggestive given the sample size and the level of aggregation of the analysis, we can conclude that the regime was able to use sanctions effectively to boost its support to a level that it was unable to achieve before or after despite the many populist initiatives that were implemented throughout the period. This should thus be taken as plausible evidence of yet another unintended consequence of the sanctions in the Italian case. Far from giving the final blow to the Italian economy and the war effort, they instead provided a powerful propagandist argument that allowed the regime to reach an unprecedented peak of popularity.

Conclusion

In this chapter, we first explored the literature and discussion of the League of Nations and economic sanctions, particularly why sanctions have failed or at least performed poorly. The case of the Italo-Ethiopian war is intriguing, since it seriously undermined the status of the League as broker in international conflicts, which was more or less its *raison d'être*. The conflict was particularly brutal, featuring the use of many illegal weapons and tactics, and it created an international uproar. However, the bureaucratic solutions offered by the League, based on its consensus governance practices, were slow and limited. Bigger nations, like the UK and France, were reluctant to impose heavier sanctions. This inability to impact Italy's behaviour reflected some past disappointments for many nations, in the sphere of disarmament in particular.

If the sanctions were limited in scope and duration, mostly targeting military goods, what were the actual impacts on Italy? There are a multitude of ways one can assess the impacts, and we have explored only some of them. First, the foreign trade data disaggregated by commodity type confirm our initial impression that the sanctions, by and large, failed to achieve the goal of disrupting Italian trade significantly, and therefore to undermine the Italian capacity to continue the war effort. The only significant effect was on imports of weapons from member countries, which did drop to zero between 1935 and 1936. Italy, however, managed to comfortably substitute such goods with imports from Germany, which shows the shortcomings of limited international coordination when it comes to economic sanctions. Therefore, Italy's primary response to League sanctions was to move closer to Germany economically (an adaptation) and militarily (a counter-measure).

The failure to use economic sanctions to force peace was freshly interpreted as 'evident proof of the fact that those in positions of responsibility either did not know how to handle the economic weapon, or did not dare to use it properly, or both' (Bonn 1937: 361). While failing to achieve sizeable economic effects (at least in the aggregate and based on trade patterns), sanctions had several unwanted consequences, which clearly show up in the trade data. First, they pushed Italy into a much closer commercial relationship with Germany, which became the main commercial partner in relative and (for imports) absolute terms between 1936 and 1940. This unwanted consequence might have certainly played a role in contributing to the progressive political alignment between the two countries after 1936. This was also the reason why the UK and France did not want to impose sanctions on coal and oil imports, yet the outcome was the same. Second, sanctions also pushed Italy to speed up the transition to autarky for key commodities – as visible from the decline in imports of commodities that were not directly targeted by the sanctions, chiefly coal – likely due to uncertainty regarding future actions of the League and therefore a need to speed up independence on strategic commodities.

Sanctions seem to have hindered Italy's development of military capacity in a limited sense, respective of its European rivals, thus thwarting Mussolini's dreams of empire. While Germany and Japan had already moved towards war economies in the late 1930s, Italy's relative military capabilities declined in the same way as the British and French did. Also, Italy's naval ambitions were at least hindered by the war and the sanctions. Overall, Italy's national material capabilities also declined, perhaps suggesting that the imposition of coal and oil sanctions could have had a significant impact if adopted. However, the war did provide the authoritarian regime a domestic popularity boost, along with cleverly designed propaganda efforts, which could be seen in the popularity of the leaders' names among Italian families. The rise in the popularity of the name Benito seems to have coincided with the period of sanctions, which is in line with findings from other similar conflicts. External international pressure was manipulated in the media by the fascists to increase their own domestic appeal.

In general, the failure of economic sanctions against Italy certainly played a role in shaping later economic, political, and military developments that ultimately led to the breakdown of the international order and World War II. It also hastened the decline and image of the League of Nations, and most likely emboldened authoritarian leaders in their plans for conquest. These dictators probably also learned that economic sanctions are not necessarily very effective if the international community is divided and that such pressure can be used domestically to prop up the regime among the population.

References

Albers, T. 2021. 'The Trade Channel of the Great Depression', *Working Paper*.

Alexseev, M. A., and H. E. Hale. 2020. 'Crimea Come What May: Do Economic Sanctions Backfire Politically?', *Journal of Peace Research* 57(2): 344–359.

Baer, G. W. 1973. 'Sanctions and Security: The League of Nations and the Italian–Ethiopian War, 1935–1936', *International Organization* 27(2): 165–179.

Baffigi, A. 2011. 'Italian National Accounts 1861–2011', *Quaderni di storia economica*, No. 18. Banca d'Italia, Roma.

Bělín, M., and J. Hanousek. 2021. 'Which Sanctions Matter? Analysis of the EU/Russian Sanctions of 2014', *Journal of Comparative Economics* 49(1): 244–257.

Bertazzini, M. C. 2020. 'Towards an Economic History of Italian Colonialism', *Rivista di storia economica* 36(3): 299–343.

—— 2022. 'The Long-Term Impact of Italian Colonial Roads in the Horn of Africa, 1935–2015', *Journal of Economic Geography* 22(1): 181–214.

—— 2023. 'The Effect of Settler Farming on Indigenous Agriculture: Evidence from Italian Libya', *Economic History Review* 76(1): 31–59.

Bonn, M. J. 1937. 'How Sanctions Failed', *Foreign Affairs* 15(2): 350–361.

Carillo, M. 2021. 'Agricultural Policy and Long-Run Development: Evidence from Mussolini's Battle for Grain', *Economic Journal (London)* 131(634): 566–597.

—— 2022. 'Fascistville: Mussolini's New Towns and the Persistence of Neo-fascism', *Journal of Economic Growth* 27(4): 527–567.

Clark, G. 2021. 'Social Mobility in Historical Economics', in Alberto Bisin and Giovanni Federico (eds.), *The Handbook of Historical Economics*, pp. 719–748. Cambridge, MA: Academic Press.

Davis, L. E., and S. L. Engerman. 2006. *Naval Blockades in Peace and War: An Economic History since 1750*. Cambridge: Cambridge University Press.

De Felice, R. 1974. *Mussolini. Mussolini il duce: 1. Gli anni del consenso: 1929–1936*. Turin: Einaudi.

Donaldson, M. 2020. 'The League of Nations, Ethiopia, and the Making of States', *Humanity: An International Journal of Human Rights, Humanitarianism, and Development* 11(1): 6–31.

Dunham, L. 1936. 'Effects of Sanctions', *Social Science* 11(4): 365–373.

Eloranta, J. 2002. '"Weak" European States in the International Arms Trade, 1920–1937: The Impact of External Threats, Market Forces, and Domestic Constraints', *Scandinavian Economic History Review* 50(1): 44–67.

——— 2009. 'Rent Seeking and Collusion in the Military Allocation Decisions of Finland, Sweden, and Great Britain, 1920–38', *Economic History Review* 62(1): 23–44.

——— 2011. 'Why Did the League of Nations Fail?', *Cliometrica* 5(1): 27–52.

——— 2017. 'Pro Bono Publico?: Demand for Military Spending Between the World Wars', *Essays in Economic and Business History* 35(2): 99–142.

Endaylalu, G. A. 2018. 'Mustard Gas Massacres and Atrocities Committed by Italy in 1939 against the Inhabitants of Menz, Merhabete, and Jamma in Amesegna Washa/Zeret Cave', *Cultural and Religious Studies* 6(9): 501–530.

European Realignment. 1938. *The Military Engineer*, 30(171): 189–190.

Federico, G. 1998. 'Italy's Late and Unprofitable Forays into Empire', *Revista de Historia Economica – Journal of Iberian and Latin American Economic History* 16(1): 377–402.

Federico, G., S. Natoli, G. Tattara, and M. Vasta. 2011. *Il commercio estero italiano: 1862–1950*. Rome: Laterza.

Felbermayr, G., A. Kirilakha, C. Syropoulos, E. Yalcin, and Y. V. Yotov. 2020. 'The Global Sanctions Data Base', *European Economic Review* 129: 103561.

Ferris, K. 2006. '"Fare di ogni famiglia italiana un fortilizio": The League of Nations' Economic Sanctions and Everyday Life in Venice', *Journal of Modern Italian Studies* 11(2): 117–142.

Gardner, L., and J. Eloranta. 2021. 'War and Empire', in Stephen Broadberry and Kyoji Fukao (eds.), *The Cambridge Economic History of the Modern World. Volume 2: 1870 to the Present*, pp. 526–550. Cambridge: Cambridge University Press.

Gordon, J. 2019. 'The Hidden Power of the New Economic Sanctions', *Current History* 118(804): 3–10.

Gram-Skjoldager, K. 2020. 'Lilliputians for Peace: Scandinavian Internationalism and International Disarmament c. 1880–1940', in Boris Barth and Rolf Hobson (eds.), *Civilizing Missions in the Twentieth Century*, pp. 109–123. Leiden: Brill.

Grip, L., and J. Hart. 2009. *The Use of Chemical Weapons in the 1935–36 Italo-Ethiopian War*. Stockholm: SIPRI Arms Control and Non-proliferation Programmme.

Guriev, S., and D. Treisman. 2020. 'The Popularity of Authoritarian Leaders: A Cross-National Investigation', *World Politics* 72(4): 601–638.

Higgs, R. 2011. 'Are Questions of War and Peace merely One Issue among Many for Libertarians?', *The Independent Review* 16(2): 307–312.

Housden, M. 2014. *The League of Nations and the Organization of Peace*. Abingdon: Routledge.

Hovi, J., R. Huseby, and D. F. Sprinz. 2005. 'When Do (Imposed) Economic Sanctions Work?', *World Politics* 57(4): 479–499.

Hufbauer, G. C., J. J. Schott, and K. A. Elliott. 1990. *Economic Sanctions Reconsidered: History and Current Policy*, vol. 1. Washington, DC: Peterson Institute for International Economics.

Ikonomou, H. A. 2021. 'The Administrative Anatomy of Failure: The League of Nations Disarmament Section, 1919–1925', *Contemporary European History* 30(3): 321–334.

Jones, L. 2015. *Societies under Siege: Exploring How International Economic Sanctions (Do Not) Work*. New York: Oxford University Press.

Jurajda, Š., and D. Kovač. 2021. 'Names and Behavior in a War', *Journal of Population Economics* 34(1): 1–33.

Kadera, K., and G. Sorokin. 2004. 'Measuring National Power', *International Interactions* 30(3): 211–230.

Knox, M. 2000. *Common Destiny: Dictatorship, Foreign Policy, and War in Fascist Italy and Nazi Germany*. Cambridge: Cambridge University Press.

Labanca, N. 2002. *Oltremare: Storia dell'espansione coloniale italiana*. Bologna: Il Mulino.

Mehrl, M., and P. Thurner. 2023. 'The Interwar Period International Trade in Arms (IPITA): A New Dataset', *Journal of Conflict Resolution* 69(2–3): 518-539.

Mulder, N. 2022. *The Economic Weapon: The Rise of Sanctions as a Tool of Modern War*. New Haven, CT: Yale University Press.

Özdamar, Ö., and E. Shahin. 2021. 'Consequences of Economic Sanctions: The State of the Art and Paths Forward', *International Studies Review* 23(4): 1646–1671.

Pala, T. 2021. 'The Effectiveness of Economic Sanctions: A Literature Review', *NISPAcee Journal of Public Administration and Policy* 14(1): 239–259.

Pape, R. A. 1997. 'Why Economic Sanctions Do Not Work', *International Security* 22(2): 90–136.

Peksen, D. 2019. 'When Do Imposed Economic Sanctions Work? A Critical Review of the Sanctions Effectiveness Literature', *Defence and Peace Economics* 30(6): 635–647.

Rauch, C. 2017. 'Challenging the Power Consensus: GDP, CINC, and Power Transition Theory', *Security Studies* 26(4): 642–664.

Renwick, R. 1981. *Economic Sanctions*. Cambridge, MA: Center for International Affairs, Harvard University.

Ristuccia, C. A. 2000. 'The 1935 Sanctions against Italy: Would Coal and Oil Have Made a Difference?', *European Review of Economic History* 4(1): 85–110.

Sbacchi, A. 2005. 'Poison Gas and Atrocities in the Italo-Ethiopian War (1935–1936)', in Ruth Ben-Ghiat and Mia Fuller (eds.), *Italian Colonialism*, pp. 47–56. New York: Palgrave Macmillan.

Singer, J. D. 1988. 'Reconstructing the Correlates of War Dataset on Material Capabilities of States, 1816–1985', *International Interactions* 14(2): 115–132.

Souva, M. 2023. 'Material Military Power: A Country-Year Measure of Military Power, 1865–2019', *Journal of Peace Research* 60(6): 1002–1009.

Stone, D. R. 2000. 'Imperialism and Sovereignty: The League of Nations' Drive to Control the Global Arms Trade', *Journal of Contemporary History* 35(2): 213–230.

Strang, G. B. 2008. '"The Worst of All Worlds": Oil Sanctions and Italy's Invasion of Abyssinia, 1935–1936', *Diplomacy and Statecraft* 19(2): 210–235.

Toniolo, G. 1980. *L'economia dell'Italia fascista*. Roma-Bari: Laterza.
Tosi, L. 2017. 'The League of Nations: An International Relations Perspective', *Uniform Law Review* 22(1): 148–157.
Walters, F. P. 1952. *A History of the League of Nations* (2 vols.). New York: Oxford University Press.
Wemlinger, C. 2015. 'Collective Security and the Italo-Ethiopian Dispute before the League of Nations', *Peace and Change* 40(2): 139–166.
Widener, N., and J. Eloranta. 2020. 'Who Rules the Airwaves? The Influence of Radio in the 1946 and 1948 Argentine National Elections', *Configurações. Revista Ciências Sociais* 26: 125–150.
Zimmern, A. 1935. 'The League's Handling of the Italo-Abyssinian Dispute', *International Affairs (Royal Institute of International Affairs 1931–1939)* 14(6): 751–768.

5 Economic Warfare against Japan, 1931–1945

Tetsuji Okazaki and Akira Okubo

Introduction

Japan participated in World War II as one of the Axis Powers from December 1941 and continued to fight in the war until August 1945, despite Germany and Italy having surrendered to the Allied Powers several months earlier. World War II had a long prehistory for Japan. The tension between Japan and the United States and United Kingdom dated back to September 1931, when Japan invaded Manchuria, motivated by ideas of economic warfare and autarky that had prevailed among middle-class army officers since the early 1920s, following the experiences of these officers during World War I.

Japan began to construct a sphere of autarky by integrating Manchuria and northern China in the early 1930s, incurring criticism and economic sanctions from the United States and United Kingdom for its endeavours. As we describe in the following sections, self-reinforcing cycles occurred involving Japan's aggressions to achieve an autarky and economic sanctions imposed by the United States and United Kingdom, which finally resulted in war between Japan and these two nations. During the war, the United States imposed a strict blockade on Japan's war economy using its military power. These sanctions caused serious damage to Japan's wartime economy, but Japan made great efforts to adapt. As a result, although there was ultimately a limit to Japan's adaptation and endurance, it was able to continue fighting the war for more than three and a half years.

In this chapter, we describe the self-reinforcing cycles of economic sanctions imposed by the Western countries and the aggressions by Japan, as well as Japan's adaptation to the economic sanctions during World War II.

The authors are grateful to Stephen Broadberry, Mark Harrison, and other participants at the Economic Warfare Conference in Venice in 2024, and Tomoko Masuda, for their valuable comments. All remaining errors are our own.

The International Politics of Economic Sanctions on Japan: The League of Nations and the United States

The question of whether economic pressure should be imposed on Japan was a key issue in international politics during the decade preceding the Pacific War. The changes in international policy towards Japan during this time can be considered by dividing the decade into three periods. First, between 1931 and 1933, member states of the League of Nations and the United States considered their response to the 1931 Japanese invasion of Manchuria. Second, between 1933 and 1937, there was a period of continued international tensions stemming from Japan's encroachment in the north-east of China combined with failed attempts at rapprochement between Japan and the West. Third, between 1937 and 1941, in response to the commencement of the Second Sino-Japanese War, the United States gradually embarked on its first serious efforts to impose sanctions on Japan. This third period ended with the commencement of the Pacific War in December 1941 and the complete severance of economic and diplomatic relations between Japan and the United States.

On 18 September 1931, elements of the Japanese army staged an explosion ostensibly by the Chinese on the Japanese-controlled South Manchuria railway near the city of Mukden. The Japanese army, with government approval following soon after, used the incident as a pretext to invade China's north-eastern provinces, commonly known as Manchuria. On 21 September, the Chinese Nationalist government in Nanjing requested the League of Nations to respond, with the goal of galvanising international support and pressuring Japan to withdraw from Manchuria (Thorne 1972: 131–134; Craft 2000).

However, the Western reaction to the incident was cautious. Most Western leaders lacked the appetite to involve themselves in a Far Eastern conflict in the midst of a severe economic depression. The permanent members of the Council of the League of Nations were united in opposition to the application of sanctions. According to Sir John Simon, the British Foreign Secretary, 'the only thing the Council can do is to avoid threatening Sanctions and to give good advice and to appeal to everybody to behave' (Butler and Bury 1960: 921). The United States, which was not a member of the League but closely associated with the negotiations, was equally reluctant. Despite public criticism of Japan by US Secretary of State Henry Stimson, President Herbert Hoover was decidedly opposed to the idea of sanctions, urging that Western countries 'not to stir the boiling pot' (Jeansonne 2012: 344). After months of discussion, the League merely decided to launch a fact-finding mission headed by Lord Lytton, a British peer. The Japanese government had been concerned that sanctions would be raised as a possibility under Article 16 of the Covenant of the League of Nations and was relieved to learn that the leading Western powers preferred a moderate solution (Higuchi 2021: 29–32).

Disdain for the concept of sanctions was not uncommon among policy makers of the era. In February 1932, Sir Maurice Hankey, the British Cabinet Secretary, stated that '[a]fter the present failure [regarding Manchuria], following Corfu and Vilna, no-one is ever likely to believe in sanctions, and they will become more and more a dead letter. Personally, I would like to see them got rid of' (Thorne 1972: 240). Many British officials held the 'sanctionist approach' of Article 16 in contempt (Steiner 1993: 52). They preferred the League to be a forum of consultation, rather than risking embarrassment or worse consequences through attempts at coercion (Obiya 2021).

Detailed governmental studies on sanctions also advocated caution. In March 1932, the British government produced a secret report on the possibility of applying sanctions to Japan. The report estimated that sanctions would have negligible effects without the cooperation of the United States. Even with US cooperation, Japan could exploit loopholes with relative ease, and effective enforcement would require a state of war. The report raised the issue of a 'double-edged effect', with impacts not just on Japan but also on the economies of the British Commonwealth, and the dangers of driving Japan into a collision course with the sanctioning powers (ATB 1932).

The Lytton Commission, assigned by the League to investigate the Mukden incident, released its report on 2 October 1932. The report was written to avoid a major fallout between Japan and the League, and it adopted a balanced approach in the sense that, while acknowledging Japan's treaty rights in China and sympathising with Japanese concerns regarding China's anti-Japanese boycotts, it denied Japanese claims that their military actions were an act of legitimate self-defence (Nish 2009: 173–179). The 139-page report, which made no mention of even the possibility of imposing sanctions, was well received among Western diplomats. Many of them wished the whole affair to be 'filed and forgotten', to initiate reconciliation with Japan, while avoiding recognition of the Japanese-imposed puppet state of Manchukuo (Thorne 1972: 290). Such conciliatory attitudes generally persisted even after the Japanese army invaded Jehol province in January 1933 and advanced towards the Great Wall.

In contrast, the Japanese government was in no mood for reconciliation. The Lytton Report was poorly received in Japan. Nationalists were frustrated with the Western refusal to recognise the legitimacy of Manchukuo and advocated for Japan to leave the League (Nish 2009: 184). Furthermore, the Japanese government calculated that leaving the League would lessen the risk of being sanctioned under the Covenant because, although sanctions were applicable to non-members, the procedures for conflict resolution were designed primarily for disputes between member states. Moreover, Japanese diplomats had observed that smaller powers were more sympathetic to the plight of China, whereas the major powers were conciliatory toward Japan. Hence, leaving the League and focusing on bilateral talks with the major powers seemed a less embarrassing and potentially more fruitful course for Japan than remaining a member (Higuchi 2021: 52, 58–59). Thus, after the League Assembly adopted a statement based on the Lytton Report on 24 February 1933, which denied the legitimacy of Manchukuo, the Japanese government withdrew from the League.

On 31 May 1933, Japan and China signed a bilateral ceasefire agreement at Tanggu. Japan was able to secure its conquests with minimal international repercussions. The non-recognition of Manchukuo was the limit of Western resistance to Japan during this phase.

A minor exception to this lacklustre response was the short-lived British arms embargo of February–March 1933, which was imposed in response to the fighting in Jehol. The embargo was aimed at both Japan and China, and avoided differentiating between the aggressor and the victim in the same spirit as the subsequent American Neutrality Acts. However, there were advocates within the British political sphere who argued for the embargo to target Japan alone, and the embargo marked a downturn in Anglo-Japanese arms trade relations, which had been close until the 1920s (Thorne 1970). Anglo-Japanese economic relations steadily deteriorated in the mid-1930s. From April to May 1933, Britain abrogated several commercial treaties between its colonies and Japan. The decision to do so was not meant as a sanction but was a protectionist response to intense lobbying from the Lancashire cotton industries as a result of an overflow of Japanese trade goods caused by a weaker yen. The increased barriers limiting access to the markets of the British Empire hampered the recovery of the Japanese textile industry and further cultivated anti-British feelings in Japan (Sharkey 2000).

In the mid-1930s, Neville Chamberlain, the British Chancellor of the Exchequer, led a British attempt to improve relations with Japan to stabilise the Far East and focus British rearmament efforts toward Europe. In 1934, British and Japanese officials exchanged ideas on a possible Anglo-Japanese non-aggression pact. Concurrently, a mission of the Federation of British Industries visited Japan and Manchuria to improve business relations and probed the possibility of investing in Manchuria. Both initiatives fell through, despite Chamberlain's efforts to persuade the Cabinet and Foreign Office, because most British officials were more concerned with the damage that an Anglo-Japanese agreement would cause to Britain's relations with China and the United States, both of which were critical of Britain's rapprochement with Japan (Bennett 1992).

Chamberlain was undeterred by this setback, and in 1935 pursued a new initiative, inviting Japan to join a British-led financial rescue package for China. China faced economic difficulties owing to spiking silver prices and sought to leave the traditional silver standard. The British government sent its chief economic adviser, Sir Frederick Leith-Ross, on a mission to assess the Chinese financial situation and assist in reforms. During the Leith-Ross mission from September 1935 to June 1936, the British attempted to persuade Japan to contribute to an international loan package for China. However, the Japanese saw the British initiative as a ploy to restrict their freedom of action in China and declined to participate. Chinese currency reforms were implemented under British leadership and a new Chinese currency, the fapi, which was pegged to sterling, was introduced in November 1935. The currency reform was well received in China and helped to stabilise the economy. As a result, the Chinese leaders gained the confidence to resist Japan. However, the Japanese government and army were frustrated with China's closer relations with Britain and the circulation of the fapi in north China, where Japan was establishing buffer regimes to secure Manchukuo (Hatano 1978; Best 2013).

On 7 July 1937, Japanese and Chinese troops exchanged fire on the outskirts of Beijing close to the Marco Polo Bridge. The Japanese government decided to send reinforcements and escalate the conflict. The Chinese government also chose escalation to bolster resistance. The conflict spread to Shanghai in August and, by the end of the year, Japan occupied several key cities, including Nanjing, causing mass harm. It was a full-scale Sino-Japanese War in all but name because both governments avoided declaring war to bypass the United States Neutrality Act.

The Neutrality Act, initially passed in 1935 and renewed in January 1937, prohibited arms exports to all belligerents at war. President Franklin Roosevelt, being sympathetic to China, decided not to apply the Neutrality Act to the undeclared Sino-Japanese War to keep war provisions flowing to China. However, despite his famous 'quarantine' speech of 5 October 1937, which stressed the need to cordon off aggressor states, isolationism was at its height in the United States and

Roosevelt was not ready to apply sanctions to Japan. The Japanese sinking of US gunboat *Panay* on the Yangtze River in December drove Roosevelt to consider options to seize Japanese assets, impose an embargo on oil imports, and blockade the Japanese, with British cooperation. Yet he decided against forceful economic measures because of the risk of provoking an armed reaction by Japan. Moreover, the British were not ready to cooperate (Dallek 1995: 146–157). The United States did little to damage the Japanese economy until mid-1938 apart from private anti-Japanese boycott campaigns.

For the British government, the outbreak of the Sino-Japanese War was a further setback to its already stagnant efforts to improve Anglo-Japanese relations. The Foreign Office, led by Anthony Eden, advocated supporting China's war effort. However, Chamberlain, who became Prime Minister in May 1937, held the view that risking a confrontation with Japan was 'suicidal', considering the parallel threats in Europe. When the British government contemplated the possibility of imposing sanctions against Japan in the autumn of 1937, the Foreign Office was supportive, but the Treasury, the service departments, and most Cabinet members were united in their disapproval. A governmental study on the possibility of applying sanctions to Japan reiterated the findings of 1932 that sanctions would have limited effects without the support of the United States. The report observed that Japan's vulnerability lay in its textile exports, along with imports of iron ore, machine parts, and especially oil, which the United States dominated. However, Japan had large oil reserves and the war in China was not particularly heavy on oil consumption. Hence, the study concluded that even with the United States on board, the sanctions would not take effect for one or two years (ATB 1937; Best 1995: 38–44; Strang 2019). The first notable intervention by Britain occurred only in March 1939 when it authorised a loan of £5 million to China (Lee 1973: 164).

Essentially, international coordination to restrain Japan's aggressions failed. In November 1937, signatories of the Nine Power Treaty of 1922 met in Brussels to discuss Japan's violation of this treaty, which was designed to preserve the territorial integrity of China. A coordinated boycott on Japanese goods and a ban on credit to Japan were discussed, but both the United States and Britain opposed strong measures. The conference concluded by merely reaffirming principles (Lee 1973: 70–77). In 1938, the League of Nations discussed the possibility of adopting sanctions under Articles 16 and 17 of the Covenant, pressed by China and supported by the Soviet Union. On 30 September, the League Council adopted a report recognising that member states were entitled to impose economic sanctions against Japan. However, due to

British and French insistence, implementation was left to the discretion of individual member states and consequently no state acted upon it (Walters 1960: 738; Higuchi 2021: 187, 214).

The continuing Japanese invasion of China and aerial bombardments of Chinese cities gradually led Roosevelt to adopt measures to hinder the Japanese war effort. In June 1938, Roosevelt ordered a 'moral embargo' against Japan on aircraft armaments, engine parts, accessories, aerial bombs, and torpedoes. In December, he approved a $25 million loan to China. In December 1939, the 'moral embargo' list was expanded to include molybdenum, aluminium, and equipment required for producing aviation fuel. In January 1940, Roosevelt's decision to abrogate the United States–Japan commerce treaty of 1911 came into effect, clearing the way for further trade restrictions. The fall of the Netherlands and France between May and June 1940 led the Japanese to pressure the cornered Europeans for concessions in South East Asia. In July, to reassure European allies and China in their resistance to Japan, and to send a message to Japan, Roosevelt restricted exports to Japan through licensing of aviation fuel and high-grade scrap metal. In September, the list was expanded to include iron and steel scrap. Undeterred, Japan signed the Tripartite Pact with Germany and Italy on 27 September. In early 1941, the United States' effective embargo expanded to include copper, brass, zinc, bronze, nickel, and potash. Furthermore, in March, the Lend–Lease Act came into force, invigorating US assistance to countries resisting the tripartite powers. China was granted eligibility for Lend–Lease assistance and received $26 million worth of material in 1941 (Newcomb 1941; Young 1963: 207; Dallek 1995: 192–196, 238–241, 273; Miller 2007: 77ff.).

As the Sino-Japanese War expanded, Japanese officials became increasingly concerned about the possibility of private anti-Japanese boycott campaigns escalating into government-led sanctions. A special committee of Japan's Planning Board (*Kikakuin*) was tasked to consider the possibility of Western sanctions, and studied the precedent of League sanctions imposed on Italy. Japanese officials were aware of their vulnerability to Western sanctions but believed that damage could be mitigated by increasing domestic production, and that retaliatory measures targeted at Western possessions in China could alleviate the asymmetry somewhat. According to historian Akio Watanabe, the US adoption in the early period of the Sino-Japanese War of 'intermediate measures', which fell between full-scale sanctions and inaction, complicated Japanese perceptions of US intentions. These actions empowered the 'hawks' in Tokyo, who believed that Western sanctions would be manageable in the short term and that, in the long term, Japan would gain self-sufficiency by taking over Western possessions in South East Asia (Watanabe 1985).

The United States was not alone in restricting trade with Japan and assisting China. The Soviet Union was the most active supporter of China during the early period of the war. The Soviets aided China with credits that amounted to $250 million by mid-1939, and substantial military equipment, including tanks and aircraft (Young 1963: 125; Haslam 1992: 92–94). In May 1938, Australia, responding to public anger at Japanese aggression, not only ousted Japan from a planned iron ore project in the Yampi Sound but also banned all iron ore exports to Japan. Pig iron exports to Japan continued, but not without controversy. In November, workers at Port Kembla refused to load pig iron shipments bound for Japan. The strike was lifted in January 1939, when the government promised the workers to strengthen its policy stance against Japan (McDougall 1977; Tsokhas 1995). The Netherlands also decreased resource exports to Japan from 1937 to 1939. After the fall of the Dutch mainland in 1940, Japan pressured the Dutch East Indies to increase resource exports, particularly oil. The Dutch authorities in Batavia yielded somewhat by increasing exports to Japan but held out on accepting inflated Japanese demands (Mook 2011: 15, 36–59; Iwama 2018: 51–72). By 1940, Britain had become more proactive in restricting trade to Japan. It assisted Batavia to resist Japanese pressure and coordinated with Washington to block resource exports from South America to Germany and Japan (Best 1995: 148–150). France, although cautious on sanctions, was the earliest Western power after the 1937 outbreak of war to provide China with a notable loan, equivalent to US$5 million, in April 1938. In September, France banned exports of iron ore from Indochina to Japan. Furthermore, French Indochina evaded persistent Japanese pressure for closure and functioned as a major route for supplies to China until Japan occupied northern Indochina in September 1940 (Young 1963: 72; Dreifort 1991: 135–145, 152).

The fatal decisions that set Japan and the United States on a collision course were made in the summer of 1941. In July 1941, Japan occupied southern Indochina to gain bases for a southward expansion. The United States immediately responded by freezing Japanese assets on 25 July 1941. Britain and other Western governments followed suit shortly after. On 1 August, the United States effectively banned, through strict licensing, all oil exports to Japan. With oil reserves declining, the Japanese military pressed for war. On 6 September, the Japanese government and emperor decided to commence war with the United States, Britain, and the Netherlands from late October (later postponed to early December) if diplomacy failed to resolve the situation. Roosevelt, aware of Japanese intentions from signal intelligence and advised by China and Britain to hold firm, refused to resupply oil to Japan unless it withdrew from China. Diplomacy on its own terms having failed, Japan launched its attack on 7 December (Iriye 1987: 148–184).

The Idea of Autarky: Building the Japan–Manchuria–China Economic Bloc

World War I had a considerable impact on the ideas and behaviour of the Japanese army. Experiencing the first total war in human history, the army, particularly the middle-class officers, came to consider broader preparation for a coming total war – including reforms of Japan's military, political, and economic systems – as essential. These army officers organised informal study groups, the most influential of which was *Issekikai*, set up in 1929. Many field grade officers were members of *Issekikai*, including Tetsuzan Nagata, Seishiro Itagaki, Kanji Ishihara, Renya Mutaguchi, Teiichi Suzuki, and Hideki Tojo[1], all of whom became major players in the sequence of incidents and wars in the 1930s and 1940s (Kato 2007: 2–3; Japan Broadcasting Corporation 2015: 124–130; Furukawa 2016: 96–97).

Some of these officers, in particular Kanji Ishihara, devised the idea of enhancing Japan's economic power based on industries and natural resources within its territory (Johnson 1982: 116; Ito 1989: 326–327). Ishihara stayed in Germany from 1923 to 1924 to study the cause of Germany's defeat in World War I. Through these studies, he developed an understanding that to win a long-lasting battle, it was important to establish conditions that would enable endurance of an economic blockade by the enemy. Specifically, he considered that Japan should fight a long-lasting ground battle for the resources of the East Asian continent (Kato 2007: 94–97). When he was an instructor at the Military Staff College of the army, Ishihara reported at an informal meeting of middle-class officers that Japan would be able to continue the war without any trouble if it could utilise the resources of the whole of

---

[1] Tetsuzan Nagata, one of the founders of *Issekikai*, became the Director of Military Affairs, the Ministry of the Army, but he was assassinated by a radical army officer in the building of the Ministry of the Army in 1935. Seishiro Itagaki and Kanji Ishihara initiated the Manchurian Incident in 1931, when they were staff officers of the Kwantung Army. Renya Mutaguchi became the commander of the First Regiment of the China Stationing Army, and initiated the Marco Polo Bridge Incident in July 1937. Teiichi Suzuki was President of the Planning Board and Hideki Tojo the Prime Minister when Japan started the Pacific War in 1941.

mainland China (Kato 2007: 100–101). In 1928, Ishihara transferred to the military staff of the Kwantung army, which took charge of the Kwantung Province of China as well as the area along the railroads of the South Manchurian Railways, which Japan had obtained through the Russo-Japanese War in 1905. As a member of the military staff of the Kwantung army, Ishihara had an opportunity to put his ideas on autarky into practice. In an article written in 1929, he argued that it was necessary to make an economic plan for the area including Japan, Manchuria, and northern China on the assumption that this area would face an economic blockade (Kato 2007: 103).

In September 1931, the Kwantung army commenced aggressions against the whole of Manchuria, using as a pretext the staged explosion of a South Manchurian Railways railroad, which had been planned and executed by the Kwantung army itself. One of the reasons for this aggression was the idea of Ishihara that Japan should occupy Manchuria as a first step in preparation for a long-lasting war in the future. By the end of 1931, the Kwantung army occupied almost all of Manchuria. In March 1932, a puppet country, Manchukuo, was founded, with Puyi, the last Emperor of the Qing Dynasty, as the Emperor of Manchukuo. Japan officially recognised Manchukuo by concluding the Japan–Manchukuo Protocol in September 1932 (Tomatsu 2015: 94–96; Furukawa 2016: 99).

The foundation of Manchukuo became the starting point of Japan's efforts to establish an autarky, as well as the start of the tensions with the United States and United Kingdom. Immediately after its occupation of Manchuria, the Kwantung army embarked on the project of developing the Manchurian economy as part of Japan's autarkic sphere. This project and the supervision of the Manchukuo government can be considered in terms of two sub-periods: 1932–1936 and 1937–1941. In the first period, from 1932 to 1936, the Kwantung army focused on establishing public security and the construction of economic infrastructure, including monetary and fiscal systems. Semi-public corporations (also known as 'special corporations' and 'quasi-special corporations') were founded for each essential industry, thus leading to the monopolistic development of industry under the supervision of the Kwantung army. The capital for these semi-public corporations was provided by the Manchukuo government and the South Manchurian Railways. This approach to developing industries reflected the anti-capitalist ideology shared by middle-class Japanese army officers. Indeed, in a December 1931 document, the Staff Section of the army stated that 'we will not allow monopolisation of profit by Japanese capitalists in Manchuria' (authors' translation) (Hara 1972: 4–9; Yamamoto 2003: 28).

In late 1935, the Ministry of Army, Japan, considered updating the Manchurian development plan, given the experience until then. A trigger was the transfer of Kanji Ishihara to the role of chief of the Operation Section of the General Staff Office. Observing the progress of the Soviet Union's Second Five-Year Plan, he considered it necessary to accelerate Manchuria's industrial development, given that it shared a border with the Soviet Union. In June 1936, the General Staff Office sent a document to the Manchukuo government requesting an acceleration of industrial development in Manchuria to prepare for war with the Soviet Union. The General Staff Office intended to develop the strategic industries necessary for enduring a war in the area encompassing Japan, Manchuria, and northern China (Hara 1972: 57–58).

Meanwhile Ishihara organised an informal institution, the Research Institute for the Public Finance and Economy in Japan and Manchuria (RIPFEJM; in Japanese, *Nichiman Zaisei Keizai Kenkyu-kai*), inviting Masayoshi Miyazaki, a representative of the Tokyo office of the Research Institute of the South Manchuria Railways (RISMR) to participate. In July 1936, RIPFEJM drafted a five-year plan for developing industries in Japan and Manchuria, which, combined with one produced by the RISMR, came to form the basis of the official plan to develop the Manchurian economy during the period from 1937 to 1941. After examination of the drafts and negotiation with the General Staff Office of the army, the Ministry of the Army, and the Kwantung army, 'The Five-Year Plan for Manchurian Industrial Development' was finalised in January 1937, and the Kwantung army instructed the Manchukuo government to implement the plan (Hara 1972: 57–65).

The plans by the RIPFEJM and the RISMR covered Japan as well as Manchuria. The Ministry of Army used them to establish the 'Outline of the Five-Year Plan of Important Industries' in May 1937, covering both Japan and Manchuria. The production targets established for the 'important industries' are shown in Table 5.1. Notably, the plan was quite ambitious. For example, production of aircraft and pig iron were expected to be 7.8 and 5.2 times their 1936 levels by 1941. Furthermore, the role assigned to Manchuria was substantial. In 1941, Manchuria was expected to be responsible for 30 and 34.8 per cent of aircraft and iron ore production, respectively.

The Ministry of Army requested the Cabinet (the first Cabinet of Fumimaro Konoe) to implement the Japanese part of the Five-Year Plan in June 1937. The Cabinet accepted the plan, and Minister of Finance Okinori Kaya and Minister of Commerce and Industry Shinji Yoshino announced 'The Three Principles of Public Finance and Economy'. These were: (1) expansion of production capacity; (2) maintenance of

Table 5.1 *Outline of the 'Five-Year Plan of Important Industries'*

	Units of production	1941 target, Japan	1941 target, Manchuria	1941 actual, Japan	1941 actual, Manchuria	1936 actual, Japan
Aircraft	Items	7,000	3,000	6,260	–	1,280
Automobiles	10,000 items	9	1	4	–	1*
Machine tools	10,000 items	45	5	5	–	2
Steel products	10,000 tons	700	300	437	46	432
Pig iron	10,000 tons	750	400	472	142	222
Iron ore	10,000 tons	1,050	1,200	303	424	125
Gasoline	10,000 kl	190	140	103	–	65
Alcohol	10,000 kl	45	5	24	–	3**
Benzol	10,000 kl	14	6	5	–	–
Heavy oil	10,000 kl	135	100	47	13	46
Coal	10,000 tons	7,200	3,800	6,241	2,452	4,790
Aluminium	10,000 tons	7	3	7	1	0
Magnesium	10,000 tons	6	3	3	0	1*
Ship	10,000 tons	86	7	31	0	25*
Electricity	10,000 kw	1,117	140	82	107	654

Sources: Inaba et al. (1963); Kokumin Keizai Kenkyu Kyokai and Kinzoku Kogyo Chosakai (1946), Toyo Keizai Shinpo-sha (1950).
Key: – indicates not available. *Excludes production in the colonies. **1937.

the international balance of payments; and (3) adjustment of the demand and supply of commodities. The three principles implied that the government would implement the policies for the expansion of production capacity requested by the army under the constraint of maintaining the international balance of payments and, to do so, it would impose controls on demand for and supply of commodities (Hara 1980: 7–8).

As stated above, by June 1937, the plan for expanding the production capacities of strategic industries in both Japan and Manchuria was ready to be implemented, when the military and economic environment changed drastically. On 7 July 1937, the Second Sino-Japanese War broke out. The Kwantung army intended to occupy northern China to 'secure their backyard' in preparation for the war with the Soviet Union. The Kwantung army expected that the operation would end quickly and, indeed, it had occupied Nanjing by December 1937. However, contrary to expectations, the Chinese government continued to resist even after the fall of Nanjing, moving the capital to Chongqing.

The war with China had positive and negative impacts on the plan for autarky. On the one hand, by occupying northern China, the

Japan–Manchuria economic bloc was extended to become the Japan–Manchuria–China economic bloc, enabling Japan to acquire natural resources that had been lacking in Japan and Manchuria, such as high-quality iron ore and coking coal. On the other hand, the war undermined the assumptions of the plan for expanding production capacity. First, the plan had assumed peace during its term, but instead Japan and Manchukuo were required to allocate resources for the war effort at the same time as attempting to expand capacity. Second, the aggression towards China caused further backlash from the United States and United Kingdom, finally resulting in them imposing economic sanctions on Japan, as described in the next section.

Economic Sanctions and Reaction I: Building the Great East Asia Co-prosperity Sphere

The first step in the imposition of economic sanctions on Japan by the United States occurred in July 1939, when Japan was notified of the cancellation of the Japan–United States Commerce and Navigation Treaty. The cancellation enabled the United States to impose economic sanctions on Japan at its discretion from January 1940 (Yoshida 2007: 6–7; Kitaoka 2011: 196–197). The Japanese government and the military regarded the outbreak of World War II in September 1939 and the success of Germany's aggression as a chance to address Japan's difficult situation. In September 1940, Japan advanced its army to the northern part of French Indochina, intending to close the route for aid from the United States and United Kingdom to China. Japan also intended to establish a base for the expansion of its sphere to South East Asia (Yoshida 2007: 3–5), motivated by the acquisition of natural resources lacking in the Japan–Manchuria–China economic bloc, including petroleum, bauxite, and rubber (USSBS 1946: 11–14; Nakamura 1977: 112). Meanwhile, Japan approached Germany and Italy and signed the Tripartite Pact in September 1940 to restrain the United States and United Kingdom.

Japan's actions in advancing into the northern part of French Indochina and signing the Tripartite Pact incurred the imposition of severe economic sanctions by the United States. In October 1940, the US imposed a total ban of steel scrap exports to Japan (Asahi Sinbun-sha 1941: 180–181; Furukawa 2016: 161–162). These sanctions had serious implications for Japan because its iron and steel industry was heavily dependent upon scrap imported from the United States as raw material for steelmaking, as discussed in more detail in the next section.

However, the sanctions were not effective in checking Japan's aggression towards South East Asia. On the contrary, the hardliners opposed to the

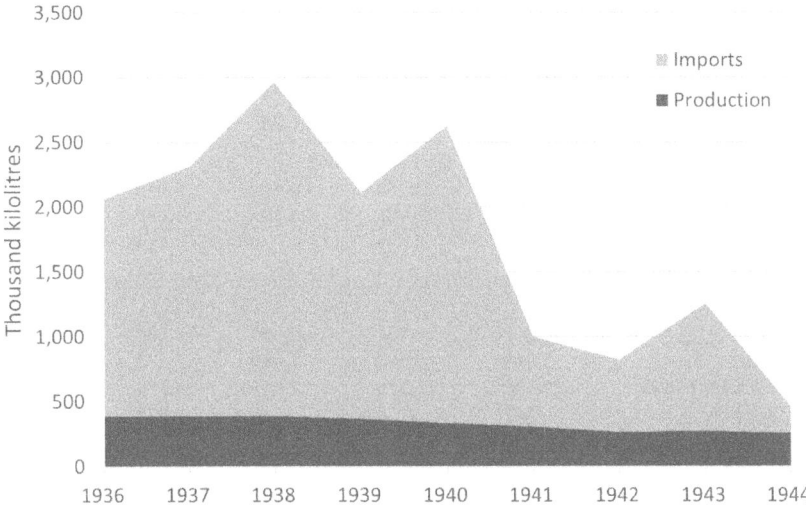

Figure 5.1 Japan's supply of crude oil, 1936–1944 (thousand kilolitres)
Source: Resources Agency (1951: 7, 77).

United States gained strength in the Japanese army and navy as a result of this measure (Yoshida 2007: 6–7). In July 1941, Japan advanced the army to the southern part of French Indochina. The United States immediately imposed further economic sanctions, totally banning exports of petroleum to Japan and freezing Japan's assets in the United States. Following the US example, the United Kingdom and the Netherlands also froze Japan's assets in their territories (Hara 1976a: 261–262).

As indicated in Figure 5.1 and Table 5.2, in 1940 Japan was highly dependent on crude oil imports, with the United States and Dutch East Indies accounting for 76.7 and 14.6 per cent, respectively, of Japan's petroleum imports. Hence, disruption of imports from these countries was critical to Japan, given that petroleum was essential for waging war. In this sense, the ban on petroleum exports to Japan was the last card for the United States to gain concessions from Japan. In the negotiations in 1941, the United States requested Japan to withdraw its military forces from China and French Indochina.

Again, however, the economic sanctions were not successful in gaining concessions from Japan. The Japanese government, the military, and the Emperor made a decision to enter into war with the United States, the United Kingdom, and the Netherlands. They calculated that Japan's petroleum stocks would be depleted within two years under the economic sanctions, and hence Japan would no longer be able to resist

Table 5.2 Japan's imports of petroleum, 1939–1943 (thousand yen)

	1939	1940	1941	1942	1943
Total	253,625	352,460	336,247	23,989	83,960
From areas that Japan occupied before the Pacific War:					
Subtotal	2,055	2,988	4,109	4,012	7,086
– Manchuria	2,055	2,962	4,109	4,012	7,086
– China	0	26	0	0	0
From areas that Japan absorbed into the Great East Asia Co-prosperity Sphere during the Pacific War:					
Subtotal	36,208	56,901	60,152	16,660	76,661
– Borneo	5,963	5,581	3,089	7,202	18,719
– Dutch East Indies	29,718	51,316	57,058	8,379	45,882
– Singapore	527	0	0	1,077	12,060
From other areas:					
Subtotal	215,363	292,572	271,986	3,317	212
– United States	200,393	270,371	259,483	2,538	212

Source: Ministry of Finance, *Annual Return of the Foreign Trade of Japan*, various issues.

pressure from the United States; however, war would give Japan a chance to establish its autarky by occupying South East Asia, including the Dutch East Indies and Malaya (USSBS 1946: 10–11; Nakamura 1977: 115; Yamamoto 2011: 17).

Based on these considerations, Japan started the war on 8 December 1941 (Japan time). In the six months that followed, the optimistic scenario of the Japanese government and the military seemed to become reality. Japan occupied a broad area of South East Asia, including French Indochina, the Dutch East Indies, Malaya, Singapore, Borneo, and the Philippines, and named the whole area under Japan's administration the 'Great East Asia Co-prosperity Sphere' (Hara 1976b: 9; Nakamura 1977: 118; Yamamoto 2011: 17–18).

Economic Sanctions and Reaction II: Adaptation of Industries

The Battle over Sea Lanes and the Mass Production of Merchant Ships

The 'Great East Asia Co-prosperity Sphere' was endowed with most strategic natural resources, and it appeared that Japan had finally established its autarky by occupying this sphere. An important point was that mainland Japan and the occupied areas in East and South East Asia were separated by the sea. Hence, for Japan to utilise the sphere's natural resources for its industrial production, it was necessary to transport them via sea from the occupied areas to Japan. This situation made the battle over sea lanes crucial for both Japan and the United States (Cohen 1949: 104–109).

When the war commenced, the Japanese navy was not well prepared for defending the sea lanes from submarines over a wide area including South East Asia. When World War I broke out, the navy established the Special Department for European War History to study the experience of the war, including the British navy's anti-submarine operations for safely escorting merchant ships through sea lanes. However, despite these studies, the knowledge gained was not reflected in the subsequent preparations for the war. When the Pacific War broke out, sea transportation defence was included in the missions of the Third Section of the Bureau Armament, the Ministry of the Navy. However, the retrospective reflections of an ex-lieutenant from this section suggested that they were overwhelmed with another mission: drafting merchant ships (War History Section 1971: 13–18). In November 1943, the Marine Escort General Headquarters was established in the navy when losses of merchant ships reached a critical level. In his speech on opening the General Headquarters, President of the Naval General Staff Shushin Nagano stated: 'Founding the Marine Escort General Headquarters now may be like calling a doctor after a patient fall[s] critically ill, but I ask all of the concerned officers to make wholehearted efforts in this national crisis' (War History Section 1971: 301–303, authors' translation).

Just before the Pacific War was declared, a navy lieutenant, Atsushi Oi, who later joined the Marine Escort General Headquarters when it was founded, attempted to inform the naval officers that obtaining oil in the Dutch Indies and transporting it to Japan were completely different issues, arguing that the sea transportation was the most difficult aspect; however, his arguments were dismissed (Oi 1983: 33–34). The negative attitude of the navy to the merchant ship escort reflected its conventional strategy of focusing on decisive encounters between fleets (War History Section 1971: 7–8).

Before the Pacific War, the US Navy also focused on decisive encounters between fleets. However, the Japanese attack on Pearl Harbor and the serious damage to the Pacific Fleet completely changed its strategy. Immediately after the attack, the headquarters of the US Navy gave the order for unlimited submarine and air attacks on Japan. One of the reasons for the change in strategy was that the US had lost a substantial part of its Pacific Fleet. The US Navy followed the example of the German submarine operations during World War I and World War II in conducting unlimited submarine and air attacks (War History Section 1971: 183–184). Initially, however, its submarine operations were not very successful because of the low quality of its torpedoes; issues with detonating devices and depth sensors prevented torpedoes from exploding. In early 1943, when these problems were fixed, the efficiency of the submarine operations was enhanced. Furthermore, the US Navy adopted a new tactic of attacking merchant ships with a group of submarines, which made the operations highly effective (War History Section 1971: 183–184, 291–292).

The evolution of the submarine operations of the US Navy was reflected in the damage to Japanese merchant ships. The dotted lines in panels (a) and (b) of Figure 5.2 indicate the gross tons of sunk cargo ships and tankers, respectively. Even in the first and second quarters of 1942, when Japan prevailed in the Western Pacific Ocean, more than 150,000 gross tons (GT) of cargo ships were sunk in each quarter as a result of attacks by the US Navy. After the Midway Sea Battle in June 1942, the quantity of sunk cargo ships in the third and fourth quarters of 1942 increased to 300,000–400,000 GT in each quarter. These losses were much larger than anticipated by the military, as reported at the Liaison Conference between the government and the Imperial Headquarters on 23 October 1941, where the propriety of opening the war with the United States, United Kingdom, and Netherlands was discussed. At that conference, the military reported that it had anticipated merchant ship losses of 800,000–1 million GT annually – that is, losses of 200,000–250,000 GT quarterly (Staff Headquarters of Army 1967: 369). In the third quarter of 1943, cargo ship losses rose even higher, exceeding 600,000 GT. In addition to cargo ships, substantial quantities of tankers were sunk. In 1943, such losses amounted to 20,000–70,000 GT each quarter; in the first quarter of 1944, losses of tankers increased very sharply to more than 200,000 GT.

In May 1942, facing huge losses of cargo ships and tankers, the government and the navy took the drastic measure of adopting the 'Planned Shipbuilding' scheme, the aim of which was to mass-produce merchant ships (Okazaki2025). This scheme had the following components. First, the administration of shipbuilding was transferred from the Ministry of Communication to the Ministry of the Navy, so that the navy could coordinate the building of naval and merchant ships. In addition, it was expected that the political power of the navy would ensure the distribution of materials for shipbuilding. Second, private shipyards concentrated on building the Wartime Standard Vessels, for which priority was given to mass production and saving materials at the cost of cruising speed and durable years, especially in the case of the Second Wartime Standard Vessels designed by the Technical Department of the navy in late 1942. Each private shipyard was assigned to build one or two types of Wartime Standard Vessels. Third, the Technical Department of the navy managed shipbuilding at private shipyards using a 'bar chart' system to

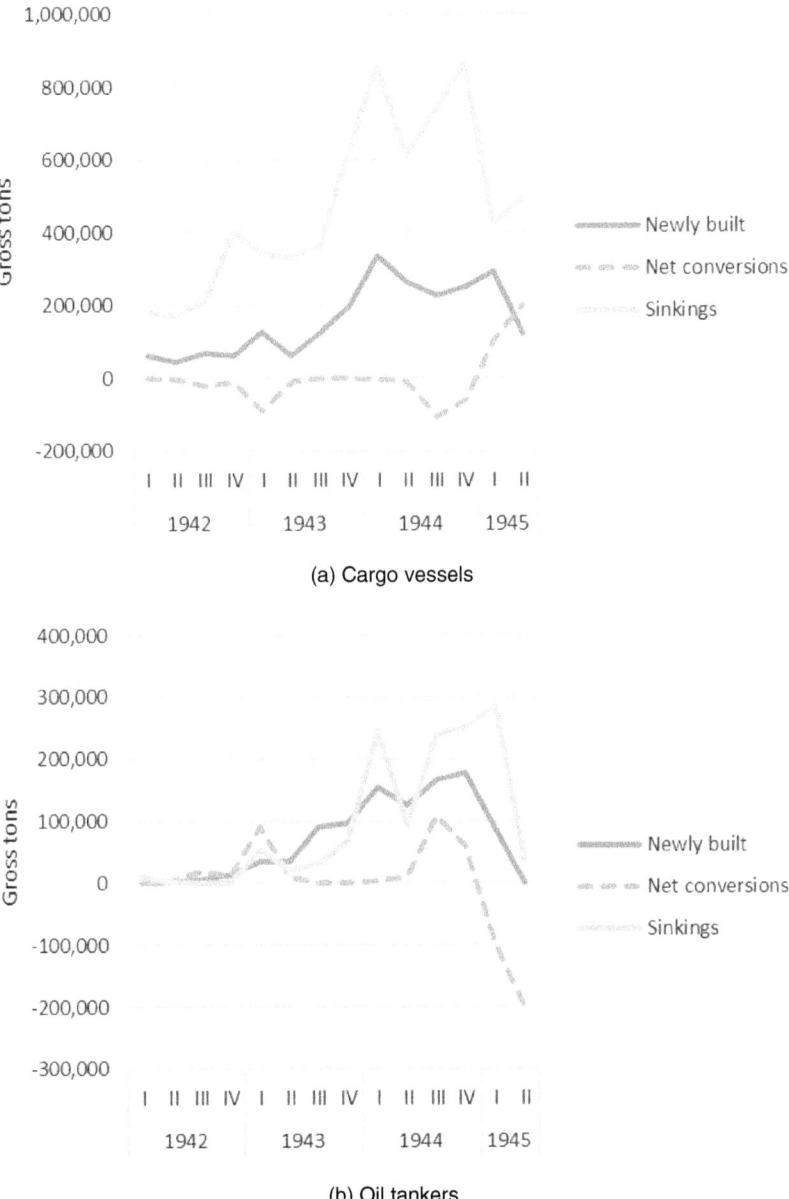

Figure 5.2 Japan's merchant shipping: gains and losses, 1941–1945
Source: Oi (1983: 383–389).

plan and illustrate the timeline for building each ship at each shipyard. Finally, Wartime Standard Vessels were purchased by a public organisation, Industrial Equipment Corporation, from shipyards to sell to marine shipping companies. Under this scheme, private shipyards not only adopted basic technological innovations, block building, and electric welding, but also devised various initiatives at the shop-floor level in customising the design of the Wartime Standard Vessels and improving operations, which resulted in sharp increases in production and labour productivity, as well as reductions of shipbuilding times.

The effect of the Planned Shipbuilding scheme is reflected in Figure 5.2. The quantity of newly built cargo ships increased from around 60,000 GT in each quarter in 1942 to 200,000–300,000 GT in each quarter in 1944. In addition, the quantity of newly built tankers increased from around 60,000 GT in each quarter in 1942 to around 250,000 GT in each quarter in 1944. Furthermore, substantial numbers of cargo ships were converted to tankers, reflecting the strategy of giving priority to transporting petroleum from the Dutch East Indies to Japan.

It is apparent that the loss of merchant ships exceeded the rate at which they could be replaced by shipbuilding despite the sharp acceleration in production under the Planned Shipbuilding scheme. To evaluate the contribution of the scheme, panels (a) and (b) of Figure 5.3 present simple simulations based on assuming that the quantity of newly built ships and net conversions are fixed at the average for 1942, before the Planned Shipbuilding scheme was fully implemented. Figure 5.3 illustrates how swiftly and how much earlier Japan's marine shipping capacity would have collapsed if the shipbuilding had not been accelerated from 1943. In this sense, the mass production of merchant ships under the Planned Shipbuilding scheme was an adaptation of the Japanese economy to the blockade that was effective to some extent.

Adaptation of the Iron and Steel Industry

The iron and steel industry was the industry most seriously and negatively impacted by the economic sanctions in the early stages. As mentioned, the United States banned steel scrap exports to Japan when the Japanese army advanced to the northern part of French Indochina in September 1940. Figure 5.4 indicates the consumption of scrap and pig iron by the Japanese iron and steel industry for steelmaking. As shown, the industry consumed much larger quantities of scrap than of pig iron. In 1939, more than half of Japan's scrap was imported, and 98.9 per cent of its total scrap imports came from the United States.

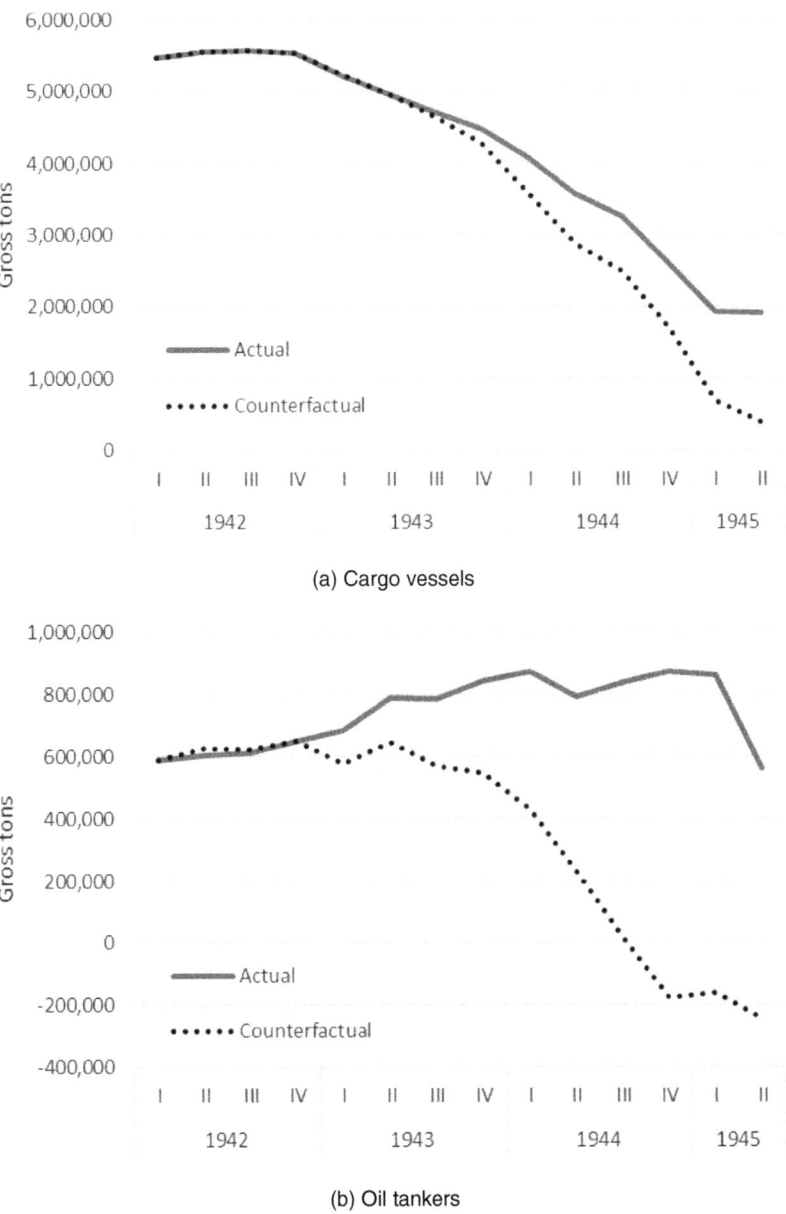

Figure 5.3 Japanese shipbuilding: actual and counterfactual, 1942–1945
Source: Actual quantities are from Oi (1983: 383–389). Counterfactual quantities are calculated by the author.

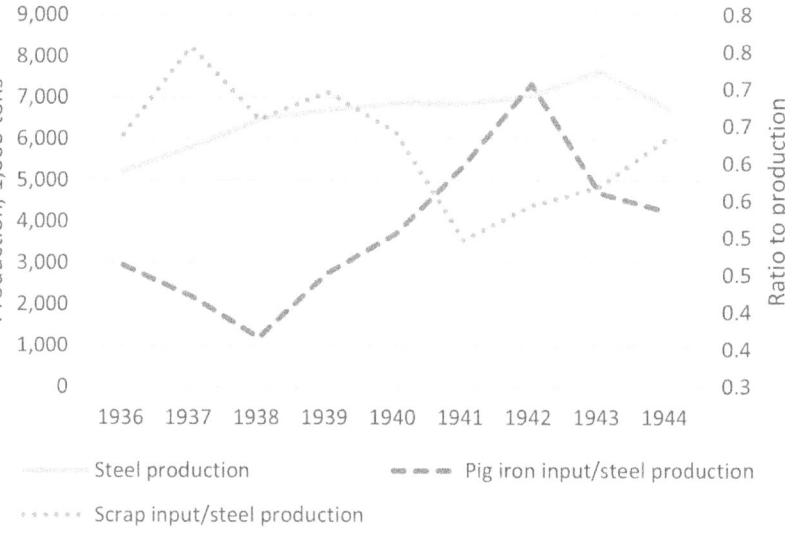

Figure 5.4 Pig iron and scrap iron in Japan's steel production, 1936–1944
Source: Japan Iron and Steel Federation (1961: 1, 3).

In 1940, scrap imports from the United States halved, and in 1941 they were almost zero (Table 5.3).

To cope with this difficult situation, the government decided to expand production equipment for the integrated production of pig iron and steel to overcome its dependency on imported scrap. Simultaneously, the government stressed the importance of collecting domestic scrap and asked for the Japanese people's cooperation in doing so.[2] Indeed, the government carried out a 'Special Collection of Iron and Steel' for public institutions from April 1941, and for private establishments from July 1941. Furthermore, in September, the Metal Collection Act was legislated, which authorised the compulsory collection of metal. In November 1942, metal collection was expanded to ordinary households (Asahi Shinbun-sha 1944: 118). From April 1943, metal collection was related to the policy of industrial adjustment. That is, the government ordered 'non-essential' establishments to close and scrap their equipment, which was then used for steelmaking (Asahi Shinbun-sha 1945: 118–119). As indicated in Table 5.3, the domestic supply of scrap more than doubled between 1939 and 1943.

---

[2] *Asahi Shinbun*, 28 December 1940.

Table 5.3 Japan's supplies of scrap iron, 1936–1944 (thousand tons)

	1936	1937	1938	1939	1940	1941	1942	1943	1944
Total	3,337	4,394	4,265	4,660	4,405	3,399	3,830	4,356	4,269
From:									
Domestic supply	1,840	1,974	2,907	2,105	3,014	3,196	3,791	4,326	4,047
Imports, total	1,497	2,420	1,358	2,555	1,391	203	39	30	222
From areas that Japan occupied before the Pacific War:									
Subtotal	61	55	77	28	17	24	36	19	219
– Manchuria	31	44	47	3	0	5	11	9	199
– China	30	11	30	25	17	20	25	10	20
From areas that Japan absorbed into the Great East Asia Co-Prosperity Sphere during the Pacific War:									
Subtotal	0	0	0	0	0	0	0	0	0
From other areas:									
Subtotal	1,466	2,376	1,280	2,527	1,374	179	3	11	3
– United States	1,028	1,777	1,007	2,175	1,116	109	1	0	0
– Britain	6	6	4	2	0	0	0	0	0
– India	139	200	82	107	78	1	0	0	0
– Australia	57	84	30	93	66	4	0	0	0
– Others	206	298	157	151	114	65	2	11	3

Source: Japan Iron and Steel Federation (1961: 6 and 14).
Note: Total supply equals total consumption; domestic supply equals total supply minus imports.

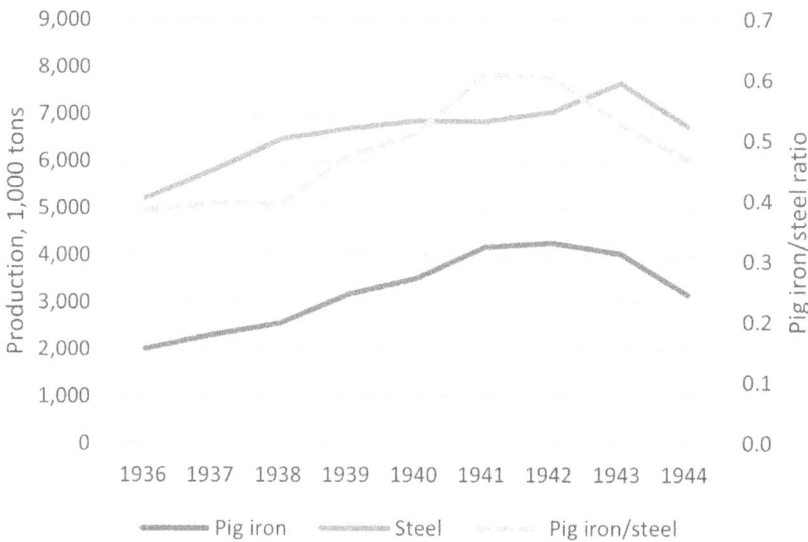

Figure 5.5 Japan's iron and steel production, 1936–1944
Source: Japan Iron and Steel Federation (1961: 1, 3).

From the time of the government's decision in December 1940, pig iron production in Japan increased consistently (Figure 5.5). Based on the increase in pig iron production, the ratio of pig iron to scrap in steelmaking rose (Figure 5.4). While the consumption of scrap per unit of steel declined sharply from 1939, the consumption of pig iron per unit of steel increased sharply. In other words, the Japanese iron and steel industry substituted pig iron for scrap to cope with the embargo on scrap exports to Japan by the United States.

To produce pig iron, Japan required iron ore, and it was largely dependent on imports for its supply (Table 5.4). In 1939, more than 80 per cent of Japan's total iron ore supply was imported, and only 22 per cent of its imports came from Japan's overseas sphere, from Korea, Manchuria, and China. During the Pacific War, Japan occupied major areas from which it had imported iron ores before the war. However, as iron ores were heavy and bulky, it was difficult to transport them to Japan during the war when there were severe constraints on marine shipping capacity. Nevertheless, the total supply of iron ores increased until 1941, and remained at a fairly high level until 1944. The major sources of iron ores were imports from China, domestic production, and stocks. Importing from China was relatively easy because China was geographically close to Japan, but also the sea lane between Japan and China in the

Table 5.4 *Japan's supplies of iron ore, 1936–1944 (thousand tons)*

	1936	1937	1938	1939	1940	1941	1942	1943	1944
Total	3,476	4,126	3,906	6,061	6,392	8,136	7,365	7,118	5,230
From:									
Production	620	602	771	836	1,123	1,253	1,796	2,510	3,003
Stock disinvestment	–936	433	904	–280	–79	275	1,148	581	–91
Imports, total	4,023	3,313	3,212	4,949	5,129	5,676	4,363	4,001	2,107
From areas that Japan occupied before the Pacific War:									
Subtotal	1,495	900	517	1,099	1,661	3,444	4,231	3,865	2,059
– Korea	243	302	367	401	439	766	605	235	610
– Manchuria	0	2	3	12	47	52	86	3	2
– China	1,252	596	147	686	1,175	2,626	3,540	3,627	1,447
From areas that Japan absorbed into the Great East Asia Co-Prosperity Sphere during the Pacific War:									
Subtotal	2,261	1,954	2,162	3,265	3,250	2,103	76	123	48
– Malaya	1,691	1,633	1,600	1,937	2,041	1,193	76	38	0
– Philippines	570	321	562	1,328	1,209	910	0	85	48
From other areas:									
Subtotal	267	459	533	585	218	129	56	13	0

Source: Japan Iron and Steel Federation (1961: 6–7), Toyo Keizai Shinpo-sha (1950: 264). Imports from Korea in 1943 and 1944 were obtained from Toyo Keizai Shinpo-sha (1950). Total imports in those two years include imports from Korea.
Note: Stock disinvestment equals total consumption minus production minus imports.

East China Sea was relatively safe from submarine attacks by the US Navy. Thus, Japan's maintenance of its iron ore supply enabled its maintenance of pig iron production and thereby of steel production until 1944.

The Limit of Adaptation

There was a limit to the extent to which Japan could adapt to the blockade as it become increasingly strict. As mentioned in the previous section, although merchant shipbuilding increased very sharply, the increase in the loss of merchant ships was still sharper, and the stock of ships for importing natural resources, therefore, continued to decline. The impact of this decline on Japan's marine shipping capacity is reflected in the decline of imports at the macro level (Figure 5.6). Real imports to Japan (in 1934–1936 prices) declined from 5,474 million yen in 1940 to 2,445 million yen in 1944. Real gross national product (GNP) was 20,796 million yen in 1940 and 20,634 million yen in 1944. The fact that real GNP was maintained despite the sharp decline in imports indicates the effectiveness of Japan's adaptation efforts to substitute domestic materials for the imported materials that were no longer

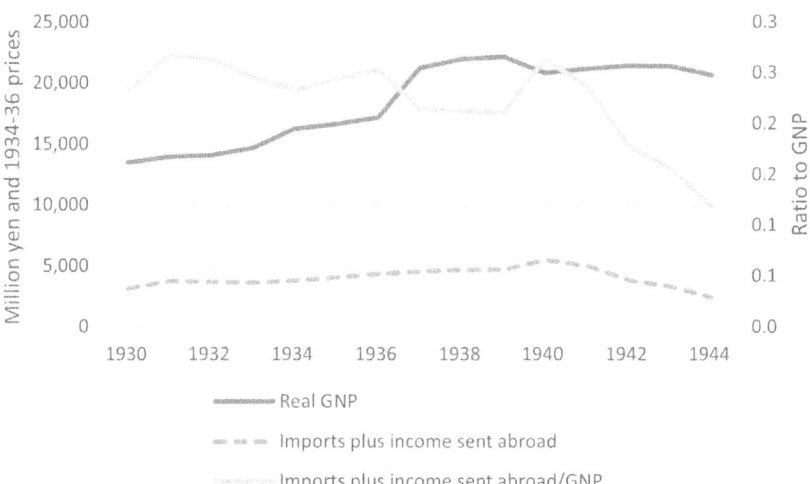

Figure 5.6 Blockade, import substitution, and Japan's real GNP, 1930–1944
Source: Economic Planning Agency (1961); Kokumin Shotoku Hakusho (Yearbook of National Income), 1959 issue.

available. These efforts were exemplified by the iron and steel industry discussed above. Nevertheless, despite these efforts, Japan was not able to increase production.

The stagnation of production highlighted the various trade-offs being made. At the macro level, increasing military expenditure suppressed private consumption. Figure 5.7 clearly illustrates this trade-off. In the period from 1937 to 1944, when Japan was at full-scale war, real private consumption and real government expenditure were negatively correlated, exemplifying the typical 'guns/butter' trade-off of wartime. Declines in private consumption affected the Japanese people's nutrition. As shown in Figure 5.8, food consumption measured in calories declined continuously from 1937. The deterioration in nutritional status was reflected in children's physical development. In December 1943, the Ministry of Welfare conducted a nutritional status survey (Research Institute of the Ministry of Welfare 1998), which provides data on heights and weights for two cohorts born in 1924 and 1931. Figure 5.9 shows the age–height profiles of boys (girls) in the industrial and agricultural/fishing areas in panels (a) and (b) ((c) and (d)), respectively. It is evident that the growth in height for children born in 1931 is lower

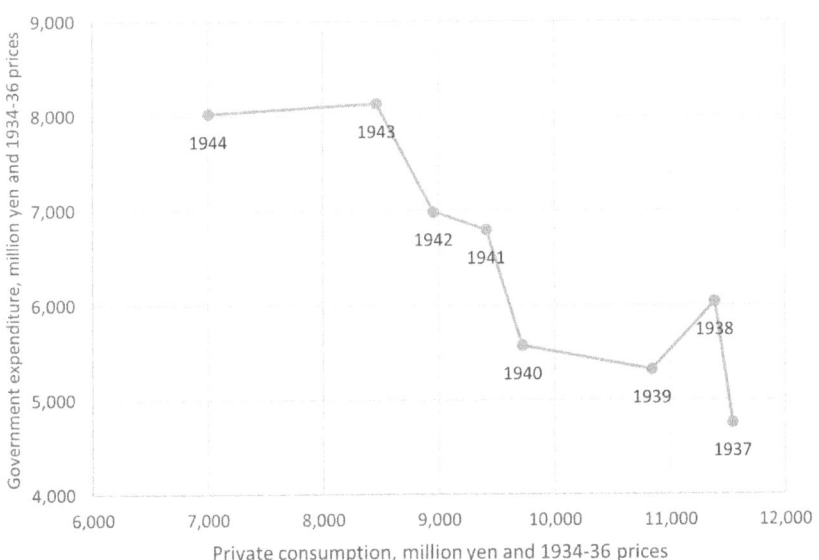

Figure 5.7 The government expenditure/private consumption trade-off: Japan, 1937–1944
Source: as Table 5.6.

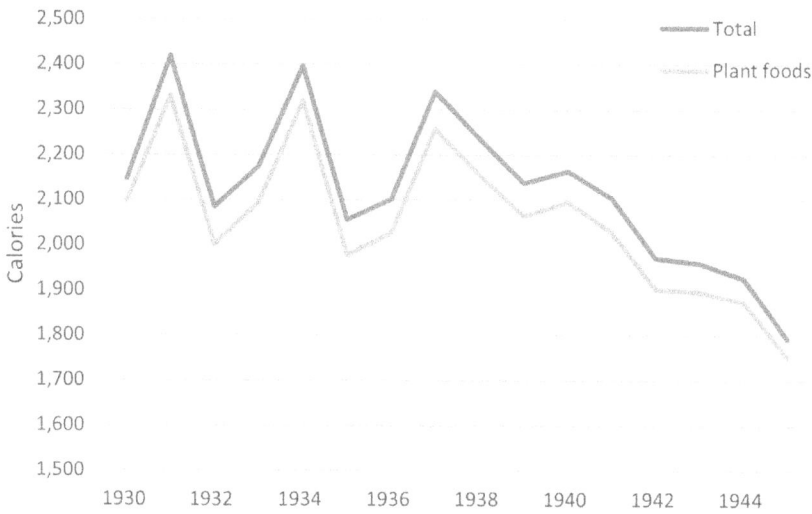

Figure 5.8 Food consumption per capita: Japan, 1930–1945 (calories)
Source: Nutrition Section of the Public Health Bureau, Ministry of Welfare (1946).

than that for children born in 1924 in the industrial area, whereas children in agricultural/fishing areas were not affected. This implies that the nutritional status in the industrial area deteriorated from the late 1930s.

The literature on the Japanese war economy has emphasised that the deterioration of people's living standards during the war was serious and that the Japanese people stoically adapted and endured this deterioration (Nakamura 1971; Yamazaki 1979). This view is supported by Figures 5.7, 5.8, and 5.9, but there was nevertheless a limit to this endurance. The 'Material Mobilization Plan' for April–June 1945 gave higher priority to food supply than to materials for munitions production. This was because the government and the military were concerned with social instability (Okazaki 1997). In other words, in the final stage of the war, the government and military changed the balance in the guns/butter trade-off towards the latter.

Finally, there was a trade-off between naval shipbuilding and merchant shipbuilding. Because private shipyards built substantial quantities of naval ships in the pre-war period, there was potential conflict between naval and merchant shipbuilding. This is indeed one of the reasons why the navy took charge of both merchant and naval

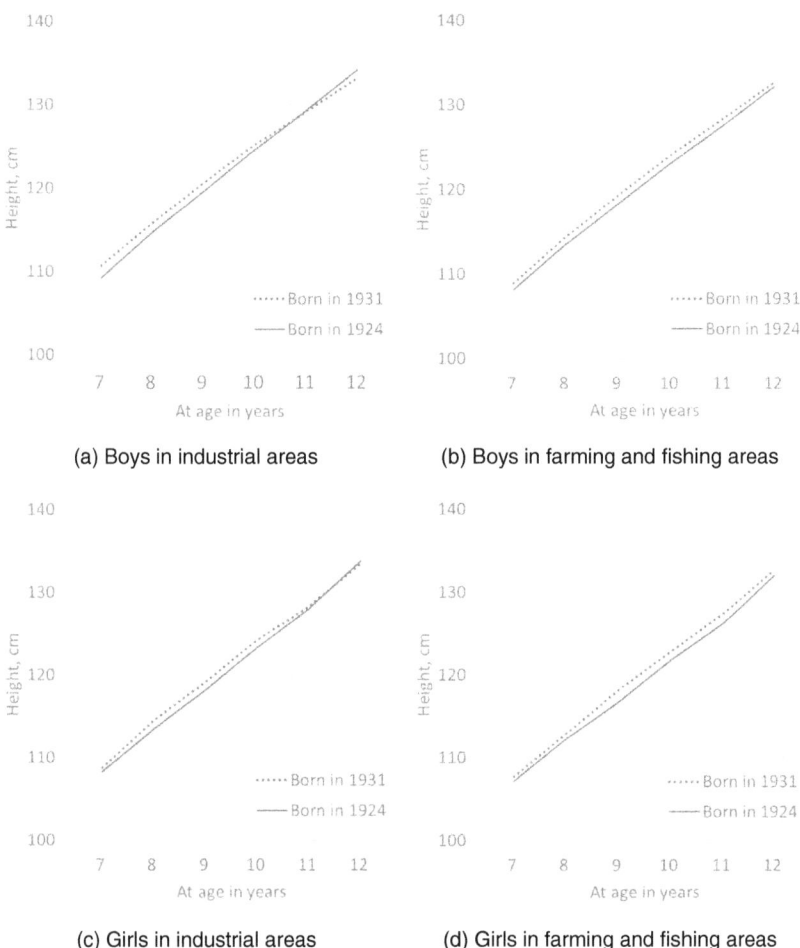

Figure 5.9 Height for age of Japanese children born in 1924 and 1931 (cm)
Source: Research Institute of the Ministry of Welfare (1998).

shipbuilding in 1942. Figure 5.10 shows the quantity of naval ships built at naval and private shipyards, indicating that private shipyards built more naval ships than did naval shipyards during the Pacific War. However, the ratio of naval ships in the total quantity of ships built by private shipyards declined sharply in this period. This suggests that the sharp increase in merchant shipbuilding constrained naval shipbuilding

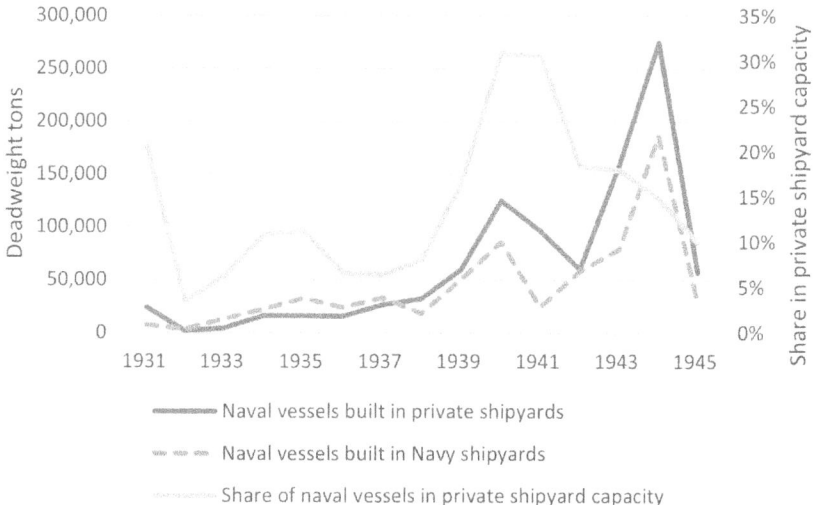

Figure 5.10. Naval shipbuilding by private and navy shipyards: Japan, 1931–1945

Source: Ministry of Transportation (1953: 164–165); Toyo Keizai Shinpo-sha (1950: 492).

Note: Calculation of the share of naval vessels in private shipyard capacity requires conversion of gross into deadweight tons at the rate of 1.1:1 (see Okazaki 2025).

by private shipyards, which was also an effect of the submarine attacks by the US Navy.

Conclusion

Japan's participation in World War II was a consequence of self-reinforcing cycles of Japan's aggressions in East Asia and the economic sanctions imposed on Japan by the Western countries. The motivation for Japan's aggressions was to construct an autarkic sphere that would enable it to endure future total war. However, the aggressions themselves incurred economic sanctions by the Western countries. In particular, the embargoes on steel scrap and petroleum imports to Japan by the United States caused serious damage to the Japanese economy, which finally pushed Japan to open the war with the United States, United Kingdom, and Netherlands.

During the war, the United States blocked transportation of natural resources to Japan from the Great East Asia Co-prosperity Sphere using its naval power, particularly submarine attacks on Japanese ships. Japan managed to adapt to this blockade strategy of the United States by adopting various measures, including accelerating merchant shipbuilding to maintain the marine shipping capacity and substituting domestic resources for imported raw materials. Although limits were ultimately reached, these measures for adaptation enabled Japan to continue the war for more than three and a half years.

References

Advisory Committee on Trade Questions in Time of War (ATB). 1932. 'Economic Sanctions against Japan', CAB 4/21/1083-B, The National Archives, Kew.
  1937. 'Economic Sanctions against Japan', CAB 4/26/1365-B, The National Archives, Kew.
Asahi Shinbun-sha. 1941. *Asahi Keizai Nenshi [Asahi Economic Yearbook]*, 1940 issue. Tokyo: Asahi Shinbun-sha (in Japanese).
  1944. *Asahi Keizai Nenshi [Asahi Economic Yearbook]*, 1942/1943 issue. Tokyo: Asahi Shinbun-sha (in Japanese).
  1945. *Asahi Keizai Nenshi [Asahi Economic Yearbook]*, 1944 issue. Tokyo: Asahi Shinbun-sha (in Japanese).
Bennett, Gill. 1992. 'British Policy in the Far East 1933–1936: Treasury and Foreign Office', *Modern Asian Studies* 26(3): 545–568.
Best, Antony. 1995. *Britain, Japan and Pearl Harbor: Avoiding War in East Asia, 1936–41*. Abingdon: Routledge.
  2013. 'The Leith-Ross Mission and British Policy towards East Asia, 1934–7', *International History Review* 35(4): 681–701.
Butler, Rohan, and J. P. T. Bury, eds. 1960. *Documents on British Foreign Policy 1919–1939*, series 2, vol. 8. London: HMSO.
Cohen, Jerome B. 1949) *Japan's Economy in War and Reconstruction*. Minneapolis: University of Minneapolis Press
Craft, Stephen G. 2000. 'Saving the League: V. K. Wellington Koo, the League of Nations and Sino-Japanese Conflict, 1931–39', *Diplomacy & Statecraft* 11(3): 91–112.
Dallek, Robert. 1995. *Franklin D. Roosevelt and American Foreign Policy, 1932–1945*. Oxford: Oxford University Press.
Dreifort, John E. 1991. *Myopic Grandeur: The Ambivalence of French Foreign Policy toward the Far East, 1919–1945*. Kent, OH: Kent State University Press.
Economic Planning Agency. 1961. *Kokumin Shotoku Hakusho [White Paper on National Income]*, 1959 issue. Tokyo: Printing Bureau of the Ministry of Finance (in Japanese).
Furukawa, Takahisa. 2016. *Showa-shi [History of the Showa Era]*. Tokyo: Chikuma Shobo (in Japanese).
Hara, Akira. 1972. '1930 nendai no Manshu keizai tosei seisaku [Economic Control Policies in Manchuria in the 1930s]', in Manshu Shi Kenskyukai (ed.), *Nihon Teikokushugi Kano Manshu [Manchuria under the Japan Empire]*, pp. 3–114. Tokyo: Ochanomizu Shobo (in Japanese).

1976a. 'Senji Keizai tosei no kaishi [Start of Wartime Economic Controls]', in Naohiro Asao et al. (eds.), *Iwanami Koza Nihon Rekishi [Iwanami Lectures on Japanese History]*, vol. 20, pp. 217–268. Tokyo: Iwanami Shoten (in Japanese).

1976b. '"Daitoa Kyoeiken" no keizaiteki jittai [Economic Reality of the "Great East Asia Co-prosperity Sphere"]', *Tochi Seido Shigaku [Journal of Agrarian History]* 71: 1–28 (in Japanese).

1980. 'Manshu Gokanen Keikaku Ritsuanshorui Kaidai [Commentary on the Documents on the Five-Year Plan for Manchuria]'. Tokyo: Ryukei Shosha (in Japanese).

Haslam, Jonathan. 1992. *The Soviet Union and the Threat from the East, 1933–41: Moscow, Tokyo and the Prelude to the Pacific War*. Basingstoke: Macmillan.

Hatano, Sumio. 1978. 'Leith-Ross no Kyokuto Homon to Nihon: Chugoku Heisei Kaikaku o Megutte [Leith-Ross Mission's Visit to the Far East and Japan's Response]', *Kokusai Seiji [International Relations]* 58: 86–104.

Higuchi, Mao. 2021. *Kokusai Renmei to Nihon Gaiko: Shudan Anzenhosho no 'Saihakken' [The League of Nations and Japanese Diplomacy: The Rediscovery of Collective Security]*. Tokyo: University of Tokyo Press.

Inaba, Masao et al., eds. 1963. *Taiheiyo senso eno Michi: Kaisen Gaiko-shi [Road to the Pacific War: Diplomatic History toward the Outbreak of the War]*, supplementary volume. Tokyo: Asahi Shinbunsha (in Japanese).

Ito, Takashi. 1989. '"Kokuse" to "kokusaku", "tosei", "keikaku" ["National policy", "policy", "control", and "plan"]', in Takafusa Nakamura and Konosuke Odaka (eds.), *Niju Kozo [Dual Structure]*, pp. 324–366. Tokyo: Iwanami Shoten (in Japanese).

Iriye, Akira. 1987. *The Origins of the Second World War in Asia and the Pacific*. London: Longman.

Iwama, Satoshi. 2018. *Asia Taiheiyo Senso to Sekiyu: Senbi, Senryaku, Taigaiseisaku [War in the Asia-Pacific and Oil: War Preparation, Strategy, Foreign Policy]*. Tokyo: Yoshikawa Kobunkan.

Japan Broadcasting Corporation. 2015. 'Kyodai soshiki "Rikugun" boso no mekanizumu [Mechanism of the Army's Rampage]', in Japan Broadcasting Corporation (ed.), *Nihonjin ha Naze Sensou ni Mukattanoka: Gaiko, Rikugun Hen) [Why Did Japanese Walk the Path to the War? Volume on Diplomacy and Army]*, pp. 118–162. Tokyo: Shincho-sha (in Japanese).

Japan Iron and Steel Federation. 1961. *Nihon no Tekko Tokei [Statistics on Iron and Steel in Japan]*, 1960 issue. Tokyo: Japan Iron and Steel Federation (in Japanese).

Jeansonne, Glen. 2012. *The Life of Herbert Hoover: Fighting Quaker 1928–1933*. New York: Palgrave Macmillan.

Johnson, Charmers. 1982. *MITI and the Japanese Miracle: The Growth of Industrial Policy, 1925–1975*. Stanford, CA: Stanford University Press.

Kitaoka, Shinich. 2011. *Nihon Seiji-shi [Political History of Japan: Diplomacy and Power]*. Tokyo: Yuhikaku (in Japanese).

Kato, Yoko. 2007. *Manshu Jihen kara Nicchu Senso e [From the Manchurian Incident to the Second Sino-Japanese War]*. Tokyo: Iwanami Shoten (in Japanese).

Kokumin Keizai Kenkyu Kyokai. 1954. *Kihon Kokuryoku Dotai Soran [Compendium of the Movement of the Basic National Resource]*. Tokyo: Kokimin Keizai Kenkyu Kyokai (unpublished, in Japanese).
Kokumin Keizai Kenkyu Kyokai and Kinzoku Kogyo Chosakai. 1946. 'Seisanryoku kakuju keikaku to sono jisseki: Sokatsu Ichiran-hyo [Production Capacity Expansion Plan and Its Results: Summary Tables] (unpublished, in Japanese).
Lee, Bradford A. 1973. *Britain and the Sino-Japanese War, 1937–1939: A Study in the Dilemmas of British Decline*. London: Oxford University Press.
McDougall, Derek. 1977. 'The Australian Labour Movement and the Sino-Japanese War, 1937–1939', *Labour History* 33: 39–52.
Miller, Edward S. 2007. *Bankrupting the Enemy: The U.S. Financial Siege of Japan before Pearl Harbor*. Annapolis, MD: Naval Institute Press.
Ministry of Transportation. 1953. *Kaiun Tokei Yoran [Statistical Handbook on Marine Shipping]*, 1952 issue. Tokyo: Ministry of Transportation (in Japanese).
Mook, H. J. Van. 2011. *The Netherlands Indies and Japan: Their Relations 1940–1941*. Abingdon: Routledge (original work published in 1944).
Nakamura, Takafusa. 1971. *Senzen-ki Nihon Keizai Seisho no Bunseki [Analysis of the Growth of the Japanese Economy in the Pre-war Period]*. Tokyo: Iwanami Shoten (in Japanese).
  1977. 'Senso Keizai to Sono Hokai [War Economy and Its Collapse], in Naohiro Asao et al. (eds.), *Iwanami Koza Nihon Rekishi [Iwanami Lectures on the Japanese History]*, vol. 21, pp. 110–160. Tokyo: Iwanami Shoten (in Japanese).
Newcomb, Robinson. 1941. 'American Economic Action Affecting the Orient', *Annals of the American Academy of Political and Social Science* 215(1): 133–139.
Nish, Ian. 2009. *Japan's Struggle with Internationalism: Japan, China and the League of Nations, 1931–3*. Abingdon: Routledge (originally published in 1993).
Nutrition Section of the Public Health Bureau, Ministry of Welfare. 1946. 'Showa 21 nendo kokumin eiyo jokyo chosa [Survey on the Nutrition Status of the People in 1946 FY]. www.digital.archives.go.jp/DAS/meta/listPhoto?LANG=default&BID=F2007021516453307030&ID=&TYPE= (unpublished, in Japanese).
Obiya, Shunsuke. 2021. 'Between "Coercive League" and "Consultative League": A Reappraisal of Debates Surrounding the "Reform" of the League of Nations', *International Relations of the Asia-Pacific* 21(3): 465–492.
Oi, Atsuhi. 1983. *Kaijo Goei-sen [Convoy Escort]*. Tokyo: Asahi Sonorama (in Japanese).
Okazaki, Tetsuji. 1997. *Kogyoka no Kiseki: Keizai Taikoku Zenshi [The Path to Industrialisation: Prehistory of the Economic Giant]*. Tokyo: Yomiuri Shinbun-sha (in Japanese).
  2025. 'Planning Mass Production of Merchant Ships in Japan during the Pacific War', in Jari Eloranta, Jeremy Land, Elina Kuorelahti, and Price Fishback (eds.), *The Routledge Economic History of War*, pp. 296–312. Abington: Routledge.

Research Institute of the Ministry of Welfare. 1998. 'Kokumin eiyo no genkyo ni kansuru chosa hokoku [Report of the Survey on the Nutrition Status of the People], in Shun Kaneko (ed.), *Senji-ka Kokumin Eiyo no Genkyo Chosa Hokokusho (Showa 18 nen [Report on the Nutrition Status Survey during the War]*, pp. 1–427. Tokyo: Fuji Shuppan (originally printed in 1943, in Japanese).

Resources Agency. 1951. *Sekiyu Tokei Nenkan [Yearbook on Petroleum Statistics]*, 1950 issue. Tokyo: Agency of Natural Resources (in Japanese).

Sharkey, John. 2000. 'Economic Diplomacy in Anglo-Japanese Relations, 1931–41', in Ian Nish and Yoichi Kibata (eds.), *The History of Anglo-Japanese Relations, 1600–2000: Volume II: The Political-Diplomatic Dimension, 1931–2000*, pp. 78–111. Basingstoke: Macmillan.

Staff Headquarters of Army, ed. 1967. *Sugiyama Memo [Sugiyama Memorandums]*, vol. 1. Tokyo: Hara Shobo (in Japanese).

Steiner, Zara. 1993. 'The League of Nations and the Quest for Security', in R. Ahmann, A. M. Birke, and M. Howard (eds.), *The Quest for Stability: Problems of West European Security 1918–1957*, pp. 35–70. Oxford: Oxford University Press.

Strang, G. Bruce. 2019. 'Imperial Hubs and Their Limitations: British Assessments of Imposing Sanctions on Japan, 1937', in T. G. Otte (ed.), *British World Policy and the Projection of Global Power, c. 1830–1960*, pp. 276–304. Cambridge: Cambridge University Press.

Thorne, Christopher. 1970. 'The Quest for Arms Embargoes: Failure in 1933', *Journal of Contemporary History* 5(4): 129–149.

1972. *The Limits of Foreign Policy: The West, the League and the Far Eastern Crisis of 1931–1933*. London: Macmillan.

Tomatsu, Haruo. 2015. 'Manshu Jihen kara Kokusai Renmei dattai e [From the Manchurian Incident to the Withdrawal from the League of Nations]', in Kiyotada Tsutsui (ed.), *Showa-shi Kogi: Saishin Kenkyu de Mioru Senso eno Michi [Lectures on the History of the Showa Era: The Road to the War Revealed by Recent Studies]*, pp. 89–106. Tokyo: Chikuma Shobo (in Japanese).

Toyo Keizai Shinpo-sha. 1950. *Showa Sangyo-shi [Industrial History of the Showa Era]*, vol. 3. Tokyo: Toyo Keizai Shinpo-sha (in Japanese).

Tsokhas, Kosmas. 1995. '"Trouble Must Follow": Australia's Ban on Iron Ore Exports to Japan in 1938', *Modern Asian Studies* 29(4): 871–892.

United States Strategic Bombing Survey (USSBS). 1946. 'The Effects of Strategic Bombing on Japan's War Economy', *Final Reports of the United States Strategic Bombing Survey 1945–1947* (National Archives Microfilm Publications).

Walters, F. P. 1960. *A History of the League of Nations*. London: Oxford University Press.

War History Section, Institute for Defense Study, Agency of Defense. 1971. *Kaijo Goei-sen [Battle to Escort Merchant Ships]*. Tokyo: Asagumo Shinbun-sha (in Japanese).

Watanabe, Akio. 1985. 'Eibei ni yoru Keizai-seisai no Kiki to Nihon no Taio: 1937–1939 [Japan's Response to the Economic Sanctions of the United States and England, 1937–1939]', in Kindai Nihon Kenkyu-kai (ed.),

Nihon-gaiko no Kiki-ninnshiki [Threat Perception in Japanese Diplomacy], pp. 221–244. Tokyo: Yamakawa.

Yamamoto, Yuzo. 2003. *'Manshukoku' Keizaishi Kenkyu [Research on the Economic History of 'Manchukuo']*. Nagoya: Nagoya University Press (in Japanese).

2011. *'Daitoa Kyoeiken' Keizaisshi Kenkyu [Economic History of the 'Greater East Asia Co-prosperity Sphere']*. Nagoya: Nagoya University Press (in Japanese).

Yamazaki, Hiroaki. 1979. 'Nihon Senso Keizai no Hokai to sono Tokushitsu' [Collapse of the Japanese War Economy and Its Characteristics], in the Institute of Social Science, the University of Tokyo (ed.), *Senji Keizai [War Economy]*, pp. 3–66. Tokyo: University of Tokyo Press (in Japanese).

Yoshida, Hiroshi. 2007. *Ajia Taiheiyo Senso [The Asia-Pacific War]*. Tokyo: Iwanami Shoten (in Japanese).

Young, Arthur N. 1963. *China and the Helping Hand, 1937–1945*. Cambridge, MA: Harvard University Press.

6 War of Attrition
Economic Warfare between Britain and Germany in World War II

Mark Harrison and Hans-Joachim Voth

Britain and Germany attacked each other's economy continuously from the start to the finish of World War II. The main forms of economic warfare were blockade and bombing.[1] Naval power was the primary instrument of blockade, sometimes supported from the air, and Britain and its allies did their best to force Germany's neutral trading partners to comply with the blockade using diplomatic pressure and economic threats. Strategic bombing was the domain of long-range air power.

After the opening moves, World War II quickly became a war of attrition. Attrition was brought about by the simultaneous attack on the adversary's armed forces and its economy. The armed forces suffered attrition on and near the battlefield. The economy had to replace the losses of equipment, and civilians were drafted to compensate for casualties. At the same time the economy suffered attrition from blockade and bombing. These economic losses could be mitigated, but not eliminated, by adaptation – by the efforts of civilians to economise on lost supplies and capacities and find substitutes for them. Fighting power was diverted to defend the economy in the air and at sea, and these countermeasures led to further military losses.

There was a limit to adaptation. This limit was not well defined or readily observed. It was psychological as well as material, and this was captured by official worries about civilian morale. Neither side knew where its own limit lay and, for obvious reasons, no government wanted to risk finding out. Concerns over the limit of civilian endurance haunted the authorities long before morale began to sag. Eventually, even extraordinary civilian sacrifices might fail to release sufficient resources to sustain the country's fighting power.

The authors thank Richard Overy, Duncan Weldon, and all others who met in Venice in January 2024 for comments, and Jonas Scherner for helpful advice.

[1] Other forms of economic warfare, of equal interest but less importance, were the pre-emptive purchasing of neutral supplies and sabotage.

This chapter is divided into four main sections. In the first, we briefly outline the plans and preparations for economic warfare of Britain and Germany. In the second, we discuss how economic warfare was conducted. In these first two sections, we consider separately blockade, the traditional instrument of economic warfare, and the novel instrument, strategic bombing.

The third and fourth sections of the chapter address the adaptation of each country to the economic warfare of the adversary, first Britain and then Germany. We follow this order for two reasons. One is that blockade and bombing interacted in their effects on each country's economy; it would be confusing to discuss adaptation to either instrument out of the context created by the other. And the other reason is that each country's response to being blockaded and bombed was idiosyncratic, so that the country outcomes of economic warfare were entirely different.

Britain and Germany both had allies, and their contributions are discussed where appropriate. British cooperation with France (until June 1940), the Soviet Union (after June 1941), and the United States (after December 1941) was far closer and more substantial than the very limited coordination of the Axis powers.

Plans and Preparations

The powers' previous experience of blockade, and inexperience of bombing, ensured that the two aspects of economic warfare proceeded quite differently. For blockade, the plans of each side were well prepared and largely anticipated by the other. The Allies, certain of naval dominance, planned to blockade Germany at sea, more or less on the lines of World War I.

German leaders feared the prospect of Allied blockade. In their minds, the events of 1918 cast a long shadow. Then, amid spreading malnutrition and a wave of industrial strikes, German morale had crumbled, and revolution had broken out. In public opinion, one important cause was the Allied blockade (Collingham 2011: 25–26; see also Chapter 3). But the fear of another blockade did not act as a restraint. Rather, it drove the National Socialists to bet on autarky (Scherner 2024: 11).

With Hitler in power, Germany prepared for blockade by two means. One was to make the German economy self-sufficient in deficit war materials including iron ore (for steel), oil, and rubber (Overy 1994; Toprani 2019). These measures were far from fully effective; food remained a major deficit commodity. The National Socialist authorities supported agriculture and controlled the market, but food self-sufficiency remained beyond their reach. The result was that Germany's economic war preparations became a plan to 'feed the war by war'. This meant to bring forward the conquest of the region to Germany's east with the genocidal intention of diverting its food surplus to German mouths (Dallin 1957; Tooze 2007: 476–485). It was an accident of the war's evolution that in 1940 Hitler found himself occupying Western (not Eastern) Europe. When the war in the West became stalemated, his attention turned naturally to the East.

As soon as war broke out in the West, both sides put their plans for blockade into effect. From the start, the Allies exercised the same naval dominance as in the previous war. They largely closed the North Sea and the Atlantic to German vessels and placed neutral shipping under close control.

While German warships made periodic attempts to break out onto the high seas, the war at sea relied largely on ocean-going submarines. Bizarrely, given the effectiveness of U-boats during World War I, the strength of the Royal Navy, and the certain expectation of renewed blockade, Nazi Germany invested more in its surface fleet than in submarines. Battleships were built that saw little or no action (von der Porten 1969). Germany entered World War II with just fifty-six operational submarines, barely more than a third of its strength in 1918.[2] Nonetheless, it launched a U-boat offensive with the aim of cutting off Allied trade and isolating the British economy. As the war progressed, it pursued it with growing seriousness.

By contrast, plans for economic warfare from the air did not exist in 1939. This is not because air power was underestimated. Rather, it was overestimated. Public opinion everywhere was convinced of the power of airplanes to attack suddenly, wreck cities, kill very large numbers of civilians, and terrorise the survivors (Overy 2014: 18–57). For this reason, long-range bombers were valued for their deterrent value more than as a means of victory. In the opening months of the war, both sides were mutually deterred, each fearing to strike the first blow.

When deterrence failed, airmen were ordered to take the offensive. What form it should take was far from clear. On the German side, following the poor results of Gotha and Zeppelin raids during World War I, air rearmament had been focused on close air support. Hitler was prepared to consider independent air operations, including the bombing of economic and civilian targets, but he was naturally sceptical and easily

---

[2] Each battleship cost forty Type VII U-boats. The submarine fleet could have been three times larger without the *Bismarck* and the *Tirpitz*, the two great battleships of the German navy.

dissuaded by poor initial results. The German air force never acquired a fleet of four-engined strategic bombers. Later in the war, he authorised the V-weapon campaign against British and West European cities under Allied control, when massive Allied bombardments had become a source of embarrassment.

On the Allied side, the independent role of air power was taken for granted. Beyond that, a division opened up between the advocates of indiscriminate versus selective or 'precision' bombing (e.g. Webster and Frankland 1961, vol. 1: 337–363; Overy 2014: 307–321; Biddle 2015: 495–499).

The division was formed by the gap between apparent technological possibilities and limited practical experience. Charles Portal, chief of Britain's Air Staff from 1940, and Arthur Harris, head of RAF Bomber Command from 1942, laid emphasis on the psychological effects of bombing on civilian communities. They favoured the relatively indiscriminate bombing of industrial cities and ports, with the aim of 'dehousing' and demoralising Germany's war workers (and incidentally killing them in considerable numbers).

By contrast, American air force generals such as Carl A. Spaatz, commander of the USAAF in Europe from May 1942, and Ira C. Eaker, commander of the US Eighth Air Force from December 1942, advocated the precision bombing of selected production facilities. Pre-war doctrine had led the USAAF to early investment in heavy bombers like the B-17 'Flying Fortress'. American airmen also put much trust in the Norden bombsight, claiming unprecedented accuracy from high altitude (Pardini 1999). With proper target selection, the resulting shortages of key commodities were expected to ripple through the supply of war, inducing a progressive collapse.

The story is sometimes oversimplified. Two qualifications are essential. For one, the British tried precision bombing in 1939 and 1940. Portal saw Germany's oil industry as a particularly attractive target. But the British experience was that precision required daylight, and in daylight aircraft losses were prohibitive. In darkness, nothing smaller could be hit than a city. Learning the same lesson in 1943, the Americans shifted their bombsights when necessary to more feasible but less discriminating targets such as cities (Biddle 2015: 492, 514).

A second qualification, essential in hindsight, concerns the selection of targets for precision bombing. The dominant framework started from the economics of inter-industry linkages created between the wars by Wassily Leontief, whose wartime employment was with the Office of Strategic Services (Bollard 2019: 190–196). Under this influence, American targeting looked for facilities supplying the intermediate goods most in demand for a range of final war products and for military activity. Ball-bearing factories and synthetic oil plants became the canonical cases.

An alternative framework existed, however – one that emphasised the spatial character of inter-industry linkages. The German economy relied heavily on railways and waterways to distribute coal and ores to its metallurgical, chemical, and engineering plants and to deliver war products to the Western and Eastern front lines, which, by 1942, were far from Germany's borders (Mierzejewski 1988: 22–60). The idea of targeting transport linkages also found expert advocates on both sides of the Atlantic, and eventually a high-level British convert in Arthur Tedder, chief of Air Staff from 1940 and deputy Supreme Allied Commander from January 1944 (Mierzejewski 1988: 80–81).

The Conduct of Economic Warfare

The Blockades

At first the Allied blockade of Germany followed closely the lines of World War I (described in Chapter 3). The first instrument of the blockade was 'control at sea', which relied on Britain's naval dominance. German warships and flag shipping were driven from the North Sea, leaving only the Baltic for German maritime trade. As exceptions go, the Baltic was far from insignificant because it allowed Germany to trade with the Soviet Union, then an ally, and neutral Sweden. On its own, therefore, the Royal Navy could not prevent Germany from trading with allies and neutrals, or from using the neutral neighbours as intermediaries for trade with the rest of the world.

The situation was greatly worsened in June 1940 by Italy's entry into the war and the fall of France. The Royal Navy could no longer control maritime shipping off the entire coastline of Western Europe and North Africa. This sealed the shift from 'control at sea' to 'control at source', in other words the direct regulation of neutral exports to Germany (Medlicott 1952, vol. 1: 415–417).

The blockade's second instrument, 'control at source', drew the Allies into the direct regulation of neutral trade. The underlying purpose was to support Allied economic warfare against Germany, but the means were coercive sanctions on Germany's neutral friends and neighbours, based on Allied naval and commercial dominance, diplomatic pressure, and veiled threats (Golson 2016).

Allied regulation of neutral trade began with the prior certification of vessels and cargoes; only this could avert seizure (not indefinitely, but pending arbitration by an international prize court), so the so-called navicert became the essential prerequisite for neutral shipping to pass the Allied blockade. A related instrument was the capacity to 'blacklist' (or sanction) supposedly neutral agents as hostile. A vessel without a navicert, or a blacklisted agent, would be denied market access anywhere in the world under Allied control.

Even these arrangements left room for Germany to benefit from neutral trade. Navicerts and blacklisting could not stop Germany's neutral neighbours, such as Switzerland and Sweden, from exporting or re-exporting war materials to Germany. Germany's access to Swedish iron ores was a particular source of concern (Milward 1977: 308–313).[3] As in the previous conflict, the answer was sought in war trade agreements with Germany's neutral neighbours. The Anglo-Swedish agreement of 1939 committed Britain to allow Swedish imports up to the pre-war level, while Sweden was not to exceed the pre-war level of its exports to Germany (and not to re-export goods to Germany that had potential war uses) (Medlicott 1952: 141–152). While the German prospect of victory remained alive, however, British diplomatic pressure was not all-powerful, and Germany was able to import Swedish ores through most of the war.

While the wartime evolution of the Allied blockade of Germany is not without interest, its greatest effects were arguably felt even before the war began. As discussed below, anticipation of the blockade drove Germany's war preparations and channelled its aggression in two directions, overland towards the wheatfields of Ukraine and under the sea around the British coastline.

The German blockade of Britain began in the early weeks of the war, but it did not become fully effective until the fall of France in the summer of 1940. While warships and planes played a role, the main burden fell on submarines. During the war, Germany produced approximately 1,100 submarines (USSBS 1945a: 69). Operational numbers averaged 118 through the war, ranging from a low of 22 in January 1940 to 240 in April 1943 as the Battle of the Atlantic reached its turning point (Davis and Engerman 2006: 295–296).

The main protection of merchant shipping against submarines was found, as in World War I, in escorted convoys. An advantage was that, while the number of escort vessels required increased with the perimeter of the convoy, the number of vessels protected increased with its square. This advantage of convoys more than compensated for the disadvantage

---

[3] The concern of the time was heightened by the belief that the German economy was fragile, so that its industry would collapse in weeks if the supply could be cut (Salmon 1981). Twenty years after the war, the idea was revived by Karlbom (1965), before being buried by Milward (1967).

that each had to proceed at the speed of the slowest vessel (Davis and Engerman 2006: 262).

At the beginning of the war, the main Allied and neutral nations (Britain, France, the United States, and Norway) had more than 30 million gross tons of shipping capacity (almost 20m tons were under a British flag). During the war, 21.5 million tons were lost to enemy action. Submarines accounted for three-quarters of sinkings (Davis and Engerman 2006: 268–270). More than 30,000 merchant seamen died. From 1943, however, the rate of American shipbuilding was more than enough to cover losses.

Figure 6.1 shows the monthly losses of Allied and neutral shipping to submarines against the numbers of German submarines operating at sea. There were three turning points in the campaign. The first two were favourable to the U-boats: the fall of France in mid 1940, which removed an adversary and provided new Atlantic bases; and US entry into the war in December 1941, which greatly increased the number of unescorted shipping targets for submarine attack. The overall situation turned in the Allied favour only in the summer of 1942 after American shipping was placed under an escort regime and Eastern seaboard towns under a blackout.

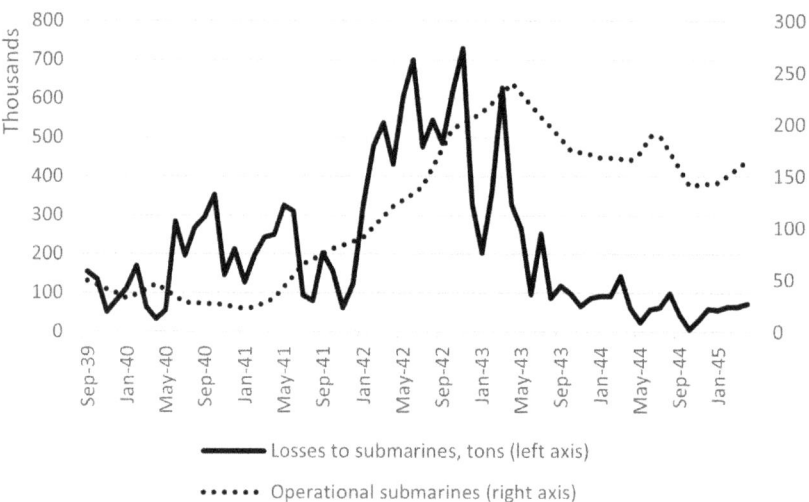

Figure 6.1 Germany's operational submarines and the sinking of Allied and neutral shipping, 1939–1945

Source: Monthly data from Davis and Engerman (2006: 298–300). Shipping losses are those attributed to submarine warfare (around three-quarters of all losses).

The German ocean-going submarines of World War II were far more capable than those of World War I. However, the Allies too improved the organisation and technology of anti-submarine warfare, especially from the air, and air cover was extended from the coasts to the mid-Atlantic (Davis and Engerman 2006: 266–286). As a result, Figure 6.1 shows, between each of the turning points the level of sinkings gradually declined. The growing disadvantage of the U-boats is represented more starkly in Figure 6.2, which captures the attacker's gain (the Allied and neutral ships sunk), relative to the cost (the number of submarines lost). Each advance made by the submariners soon disappeared.

While we will focus below on how Britain adapted to the German blockade, there were implications beyond the British predicament. By 1942 the newly Allied powers were engaged in a cooperative project that had begun with aid from Britain to the Soviet Union in 1941 and now continued, on a much larger scale, with American aid to both Allies (Harrison 1996: 128–154). This increased the value of Atlantic shipping as a target for German submarines.

Economic cooperation among the Allies was essentially the same process as economic warfare among enemies, but with opposite sign

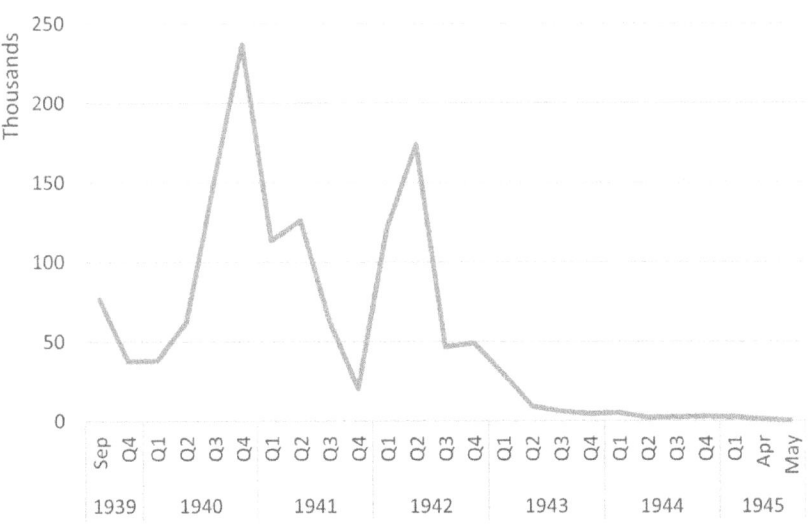

Figure 6.2 Allied and neutral shipping tonnage sunk per U-boat lost, September 1939–May 1945

Source: As Figure 6.1. Monthly data are reported here on a quarterly basis (except as shown for opening and closing months) because, in some months, no submarines were sunk. In consequence there is some smoothing.

(Harrison 2025). Where economic warfare destroyed resources and disrupted supply chains, Allied cooperation created them. Where economic warfare forced societies up against their limits, economic cooperation allowed breathing space. Control of the Atlantic was the essential condition for Allied cooperation. If the German submarine campaign had succeeded in isolating Europe from America, more would have been at stake than the future of Britain.

By contrast, Germany and Italy failed to integrate their war economies because they were allies: neither could coerce the other, so cooperation disappeared into the space between them (Scherner 2022).

The Bombing Offensives

The war's first months were unexpectedly characterised by a mutual reluctance to send bombers against each other's cities. The equilibrium was upset by the Battle of Britain, which ended German hopes of a speedy victory over the United Kingdom. By this point, each side had begun to raid the other's towns, aiming directly at port facilities and military-industrial targets. Each soon discovered how difficult it was to hit anything with precision. At this time, each side deployed relatively lightweight bomber aircraft in relatively small numbers. Thus, the first blows exchanged in 1940 and 1941 were relatively minor.

More important were the effects on the leaders' thinking. On the German side, Hitler concluded that bombing the British war industries was a waste of effort. Since daylight mastery of the air over Britain was out of reach, he shifted focus to the Eastern front (Overy 1980: 47). By contrast, the British, shortly joined by the Americans, came up with a different answer: to try much, much harder (e.g. Webster and Frankland 1961, vol. 4: 259–260). Attacking Germany by air was also important for morale: it showed that Britain and America were indeed at war with Germany – and it showed their Soviet ally that they were committed to the cause. The consequences are visible in the tonnage of bombs that each side went on to drop on one other (Table 6.1). At first these were nearly equal. In 1942 a large Allied advantage emerged and widened thereafter. By the end of the war, Allied bomb tonnage dropped on Germany exceeded the German total on Great Britain by more than twenty-five times.

The Allied air offensive evolved over time in several dimensions. Between the fall of France and US entry into the war, British strategy remained caught between over-ambition and lack of means. In his Cabinet memorandum of September 1940, Churchill remarked: 'the Bombers alone provide the means of victory': the goal he set for them

Table 6.1 *Bomb tonnage on the UK and on occupied Europe, 1940–1945*

Year	German bomb tonnage on UK	Allied bomb tonnage on occupied Europe	Allied/German ratio
1940	36,844	14,631	0.397
1941	21,858	35,509	1.62
1942	3,260	53,755	16.5
1943	2,298	226,531	98.6
1944	9,151	1,188,577	130
1945	761	477,051	627
Total	74,172	1,996,054	26.9

Notes: The German figure includes V-weapons (used from June 1944 to March 1945). For Allied bombing, the figures used here are those most nearly comparable to the German figures: the total tonnage dropped by the long-range bombers of RAF Bomber Command and the 8th and 15th US Army Air Forces, making 2.0 million tons of high explosives. A larger figure, 2.7 million tons, is the total of bombs dropped by all Allied air forces on all targets in the European theatre (USSBS 1945a: 1).
Source: Figures in tons are from Overy (1980: 120). Ratios are calculated from the figures given in the source.

was to 'pulverise the entire industrial and scientific structure on which the war effort and economic life of the enemy depends' (Richards 1953: 229). But the means available at the time gave no realistic prospect of that.

Several steps led to more realistic ambitions. June and December 1941 saw the Soviet Union and the United States enter the war. While the plight of the Soviet Union presented new demands for military aid, the United States offered immense resources. In January 1942, the Washington Conference committed the newly allied British and Americans to open a 'second front' on the continent of Europe in 1943. A year later, the Casablanca Conference of January 1943 committed their bombers to 'the progressive destruction and dislocation of the German military, industrial and economic system, and the undermining of the morale of the German people to a point where their capacity for armed resistance is fatally weakened'; but it also postponed the invasion of France to 1944. The Combined Chiefs of Staff defined 'fatal weakening' as 'meaning so weakened as to permit initiation of final combined operations on the Continent' (Webster and Frankland 1961, vol. 4: 273–283).

At the start of 1940, RAF Bomber Command had 438 bombers available, none of them of the heavy four-engined type (BBSU 1998: 41). By 1943 (all figures are for January) the number had risen to 839, of which 551 were heavy bombers; and by 1945 the numbers were 1,617 and 1,096 respectively. Meanwhile the numbers of heavy bombers available to the 8th and 15th US Air Forces in Europe had grown from 156 at the start of 1943 to 3,115 in 1945.[4]

The early years provided opportunities to learn. In 1940 and 1941, RAF Bomber Command was focused on attacks on U-boat facilities, the oil industry, and railways. The British learned that German air defences made daylight bombing prohibitively dangerous. At night the bombers could fly more safely, but in darkness they could not find any target smaller than a town (BBSU 1998: 2–9, 53–54). From this grew the British practice of nighttime town raids or 'area bombing', set out in a directive of February 1942. The logic was that, given the difficulty of hitting particular facilities, the best way to suppress production was to destroy the workers' neighbourhoods, including housing and essential public services.

Arriving in Europe during 1942, the US Eighth Army Air Force brought with it the belief that night raids were ineffective and a renewed commitment to precision bombing in daylight. The Allied Pointblank directive of June 1943 set the priority for the combined bomber offensive as German fighter production, alongside submarine shipyards and the industries for military vehicles, ball-bearings, and synthetic oil and rubber. The Americans began daylight operations against Germany's ball-bearing and fighter plants in the summer of 1943 but suffered heavy losses. Precision bombing required not only daylight but the suppression of German fighter cover. Until German airspace could be made safe for daylight bombing, the RAF would continue to pound the built-up areas of the industrial towns by night (BBSU 1998: 10–16). This began to change in 1944, when long-range fighters started to cover long-distance daylight raids. German air power weakened, and the scope of Allied operations against Germany widened. The RAF did not stop raiding German towns by night, but it also began to share the effort of daylight raids on German manufacturing and transport facilities.

The British and American approaches to the bombing war never fully converged. The American commitment to precision bombing in daylight was visible whenever circumstances appeared to permit. By contrast, the British left the path of area bombing reluctantly and only when pressed (Biddle 2015: 516). Nonetheless, pressure and circumstances were

---

[4] The greater number of the American bombers was offset by lighter bomb loads; this was a consequence of their heavier armament and armour, which turned out to be of less utility than expected.

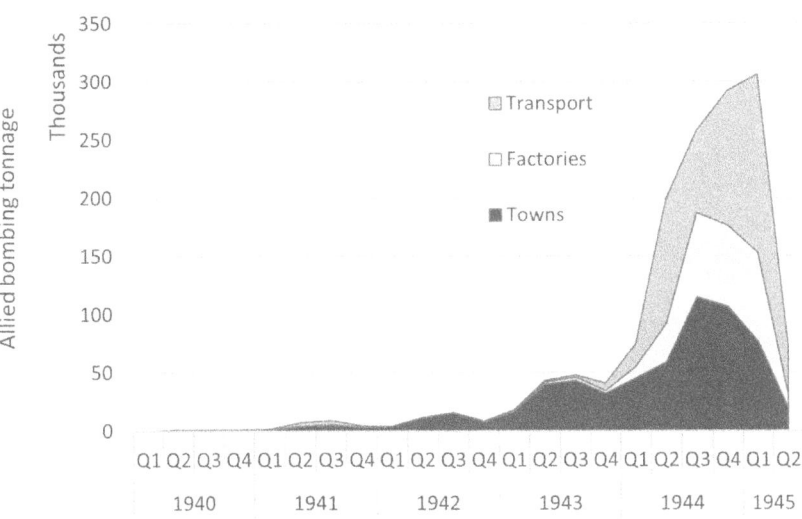

Figure 6.3 Allied bombing of economic targets in Axis Europe, 1940–1945 (thousand tons)
Source: Quarterly data from USSBS (1945b: 2–5). These figures cover approximately three-quarters (1.425 million) of the 2 million tons of Allied bombs dropped by RAF Bomber Command and the U.S. 8th and 15th Air Forces and listed in Table 6.1. Economic targets included towns (43 per cent), industrial facilities (20 per cent), and transport facilities (37 per cent). The remaining 575,000 tons were dropped on 'other targets', including submarine pens and airfields, in support of military operations.

sufficient to bring about a rough merging of the two national efforts in the closing stages of the war (O'Brien 2015: 321–325).

Figure 6.3 shows the main developments of the Allied air offensive. There were two turning points. Through the first quarter of 1943, although already horrifying for those living under it, the bombing of Germany was just a foretaste. The quarterly average of bomb tonnage up to then was just 7,000 tons. The second quarter of 1943 saw the RAF open the Battle of the Ruhr, a new campaign against the industrial towns of western Germany. This was the first turning point, described by Tooze (2007) and Biddle (2015). The quarterly average of bomb tonnage stepped up by an order of magnitude, to more than 50,000 tons. American daylight raids on industrial targets began at the same time but were curtailed after heavy losses.

The second turning point arrived in the second quarter of 1944. American bombers gained access to southern Germany from the Italian base of Foggia. The problem of daytime bombing was solved by long-

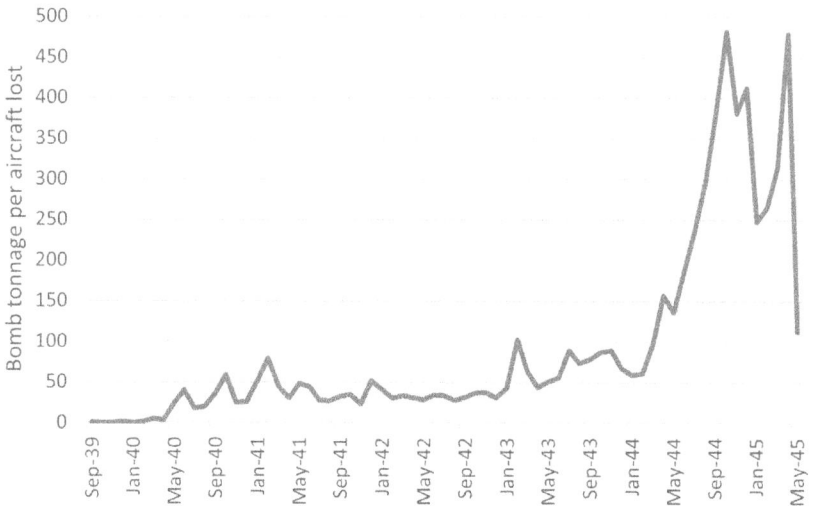

Figure 6.4 Bomb tonnage dropped by RAF Bomber Command per airplane lost, 1939–1945

Source: Monthly data from Webster and Frankland (1961, vol. 4: 431–436, 455–457). Figures cover all Bomber Command operations, not just those directed against economic targets.

range fighter escorts. As a result, German fighter strength was rapidly degraded, while Allied bombers ranged over all German air space by night and day. Now the quarterly average of bomb tonnage rose by another order of magnitude, this time to 225,000 tons. While town raids continued to increase in scale, they were more than matched by the scale of attack on other targets: a new carousel of industrial facilities, and a vast campaign against German transportation.

It was only in this final phase that Allied bombing became decisively less costly to the Allies. Figure 6.4 shows the monthly bomb tonnage dropped by RAF Bomber Command per aircraft lost. For most of 1941 and 1942, the RAF was able to deliver barely 50 tons of bombs for every aircraft lost. In 1943, the number rose towards 100, but did not clearly exceed it until April 1944, rising thereafter to almost 500 tons in the autumn.

Adapting to Economic Warfare: Britain

War Production and Bombing

Britain entered the war with a relatively large, diversified, and rapidly growing defence industry (e.g. Edgerton 2006: 15–58). Shipyards were beside major harbours (Barrow, Birkenhead, Belfast, Glasgow, Southampton). Factories for guns, shells, planes, and military vehicles were in population centres already specialised in engineering and metallurgy (London, the Midlands, Manchester). As a result, there was no shortage of potential targets.

The pre-war growth of the defence industry was governed by competing considerations (Hornby 1958: 203–208, 285–298). Rearmament presented opportunities for dispersal of war production to the north and west of the country. Even before rearmament became urgent, the government's regional policy of levelling up was one factor promoting greater dispersal. As the threat of war increased, with it arose fear of bombing, and in 1935 London and the East of England were designated a 'danger zone' from which war production should be removed.

Unsurprisingly, powerful frictions worked against these seemingly compelling considerations to keep war production where it was. The urgency of rearmament focused decision makers on quick results. Economies of scale and agglomeration would be lost if scattered small factories took the place of large ones and if new capacity was located at a distance from specialised suppliers, habituated workers, and experienced managers. Finally, the increasing range of modern aircraft caused the safe areas to shrink.

As a result, the main progress in dispersal of the defence industry was limited to a few ammunition plants and ship repair facilities. Many new establishments, including 'shadow' factories and dispersal factories, were based around London and the Midlands.

In 1940 and 1941, the Luftwaffe paid considerable attention to the main centres of wartime production and distribution (especially ports). In the year to July 1941 there were 41,000 deaths and a similar number of serious injuries, and a million people were made homeless (Webster and Frankland 1961, vol. 4: 258). The effects on production were modest and, for the most part, transient. Figures for electricity consumption in cities that experienced bombing suggested that economic activity fell immediately by 10–25 per cent, but in nearly all cases returned to normal within ten days. Coventry was an exception: after the raids of November 1941, the city took six weeks to recover (Overy 2014: 114).

Other effects were more persistent. Most important was the diversion of major resources to air defence and the emergency services. The numbers engaged in air raid precautions and emergency responses rose to 700,000 full-time and 1.5 million part-time personnel by 1941 (Overy 2014: 115). Resources were diverted from Britain's war effort in other theatres: the Mediterranean, and beyond. As a result, Britain was less able to resist the U-boat offensive in the Atlantic, German and Italian aggression in Greece and North Africa, and Japanese aggression in the Far East, and less capable of offensive operations.

Another diversion of resources arose from the immobilisation of Britain's east coast ports after the fall of France (Hancock and Gowing 1949: 253, 260). The western ports became congested, forcing ships to lie idle at the docks and so reducing their effective carrying capacity. Once unloaded, the supplies arriving on the west coast had to be rerouted to their destinations, so that the railways also suffered congestion, slowdown, and reduced capacity.

The German bomber offensive diverted British economic fighting power in 1940 and 1941, but this falls short of strategic success. On the contrary, 1940 and 1941 were years in which war production climbed and the workforce was comprehensively mobilised into uniform and war work (Harrison 1993). Indirect evidence of German success might have been signalled by crumbling civilian morale (the 'will to make war', as defined by USSBS 1945a: 95) or by indicators of declining health and work capacity of civilians. But there is little to no evidence of either (Mackay 2003: 248–265; Overy 2014: 169–196; Todman 2016, vol. 1: 515–524; 2020, vol. 2: 7–16).

To summarise, the German air offensive imposed serious costs on the British economy but did not put at risk Britain's military defence or social stability. If the aim was to undermine or destroy Britain's economic fighting power, the outcome was a clear failure.

Food and the Submarine Blockade

Before World War II, Britain imported more than three-quarters of wheat and flour, oils and fats, butter, cheese, and sugar (Hammond 1951: 394). The Battle of the Atlantic was hard fought and costly to both sides. By 1942, as Table 6.2 shows, Britain's quarterly food imports were running at just half the rate of the first nine months (October 1939 to June 1940). The loss of imports was only partly mitigated by a substantial increase in home production. Yet, after a dip at the end of 1939, British food stocks never fell below the pre-war level.

The war saw sweeping changes in the composition of the British diet, which became much more vegetarian and considerably more monotonous. The sharpest declines were in the consumption of sugar, fruit, fish and poultry, and tea and coffee, all of which were rationed. The largest increases were in the consumption of grains and potatoes, which were the most important sources of energy. These were never rationed, which speaks to the adequacy of the food supply, if not its variety (Hammond 1951). The result, also shown in Table 6.2, was that the calories

Table 6.2 *Food availability in the UK, 1939–1945*

	Pre-war	1939	1940	1941	1942	1943	1944	1945
Imports under Ministry of Food (m tons and quarterly rate)	–	5.5*	3.8**	3.7	2.7	3.0	2.8	–
Home production, crops (m tons):								
– Wheat	1.7	1.6	1.6	2.0	2.6	3.4	3.1	2.2
– Potatoes	4.9	5.2	6.4	8.0	9.4	9.8	9.1	9.8
– Sugar beet	2.7	3.5	3.2	3.2	3.9	3.8	3.3	3.9
– Vegetables	2.4	2.4	2.6	2.9	3.7	3.1	3.4	3.2
Home livestock (m head and mid year)								
– Cattle	–	8.9	9.1	8.9	9.1	9.3	9.5	9.6
– Sheep and lambs	–	26.9	26.3	22.3	21.5	20.4	20.1	20.2
– Pigs	–	4.4	4.1	2.6	2.1	1.8	1.9	2.2
– Poultry	–	74.4	71.2	62.1	57.8	50.7	55.1	62.1
Food stocks at end-of year (m tons)	10.5	7.5	10.6	13.4	13.7	15.8	15.0	–
Energy consumed (thousand calories per person, average)	3.0	–	2.8	2.8	2.9	2.8	–	–

Key: *October 1939 to June 1940. ** July to December 1940.
Sources: Imports taken or calculated from Hancock and Gowing (1949: 206, 357). Home production from Hammond (1951: 393). Food stocks from Hancock and Gowing (1949: 207, 358). Energy consumed from Hammond (1951: 387), the figures given there being rounded to the nearest 100 calories in accordance with discussion in the accompanying text.

consumed per person remained essentially constant throughout the war, while their distribution was probably somewhat equalised by rationing.

A series of interventions brought this about. Shipping space was rationed. Bulky and perishable foods were to be produced at home. Luxury foods were rationed. Food was subsidised and farmers were paid to plough up grassland and focus on arable crops.

While food supplies remained adequate, the same cannot be said of other consumer products. Civilian supplies of cloth and clothing, fuel and access to transport services, and consumer durables of all kinds were severely restricted (Table 6.3).

As for health and longevity, adult death rates, which had trended down through the inter-war years, rose in 1939 and rose again in 1940. The spike was temporary, however. By 1942 adult mortality was once again below the pre-war level and thereafter continued downward along the pre-war trend (Figure 6.5). Infant mortality followed a similar pattern,

Table 6.3 *Real civilian outlays on consumer goods in Germany and the UK, 1938–1944 (% of 1938)*

Year	United Kingdom % of 1939	Germany % of 1940	Germany Rebased to 1939
1939	100	108	100
1940	87	100	93
1941	81	97	90
1942	79	88	81
1943	76	87	81
1944	77	79	73

Source: Columns 1 and 2 from BBSU (1998: 76). Column 3 is calculated from the source.

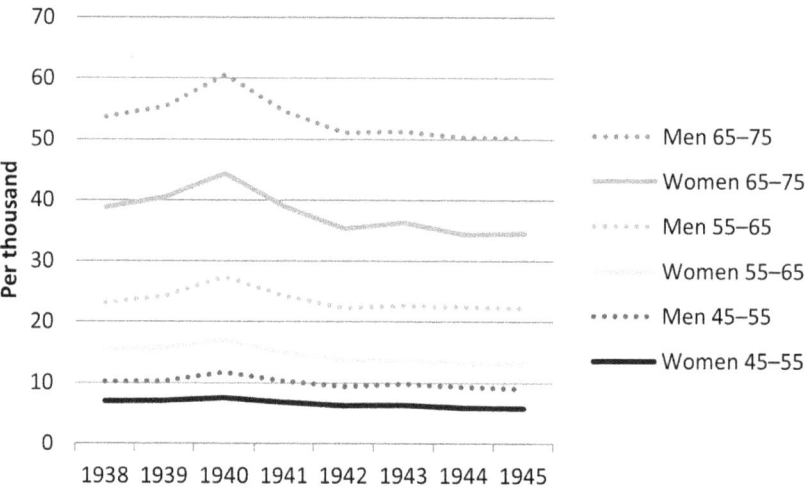

Figure 6.5 Adult civilian male and female death rates at ages 45–75 years in the UK, 1938–1945
Source: Annual data from Titmuss (1950: 521). Causes of death exclude operations of war.

spiking in 1940 and thereafter declining. By contrast, the pre-war downward trend of stillbirths was barely disturbed by the outbreak of war (Figure 6.6).

It would be rash to conclude that public health posed no issues for the British civilian authorities in wartime. On the contrary, air raids, evacuations, and the unprecedented wartime mixing of the civil population presented stiff tests. Among these (Table 6.4) were upticks of notifiable

Table 6.4 *Notifiable infectious diseases per 10,000 residents of the United Kingdom, 1939–1945*

Year	Dysentery	Diphtheria	Pulmonary tuberculosis	Scarlet fever	Typhoid fever
1939	0.6	12.1	11.2	19.6	0.4
1940	1.0	13.1	11.4	15.9	0.8
1941	1.9	13.4	12.4	14.4	1.2
1942	2.0	10.8	12.9	20.8	0.2
1943	2.2	9.1	13.3	27.5	0.2
1944	3.6	6.4	13.3	22.1	0.2
1945	4.3	5.1	12.7	17.8	0.1

Sources: Calculated from total notifications in CSO (1995: 19), normalised by the mid-year resident population (1939) and civil population (1940–1945) from LCES (1970: 8).

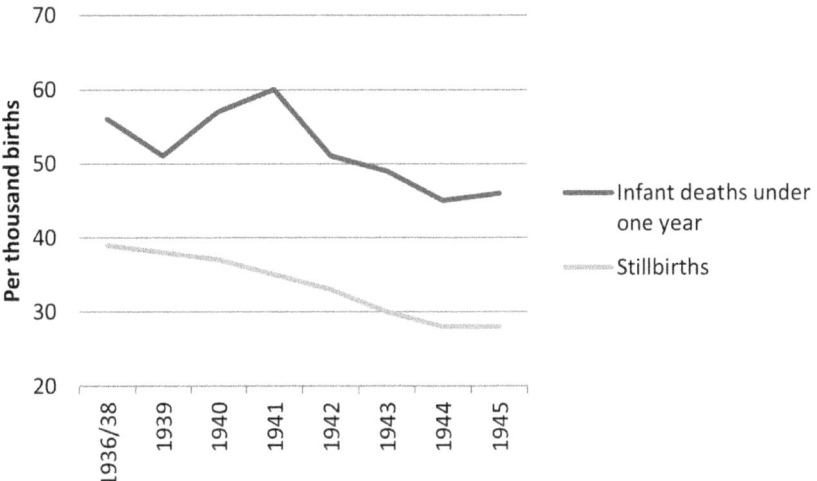

Figure 6.6 Infant deaths and stillbirths in the UK, 1936/38 (average)–1945
Source: Annual data from Titmuss (1950: 524).

infections. Dysentery, pulmonary tuberculosis, and scarlet fever were persistent; typhoid fever spiked in 1941, then died away. Infectious diseases did not, however, develop into a serious threat.

Living with food rationing, like living under bombardment, occasioned grumbling in queues and in shelters, but did not undermine morale in the form of expectations of victory and willingness to work.

To summarise, Britain survived blockade despite substantial dependence on food imports. Adaptation to blockade, like adaptation to bombing, was costly. In Britain's case, however, the price of survival did not bear heavily on the war effort. Much grassland was ploughed up for arable cultivation. While the agricultural workforce grew by more than 10 per cent, the increase was entirely made up of people drawn out of inactivity. Growing use of agricultural machinery also helped: domestic tractor production increased by 250 per cent from 1938 to 1943 (CSO 1995: 46, 67, 176). The turn to home production and the growing consumption of bread and potatoes reduced import requirements (Table 6.2), saving 50 million tons of shipping capacity, or nearly two years of peacetime non-oil imports (Olson 1963: 128).

Other countries that entered the war nearly or entirely self-sufficient struggled and sometimes failed to feed their populations. They failed because they were poorer at the outset, and so began the war with fewer inessential uses of food; or because their economies were insufficiently integrated, so that wartime shortages could not be mitigated by efficient substitutions; or both.

Adaptation and Its Limits: Germany

Neutralising Blockade

Scarred by the experience of blockade in the previous war, German leaders prepared for the same in the next one. As already discussed, they planned to feed Germans at war at the expense of the territories conquered in the east.

Conquest yielded major resources for the Germany economy, for which the figures given in Table 6.5 represent a lower bound. Klemann and Kudryashov (2012: 99) estimate the net wartime contribution of occupied and 'dependent' Europe to the German war economy at RM93.6 billion, close to a full year of pre-war German GDP. But, of that sum, only RM9.3 billion, or one-tenth, came from the occupied east, with another RM8.9 billion from northern and eastern Europe.[5] Measured at pre-war prices, the annual volume of net imports reached at least 20 billion in 1942 and 1943, representing 15 per cent of Germany's GNP in those years. In 1943, 70 per cent of German revenues from the major channel of exploitation, the 'occupation costs' that Germany

---

[5] The figure of RM8.9 billion is based on summing the subtotals for Albania, Bulgaria, Croatia, Finland, Hungary, Romania, and Slovakia.

Table 6.5 *Germany's gross national product and resources available, 1938–1943 (billions of Reichsmarks and 1939 prices)*

	1938	1939	1940	1941	1942	1943
Government expenditures	33	45	62	77	93	109
Consumer expenditures	70	71	66	62	57	57
Gross domestic investment	13	14	10	7	6	5
Net exports	1	−1	−9	−15	−20	−21
GNP, total	117	129	129	131	136	150
Resources available, total	116	130*	138	146	156	171

Source: Klein (1959: 257). The total of resources available is either the sum of government and consumer expenditures and gross domestic investment, or GNP plus net imports (net exports with opposite sign). For 1944, Klein provides only a figure for real consumer expenditures – RM53 billion, 7 per cent less than in 1943.
* Corrected from 126 in the source.
The reader should treat all the figures in this table with circumspection. They provide only a rough guide to general trends and orders of magnitude. Real consumer expenditures may be overstated. Gross domestic fixed investment is certainly understated (although inventory investment may also be overstated), and some investment costs may be hidden in the figures for government expenditure. Finally, the contribution of the occupied territories to wartime resources available is certainly understated. In more detail:

(a) The level of household consumption may be overstated. A recent benchmark estimate of Germany's GNP for 1936, based on input–output data from the 1936 industrial census, yields RM53.2 billion of private consumption in 1936 (Fremdling and Staeglin 2014: 377), around 5 per cent less than Klein's (1959: 252) 55.8 billion in the same year.
(b) The level of domestic investment may be understated. The Fremdling–Staeglin benchmark for Germany's GNP in 1936 shows RM11.4 billion of gross fixed capital formation, nearly twice the 6.2 billion found by Klein in the same year. (For inventory investment, however, the discrepancy, although smaller, runs the other way: RM3.0 billion according to Klein, 1.4 billion according to Fremdling and Staeglin.) Independently, Scherner (2010, 2013) has identified various large and consequential omissions from the investment series available to Klein. Consistently, he finds industrial fixed investment of RM2.65 billion in 1936 (Scherner 2010: 438) compared with the previously accepted figure of RM2.16 billion. Of greater significance is the discrepancy Scherner finds for the war years. Summing over the three years from 1941 to 1943, Klein (1959: 256) valued gross domestic investment at current prices at RM19 billion. But this sum is equalled or even exceeded by the RM19.1 billion that Scherner was able to find over the same period for *industrial fixed investment alone*.
(c) Net imports are underestimated, potentially by billions of Reichsmarks. Germany was able to exploit its occupied territories through many channels, not all of which were accounted for at the time. The figures omit, for example, foreign goods purchased and consumed by the German armed forces abroad without entering the country. They also omit the value of foreign goods seized and consumed without payment. Various estimates are available (Klemann and Kudryashov 2012: 75–117; Scherner 2012), but have not been compiled for national accounting purposes.

levied on its occupied territories, came from western Europe. More than 40 per cent came from France alone (Abelshauser 1998: 143). France overall contributed resources equal to 9 per cent of German GDP (Milward 1977: 140).

The eastern territories made a larger contribution in the form of labourers. By 1944, one in five German civilian workers in industry, transport, and agriculture, was a foreigner (Abelshauser 1998: 161). A war designed to subjugate or kill Europe's undesirable foreigners brought more than 7 million of them into the heart of Germany.

Despite additional resources from conquest, German civilians were increasingly exposed to war mobilisation, blockade, and bombing. By 1943 real civilian consumption in Germany was already 20 per cent down on its 1939 peak. In early 1943, Germany's colonial sphere reached its maximum extent, after which it began to shrink. At the same time, as shown below, Allied bombing was starting to drive Germany's aggregate production below its full potential, shifting pressure into the civilian sphere.

The ultimate failure of German plans to pre-empt the Allied blockade by war prompted the official historian to conclude:

Fear of the consequences of the blockade played a part in drawing Germany into the Russian adventure and the two-front war which ultimately proved so disastrous for her; perhaps one could say that in this sense the fear of blockade may have been more important than the blockade itself in bringing her to ultimate defeat. (Medlicott 1959: 646)

War Production and Bombing

The salient fact of the German war economy was the growth of war production despite the suffocating pressure of relentless blockade and bombing. The index of war production compiled by Rolf Wagenführ showed a threefold increase from the first months of 1941 to the summer of 1944 (USSBS 1945a: 33). The 'production miracle' made a mockery of efforts to find a close link from Allied bombing to the German war effort.

The success of German war production should not be taken entirely at face value. There were elements of 'mirage' in the 'miracle' (Scherner and Streb 2016). The index was designed to promote the image of Minister of Munitions Albert Speer. It concealed occupied Europe's contribution and emphasised the growing supply of 'big ticket' items while quality and reliability declined. Still, the achievement was real to a considerable extent.

The Allied air offensive did not prevent the production miracle. Its contribution was to force Germany to defend against the bombers and adapt to continuous bombing. The costs of defence alone were many and heavy. Of the 93,000 military aircraft that Germany produced after 1941, more than half were fighters. From 1942, more fighter aircraft were deployed in the West and over Germany than in the East (O'Brien 2015: 290–291).

Both sides lost around 40,000 aircraft. Plane for plane, the Allies lost more aircrews and more valuable machinery. In 1943, for this reason, German air commanders calculated they could win the war of attrition in the air (O'Brien 2015: 337). But they did not reckon with the Allies' greater economic capacity to replace losses.

From the summer of 1943, German air power was in decline. German fighters were concentrated over the homeland and were used up in air defence. While Allied bomber streams attacked airframe and aeroengine plants, the long-range fighters that escorted them were also given free rein to attack German fighters and airfields. The turnover of pilots accelerated. Accident rates rose with non-combat losses. The Luftwaffe went into a tailspin from which it did not recover. By 1944, 30 per cent of German fighter pilots were dying each month, while replacements were insufficiently trained for their own survival (O'Brien 2015: 293–297, 336–339). Such losses, being unsustainable, marked the beginning of the end. The simultaneous no-shows of German air power over the Normandy landings (June 1944) and the Bagration operational area (which annihilated Army Group Centre Operation in the East in June and July 1944) were directly attributable to the Allied bomber offensive. Without air support, the combined arms approach that had underpinned early German victories was gone.

Allied air raids also drew German labour resources and armament into air defence and bomb repair. More German troops served in air defence from 1943 onwards than in Stalingrad. Albert Speer recalled that German air defence in 1944 required proportions of Germany's output of armament, heavy ammunition, and optical and electronic products varying from one-fifth to one-half. He put the numbers engaged in air raid precautions and bomb repair in 1944 at 1 to 1.5 million (Webster and Frankland 1961, vol. 4: 381, 393–394).

On top of the costs of defence, Germany also had to adapt economically and pay the costs of adaptation. The canonical case is the 1943 raids on Schweinfurt, where Germany's ball-bearing factories were concentrated. The attack destroyed up to half the existing capacity. Yet 'there is no evidence that the attacks on the ball-bearing industry had any measurable effect on essential war production' (USSBS 1945a: 6).

Mançur Olson (1962) later showed how Germany's war effort adapted quickly to the blow: by a ripple of economising and substitution. Before the Schweinfurt raids, Germany's ball-bearing supplies were already more than adequate. In the face of sudden shortage, it was not difficult to concentrate remaining supplies on war production where they were most needed. The German war economy retained considerable slack until 1944, facilitating adaptation to the combined impact of blockade and bombardment.

While taking up slack helped with adaptation in the short term, there was also the creation of new capacity. Allied bombing is thought to have destroyed one-sixth of the industrial fixed capital stock in the future zone of British–American occupation. But damaged capacities could be quickly rebuilt and augmented on a surprising scale. By 1945, the gross value of fixed industrial assets in west Germany was 20 per cent larger than in 1936 – and one-third of this gross value was less than five years old (compared to only 9 per cent in 1935) (Abelshauser 1998: 167–168).

The new capital created in wartime Germany was costly. The 4,100 factories that were relocated in the twelve months up to November 1944 absorbed more 70 per cent of available construction materials. This was one of the two great wartime projects of industrial dispersal, the other being the Soviet evacuation and relocation of industrial assets out of the path of the invading German armies in1941 and 1942. The heavy costs of new industrial construction had to be taken from somewhere. At first, they came from the remaining reserves of civilian consumption. As the war progressed and the scope for civilian adaptation dwindled, the risk would arise that more new facilities could be built only at the expense of new war production.

The new industrial facilities were also not as productive as those they replaced. To reduce their vulnerability to repeated raids, they were dispersed away from existing industrial centres, and external economies were lost in the process (Overy 1994: 373–374). Dispersal also undermined efforts at cost-cutting through rationalisation and centralisation. German sources estimated large production losses from this alone – for example, up to half of the potential supply of Messerschmitt fighters from the summer of 1943 to early 1944 (O'Brien 2015: 78). Moreover, the dispersed facilities were more exposed to disruption of railway transportation (USSBS 1945b: 158–159), so they had to carry larger stocks, reducing efficiency further.

War production suffered not only from the dispersal of capital. It was also impeded by the scattering of the workforce following Allied air raids. By the end of the war, two-fifths of the urban housing stock of Western Germany and West Berlin had been destroyed. At the same time, residential investment came to a standstill. At the war's end, the shortage of urban dwelling units stood at 4.3 million. Because of this, German towns were depopulated, losing 2.3 million inhabitants by 1946 (compared to 1939). As Vonyo (2012) has shown, the housing shortage became a major drag on industrial recovery that persisted for years after the war.

How did German war production and fighting power respond to Allied bombing as the war progressed? The sources fall into two categories: insider estimates found after May 1945 in contemporaneous German documents or reported afterwards by German officials to Allied interrogators; and independent estimates constructed afterwards by the Allied bombing surveys (USSBS 1945a; BBSU 1998).

An advantage of the insider accounts is that they are rich in narrative. On the other side, it is hard to identify any German source with a clear commitment or other reason to tell the truth. The explicit mission of both Allied post-war survey teams was to reach unbiased conclusions. The US team was large and relatively independent. The smaller British team was led by Sir Solly Zuckerman, a respected scientific adviser, though not a disinterested party: in wartime he was Tedder's ally in advocating the bombing of German transportation.

Both Allied reports presented and deployed much data. For causal inference they relied considerably on narrative and judgement. However, they introduced two methods that offered a firmer basis for identifying causation: differences-in-differences and the construction of counterfactual series.

Both Allied teams exploited variations in the intensity of bombing across German towns to estimate the effects of town raids (shown in Table 6.6). The Americans estimated losses of total ('Reich') production year by year from a sample of ten cities. Based on the known destruction of these towns and their contributions to industrial production, the loss of production was found to have reached 2.5 per cent in 1942, 9 per cent in 1943, and 17 per cent in 1944. This did not show the effect on war production, however.

The British team compared twenty-one towns that were heavily bombed to fourteen that were largely untouched. Monthly data by town and by industrial branch from April 1943 to June 1944 showed that total output rose everywhere, but the bombed towns fell short of the control group by 13.7 per cent. The war production lost through bombing was much less, however – only 6 per cent, and the loss diminished over time. This indicated that 'with increasing experience of air attack, the Germans became more skilled at diverting the effects of air attack onto the civilian sector of industry' (BBSU 1998: 95). Generalised to Germany as a

Table 6.6 *German production, 1942–1945: Allied estimates of reduction attributed to Allied area bombing (% of estimated potential)*

	USSBS estimate of loss of Reich production	BBSU estimate of loss of all industrial production	BBSU estimate of loss of war industry production
1942	2.5	0.7	0.5
1943	9.0	–	–
First half	–	3.5	3.3
Second half	–	10.5	6.9
1944	17.0	–	–
First half	–	5.7	2.4
Second half	–	9.0	2.6*
1945 (Jan.–April)	6.5	12.2*	3.7*

Sources: Webster and Frankland (1961, vol. 4: 482–483); see also BBSU (1998: 93,96).
USSBS (United States Strategic Bombing Survey): Over a sample of ten German cities, an index is constructed to show the intensity with which a city was bombed and the months of lost output associated directly and indirectly with the bombing. The loss of 2.71 per cent of annual Reich production over the ten cities is averaged over the 39,900 tons of bombs dropped on them. Extrapolation to area bombing of the Reich as a whole yields the figures shown.
BBSU (British Bombing Survey Unit): The 'estimated percentage loss attributable to all town area attacks allowing for the lag in effects on industry ... All percentages are in terms of the corresponding estimated potential production in the absence of town raids'. Figures for the first four months of 1945 are calculated 'as though they took place over a six months' period'. Figures marked with an asterisk (*) are 'particularly conjectural, as they assume that war production could be maintained relative to all production as well as it was in January–June 1944'.

whole, these findings suggested modest losses of overall war production (Table 6.4 again).

These studies were limited to the effects of area raids, which became a much smaller proportion of the total effort in 1944. The effects might be understated, however, because the method of differences-in-differences necessarily excluded spillover effects on the economy as a whole.

A more comprehensive picture emerges from the efforts of the British team to construct a counterfactual index of potential war production. They estimated the capacities of every plant in every branch of German war industry quarter by quarter through the war and added them up on the same basis as Wagenführ's index of war production.

Comparison of actual and potential war production (Figure 6.7) shows two turning points. One is marked in the second quarter of 1943, when

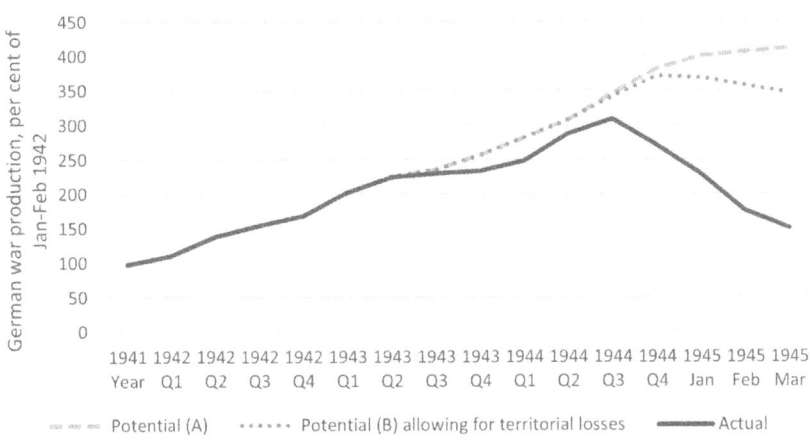

Figure 6.7 German war production, potential and actual, 1941–1944 (% January–February 1942)
Source: Quarterly data from BBSU (1998: Figure 20, facing page 90). Actual production is the Wagenführ index; potential production is the same adjusted by the BBSU.

German war production first slowed and began to fall short of potential. Another is marked in the third quarter of 1944, when German war production peaked, turned down, and began to fall absolutely.

The idea that Allied bombing first forced German war production below its potential in spring 1943 is consistent with the BBSU differences-in-differences estimate of town raid effects (Table 6.6) and narrative accounts of the Ruhr campaign from March to July 1943 (USSBS 1945b: 146; Tooze 2007: 596–598; Biddle 2015: 501–503). O'Brien (2015: 298) tells another story, different in substance but consistent in timing.

The collapse of German war production began around the time Allied forces approached Germany's frontiers. To control for territorial losses, they were counted separately in the potential war production series. Figure 6.7 shows that potential output on German-controlled territory began to turn down in early 1945; in contrast, the collapse of war production began earlier and proceeded more rapidly than territorial losses could explain.

The BBSU found a consistent explanation of the final collapse in the transportation campaign in the attack on German transport (railways, canals, and bridges). The attack began in the early months of 1944, intensified in September as Allied control of France was consolidated, and eventually absorbed more than a quarter of the overall Allied

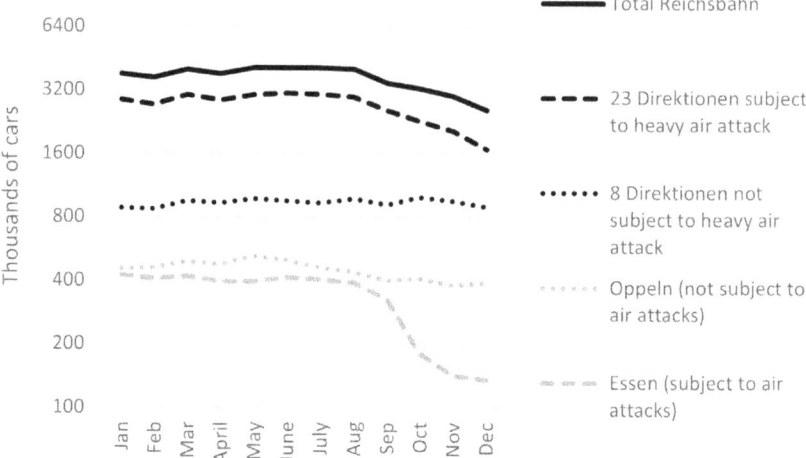

Figure 6.8 Effects of Allied bombing on German railway wagon loadings across Reichsbahn Direktionen, January–December 1944
Source: Monthly data from BBSU (1998: Figure 47).

bombing effort (Mierzejewski 1988: 102–161). Using differences-in-differences, the British team found a causal effect of bombing on German railway shipments. Monthly data for thirty-one railway districts through 1944 showed a precipitate decline of railway shipments that began in August (Figure 6.8). The decline was fully explained by the twenty-three districts that were attacked from the air. Districts that were not attacked showed no loss of performance. Thus, the attack on the railways was effective.

Finally, the disruption of the railways could be linked to the decline of war production. Over the ten months up to the end of the war, the decay of German war production appeared to respond to the decline of railway shipments with a lag of one or two months (Figure 6.9). By implication, the transportation campaign had at last pushed Germany's war industries up to and over a cliff edge.

Table 6.7 summarises a conjecture. The bombing war can be separated into three phases. In the first phase of the bombing campaign, Allied bombing of German economic targets ran at 7,000 tons per quarter, of which 1,000 were dropped on transport facilities. War production was unaffected, because Germany's civilian economy was fully capable of adapting and protecting the war effort. In the second phase, the intensity of Allied bombing rose to 81,000 tons per quarter, of which transport accounted for 27,000. Now adaptation became insufficient, so there

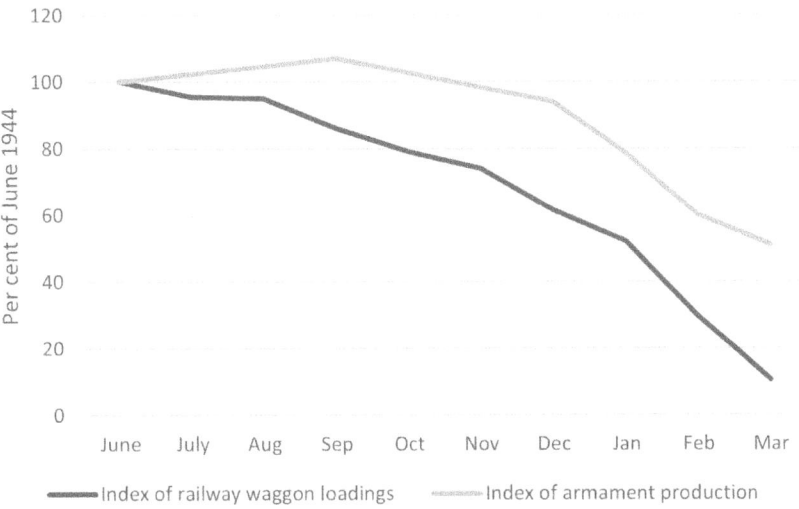

Figure 6.9 War production and railway loadings, June 1944–March 1945 (% of June 1944)
Source: Monthly data from BBSU (1998: Figure 42). Mierzejewski (1988: 198) gives a similar chart, comparing German monthly war production with monthly railway loadings in total and of hard coal, covering a longer period, January 1943 to March 1945.

were observable effects: German war production paused its growth and fell short of potential for the first time. Growth resumed with small but persistent losses of 16 index points per quarter. In the final phase, Allied bombing increased again, averaging 285,000 tons per quarter and 113,000 tons on transportation. With the German economy pushed beyond its limit, adaptation stopped. Quarterly losses of war production rose to 123 index points per quarter, signifying an irretrievable collapse.

Why was the attack on German transportation effective when all else seemed to fail? On this interpretation, when every railway interchange, canal, and bridge had been destroyed, every supply chain was broken. When nothing could move, production stopped, and military resistance also came to an end (O'Brien 2015: 349–357).

The Exhaustion of Civilian Reserves

The intention of economic warfare was to make the costs of adaptation and countermeasures so heavy that Germany could no longer sustain them. Did this happen? The evidence can be found in available measures of nutrition, morbidity, mortality, and morale of the German civilian population.

Table 6.7 *Germany's war production shortfall and Allied bomb tonnage on economic targets in three periods, 1941–1945*

Period	Germany's shortfall of war production, index units per quarter		Allied bomb tonnage, thousands per quarter Total	Allied bomb tonnage, thousands per quarter, of which, on transport
1. Apr 41–Mar 43	0	(complete adaptation)	7	1
2. Apr 43–Jun 44	–16	(partial adaptation)	81	27
3. Jul 44–Mar 45	–123	(collapse)	285	113

Notes and sources: Germany's war production shortfall is actual war production less potential war production allowing for territorial losses, as shown in Figure 6.7. Index units are percentages of the January–February 1942 monthly average level of production. Allied bombing tonnages are as shown in Figure 6.3. Period 1 starts with the Allied bombing of economic targets. Period 2 begins when German war production first fell below potential (although not yet at its peak). Period 3 starts when German war production began to fall.

Nutritional standards were already problematic for the mass of German people before the war. Under pre-war rearmament, according to Baten and Wagner (2002), mortality failed to improve in Germany at rates observed elsewhere in Europe in the inter-war years. The immediate reason was the greater prevalence in Germany of infectious and parasitic diseases associated with poor nutrition of the urban population. Behind the poor quality of food supplies to towns and cities lay the pressures of military mobilisation, price controls, and the disintegration of the German food market. Even before the war, German consumers were already making a down-payment on the price of their leaders' war ambitions.

On the eve of war, the German authorities introduced food rationing. The arrangements were both more and less comprehensive than those made in the United Kingdom. In Germany, rationing was not applied to the agricultural population, because farmers and farm workers were expected to be 'self-sufficient'. For others, the German system covered a wider range of foodstuffs, including bread (from the start) and potatoes (eventually); these were never rationed in the UK.

As Table 6.8 suggests, the energy and protein content of rations for a German working family was adequate at first, judged by the rather poor standards of the pre-war years. It then declined in steps that were particularly marked in April 1942, May 1943, and October 1944, ending at a level that was altogether inadequate.

Table 6.8 *Energy content of food rations for a German worker family member, 1939/40–1945/46*

Years	kCalories per day
1939/40	2,435
1940/41	2,445
1941/42	1,928
1942/43	2,078
1943/44	1,981
1944/45	1,671
1945/46	1,412

Source: Abelshauser (1998: 155).

Table 6.9 offers a more granular picture that distinguishes between energy and proteins. In wartime, workers performing heavy labour and children were given priority. Those performing heavy work received more calories and more protein than regular workers.. In proportion to their body weight, older children were assigned more calories and younger children were given more protein. The result was that the entitlements of those employed in heavy work declined at half the rate of others. By the end of 1944, those engaged in 'normal' work had lost up to 15 per cent of their calories and almost one-quarter of their protein intake – more, if we allow for unobserved quality deterioration.

These entitlements applied to non-agricultural households. In farming communities, 'self-sufficient' households retained a substantial advantage (Buchheim 2010: 315). For urban dwellers, the significance of nutritional deficits was cumulative. An SS report of 1943 on intellectual workers, who lacked access to ration supplements for 'heavy' work, referred to 'severe fatigue, lack of concentration and greater irritability', associated with significant weight loss since the war began (Buchheim 2010: 322).

Urban residents often traded illegally for farmers' food surpluses. The black market increased the farmers' incentive to hide produce from government procurement officials. It increased food availability in towns but disrupted the supply of rationed food. The growing shortfall of rations was both debilitating and demoralising. Ration cuts tended to follow military setbacks, undermining the regime's propaganda of inevitable victory. The regime's attitude to the black market vacillated between tightening rules and easing enforcement (Buchheim 2010: 311, 314).

There was a physical toll on health. Table 6.10 compares the incidence of notifiable diseases in wartime Germany to other places and times.

Table 6.9 *Feeding worker households in Germany in World War II: rationed energy and protein from six food groups, by main breadwinner's type of work and age of children (% average consumption in 1937)*

	Heavy work, older children	Heavy work, younger children	Normal work, older children	Normal work, younger children
Energy:				
End 1939	100	100	91	91
Mid 1942	93	92	85	84
End 1944	96	94	87	85
Protein:				
End 1939	98	100	86	88
Mid 1942	83	82	73	73
End 1944	87	87	76	77

Notes: The six food groups covered in this table are bread and flour, meat, fats, whole milk, eggs, and sugar and jam; fruit and vegetables (especially potatoes, rationed from April 1942) are not counted. The baseline is average consumption of a family of five (two adults and three children) with an annual income of 2,500–3,000 Reichsmarks in 1937. In wartime, rations were differentiated by class of employment (heavy labour attracted more energy and protein) and age (older children were given more calories while younger children were given more protein). In all cases the energy and protein content of rations is shown for a family of five. Older children in the table were 14, 10–13, and 3–6 years of age; younger children were 12, 7, and 1½ years.

Sources: Family rations are from Buchheim (2010: 317). Energy and protein are converted on the basis of Gebhardt and Thomas (2002) as follows: bread and flour (#419 bread, whole wheat); meat (#764 fresh pork chop, lean and fat); fats (#154 butter, unsalted); whole milk (#118); eggs (#140 one medium size, raw); sugar and jam (#1024 white granulated sugar). These conversions likely overstate the absolute quality of German wartime foodstuffs, but they suffice to give relative weights for the index numbers reported in the table. No allowance is made for the deterioration of food quality from 1937 to the war years, described by Buchheim (2010: 319).

German civilians experienced waves of diphtheria, pulmonary tuberculosis, and scarlet fever. For diphtheria and scarlet fever, the burden was heavier than in World War I. Germany also suffered more widespread infections than the United Kingdom in World War II for these illnesses, though British authorities struggled to contain TB and dysentery to some extent (Table 6.4).

Eventually, German civilians began to die. Until 1943 (as Figure 6.10 indicates), they had died no more frequently than in England and Wales. After 1943, there are no more statistics for Germany as a whole. But the Bavarian authorities' records through the remaining war years have been kept. They show that mortality rose sharply in 1944, and again in 1945

Table 6.10 *Notifiable infectious diseases per 10,000 residents in Germany in the two world wars*

Year	Dysentery	Diphtheria	Pulmonary TB	Scarlet fever	Typhoid fever	Typhus (spotted fever)
World War II						
1938	0.8	21.8	8.9	16.1	0.9	0.0
1939	0.9	20.6	10.5	18.5	0.8	0.0
1940	1.8	19.6	13.3	19.2	1	<0.1
1941	1.2	24.1	13.4	34.3	1.9	0.1
1942	1.7	33.4	16.1	48.7	1.8	0.3
1943	0.8	33.5	17.4	48.4	1.9	0.4
1944	0.8	33.6	17.1	32.2	1.3	1.8
World War I						
1914	0.9	19.2	–	15.8	2.6	0
1915	1.2	26.1	–	22.7	3.2	1
1916	1.5	29.9	–	14.3	2.2	<0.1
1917	10.5	26.7	–	7.4	4.6	<0.1
1918	4.8	24.8	–	6	3.7	<0.1

Source: Süss (2003: 442).

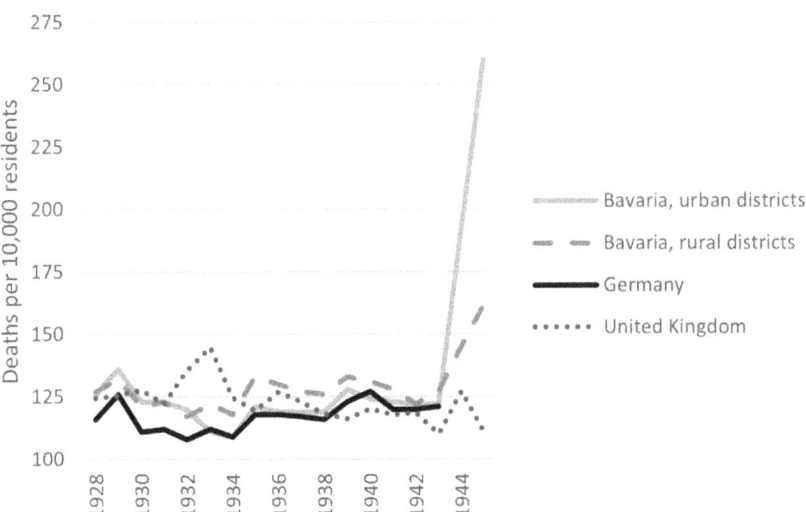

Figure 6.10 Mortality in Germany (including Bavaria by urban and rural districts), 1928–1945, compared to the United Kingdom
Source: Annual data from Süss (2003: 447).

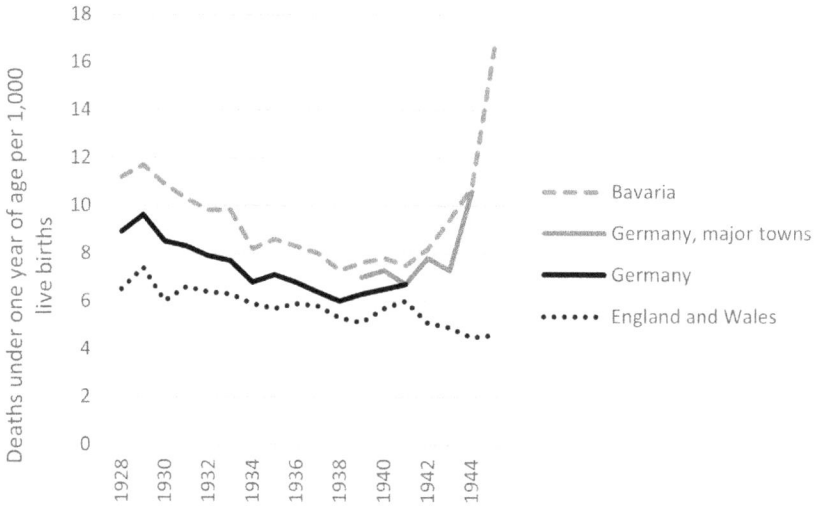

Figure 6.11 Infant mortality in Germany (including Bavaria), 1928–1945, compared to England and Wales
Source: Annual data from Süss (2003: 447).

(but most of that year fell after the German surrender). In the Bavarian countryside in 1944, the crude death rate rose from 127 to 145 per 10,000. In Bavarian towns, the increase was far greater, from 122 to 191 – and 1945 saw further increases. Infant mortality rose in Bavaria in 1944 and 1945, and also in Germany's major cities (Figure 6.11). Heightened morbidity and mortality in the last year of the war point to a critical deterioration of the conditions of civilian life.

Finally, we address civilian morale. Allied bombing and food shortages weakened civilian support for National Socialist leadership and war aims. Official records, secret Gestapo reports, captured correspondence, and interrogations suggest several conclusions. Bombing directly affected more than 25 million German civilians, or one-third of the population. It increased the desire for an end to the war, willingness to surrender, and distrust in leaders, exacerbated by inadequate air raid precautions and poor shelter access.

Nazi officials were intensely concerned about civilian morale and bombing's impact on citizens' perception of leaders and war aims (USSBS 1945a: 97–98). Bitter jokes circulated, contrasting Nazi boasts with the devastation of German cities. After the Hamburg raid in 1942, party officials were confronted by outraged citizens. Many hid their party insignia, and citizens stopped using 'Heil Hitler'. Speer feared a few more attacks like Hamburg would finish Germany. Support for bombed-out civilians became a priority, with special staff created to repair buildings and increased production of furniture and textiles.

The American bombing survey found 'diminishing returns': bombing was bad for morale, but those who survived heavy bombing were not more demoralised than others who experienced 'lighter' bombing (USSBS 1945a: 96).

Did morale matter? As the American survey notes, government documents of the time 'consistently assert that air attacks were undermining morale and producing defeatism, but they usually claim that no matter how the civilians thought and felt, their behaviour showed no active opposition to the war ... depressed and discouraged workers were not necessarily unproductive workers' (USSBS 1945a: 97). If so, morale was irrelevant to the war's progress.

Such scepticism is undermined by recent research using new data and modern methods. Contrary to USSBS findings, Adena et al. (2020) show that bombing stimulated civilians to resist the regime and damaged military productivity. They measure civilian morale by the frequency of treason trials for anti-Nazi activity, and military morale by the victory rates of ace fighter pilots. Anti-Nazi resisters and ace fighter pilots exemplify the extraordinary efforts that can make a difference in war.

The study of civilian morale is based on a sample of 911 cities, of which almost half were bombed at least once (Table 6.11). The bombed cities accounted for nearly all (86 per cent) of resistance episodes; thus, resistance was 6.9 times more likely in bombed cities than in those spared. Considering only the cities that were bombed at least once, the timing of resistance tells a similar story. In a month without bombing, the likelihood of a resistance group starting to operate was just 7.6 per cent. The risk more than doubled, reaching 17.6 per cent, in the month such a city was bombed.

The catastrophe engulfing Germany's towns had indirect military effects. Fighting men were kept informed through home visits, letters, and emergency postcards from those made homeless. Many came back from home leave in distinctly low spirits (Hastings 2000: 27). The bombing of an ace fighter pilot's hometown promptly reduced their subsequent aerial victory rate, and repeated bombing magnified the effect.

The same research finds that bombing was not the only way to lower German civilian morale. Access to BBC radio news complemented Allied bombing, each augmenting the other's effect in stimulating resistance. BBC broadcasting was far cheaper in lives and resources than Allied bombing.

Table 6.11 *Bombing frequency and risk of resistance, Germany, 1943–1944*

(a) Resistance in towns that were bombed once or more versus towns never bombed

	Total	Never bombed	Bombed once or more
Towns	911	457	398
Any resistance?	56	8	48
Resistance risk	6.1%	1.8%	12.1%
Odds ratio	–	–	6.9

(b) In towns that were bombed once or more, resistance starts in town/months when bombing took place versus town/months without bombing

	Total	Without bombing	Bombed once or more
Town-months	10,704	9,150	1,554
Resistance starts?	972	698	274
Resistance risk	9.1%	7.6%	17.6%
Odds ratio	–	–	2.3

Source: Adena et al. (2020) – author's communication.
Note: Cases of resistance are counted in the month of instigation based on court records. The odds ratio is the risk of instigation of resistance in a town (town/month) where (in which) bombing took place as a multiple of the risk in the absence of bombing.

The morale dimension of bombing led Germany into its most ambitious and costly technology project. The V-weapons programme was intended to terrify Allied populations and shore up German domestic morale. It cost Germany a share of national resources equivalent to the Manhattan Project but did the Allies little damage (O'Brien 2015: 335).

In summary, when the supply of war was attacked, the civilian economy acted as a shock absorber. Civilians were forced to adapt by making do with inferior substitutes and by making do with less; the effect was to free resources to fill gaps in war supplies. By 1944, the German household sector approached the limit of its adaptability. Nazi fears for morale restricted further resource transfers from the civilian sector. Germany ran out of capacity to absorb the hammer blows of economic warfare. The collapse of the war economy proceeded slowly at first, then rapidly over the war's last six months.

Conclusion

> There will come a time ... when the effects of economic war will begin to multiply themselves ... failure accumulates, battles are lost, wars are lost; and in that ultimate breakdown the effects of economic war will be completely merged with the phenomena of defeat. (Vickers 1943: 21–22)

Economic warfare was a central process of the war. Britain and Germany tried to strangle each economically and to pre-empt the other's attempt to do the same. Both had prepared for a repetition of World War I at sea – Germany through an extensive autarky programme before 1939; Britain by maintaining a large navy to ensure dominance on the seas. Neither was ready for the air war that came after 1939.

Germany and Britain were tough targets for economic warfare. Neither country was brought low by economic warfare alone. Economic warfare took time to implement and more time for its effects to ripple through the adversary's economy and for the adversary to run out of resources. The attrition arising from economic warfare was felt only in combination with attrition on the battlefield. Britain, with support from its American ally, was too tough a nut to crack. Germany lacked time (and its leaders lacked patience) for economic warfare against Britain to succeed; and it faced a wealthier adversary.

By contrast, British and Allied economic warfare against Germany largely succeeded. It succeeded only after much more time elapsed than was originally hoped and after the expenditure of extraordinary and unanticipated efforts to build a bomber force of thousands and to replace tens of thousands of planes and more than 100,000 aircrew lost. Precision bombing and the idea that, with the destruction of a few critical industries, war production would come to a halt turned out to be wishful thinking. Air attack had important military effects by diverting fighter strength, shell output, artillery, and manpower to the defence of the Reich – and by grinding down the German air force even before the Normandy landings, but it succeeded in economic terms only when combined with the pressures brought about by the Allied blockade and the Allied victories on the eastern front, in the Mediterranean, and in France.

Allied economic warfare against Germany aimed to weaken its war effort through the denial of resources – by destroying production or the means of production. The results of the air offensive, measured by the undermining of the German war effort, were imperceptible until the spring of 1943. They still disappointed through the summer of 1944, reducing German war production by no more than a few percentage points. They became fully effective only late in 1944 with the intensifying attacks on oil plants and on railway, bridges, and canals.

Allied economic warfare succeeded by forcing Germany to divert resources, economic and military, before the war and during it. Before the war, the fear of blockade drove Germany to bid for autarky, undertaking costly investments in domestic iron ores for steel and in synthetic oil, and rubber. Once the war began, the same fear spurred German ambitions to seize the food-surplus regions to the East. But, instead of freeing Germany from the fear of blockade, the Eastern front became a sink for German military power. Meanwhile the Combined Bomber Offensive forced Germany into a dispersal of war factories that was costly in labour and building materials and reduced the effectiveness of capital investments. At the same time, air defence of the homeland acquired higher priority than the pursuit of victory in the East.

To protect its war effort from the effects of economic warfare, German leaders shifted the costs of defence and adaptation onto the civilian sphere. While the German war effort thereby expanded for much longer than Allied planners hoped, civilian resources and reserves were depleted. German leaders understood that there was a limit to this process. The long shadows of 1918 limited the hardships that the Nazi regime felt it could impose on civilians. Civilian production stayed higher for longer to stave off the morale effects of Allied bombing. But eventually the point came where the losses, not only from economic warfare but from attacks on every front, could no longer be made good by civilian sacrifice. Now the damage rebounded back onto the war effort, which suddenly weakened and began to collapse.

References

Abelshauser, Werner. 1998. 'Germany: Guns, Butter, and Economic Miracles', in Mark Harrison (ed.), *The Economics of World War II: Six Great Powers in International Comparison*, pp. 122–176.. Cambridge: Cambridge University Press.

Adena, Maja, Ruben Enikolopov, Maria Petrova, and Hans-Joachim Voth. 2020. *Bombs, Broadcasts and Resistance: Allied Intervention and Domestic Opposition to the Nazi Regime during World War II*. CEPR Working Paper No. 15292. London: Centre for Economic Policy Research.

Baten, Jörg, and Andrea Wagner. 2002. 'Autarchy, Market Disintegration, and Health: The Mortality and Nutritional Crisis in Nazi Germany, 1933–1937', *Economics and Human Biology* 1: 1–28.

BBSU (British Bombing Survey Unit). 1998. *The Strategic Air War against Germany, 1939–1945*. Report of the British Bombing Survey Unit [declassified in 1956]. Introduction by Sebastian Cox. London: Frank Cass.

Biddle, Tami Davis. 2015. 'Anglo-American Strategic Bombing, 1940–1945', in John Ferris and Evan Mawdsley (eds.), *The Cambridge History of the Second World War*, vol. 1, pp. 485–526.. Cambridge: Cambridge University Press.

Bollard, Alan. 2019. *Economists at War: How a Handful of Economists Helped Win and Lose the World Wars*. Oxford: Oxford University Press.

Buchheim, Christoph. 2010. 'Der Mythos vom "Wohlleben": Der Lebensstandard der deutschen Zivilbevölkerung im Zweiten Weltkrieg', *Vierteljahrshefte für Zeitgeschichte* 58(3): 299–328.

CSO (Central Statistical Office). 1995. *Fighting with Figures: A Statistical Digest of the Second World War*. Edited by Peter Howlett. London: Central Statistical Office.

Collingham, Lizzie. 2011. *The Taste of War: World War Two and the Battle for Food*. London: Allen Lane.

Dallin, Alexander. 1957. *German Rule in Russia, 1941–1945: A Study of Occupation Policies*. London: Macmillan.

Davis, Lance E., and Stanley L. Engerman. 2006. *Naval Blockades in Peace and War. An Economic History since 1750*. Cambridge: Cambridge University Press.

Edgerton, David. 2006. *Warfare State: Britain, 1920–1970*. Cambridge: Cambridge University Press.

Fremdling, Rainer, and Reiner Staeglin. 2014. 'Output, National Income, and Expenditure: An Input–Output Table of Germany in 1936', *European Review of Economic History* 18(4): 371–397.

Gebhardt, Susan E., and Robin G. Thomas. 2002. Nutritive Value of Foods. U.S. Department of Agriculture, Agricultural Research Service, Home and Garden Bulletin 72.

Golson, Eric. 2016. 'Neutrals at War', in Jari Eloranta, Eric Golson, Andrei Markevich, and Nikolaus Wolf (eds.), *Economic History of Warfare and State Formation*, pp. 259–278. Singapore: Springer.

Hammond, R. J. 1951. *Food*, vol. 1. *The Growth of Policy. History of the Second World War: United Kingdom Civil Series*. London: HMSO.

Hancock, W. K., and M. M. Gowing. 1949. *British War Economy. History of the Second World War: United Kingdom Civil Series*. London: HMSO.

Harrison, Mark. 1990. 'A Volume Index of the Total Munitions Output of the United Kingdom, 1939–1944', Economic History Review 43(2): 659–668.

1996. *Accounting for War: Soviet Production, Employment, and the Defence Burden, 1940–1945*. Cambridge: Cambridge University Press.

2025. 'Economic Warfare and the Battlefield on the Eastern Front, 1941–1945', in Ralf Futselaar, Els Jacobs, and Ben Wubs (eds.), *We Moeten Door, We Willen Door. Festchrift voor Hein A. M. Klemann*, pp. 29–38. Leiden: Sidestone Press.

Hastings, Max. 2000. *Das Reich: The March of the 2nd Panzer Division through France, 1944*. London: Pan Books.

Hornby, William. 1958. *Factories and Plant: History of the Second World War: United Kingdom Civil Series*. London: HMSO.

Karlbom, Rolf. 1965. 'Sweden's Iron Ore Exports to Germany 1933–1944', *Scandinavian Economic History Review* 13: 65–93.

Klein, Burton H. 1959. *Germany's Economic Preparations for War*. Cambridge, MA: Harvard University Press.

Klemann, Hein, and Sergei Kudryashov. 2012. *Occupied Economies: An Economic History of Nazi-Occupied Europe, 1939–1945*. London: Berg.

LCES (London and Cambridge Economic Service). 1970. *The British Economy: Key Statistics, 1900–1970*. London: Times Newspapers.

Mackay, Robert. 2003. *Half the Battle: Civilian Morale in Britain during the Second World War*. Manchester: Manchester University Press.

Medlicott, W. N. 1952, 1959. *The Economic Blockade*, vols. 1–2. *History of the Second World War: United Kingdom Civil Series*. London: HMSO.

Mierzejewski, Alfred C. 1988. *The Collapse of the German War Economy, 1944–45*. Chapel Hill: University of North Carolina Press.

Milward, Alan S. 1967. 'Could Sweden Have Stopped the Second World War?', *Scandinavian Economic History Review* 15: 127–138.

1977. *War, Economy, and Society, 1939–1945*. London: Allen Lane.

O'Brien, Phillips P. 2015. *How the War was Won: Air-Sea Power and Allied Victory in World War II*. Cambridge: Cambridge University Press.

Olson, Mançur. 1962. 'The Economics of Target Selection for the Combined Bomber Offensive', *Royal United Services Institution Journal* 107(628): 308–314.

1963. *The Economics of the Wartime Shortage: A History of British Food Supplies in the Napoleonic War and in World Wars I and II*. Durham, NC: Duke University Press.

Overy, Richard. 1980. *The Air War, 1939–1945*. London: Europa.

1994. *War and Economy in the Third Reich*. Oxford: Clarendon Press.

2014. *The Bombing War: Europe, 1939–1945*. London: Penguin.

Pardini, Albert L. 1999. *The Legendary Norden Bombsight*. Atglen, PA: Schiffer Publishing.

Richards, D. 1953. *The Royal Air Force, 1939–1945, Volume 1. The Fight at Odds*. London: HMSO.

Salmon, Patrick. 1981. 'British Plans for Economic Warfare against Germany 1937–1939: The Problem of Swedish Iron Ore', *Journal of Contemporary History* 16(1): 53–72.

Scherner, Jonas. 2010. 'Nazi Germany's Preparation for War: Evidence from Revised Industrial Investment Series', *European Review of Economic History* 14(3): 433–468.

2012. 'Der deutsche Importboom während des Zweiten Weltkriegs. Neue Ergebnisse zur Struktur der Ausbeutung des besetzten Europas auf der Grundlage einer Neuschätzung der deutschen Handelsbilanz', *Historische Zeitschrift* 294(1): 79–113.

2013. '"Armament in Depth" or "Armament in Breadth"? German Investment Pattern and Rearmament during the Nazi Period', *Economic History Review* 66(2): 395–691.

2022. 'Incompetence or Ingenuity? Why Did Nazi Germany Not Seek Closer Wartime Economic Cooperation with Italy?', *Journal of Contemporary History* 57(3): 553–576.

2024. 'Germany, Blockade and Strategic Raw Materials in the Era of the Two World Wars', *International History Review* 46(4): 515–534.

Scherner, Jonas, and Jochen Streb. 2016. 'The Mirage of the German Economic Miracle in World War II', in Jari Eloranta, Eric Golson, Andrei Markevich, and Nikolaus Wolf (eds.), *Economic History of Warfare and State Formation*, pp. 243–258. Singapore: Springer.
Süss, Winfried. 2003. *Der 'Volkskörper' im Krieg*. München: R. Oldenbourg Verlag.
Todman, Daniel. 2016–2020. *Britain's War*: vol. 1 (2016), *Into Battle, 1937–1941*; vol. 2 (2020), *A New World, 1942–1947*. London: Allen Lane.
Titmuss, R. M. 1950. *Problems of Social Policy*. History of the Second World War: United Kingdom Civil Series. London, HMSO.
Tooze, Adam. 2007. *The Wages of Destruction: The Making and Breaking of the Nazi Economy*. London: Penguin Books.
Toprani, Anand. 2019. *Oil and the Great Powers: Britain and Germany, 1914–1945*. Oxford: Oxford University Press.
USSBS (US Strategic Bombing Survey). 1945a. Summary Report (European War), Washington, DC.
  1945b. *The Effects of Strategic Bombing on the German War Economy*. Overall Economic Effects Division, Washington, DC.
Vickers, C. G. 1943. 'Economic Warfare', *Royal United Services Institution Journal* 88(549): 14–22.
Von der Porten, Edward. 1969. *The German Navy at War*. New York: Thomas Crowell.
Vonyó, Tamás. 2012. 'The Bombing of Germany: The Economic Geography of War-induced Dislocation in West German Industry', *European Review of Economic History* 16(1): 97–118.
Webster, Charles, and Noble Frankland. 1961. *The Strategic Air Offensive Against Germany, 1939–1945, vols 1–4*. History of the Second World War: Military Series. London: HMSO.

7 No Trading with the Enemy
COCOM Commemorated

Vincent Geloso and Albrecht Ritschl

The end of World War II brought forth the beginning of the Cold War and a new type of economic sanctions. Where classical blockades tended to emphasise the importance of blocking the entry of goods (Crouzet 1964; Davis and Engerman 2006; Brauer and Van Tuyll 2008), attempts to restrict trade in the Cold War were also meant to prevent the acquisition of technological/industrial secrets that communist countries could use. These restrictions were heavily motivated by fears – which are well exemplified in Cold War era popular works such as Werner Keller's *East Minus West Equals Zero* (1962) or Jacques Bergier's *Secret Armies* (1975) – that those technologies with dual (civil and military) uses (such as nuclear technologies) could end up being used by Soviet-bloc nations to attack the West and its allies. The same fear is invoked today regarding China's intensive efforts to steal microchip technology in order to improve its military might relative to the West.

This fear was novel after World War II and it explains embargoes such as the Coordinating Committee for Multilateral Export Controls (COCOM) which began in 1949. COCOM was a shared sovereignty arrangement between nations where members (fifteen Western nations) could vote down exports of dual-use technologies by a member nation to a list of proscribed countries. These were then interlaced with the imperative to impose political pressure upon certain regimes. For example, industrial espionage was seen as one of the main ways the Soviet bloc was able to maintain itself economically for so long. Thus, preventing industrial espionage was an indirect way to keep the pressure up on the USSR.

Alongside fears of industrial espionage, the rise of communism also motivated the use of economic sanctions to promote regime change. This involved traditional policy tools such as embargoes on flows of goods to certain countries and limitations of worker mobility (so as to prevent the flows of certain services). This is most obviously the case with Cuba, which was embargoed by the United States following the accession to power of the Castro family.

In this chapter, we discuss conceptual issues surrounding COCOM and review existing evidence on economic sanctions during the Cold War. In examining the effects of the various measures imposed on Soviet-type command economies, we exploit the variation between the more industrialised economies of Eastern Europe and the more agricultural economy of Cuba. Regardless of specialisation, all the countries under Soviet influence had mobilisation economies – that is, they mobilised output in the short term at the expense of productivity growth in the long term. In that sense the institutional structure of the Soviet-type command system was self-sanctioning. Any adverse effect of external sanctions was additional to this. In the cases of Eastern Europe, we will show that a further constraint on productivity growth was the COCOM barrier to the import of technically advanced capital goods for use in industrial production. The Cuban case was different because industrial production did not make up a substantial element of Cuba's economy. Because of this, COCOM sanctions did not substantially damage Cuban aggregate productivity growth, which was held back largely by Cuba's own institutions. But Cuba was additionally damaged by the US embargo on Cuban exports, which limited access to dollars and reduced Cuban living standards.

The order of our discussion is as follows. First, we look into the importance of industrial espionage. There is evidence that it mattered (Glitz and Meyersson 2020), though perhaps not very much. We also point to evidence that claims of the extent of Soviet espionage were overblown and that incentive structures in the Soviet Union and its allies limited the ability to adapt Western technologies to their own economies (Boettke 2001).

Second, we review whether COCOM had the impact desired and any unforeseen consequences. When COCOM was imposed, the European economies were still reeling from the economic consequences of World War II, and productivity levels remained far below historical highs. This was compounded by the forced transition of Eastern Europe to collectivisation, which coincided with the breakdown of security cooperation between the former World War II allies. Low data reliability in communist economies, notably the over-reporting of investment and output, further complicates the analysis. We review efforts to correct the data and explore possible channels through which COCOM effects were transmitted. This includes evidence on the immediate aftermath of the transition to and the abandonment of state economic planning. While COCOM did matter, the evidence overwhelmingly suggests that it was socialism itself, not Western sanctions, that drove the poor economic performance of Eastern Europe at the time.

Third, we review the more classical case of the Cuban embargo imposed by the United States. We find strong evidence that it was a negative factor for Cuban living standards. However, all the available evidence points to the embargo having very small effects on output. On its own, the embargo is unable to explain much of Cuba's economic evolution since 1959. This is especially true when compared with counterfactual scenarios built on synthetic control methods to estimate the income path of Cuba absent the Castro regime (Ward and Devereux 2012; Jales et al. 2018; Devereux 2021). At best, it explains a minor part of why Cuba has stagnated economically since 1959. We also indicate that the blockade had trivial effects on non-economic outcomes such as infant mortality or life expectancy (Berdine, Geloso, and Powell 2018; Geloso and Pavlik 2021). Moreover, its effects on Cuban living standards were long compensated for by Soviet aid such that the net effects of economic sanctions were even smaller. We argue that these seemingly paradoxical results can be readily explained from an input variety perspective.

Overall, we conclude that – for the Cold War – economic sanctions had few visible political effects (positive or negative) but more visible economic consequences.

Conceptualising COCOM: Lessons of Endogenous Growth

Cold War embargoes on sensitive goods operated to inhibit technology transfers and disrupt intra-industry supply chains. In the world assumed by standard models of trade and growth, all would have access to the same technology. In that case, the effects of blocking access to Western goods could be perverse. Assuming the exporter had a comparative advantage in the sanctioned goods, the frustrated importer would have an incentive to substitute domestic production for the imports denied. Scale and learning effects could sustain such import substitution industries even after the embargoes were removed. A historical example documented by Juhasz (2018) is the rise of infant industries in France under British blockade during the Napoleonic Wars of the early nineteenth century.

Modern growth theory provides an alternative toolkit. The key is to think of manufactured outputs and capital goods as input varieties. Sanctions may affect (a) the scope of the varieties, (b) the technologies embodied in the varieties, and (c) the human capital levels connected to physical capital through capital/skill complementarities.

(a) COCOM under Smithian Growth: Curtailing Variety

Consider an economy whose main source of economic growth is an increase in product and intermediate input variety, where the total number of available varieties grows over time. New varieties may or may not in themselves be more productive than existing ones. Productivity growth is instead due to the addition of further input varieties causing increased Smithian specialisation in production (for further reading see Aghion and Howitt 2008: chapter 3).

In this Smithian growth scenario, COCOM sanctions affect production in two ways. One is to limit or deny access to certain varieties, locking the economy into producing the remaining available varieties, irrespective of whether these are particularly productive or not. In fact, eliminating any of the remaining varieties would lower output even further. Unless the sanctioned economy can successfully embark on import substitution industrialisation, it is caught in a low-level equilibrium trap where the use of old technologies may perpetuate itself.

A second effect works through Smithian economies of scope: excluding some input varieties from production may make other lines of production less productive as well. A knock-on effect of lowered productivity in manufacturing under COCOM sanctions is a slowdown in the transition of labour from agriculture into industry.

(b) COCOM under Schumpeterian Growth: Sanctioning an Economy into Technological Obsolescence

Again think of an economy with well-established intermediate input chains. Under Schumpeterian growth, creative destruction is the dominant channel of economic growth. New and more productive methods and varieties are created constantly, driving out obsolete ones (Aghion and Howitt 2008: chapter 4).

Denying cutting-edge technology through sanctions reverses this effect and may gradually push the sanctioned economy into technological obsolescence. Two effects are at work. First, reductions in the number of varieties may create negative scale and scope effects as before. The second channel is through capital productivity. An economy bereft of Schumpeterian creative destruction will miss out on modern, high-productivity varieties. This reduces output relative to free trade even if production exhibits constant returns to scale and there is no endogenous growth.

(c)   Capital/Skills Complementarities: Locking Workers into Obsolete Skills

Capital/skills complementarities open a closely related channel for COCOM effects. Different generations of equipment may require specialists with different vintage-specific skills. Not having access to more modern technologies implies that parts of the labour force will need to be trained to operate obsolete equipment. As a consequence, not just physical capital but also human capital becomes obsolete.

East Germany's Stasi and the Role of TFP: Industrial Espionage

Industrial espionage by the Soviets started well before World War II (Sibley 1999).[1] In fact, it started in the 1920s, immediately after the final victory of the Soviets against the remaining tsarist forces (Murphy 2021) when 'intelligence centres' were 'concealed in embassies, consulates, and trade missions' in major European cities (Murphy 2021: 45). During the 1930s, 'thousands of Soviet engineers, technicians, and other specialists spent months in many of America's industrial plants' (Sibley 1999: 95). Priority was given to technologies with 'military applications'. By the late 1930s, fears of industrial espionage entered political discussion, and the later defection of Soviet agents and spies such as Igor Gouzenko and Whittaker Chambers further heightened perceptions of danger from industrial espionage (Parrish 2001; Murphy 2021; Sibley 1999, 2003). Numerous government agencies began to fear that the Soviet Union was using spies to collect information not only about military technologies but also about 'assorted industrial formulae and techniques such as the processes for making synthetic rubber and producing film' (Sibley 2003: 24).

We can break these fears into two categories. The first is well represented by the work of Werner Keller's *East Minus West* (1962). Keller argued that Russia – well before it became the USSR – owed all its achievements to advances in the Western world. Given the ideological fear that the USSR caused, this argument had the logical implication that without spying or wilful transfers of technology, the USSR could not win the Cold War. In this sense, industrial espionage was a danger to the

---

[1] Industrial espionage is nothing new. Before the nineteenth century, the focus was often on key industries (e.g. textiles, steam engines) with the fear that artisans from those industries would share knowledge. Guild regulations, barriers to entry, and monopoly privileges were tools to prevent this sharing (see Robinson 1974; Miller 1999; Bertucci 2013).

West in that it would allow the USSR to overtake the United States economically. Economists would be most familiar with this claim from the well-known story of how Paul Samuelson's *Principles of Economics* contained a graphic of Soviet GDP per capita and when it was supposed to overtake that of the United States (Levy and Peart 2011).

The second can be well illustrated by Warren Nutter (1962). He reiterated the idea that that Soviet industrial capacity was in part due to 'wartime contact with the West and acquisition of Western goods' (Nutter 1962: 6).[2] In contrast to Samuelson, Nutter argued that Soviet economic growth and industrial capabilities were overstated. The fear was more about the military threat posed by the theft of technology that could be used against the United States. Proponents of this view believed there were no ways for the USSR to ever overtake the West economically. Nutter (then professor of economics at the University of Virginia) later became assistant secretary of defence in the Nixon administration.[3] His views on how the Soviet Union maintained itself through stealing Western technologies appear to have motivated Nutter's policy proposals.[4]

Unfortunately, little effort has been made to determine whether, after stealing or being given a technology, the Soviets were actually able to use it in a productive manner. More importantly, it is worth pointing out that fears like those of Keller (1962) are not about espionage *exclusively*. They are about the wilful transfer of technologies and ideas *and* industrial espionage.[5] Few systematic efforts were made to disentangle the two and to assess the economic importance of espionage by itself.

First, copying an idea or stealing a trade secret is conceptually different than being able to use them. This goes back to the economic critique of planning raised by Ludwig von Mises ([1920] 2012).[6] Mises distinguished 'technical' knowledge from 'economic knowledge'. Technical knowledge speaks to questions such as 'what material can we use to build

---

[2] See also Nutter (2019), first published in 1969. Other scholars also pointed to the heavy reliance on Western technologies by the Soviet Union (e.g. Dalrymple 1966 regarding agriculture).

[3] He had earlier been the chief of the Economic Capabilities Branch of the CIA's Office of Research and Reports

[4] There is little work on Nutter, who used to be a fixture of the Virginia School of Economics alongside future Nobel laureates James Buchanan and Ronald Coase and other influential economists like Gordon Tullock and Leland Yeager. Kuehn (2021) has written on Nutter's views regarding backing a coup in Chile after Salvador Allende's seizure of power but the work leaves many questions undiscussed. With regard to copying, see the contemporary work of Mallan (1959).

[5] See Sokolov (1994) for a discussion regarding willing transfers such as lend–lease.

[6] See Boettke (1990) for a modern elaboration.

a railway?' or specifically 'can we use titanium to build that railway?' Economic knowledge speaks to a more subtle question, 'what material should we use to build a railway?', in other words, 'what is the most economical way to do so?' In Mises, it is impossible for planners to identify the most efficient allocation of resources without price signals from markets. For this reason, acquiring Western technology does not mean that it will be deployed or used effectively. Moreover, Mises explicitly assumed – in a rhetorical exercise – that planners would be disinterested actors with no incentive misalignment with the general public. Easing that assumption only reinforces this point.[7] Mises' argument can be translated to the case of espionage by saying that acquiring the technical knowledge of a particular chemical process or a particular fabrication technique did not come with the economic knowledge about their best use. To our knowledge, no one has assessed what proportion of 'stolen' technologies was successfully adopted and employed in the USSR and thus tested whether Mises' point is empirically important.[8]

The only systematic effort that exists regarding the importance of industrial espionage is that of Glitz and Meyersson (2020) for East Germany. East Germany was widely seen as 'communism that works' and 'the communist world's high-technology leader' (Glitz and Meyersson 2020: 1059), so this sets an upper bound on the role of industrial espionage. Gathering data on close to 200,000 information receipts by the Stasi (Ministry for State Security in the German Democratic Republic), they were able to identify the sector of activity that was subjected to espionage. Merged with data about sectoral total factor productivity (TFP) by industry, they were able to determine whether variations in espionage explained variations in TFP for the different industries. In aggregate, they found that the ratio of East to West German TFP would have been 13.3 per cent smaller in the absence of industrial espionage.

At first glance, this may look like a large number. First glances are deceptive. This is a small proportion. The ratio of East German to West German TFP in 1989 is stated to be 21.8 per cent by Glitz and Meyersson (2020: 1057). Without industrial espionage, that ratio would have stood at 18.9 per cent. The difference is minuscule. To contextualise it further, all that was needed to close the gap by such a proportion

---

[7] See notably Anderson and Boettke (1993, 1997) for examples.
[8] Allen (2003) speaks of the rapid industrialisation of the USSR until 1940 but he does not discuss what share was due to industrial espionage. Nutter (1962) devoted an entire chapter to how 'forcing' the use of certain technologies to promote given industries (i.e. a particular type of industrialisation) did not tell us if the output/product mix was actually efficient. His conclusion was that it was not. This is suggestive, not definitive.

was two years of TFP growth during the reunification (i.e. post-1991) period (Burda and Hunt 2001: 22; Burda and Severgnini 2018). At the very least, these numbers suggest that industrial espionage never amounted to much in terms of allowing the USSR to match the West economically.[9]

This leaves the question of whether the USSR was able to copy technologies for military purposes. As Ingesson (2023: 817) states, attempts to study the 'results of industrial espionage' in terms of military abilities have been few. What evidence is available tends to favour the claim that it helped the USSR. The most obvious case is espionage tied to nuclear energy (see Houghton 2019). For example, Usdin (2009) used leaked materials from Soviet archives to review the infamous case of Julius Rosenberg and found that he was indeed an important collaborator with a large network that helped the USSR speed up the development of weapons of mass destruction. Ingesson (2023), as another example, studied six different Soviet aircraft systems and compared them with close Western equivalents. He deemed only one to be a near copycat, three were actually innovative, and the remaining three involved some copying of Western technologies. However, the evidence available still suggests that the effect of espionage was minimal. Moynihan (1998: 143–144) argued that the Rosenbergs' espionage sped up the development of the Soviet atomic bomb by a year at most.[10] Ingesson's evidence also suggests that the Soviets were able to develop technologies on their own, even if copying was important. This echoes Cold War contemporaries such as Lloyd Mallan (1959), who argued that, even with espionage, Soviet technological capabilities remained heavily limited and its military abilities were overstated.

Obviously, our assessment of the thin literature on the effects of espionage should not be taken as one that speaks to the effectiveness or relevance of economic sanctions. That the extent of espionage does not seem to matter a great deal does not mean that, without economic sanctions, the level would be unchanged. The small effects we just documented could be the result of the effectiveness of economic

---

[9] Above we mentioned the fear reiterated in undergraduate textbooks such as Paul Samuelson's *Principles of Economics* that the USSR would eventually overtake the United States. Levy and Peart (2011: 115) point out that with each edition of these textbooks, the proposed doomsday date was pushed back further. For example, in Samuelson's 1961 edition, the USSR was supposed to overtake the USA within 23–36 years. In the 1973 edition, it was between seventeen and thirty-five years. In the 1980 edition, it was between twenty-two and thirty-two years. This episode from the history of economic thought points in the same direction as the TFP numbers we point out above – the Soviet bloc was probably never even close to overtaking the West.

[10] Given Moynihan's political views and roles, he may have engaged in hyperbole.

sanctions. This is why the next two sections of this chapter are dedicated to the two most comprehensive forms of economic sanctions during the Cold War: COCOM and the Cuban embargo.

COCOM, Its Origins, Effectiveness, and Consequences

COCOM started officially in 1949. Efforts to switch from World War II technology transfers to the Soviet ally to a more restrictive policy began in late 1947. The political relationship between the West and the Soviets had started to sour, not the least over the political strings attached to the nascent Marshall Plan that were incompatible with a totalitarian model of society (Yasuhara 1991). Embargoes started in earnest with the Berlin blockade of 24 June 1948. Several days before, the Allied military governments had launched a unilateral currency reform in their jointly administered Trizone, the nucleus of what became the West German Federal Republic. In East Germany, the Soviet military administration responded by blocking all land access to West Berlin, which was an administrative island under Western Allied administration surrounded by Soviet-occupied East Germany. A counter-blockade by the Western Allies banned almost all cross-border trade with East Germany until the Soviet blockade was lifted in May 1949. Meanwhile, a list was drawn up of sensitive articles to be embargoed. It affected not just East Germany but the whole of the emerging communist bloc. After the passing of the US Export Control Act in 1949 and extensive secret negotiations with Western Europe's reluctant governments, an informal body named the Coordinating Committee for Multilateral Export Controls began operations in early 1950. Described as a group of mid-level diplomats and security experts, COCOM held frequent meetings in Paris to coordinate policies on embargoed items between the member governments. Leverage came initially from US financial assistance to Western Europe (Adler-Karlsson 1968). In later decades, COCOM controls oscillated between stringency and leniency depending on the temperature of US/Soviet relations. Political détente played a role in permitting large-scale exports of critical infrastructure for the East European gas and oil network of the Soviet-dominated member states of the Council for Mutual Economic Assistance (COMECON), as well as for its extension to Western Europe in the 1970s and 1980s (Henshaw 1993).

COCOM ran separate lists in the three areas of munitions and military equipment, nuclear technology, and industrial (dual-use) items. The industrial list was further subdivided into items under embargo, items under quantitative export control, and items under end-use surveillance.

The embargo list during the early 1950s was estimated to have included nearly 300 items, gradually dwindling to about 150, for which export embargoes were still upheld in the 1970s. At the same time, exceptions from the embargo could be granted, for example if the item was an essential input for a critical supply chain of non-military production whose delivery was considered politically important (e.g. Zaleski and Wienert 1980). At one point, COCOM had five different exemption procedures (Cupitt and Grillot 1997).

COCOM and the Scarring Effects of World War II

Big macroeconomic shocks may lead to persistent deviations from the previous growth path with only slow reversion to the historical steady state. This scarring effect is well documented for recent economic disruptions such as the financial crisis of 2008 or the Covid shock, where the rates of recovery to previous trends have differed markedly across countries (see e.g. Aikman et al. 2022).[11] The implementation of COCOM in the late 1940s took place in an international environment deeply scarred by World War II, with productivity still far below historical levels. Eichengreen and Ritschl (2009) document that, in Germany, TFP levels had fallen to less than a third of their historical maximum. Post-war growth rates in the economies of Europe were generally higher, the deeper the country-specific wartime shock. COCOM cannot account for these low initial productivity levels. Ritschl and Vonyo (2014) compared labour productivity as well as TFP levels and growth in both halves of post-war Germany during the early post-war period. Their principal finding is that in the immediate aftermath of World War II, Soviet-occupied East Germany had a slight initial advantage in TFP. While TFP between both halves of Germany was roughly at a par in 1948, the West German economy had visibly pulled ahead by 1950, whereas East Germany made barely any progress. Zooming in on intra-industrial trade, they argue that output and productivity losses of the East German economy were largely due to severed cross-border supply chains as well as to lost Western demand. While West German producers could draw on international, notably US supplies, East Germans had no such recourse and were either driven out of production or had to engage in costly or lower-quality import substitution. They estimate the resulting

---

[11] The seminal paper on scarring effects of recessions in recent data is Ouyang (2009), who documents persistent effects on cohort wages and attainment gaps in labour markets. Recent contributions include Huckfeldt (2022), among many others.

Table 7.1 *Real GDP per capita of four East European economies, 1950–1989 (% of West German levels)*

	1950	1960	1970	1980	1989
Czechoslovakia	79.5	58.6	52.6	50.4	47.4
Hungary	56.3	41.9	40.9	39.8	37.3
Poland	55.5	36.9	36.0	36.3	30.7
GDR	45.5	40.0	37.8	39.0	38.7
GDR (Heske)	41.6	41.1	45.2	50.9	55.2
GDR (Ritschl/Vonyo)	70.0	–	–	–	–

Sources: Maddison (2006), Heske (2013), Ritschl and Vonyo (2014); authors' calculations.

loss of labour productivity at roughly one-third, a gap that they argued may have further widened to about two-thirds by the time of reunification in 1990. Gaps in productivity vis-à-vis West Germany as the regional benchmark economy were also prevalent elsewhere in East-Central Europe (Table 7.1).

Taken from Vonyo and Klein (2019) and their underlying sources, the data clearly confirm growing productivity gaps throughout. We note the similarity between the initial gap for Czechoslovakia and the Ritschl/Vonyo (2014) estimate for East Germany, which would be consistent with the broadly similar levels of economic development of both areas prior to World War I. The sole exception is the estimate of Heske (2013) that also underlies the research of Glitz and Meyersson (2020). Not only does it start from an implausibly low initial level of East German productivity, but it also shows East Germany catching up to the West German economy. Similar concerns apply to its high 1989 endpoint estimate.

The stylised fact implicit in the beginning of COCOM and borne out by Table 7.1 is that of a substantial adverse productivity shock, followed by divergence. Under this scenario, the likely effects of trade embargoes and COCOM sanctions were strong and even increased over time. This would be at variance with standard evidence on sanctions, which suggest strong impact effects that weaken over time due to trade diversion and sanctions busting (Kohl and Klein Ressink 2019; Splinter and Klomp 2022).

COCOM Effects: Schumpeterian De-growth

The evidence gathered above is broadly consistent with constraints to Schumpeterian growth in an input variety model. Under the mechanism sketched further above, Schumpeterian growth works through inventions

(a) 1990   (b) 2022

Note: The final assembly lines in the production of East Germany's Trabant car at VEB Sachsenring, still based on U.S. vintage production equipment delivered to its precursor DKW in 1938, and on a two-stroke engine design from the early 1940s. Due to lack of steel under COCOM sanctions, the car's body was made of 'Trabiplast', a combination of synthetics and recycled cotton fibre.

Note: An ID.5 electric vehicle on an assembly line at Volkswagen in a newly erected hall on an adjacentsite, using robotized flexible production systems. See Rubin (2008) for an account of the Trabant car and of VEB Sachsenring with further references, and Broadberry and Klein (2011) on East Europe's growth lag.

Figure 7.1 Car assembly lines at the Zwickau works, East Germany
Source: (a) Richard Baker / In Pictures / Getty Images
(b) Krisztian Bocsi / Bloomberg / Getty Images

embedded in new, more productive input varieties. Denying an economy access to advanced inputs would lead to persistent divergence in productivity shock as the capital stock in the affected economies becomes technologically more and more obsolete. In the extreme, sanctions can freeze the economy and turn it into a technology museum (Figure 7.1).

The Eastern European TFP Puzzle

Delving deeper into the measurement of productivity progress in postwar Eastern Europe, a puzzle arises. The evidence collected by Glitz and Myerson (2020) suggests that Stasi espionage did little to enhance TFP, which is to say that transferring blueprints may not have been the relevant channel for technological progress or lack thereof. On the other hand, conventional wisdom on Eastern European growth has long been that TFP growth was faltering, which is seemingly in line with the evidence on labour productivity in Table 7.1.

Official data for Eastern Europe showed strong TFP growth in the 1950s and 1960s, often matching or even surpassing the figures for

Western Europe. Downward revisions of output (for East Germany, Merkel and Wahl 1991) have challenged this view, but in turn they implied very low TFP and sometimes negative TFP growth, especially for the 1980s (Ritschl 1994). Burda and Severgnini (2014) argued from simulated datasets that capital stock mismeasurement may in large part be responsible for biases in measured TFP growth. Their proposed remedies include perpetual inventory approaches to capital stock estimation. This strategy is also used by Vonyo and Klein (2019), who revised capital stock data for three Eastern European economies. According to their estimates, investment was substantially overstated in official statistics. Their principal finding is that low and declining equipment investment was an underappreciated major factor in the output decline of the Eastern bloc, whereas TFP growth declined far less dramatically than earlier research would suggest:

As Figure 7.2 shows, growth of the TFP residual calculated from the corrected capital stock data stabilised in all three economies during the 1970s and 1980s. In one case, it is even shown to have picked up. Critically, the overall trend in TFP growth from the 1960s onwards now broadly matches that of West Germany (Figure 7.3).

This brings the initial productivity differences and the reasons for subsequently low investment rates into new focus. High but falling TFP growth during the post-war period cannot itself be ascribed to COCOM. Instead, it is a symptom of a rebound from wartime disruption and of improvements in the utilisation of existing capital stock as repairs were made and networks reinstalled. This is borne out by the West German data, which show a similar fall in TFP growth, albeit from a much higher initial level. This begs the question of whether low initial levels of comparative productivity in East-Central Europe combined with lack of access to cutting-edge capital goods to create low investment. This is what early work by Nothnagel (2009) on persistent productivity shocks after World War II would suggest. In a simulated stochastic growth model, low investment emerges as a rational response to persistent low productivity after an adverse initial shock – the blanket embargo against Eastern Europe in the wake of the 1948 Berlin blockade. Calibrating the persistence of this productivity shock against data from both halves of post-World War II Germany, Nothnagel (2009) indeed finds that faster TFP recovery in West Germany is consistent with substantially higher rates of net investment there. Communist countries under the embargo were unable to import Western production technologies on a large scale. This in turn gave them good reasons not to invest too heavily in their obsolete, home-made capital goods, as the returns from these investments were too low to justify the effort.

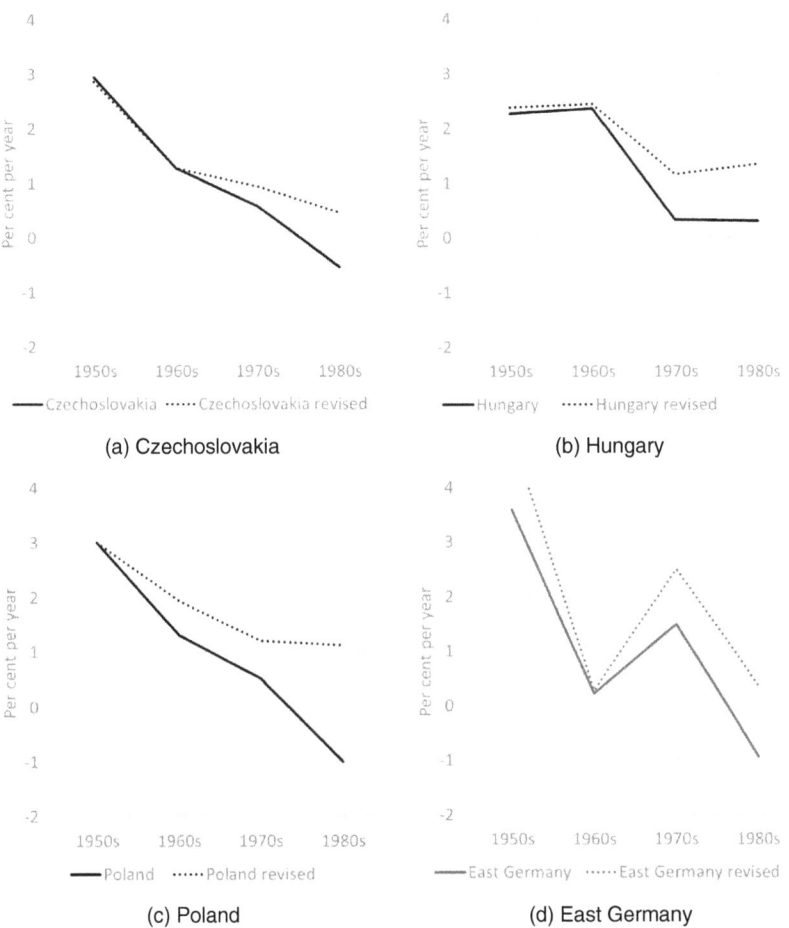

Figure 7.2 Total factor productivity growth in four East European economies: effects of revising the growth of the capital stock, 1950s–1980s
Source and notes: see text.

This is also consistent with evidence gathered and simulations produced by Kukič (2021). Employing an aggregate CES (constant elasticities of substitution) production function approach, Kukič provides evidence of substitution elasticities between capital and labour, and also of capital efficiency. If capital and labour cannot easily be substituted for each other, sanctions on capital goods have potential traction as the economy cannot easily move away from their use. Kukič indeed finds substitutability to be low (Table 7.2). He also argues that capital

Table 7.2 *Assumed capital shares and implicit elasticity of capital/labour substitution of three East European economies and West Germany*

Country	Capital share	Elasticity of capital/labour substitution
Czechoslovakia	0.4	0.1
Hungary	0.4	0.115
Poland	0.4	0.115
West Germany	0.4	0.125–0.33

Source: Kukič (2021); Henningsen, Henningsen, and Literati (2021).

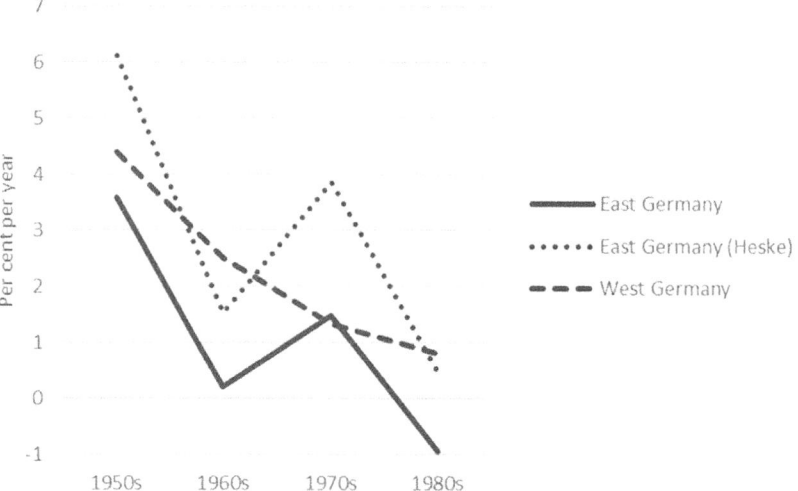

Figure 7.3 Total factor productivity growth: effects of revising the growth of the capital stock, West versus East Germany, 1950s–1980s
Source and notes: see text.

efficiency was low and declining, even with the downward-revised investment figures of Vonyo and Klein (2019).

This points to double trouble with capital and investment under socialism. On the one hand, capital goods and the Western technology they embodied were essential and not easy to replace. On the other hand, whatever capital goods were available were not allocated efficiently, accounting for much of the economic decline and exacerbating the effects of sanctions.

COCOM Effects: Smithian De-growth

If the Eastern European TFP puzzle finds its resolution in low investment instead of negative TFP growth, this points to an interpretation in terms of Smithian (de-)growth. As laid out further above, denying an economy under sanctions access to additional varieties will hamper economic growth, irrespective of whether they are more productive or not. Low economic growth then is a consequence of low investment rather than of the abnormally low TFP growth shown in Figure 7.2.

In the case of the Trabant car (Figure 7.1), political decisions were taken not to modernise models or production in spite of prototypes developed by the industry (Rubin 2008). Some of the stated reasons were ideological, a refusal to walk down the Western path towards mass consumerism. Another, more direct and pragmatic one was the lack of available resources, a sign of the low-level equilibrium trap that communist economies found themselves in.

Life after COCOM: Recovery through Embodied Technology

In this section, we review evidence by Burda and Severgnini (2018) on East Germany's productivity catch-up after 1990. The authors document that TFP grew strongly in East Germany after 1990, but not uniformly so. First, TFP growth back towards the frontier was initially strong but stalled about five years after unification. Second, they find a degree of substitutability between TFP growth and growth in the capital–labour ratio, where the latter eventually dominated. One key result of their research is that east of the former Iron Curtain, the capital–labour ratio exceeded that of the old West, while TFP levels still fell short. Applying this finding to the scenario during communism and before, this would be further evidence of productivity gains embodied in capital investment and only imperfectly reflected in TFP.

Drawing the results together, did COCOM sanctions against Eastern Europe have persistent effects? In a world where technological progress is disembodied, withholding technology should have detrimental productivity effects, irrespective of investment. While there is some evidence of such damage, it is apparently not the main channel. The dominant effect of COCOM was to deny trade in advanced production equipment that could simply have applied Western technology to production immediately upon installation. Evidence from 1948 suggests this trade effect of sanctions was strong and persistent, perhaps permanent for the duration of communist rule. Evidence from revised output and investment data suggests that communism failed to derive large benefits from the advanced technology it obtained, and that it was less than successful at import substitution policies. Evidence from after the end of communism suggests that the recovery of productivity was to a large extent driven by factory modernisation with advanced equipment, again pointing to the embodied nature of technological progress. It also implies there was not much of an effect of COCOM on industrial productivity where there was not much of an industry to be sanctioned. This will be explored in the next section.

The Cuban Embargo

The Cuban embargo has had varying objectives since its inception following Fidel Castro's accession to power. Initially, it was mostly meant as a response to the nationalisation of American-owned businesses and as a tool for containing communism. It was also meant to impose economic hardship in order to foment political change. Since the collapse of the USSR, the latter objective has been increasingly emphasised.

As the Cuban regime is still in place, it is obvious that the policy has been unsuccessful. However, there is the possibility that the embargo made the regime slightly less repressive (Lopez 1999). For example, following the collapse of the USSR, the United States enacted a tightening of the embargo in order to exert further pressure for regime change (Pickel 1998).[12] In joint response to the tightening and the collapse of the USSR, the regime responded by mildly liberalising the economy in order to prevent a strong contraction (Corralles 2004; Wilkinson 2017). The problem with this argument is that it also gives as a cause the collapse of the USSR, which cannot easily be disentangled from the embargo and its tightening. There is also the counter-claim that the embargo allowed the regime to strengthen its grip on power. Cuban officials have used the embargo as a propaganda tool to stave off discontent (Wilkinson 2017: 30).

This leaves the question of the socio-economic consequence of the embargo. On that front, there is strong evidence that claims about deleterious effects are overstated even though it is also clear that the embargo was harmful. The influential article by Garfield and Santana (1997) provides an illustration of an overstated case. It argues that the embargo imposed large health costs in terms of infant mortality. However, that work made no attempt at estimating econometrically the effects of the embargo. It simply evaluated the evolution of infant

---

[12] This included provisions to induce other countries to cooperate with the United States.

mortality after the end of the USSR (when Soviet aid vanished) and was thus unable to determine whether outcomes were affected by the embargo or by the end of Soviet aid.

More recent works – such as Geloso and Pavlik (2021) – attempted to make that econometric effort by relying on synthetic control methods. The method of synthetic control (Abadie 2021) starts by identifying a group of countries that resemble each other, except that one is treated by a shock or intervention at a point in time. Data from the pre-treatment period are used to create a composite of the untreated countries by weighting them to resemble the treated country as closely as possible. The performance of the weighted composite is then observed in the treatment period. This is the 'synthetic control'. Any difference between the performance of the treated country and of the control is interpreted as the causal effect of the treatment. Geloso and Pavlik (2021) applied this method to infant mortality in Cuba and found that the accession to power of Fidel Castro in 1959 marked the beginning of a major shortfall of Cuba's actual outcomes below the performance of the control. In fact, most of the underperformance had emerged before 1962 – when the full US embargo was enacted. The embargo appears to explain very little in terms of health outcomes. They used the same method to assess whether Soviet aid mattered and found that it too did not matter.

Jales et al. (2018) used the same method as Geloso and Pavlik but they looked at GDP per capita and export volumes instead. Their estimates suggest that the embargo did make Cubans poorer by a non-negligible proportion.

Both works point to something quite different – that Cuba largely waged economic warfare against itself. In the work of Jales et al. (2018), most of Cuba's shortfall relative to the counterfactual outcomes is assigned to the economic policies of the regime itself. Socialism and economic planning dramatically slowed down economic growth relative to the counterfactual such that Cuba was 20 per cent poorer than it could have been by the mid-1960s and close to 70 per cent poorer by the early 1990s. The embargo explains at best a third of those gaps according to Jales et al. (2018). The rest is the effect of the regime's own policies.

These proportions are probably quite conservative. Jales et al. (2018) took the Cuban regime's data at face value and did not question it. As the rising literature regarding how dictators lie about GDP statistics (Magee and Doces 2015; Martinez 2022; Alvarez, Geloso, and Scheck 2024) suggests, this was a generous move because it is bound to overstate actual performance relative to the counterfactual. Revised estimates produced by Devereux (2021) suggest that the GDP numbers used by Jales et al. (2018) are systematically greater than the true values. Feeding

Devereux's revised estimates into the calculation would thus increase the measured shortfalls compared to the counterfactual.[13] This supports the idea that perceived poverty in Cuba is the outcome of the regime's policy rather than the embargo.[14] Cuba was a rich Latin American economy by 1959 with some socio-economic indicators matching those of European economies (e.g. Italy, Austria, Spain, and Portugal) while it is now a poor Latin American economy with multiple indicators showing signs of absolute or relative regress since 1959 (Locay 2009).

Overall, the embargo against Cuba by the United States was detrimental but the extent of the damage has been overstated. That being said, any political benefits in the form of increased probability of regime transition also appear small, which makes the costs of the embargo quite large in comparison.

Concluding Remarks

Whether or not sanctions are a failure – and indeed, whether COCOM failed – is to some extent a matter of perspective. This chapter agrees with political scientists that sanctions, including COCOM, brought no measurable political gain, certainly not in the short term.

Disentangling the economic effects is more complex. The countries that provide our evidence allow us to distinguish between the more industrially developed economies of Eastern Europe and the more agricultural economy of Cuba. For an industrial economy, the first question is whether technological progress is embodied in capital goods that, if not supplied locally, must be imported and reverse-engineered by the importing country. We argue from evidence on the economic recovery of East Germany after unification that productivity progress largely came from replacing obsolete with state-of-the-art factory equipment in which technological progress was embodied. To this extent, COCOM and other sanctions on communist Eastern Europe would have worked through the trade effect: a reduction in imports of advanced capital

---

[13] A working paper by Bastos, Geloso, and Pavlik (2025) uses the Devereux data to revisit the issue and finds that the gap by the mid 1960s is far larger than in Jales et al. (2018).

[14] Geloso and Pavlik (2021) found that the regime increased infant mortality relative to the counterfactual but only from 1959 to circa 1974. Afterwards, the actual outcomes are nearly identical to those of the counterfactual. Following the revolution, the government expended considerable extra resources to the provision of health care – far in excess of most Western countries (Berdine, Geloso, and Powell 2018; Geloso, Berdine, and Powell 2020). Failing to overperform the counterfactual despite channelling far greater quantities of resources to health care suggests that performance went down. As Geloso and Pavlik (2021) find that neither Soviet aid nor the embargo had significant effects, they conclude that the regime has been largely unable to improve health outcomes.

goods. This is consistent with recent evidence on the overall meagre TFP effects of industrial espionage during the Cold War.

We also survey research on the early days of COCOM and find that the impact effect was sizeable, though not as dramatic as presented by researchers striving to paint socialist industrial policies as a successful recovery from very difficult beginnings. While those authors would argue that COCOM had little lasting effect, our research would imply that COCOM may have significantly affected the technological vintage structure of Eastern Europe's capital stock, compounding the inefficiency of the communist planning system.

COCOM would fail to have much effect on the efficiency of industry where there was little industry to start with. A side result of our discussion of Eastern Europe is that in weakly industrialised countries, Western sanctions would predominantly affect consumption patterns and living standards but not have much of an effect on TFP.

We find this result confirmed in our survey of evidence on Cuba, which was placed under strict US sanctions, without suffering much additional decline in productivity as a consequence. Clearly, to reduce productivity in an economy whose comparative advantage is in sectors other than manufacturing, sanctions on its exports might be a more effective tool.

References

Abadie, Alberto. 2021. 'Using Synthetic Controls: Feasibility, Data Requirements, and Methodological Aspects', *Journal of Economic Literature* 59(2): 391–425.

Adler-Karlsson, G. 1968. *Western Economic Warfare 1947–1967*. Stockholm: Almqvist & Wiksell.

Aghion, P., and P. W. Howitt. 2008. *The Economics of Growth*. Cambridge, MA: MIT Press.

Aikman, D., M. Drehman, M. Juselius, and X. Xing. 2022. 'The Scarring Effect of Deep Contractions', BIS Working Paper No. 1043.

Allen, Robert C. 2003. *Farm to Factory: A Reinterpretation of the Soviet Industrial Revolution*. Princeton, NJ: Princeton University Press.

Alvarez, S. P., V. Geloso, and M. Scheck. 2024. 'Revisiting the Relationship Between Economic Freedom and Development to Account for Statistical Deception by Autocratic Regimes', *European Journal of Political Economy* 85: 102577.

Anderson, G. M., and P. J. Boettke. 1993. 'Perestroika and Public Choice: The Economics of Autocratic Succession in a Rent-Seeking Society', *Public Choice* 75(2): 101–118.

1997. 'Soviet Venality: A Rent-Seeking Model of the Communist State', *Public Choice* 93(1–2): 37–53.

Bastos, J., V. Geloso, and J. Bologna Pavlik. 2025. 'The Forsaken Road: Reassessing Living Standards Following the Cuban Revolution and the American Embargo', *SSRN Discussion Paper* 5235912.
Berdine, G., V. Geloso, and B. Powell. 2018. 'Cuban Longevity and Infant Mortality: Health Care or Repression?', *Health Policy and Planning* 33(6): 755–757.
Bergier, J. 1975. *Secret Armies: The Growth of Corporate and Industrial Espionage*. Indiananpolis: Bobbs-Merrill.
Bertucci, P. 2013. 'Enlightened Secrets: Silk, Intelligent Travel, and Industrial Espionage in Eighteenth-Century France', *Technology and Culture* 54(4): 820–852.
Boettke, P. J. 1990. *The Political Economy of Soviet Socialism: The Formative Years, 1918–1928*. Boston: Kluwer Academic.
   2001. *Calculation and Coordination: Essays on Socialism and Transitional Political Economy*. London: Routledge.
Brauer, J., and H. Van Tuyll. 2008. *Castles, Battles, and Bombs: How Economics Explains Military History*. Chicago: University of Chicago Press.
Broadberry, S. and A. Klein. 2011. 'When and Why Did Eastern European Economies Begin to Fail? Lessons from a Czechoslovak/UK Productivity Comparison, 1921–1991', *Explorations in Economic History* 48(1): 37–52.
Burda, M. C., and J. Hunt. 2001. 'From Reunification to Economic Integration: Productivity and the Labor Market in Eastern Germany', *Brookings Papers on Economic Activity* 2001(2): 1–92.
Burda, M. C., and B. Severgnini. 2014. 'Solow Residuals without Capital Stocks', *Journal of Development Economics* 109: 154–171.
   2018. 'Total Factor Productivity Convergence in German States since Reunification: Evidence and Explanations', *Journal of Comparative Economics* 46(1): 192–211.
Corrales, J. 2004. 'The Gatekeeper State: Limited Economic Reforms and Regime Survival in Cuba, 1989–2002', *Latin American Research Review* 39(2): 35–65.
Crouzet, F. 1964. 'Wars, Blockade, and Economic Change in Europe, 1792–1815', *Journal of Economic History* 24(4): 567–588.
Cupitt, R., and S. Grillot. 1997. 'COCOM Is Dead, Long Live COCOM: Persistence and Change in Multilateral Security Institutions', *British Journal of Political Science* 27(3): 361–389.
Dalrymple, D. G. 1966. 'American Technology and Soviet Agricultural Development, 1924–1933', *Agricultural History* 40(3): 187–206.
Davis, L. E., and S. L. Engerman. 2006. *Naval Blockades in Peace and War: An Economic History since 1750*. Cambridge: Cambridge University Press.
Devereux, J. 2021. 'The Absolution of History: Cuban Living Standards after 60 Years of Revolutionary Rule', *Revista de Historia Economica – Journal of Iberian and Latin American Economic History* 39(1):, 5–36.
Eichengreen, B., and A. Ritschl. 2009. 'Understanding West German Economic Growth in the 1950s', *Cliometrica* 3: 191–219.
Garfield, R., and S. Santana. 1997. 'The Impact of the Economic Crisis and the US Embargo on Health in Cuba', *American Journal of Public Health* 87(1): 15–20.

Geloso, V., G. Berdine, and B. Powell. 2020. 'Making Sense of Dictatorships and Health Outcomes', *BMJ Global Health* 5(5): e002542.

Geloso, V., and J. B. Pavlik. 2021. 'The Cuban Revolution and Infant Mortality: A Synthetic Control Approach', *Explorations in Economic History* 80: 101376.

Glitz, A., and E. Meyersson. 2020. 'Industrial Espionage and Productivity', *American Economic Review* 110(4): 1055–1103.

Henningsen, A., G. Henningsen, and G. Literati. 2021. 'Econometric Estimation of the Constant Elasticity of Substitution Function in R: Package micEconCES', in N. Hashimzade and M. Thornton (eds.), *Handbook of Research Methods and Applications in Empirical Microeconomics*, pp. 596–640. Cheltenham: Elgar.

Henshaw, J. 1993. *The Origins of COCOM: Lessons for Contemporary Proliferation Controls Regimes*. Report No. 7, Henry Stimpson Center, Washington DC.

Heske, G. 2013. 'Wertschöpfung, Erwerbstätigkeit und Investitionen in der Industrie Ostdeutschlands, 1950–2000: Daten, Methoden, Vergleiche', *Historical Social Research* 38(4): 14–254.

Houghton, V. 2019. *The Nuclear Spies: America's Atomic Intelligence Operation Against Hitler and Stalin*. Ithaca, NY: Cornell University Press.

Huckfeldt, C. 2022. 'Understanding the Scarring Effect of Recessions', *American Economic Review* 112(4): 1273–1310.

Ingesson, T. 2023. 'Innovators, Copycats, or Pragmatists? Soviet Industrial Espionage and Innovation in the Military Aerospace Sector during the Cold War', *International Journal of Intelligence and CounterIntelligence* 36(3): 816–846.

Jales, H., T. H. Kang, G. Stein, and F. Garcia Ribeiro. 2018. 'Measuring the Role of the 1959 Revolution on Cuba's Economic Performance', *The World Economy* 41(8): 2243–2274.

Juhasz, R. 2018. 'Temporary Protection and Technology Adoption: Evidence from the Napoleonic Blockade', *American Economic Review* 108(11): 3339–3376.

Keller, W. 1962. *East Minus West Equals Zero: Russia's Debt to the Western World, 1862–1962*. New York: Putnam.

Kohl, T., and C. Klein Reesink. 2019. 'Sticks and Stones: Sanction Threats, Impositions, and Their Effect on International Trade', in T. Besedeš and V. Nitsch (eds.), *Disrupted Economic Relationships: Disasters, Sanctions, Dissolutions*, pp. 103–130. (CESifo Seminar Series). Cambridge, MA: MIT Press.

Kuehn, D. 2021. '"We Can Get a Coup": Warren Nutter and the Overthrow of Salvador Allende', *Research in the History of Economic Thought and Methodology* 39: 151–186.

Kukič, L. 2021. 'The Nature of Technological Failure: Patterns of Biased Technical Change in Socialist Europe', *Journal of Economic Surveys* 35(3): 895–925.

Levy, D. M., and S. J. Peart. 2011. 'Soviet Growth and American Textbooks: An Endogenous Past', *Journal of Economic Behavior and Organization* 78(1–2): 110–125.

Locay, L. 2009. 'Cuban Socioeconomic Indicators before the Revolution: An International Comparison', *Cuba in Transition* 19: 146–152.

López, J. J. 1999. 'Implications of the US Economic Embargo for a Political Transition in Cuba', *Cuban Studies* 28: 40–69.

Maddison, A. 2006. *The World Economy: Volume 1: A Millennial Perspective, Vol 2: Historical Statistics*. Paris: OECD.

Maddison, A., and T. P. Alton. 2011. 'The German Democratic Republic's Gross Domestic Product Development between 1950 and 1989', GESIS Data Archive, Cologne. ZA8387 Data file Version 1.0.0. https://doi.org/10.4232/1.10251.

Magee, C. S., and J. A. Doces. 2015. 'Reconsidering Regime Type and Growth: Lies, Dictatorships, and Statistics', *International Studies Quarterly* 59(2): 223–237.

Mallan, L. 1959. *Russia and the Big Red Lie: Exposes the Hoax of Soviet Supremacy in Missiles, Air Power, Space Medicine, Science*. New York: Fawcett Publications.

Martinez, L. R. 2022. 'How Much Should We Trust the Dictator's GDP Growth Estimates?', *Journal of Political Economy* 130(10): 2731–2769.

Merkel, W., and S. Wahl. 1991. *Das geplünderte Deutschland. Die wirtschaftliche Entwicklung im östlichen Teil Deutschlands von 1949 bis 1989*. Bonn: Institut für Wirtschaft und Gesellschaft.

Miller, L. E. 1999. 'Innovation and Industrial Espionage in Eighteenth-Century France: An Investigation of the Selling of Silks through Samples', *Journal of Design History* 12(3): 271–292.

Mises, L. von ([1920] 2012). *Economic Calculation in the Socialist Commonwealth*. Auburn, AL: Mises Institute.

Moynihan, D. P. 1998. *Secrecy: The American Experience*. New Haven, CT: Yale University Press.

Murphy, W. T. 2021. 'First Decade of Soviet Espionage in America: 1924 to 1933', *International Journal of Intelligence and CounterIntelligence* 34(1): 45–69.

Nothnagel, I. 2009. 'Westeuropas wirtschaftliche Entwicklung zwischen dem Ende des Zweiten Weltkrieges und der Ölkrise im neoklassischen Wachstumsmodell', PhD Diss., Humboldt University of Berlin.

Nutter, G. W. 1962. *The Growth of Industrial Production in the Soviet Union*. Princeton, NJ: Princeton University Press.

  2019. *The Strange World of Ivan Ivanov*. Edited and introduced by Phillip W. Magness. Great Barrington, MA: American Institute for Economic Research.

Ouyang, M. 2009. 'The Scarring Effect of Recessions', *Journal of Monetary Economics* 56(2): 184–199.

Parrish, M. E. 2001. 'Soviet Espionage and the Cold War', *Diplomatic History* 25(1): 105–120.

Pickel, A. 1998. 'Is Cuba Different? Regime Stability, Social Change, and the Problem of Reform Strategy', *Communist and Post-communist Studies* 31(1): 75–90.

Ritschl, A. 1994. 'An Exercise in Futility: East German Economic Growth and Decline, 1945–89', in N. Crafts and G. Toniolo (eds.), *Economic Growth in Postwar Europe*, pp. 498–540. Cambridge: Cambridge University Press/CEPR.

Ritschl, A., and T. Vonyo. 2014. 'The Roots of Economic Failure: What Explains East Germany's Falling Behind between 1945 and 1950?', *European Review of Economic History* 18: 166–184.

Robinson, E. H. 1974. 'The Early Diffusion of Steam Power', *Journal of Economic History* 34(1): 91–107.

Rubin, E. 2008. 'The Trabant: Consumption, Eigen-Sinn, and Movement', *History Workshop Journal* 68(1): 27–44.

Sibley, K. A. 1999. 'Soviet Industrial Espionage against American Military Technology and the US Response, 1930–1945', *Intelligence and National Security* 14(2): 94–123.

  2003. 'Soviet Military-Industrial Espionage in the United States and the Emergence of an Espionage Paradigm in US–Soviet Relations, 1941–45', *American Communist History* 2(1): 21–51.

Sokolov, B. V. 1994. 'The Role of Lend–Lease in Soviet Military Efforts, 1941–1945', *Journal of Slavic Military Studies* 7(3): 567–586.

Splinter, M., and J. Klomp. 2022. 'Do Sanctions Cause Economic Growth Collapses?', in R. Beeres, R. Bertrand, J. Klomp, J. Timmermans, and J. Voetelink (eds.), *NL ARMS Netherlands Annual Review of Military Studies 2021*, pp. 115–131. The Hague: NL ARMS. T. M. C. Asser Press.

Usdin, S. T. 2009. 'The Rosenberg Ring Revealed: Industrial-Scale Conventional and Nuclear Espionage', *Journal of Cold War Studies* 11(3): 91–143.

Vonyo, T. 2016. 'War and Socialism: Why Eastern Europe Fell Behind between 1950 and 1989', *Economic History Review* 70(1): 248–274.

Vonyo, T. and A. Klein. 2019. 'Why Did Socialist Economies Fail? The Role of Factor Inputs Reconsidered', *Economic History Review* 72(1): 317–345.

Yasuhara, Y. 1991. 'The Myth of Free Trade: The Origins of COCOM 1945–1950', *Japanese Journal of American Studies* 4: 127–148.

Ward, M., and J. Devereux. 2012. 'The Road Not Taken: Pre-revolutionary Cuban Living Standards in Comparative Perspective', *Journal of Economic History* 72(1): 104–132.

Wilkinson, S. 2017. 'A Perfect Impasse? Cuba's Move Towards the Market and the United States' Move Towards Cuba', *Economic Affairs* 37: 19–35.

Zaleski, E. and H. Wienert, eds. 1980. *Technology Transfer between East and West*. Paris: Organisation for Economic Co-operation and Development.

8 From Condemnation to Action?
United Nations Sanctions on Rhodesia and South Africa

Leigh A. Gardner and Martine Mariotti

Introduction

In 1994, the year Nelson Mandela was sworn in as the president of a newly democratic South Africa, the United Nations published an account of its contributions to the global campaign against apartheid. Boutros Boutros-Ghali, then the UN Secretary-General, wrote in the introduction that 'the struggle against apartheid extended far beyond South Africa's borders, and was one that helped to define the role that the United Nations could play in resolving seemingly intractable issues'. He admitted, however, that this process of definition had its challenges.

> While the abhorrence of apartheid became universal, it took many years of patient and persistent efforts by the United Nations to build a consensus among Member States on the desirability of going beyond mere condemnation to action, and to secure agreement on measures and to assist the oppressed people in their legitimate struggle to force the South African government to desist from its disastrous course. (United Nations 1994: 4)

The primary action available to the UN in its campaign against apartheid was the adoption of economic sanctions. Losman (1979: 1) defines economic sanctions as 'penalties inflicted upon one or more states by one or more others, generally, to coerce the target nation(s) to comply with certain norms that the boycott initiators deem proper or necessary'. This notion of boycotting distinguishes sanctions from earlier methods of modern economic warfare intended to undermine the coercive capacity of an adversary. Modern sanctions can include a range of measures, from restrictions on trade and investment, migration, the withdrawal of diplomatic recognition and even the boycotting of sports and cultural events (Davis and Engerman 2003: 187). Over the course of the twentieth century, sanctions have become a permanent part of the toolkit of international relations, and their use has accelerated rapidly since the middle of the century. In the rhetoric adopted by the UN and other international organisations, coordinated economic pressure was intended to replace armed conflict – acting as an 'antidote to war itself'. Over the course of that period, however, there have been substantial changes in the aims, scope, and implementation of economic sanctions which have generated fierce debates about whether and how sanctions can generate political change while also preventing bloodshed (Jones 2015; Jentleson 2022; Mulder 2022).

The UN's campaign against white minority regimes in Africa was not confined to the anti-apartheid struggle. Its initial interventions in Africa came primarily through the Trusteeship Council established to monitor the governance of the former League of Nations mandate territories, which became trust territories of the UN after World War II. Though there were only seven such territories, their management offered the UN the opportunity to scrutinise – and often criticise – the policies of European colonisers (McKay 1963: 37). Over the course of the 1950s and 1960s, the growing share of former colonies among UN members prompted an expansion of its remit to other dependent territories through the creation of entities like the Committee on Information from Non-Self-Governing Territories, which was intended to provide an outlet similar to the Trusteeship Committee for colonised territories without Trustee status. Beyond South Africa, other white minority regimes also became the target for UN condemnation and, at least sometimes, action. This included Southern Rhodesia following its unilateral Declaration of Independence in 1965, as well as pressure on Portugal to grant independence to its colonies (Cooper 2019: chapter 6).

Central to these efforts were fierce debates about the extent to which the UN should try to influence the internal politics of member countries, or those of their colonies. Where did sovereignty end and international cooperation begin? In addition, there was little agreement on how the UN could exercise its influence, particularly following the mixed experience of sanctions imposed by the League of Nations (discussed in Chapter 4 of this volume). As the collapse of European empires led to growing numbers of former colonies joining the UN as voting members, the UN increasingly became a forum for discussion and rethinking about what sanctions could accomplish and how they should be implemented. As Boutros-Ghali's introduction suggested, how to translate condemnation into action was not yet well defined and this lack of clarity turned the implementation of sanctions into a drawn-out process, which, in turn, shaped their impact. As colonial regimes withdrew, these debates focused increasingly on remaining white minority regimes in South Africa and Southern Rhodesia.

The sanctions imposed on South Africa and Southern Rhodesia have been the subject of considerable debate among both academics and policy makers. Perhaps surprisingly, however, they are rarely considered in comparison to one another, though both often appear as cases in wider histories of sanctions. Additionally, much of the existing literature was written while sanctions remained in place and before the end of white minority regimes in Southern Africa, and thus before it was possible to develop any narratives about the long-term impacts of the various types of sanctions imposed from the 1960s through the 1980s (Adelman 1993). This timing matters – as Jentleson (2022: 26) puts it, 'most studies of anti-apartheid sanctions against South Africa before Nelson Mandela's 1990 release from political prison deemed them a failure. Analyses since then almost all see South Africa as a success story, indeed for many an iconic case'. In the meantime, a 'renaissance' in the field of African economic history has generated a much more detailed picture of the structure and performance of African economies over the period before and during the implementation of sanctions (Austin and Broadberry 2014; Fourie 2016; Frederick, Juif, and Meier zu Selhausen 2024).

This chapter builds on these advances to reassess the origins, implementation, and effectiveness of UN sanctions in these two countries. It begins by providing a brief review of the economic history of both countries which tries to explain why, out of all of Britain's former colonies, the elites of these two countries felt willing and able to resist the global movement towards majority rule following the end of World War II. It then examines early debates in the UN General Assembly and other venues about what role the UN and its member states could or should play in pressuring these two governments to abandon discriminatory policies against non-whites. The next section shifts from debates about sanctions to examining their implementation. Finally, the chapter considers the ways in which the South African and Rhodesian economies were able to adapt to the constraints of sanctions and proposes several theories about the long-term impact of sanctions regimes. The chapter concludes by offering lessons for the wider debate on sanctions from the comparison of these two cases.

The Rise of White Minority Regimes in Southern Africa

The policies that were to become the target of condemnation by the UN were not new to Southern Africa, nor were they unique to the region. In 1952, when the UN General Assembly passed its first resolution specifically condemning apartheid, most of Sub-Saharan Africa was still governed by colonial regimes which excluded the majority from political participation. Nor was racial discrimination particular to colonies – in the United States, for example, it would be another two years before the

Supreme Court ruling in *Brown v. the Board of Education* made racial segregation of schools unlawful. However, the economic and political histories of South Africa and Rhodesia put white elites in a position to resist pressures to move towards majority rule. Instead, both countries saw the adoption of policies intended to entrench the position of that elite and strengthen, rather than weaken, repression and segregation.

Segregationist policies had been part of the political economy of both countries since the first arrival of European settlers. High transport costs meant that settlers were particularly dependent on indigenous and enslaved labour – and on keeping the price of that labour low. This was equally true of the first Dutch East India Company staff to acquire land in the seventeenth century or those who moved north to what became Southern Rhodesia in the nineteenth. In both, some of the first laws passed by colonial administrations were intended to facilitate the supply of labour for settler farms by restricting the economic options available to the indigenous population through the seizure of land and other resources (Simons and Simons 1969: 16; Maylam 2001: 77).

The discovery of minerals in the region – starting with diamonds in Kimberley in 1867, followed by gold in the Transvaal in 1886 – merely strengthened the incentives for racial discrimination. They prompted a rapid influx of capital into South Africa, the scale of which outstripped private investments in the rest of the continent combined (Frankel 1938). Both agriculture and mining depended on cheap labour to maintain profitability, and elites used their position in government to create policies that would serve their mutual needs. Stanley Trapido (1971) draws a parallel between the 'marriage of iron and rye' in Germany and what he calls the 'alliance of maize and gold' in South Africa. The structure of local institutions gave them the power to do so – in the negotiations which followed the end of the South African War (1899–1902), the British government granted the new Union of South African powers of self-government within the British Empire. This left political control in the hands of a substantial, if often fractious, group of Afrikaner and British settlers. Early legislation passed by the Union government included further restrictions on African workers which limited them to low-skilled jobs and made breach of labour contracts by black workers a criminal offence.

Mineral discoveries also provided the backdrop for the colonisation of Rhodesia when Cecil Rhodes's British South Africa Company went in search of further gold deposits to the north (Phimister 1988: chapter 1). The BSAC offered land to settlers on attractive terms to cover the initial costs of administration. Many of these settlers were poor farmers from the Cape Colony who had been forced off their land – and, as a result, many of South Africa's policies were replicated in Southern Rhodesia. The most promising land was reserved for white settlement and speculation, while African farmers were restricted to less fertile land set aside as African 'reserves' (Arrighi 1967).

Southern Rhodesia was governed by the BSAC until 1923, when the mounting costs of colonial administration combined with the failure to locate the mineral resources which had inspired its colonisation led the company to cede administrative responsibility to the British government. On this transition, the colony of Southern Rhodesia achieved self-governing status similar to that of the Union. As in the Union, this meant that domestic policies were decided primarily by officials elected locally rather than employed by the British government – but, as in South Africa, the franchise was restricted to white settlers.

In both South Africa and Southern Rhodesia, the economic upheavals of World War I and the Great Depression led to the adoption of even more restrictive legislation as both farms and mines struggled to maintain profitability among volatile global prices for exports. African landownership and labour mobility were further restricted, and rules on the marketing of maize and other agricultural goods introduced two-tier pricing systems which disadvantaged African farmers (Phimister 1988: chapter 2; Maylam 2001: chapter 5). Despite these efforts to restrict African opportunity, the struggles of poorer settlers began to reshape domestic politics in ways that would set these two colonies apart in the post-war era. In 1924, for example, the South Africa Party, which had been in power since 1912, lost to the Nationalist-Labour Pact government, which drew its support from poor whites and others who favoured independence from Britain.

This nationalistic shift was reflected perhaps most prominently in economic policy. Figure 8.1 gives GDP per capita in both countries from the late nineteenth century up to 1960. It shows that this was a period of both growth and volatility. The trade disruptions of World War I had provided some degree of natural protection for local manufacturing industries, and post-war governments in both countries pressed for continued support of structural change. The industrial foundations established during this period provided a key source of economic strength under later sanctions regimes.

By the outbreak of World War II, both South Africa and Rhodesia had more diversified economies than other parts of Sub-Saharan Africa. The war gave a further boost to processes of structural change, so that by the late 1940s manufacturing constituted a substantial share of GDP. In Southern Rhodesia, manufacturing's share of non-service-sector GDP

From Condemnation to Action?

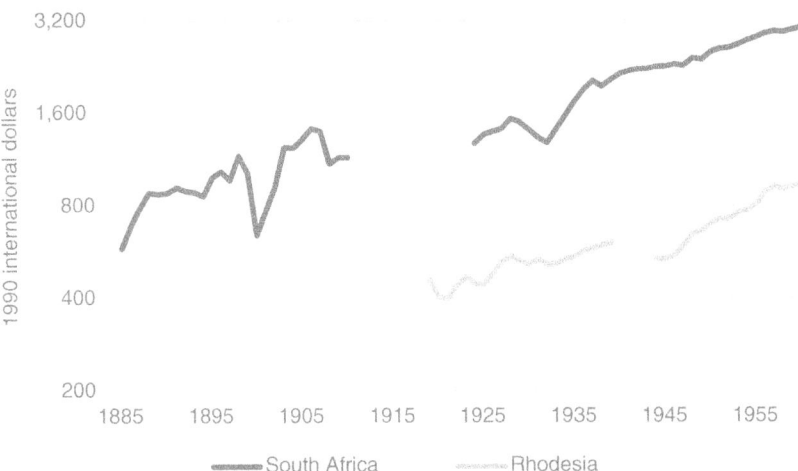

Figure 8.1 GDP per capita of South Africa and Rhodesia, 1885–1960 (1990 international dollars)
Source: Broadberry and Gardner (2022).

rose from around 25 per cent in 1939 to almost 50 per cent in 1948 (Stoneman 1976; Phimister 1988: 253). When services are included, manufacturing constituted around 17 per cent of total GDP. Agriculture also increased as a share of GDP, while mining declined (Phimister 1988: 253). In South Africa, secondary industry was 23 per cent of total GDP in 1948 (Feinstein 2005: 144). These were substantial shares in comparison to other African states. In the 1960s, for example, the share of manufactures in the tradeable output of Uganda was around 11 per cent, in contrast to 40 per cent in Rhodesia (Wood and Jordan 2000: 101).

The years immediately following the war saw both economic and political shifts throughout the region. Already a key supplier of minerals and other raw materials, Africa became even more crucial to European economies and the war effort after the fall of South East Asia to the Japanese. Demand for strategic commodities also saw unprecedented government intervention in colonial economies, while rapid urbanisation and rising prices for imported goods generated growing social and political tensions. These became evident in a wave of strikes and protests in the years before, during, and just after the war. In Southern Rhodesia, there were major strikes in 1945, 1946, and 1948. In South Africa, the 1946 African Mineworkers Strike drew a brutal response from the government which foreshadowed greater violence to come (O'Meara 1975; Mlambo 2009).

In both countries, the white minority feared that the British government would offer constitutional concessions to the African majority, as it was starting to do elsewhere in the region. This generated pressures from the white population for greater autonomy from Britain. In South Africa, the 1948 election of the National Party saw efforts to, in the words of Posel (2011: 326), 'shed the yoke of British authority'. The new government abolished British citizenship in 1951 and lowered the Union Jack in 1957. By 1961, South Africa had withdrawn from the Commonwealth and replaced sterling with a new currency called the Rand (Feingold, Fourie, and Gardner 2021).

Domestically, the government began to move from a system of racial discrimination to complete political and spatial segregation – 'apartheid'. Africans were to be citizens not of South Africa but of the so-called Bantu homelands. At the same time, laws restricting African residence in urban areas were strengthened, as were policies of job reservation and the segregation of schools. Central to this system was the 1950 Population Registration Act, which required each individual residing in South Africa to obtain an official racial classification, which was then used to determine where each person could live and work, and what rights they had under the political system in place.

The British government was concerned that a self-governing Southern Rhodesia, which had numerous economic, political, and cultural links with its southern neighbour, would attempt to merge with this newly hostile South Africa. To prevent this, in 1953 it established a new Central African Federation, which unified Southern Rhodesia with Northern Rhodesia and Nyasaland. This was done over the determined opposition of Africans in the latter two territories, who feared that Federation would facilitate the extension of Southern Rhodesia's policies of racial discrimination in land and labour law. The scale of this opposition was such that the Federation collapsed only a decade after its foundation, leading to the independence of Malawi (formerly Nyasaland) and Zambia (formerly Northern Rhodesia). This further exacerbated fears among whites that Britain would force Southern Rhodesia to move towards majority rule at the same time. Negotiations over a constitutional settlement which would have done just that failed, as the National Front Party – elected to power in 1962 – was strongly opposed to majority rule. After the failure of these negotiations, the NFP government issued a unilateral declaration of independence (UDI) in 1965.

The Federation did not last long; nevertheless it still had significant impact on the future development of the region. Investments in infrastructure, including the massive Kariba Dam hydroelectric plant, were concentrated in Southern Rhodesia. The Federation government had also used the substantial proceeds of copper mining in Northern Rhodesia to subsidise development projects in Southern Rhodesia. Manufacturing in Rhodesia also gained from access to a larger market (Gwande 2019). Later, these investments would help Southern Rhodesia blunt the impact of sanctions by bolstering the self-sufficiency of its domestic economy and by increasing the costs to neighbouring countries of cutting off economic relations.

South Africa and Southern Rhodesia were not unique in their desire to resist global movements towards democracy and majority rule in the post-war period. Settler communities in Portuguese Africa – under the dictatorship of Salazar in Portugal – did the same. However, they were unique in their ability to do so. The long history of self-rule under British colonialism had created a distinct path in which white elites framed their intent to continue the subjugation of the majority in the same terms of political self-determination as nationalist movements all over the continent (Cooper 2019). It had also shaped patterns of economic development and diversification which meant that both South Africa and Southern Rhodesia were more domestically self-sufficient than most African economies, which enabled them to manage better a period of economic isolation. The next section examines the growing international campaign against minority rule and the emergence of the UN as a forum for policy debates about how to turn that opposition into action.

Confronting Minority Regimes

What should be done about the policies of racial discrimination adopted by South Africa and Rhodesia – among many other countries at the time – became an increasingly thorny problem for the United Nations from its first foundation after World War II. India first raised the issue of discrimination against its citizens in South Africa on the floor of the UN in 1946. The response from the General Assembly was the adoption of Resolution 44(I) of 1946, which condemned the treatment of Indians as not in line with agreements made by both governments and warned that relations between the two countries were 'likely to be further impaired' if the issue was not addressed. This was to be one of a long series of similar complaints lodged by the Indian government, and supported by a growing number of other states as newly independent countries joined the UN. Responses to these complaints raised difficult questions about the jurisdiction of the UN and its capacity to influence changes in the domestic policy of member countries. These debates also foreshadowed general questions about the implementation and effectiveness of sanctions which remain live to this day.

In the early years of the UN's existence, there was no consensus on when the United Nations should, or should not, intervene to shape the policies of a government over its own people (as opposed to aggression against other states). South Africa's response to the complaints of India and other nations was to claim that the UN had no jurisdiction over domestic issues. In a statement to the General Assembly in September 1948, the South African delegate noted that attempts 'were still being made by both the Councils of the Organization and the General Assembly itself to intervene in the domestic affairs of member states'. This included 'adopting resolutions involving unjustifiable limitation on the sovereignty of states, to which no member state could reasonably submit'. This claim was challenged by representatives of other countries, who argued that the UN's charter gave it the responsibility to safeguard the rights of people living in all member countries. At stake in this debate was not only the tone of UN statements about South Africa, but also a wider precedent about the scope and limits of the UN's role and the extent to which membership in the UN meant agreeing to constraints on domestic policy – questions for which there were few precedents to help answer.

This debate had wider implications for the question of the UN's role in dealing with European empires and the process of decolonisation, which became apparent when similar questions were raised about Southern Rhodesia. In 1963, following the break-up of the Central African Federation, a group of African states led by Ghana submitted a letter to the Security Council condemning the persistence of 'undemocratic white minority rule' in the territory, and protesting in particular the proposed transfer of military technology from the United Kingdom. The British delegate immediately objected to the Council's debating the topic at all, stating that 'the item on the professional agenda today represents an abuse of the functions of the Council'. He continued on to argue that 'no situation exists in Southern Rhodesia which touches the responsibility of the Council'. His argument was that, because Southern Rhodesia remained a British colony, the UN had no right to intervene. The dispute between Ghana (and other African states) and the United Kingdom thus hinged partly on disputed definitions of Southern Rhodesia as a polity and on judgements about whether minority rule there threatened the security of other member states. Three years later, after UDI, the British government changed its position on the UN's jurisdiction over the matter. On 12 November 1965, the Foreign Secretary – temporarily taking over the role of his government's delegate to the Security Council to illustrate the gravity of the situation – stated that 'an attempt to establish in Africa an illegal regime based on minority rule is a matter of world concern'. On this basis, he asked that other UN member states join with the United Kingdom in refusing to recognise the new state, banning imports of Southern Rhodesian tobacco and exports of capital to Southern Rhodesia among several other measures. The representative from Ghana scoffed at this speech, quoting the British representative's earlier claims about jurisdiction.

Whatever the answers to questions about jurisdiction and responsibility, having jurisdiction does not by itself equal power to do anything. In a 1948 letter to the Secretary-General, the Indian representatives argued that the UN's failure to adopt an 'effective resolution' on the subject amounted to 'a tacit approval' of South Africa's policies. But what would an effective resolution look like? In a world recovering from war and keen to avoid further armed conflict, the key weapon in the UN's arsenal was economic warfare. Article 41 of the UN Charter states that

> the Security Council may decide what measures not involving the use of armed force are to be employed to give effect to its decision, and it may call upon the Members of the United Nations to apply such measures. These may include complete or partial interruption of economic relations and of rail, sea, air, postal, telegraphic, radio and other means of communication, and the severance of diplomatic relations.

Bruce Jentleson (2022: 10–11) identifies several broad types of sanctions which have been used in the second half of the twentieth century, including in the cases studied here. First are comprehensive sanctions which aim to prevent all trade. In contrast, sectoral sanctions are 'aimed at key parts of the target economy'. Common forms of sectoral sanctions include arms embargoes and energy sanctions. Targeted sanctions identify specific 'high-value targets' – including corporations, individuals, or other entities in an effort to impact elite decision making while minimising costs on the majority of the population. Secondary sanctions are those imposed on third parties outside the jurisdiction of the sanctioning state to try to force their cooperation with sanctions regimes. Finally, informal sanctions are imposed not by states but by private sector actors.

Under the League of Nations, the emphasis had been on comprehensive sanctions. Article 16 of the covenant called for the 'severance of all trade or financial relations, the prohibition of all intercourse between nationals and the nationals of the covenant-breaking state, and the prevention of all financial commercial or personal intercourse' between nationals. This demand for the complete severing of economic and financial relationships made Article 16 very difficult to implement. Cutting off all economic ties might affect some boycotting states more than others. In addition, there were debates about how the burden of such sanctions would be distributed. According to one 1931 treatise on the subject, 'a really successful food embargo ranks well in advance of torpedoing hospital ships and is somewhere near the class of gassing maternity hospitals' (Clark 1931, quoted in Losman 1979: 4). As a result of these difficulties, the League's two attempts to invoke Article 16 had little impact. The first was against Italy over the invasion of Ethiopia in 1935, addressed in Chapter 4 of this volume. The second was against Japan for the bombing of Chinese cities in 1938. In both cases, the requirement that economic relations be severed completely meant that implementation was only partial, and some member states refused to comply.

Perhaps because of the failures of Article 16, the language in the UN charter was more nuanced about the types of economic sanctions which might be imposed and did not require the complete severing of economic relations. In Jentleson's terms, the broader definition of economic warfare adopted by the UN charter reduced the barriers to imposing sanctions by allowing for sectoral and targeted sanctions. However, this flexibility also introduced new questions about the most effective scale and scope. Within the United Nations and among member governments, debates focused on three main questions. First, how likely was it that economic sanctions of whatever form could achieve their main aim, namely to exert sufficient pressure on the governments of Southern Rhodesia and South Africa that they would abandon policies of racial discrimination and move towards majority rule? Second, given the range of possibilities short of complete cessation of trade, what kinds of sanctions would have the greatest impact on policy without hurting the very people the campaign was supposed to help? Third, since UN resolutions could only be enforced through the actions of member states, how could the body best convince those states – for which the costs of imposing sanctions also varied widely – to act in a uniform way?

On the first of these questions, there was considerable doubt. In a meeting between UK and US officials in November 1961, for example, Sir Algernon Rumbold, the UK's Deputy Undersecretary for Commonwealth Relations, said that he 'doubted whether sanctions would be effective in view of the basic strength of the South African economy'. Similarly, in UN Security Council debates on Southern Rhodesia following UDI, delegates from African countries – including Ghana and Senegal – argued that sanctions were not enough and that military force was called for. 'From the continental blockade of Napoleon I against Great Britain to the present day – including the economic sanctions proclaimed against Mussolini by the League of

Nations in 1935 when that dictator attacked and invaded Ethiopia – economic sanctions have never in the end produced the results expected of them', argued the representative from Senegal.

If sanctions were to be imposed, another question was how to structure them so that they applied pressure to governments rather than the poorest in the target societies, reflecting long-running debates about the ethics of sanctions (Jentleson 2022: 27–29). Rumbold stated that one reason for the British government's opposition to sanctions was that the African majority 'would be the first to suffer' from such sanctions, along with the populations of the High Commission territories which the South African government might use as leverage. It was often difficult to disentangle the interests of the elite and the majority, as the sectors most vulnerable to sanctions were also those that employed large numbers of Africans. This was true, for example, of the tobacco sector in Southern Rhodesia. The country's dependence on tobacco should have made it vulnerable to sanctions, as it was a distinctive product that was easy for importers to recognise. The next sections show that the tobacco sector did, in fact, shrink during the sanctions era – but Losman (1979) argues that most of the costs of import bans on tobacco fell on African workers rather than the white population.

Complicating the task of selecting the right sanctions was the fact that each UN member country faced a different set of costs and benefits for each type of sanction proposed. These were not only economic but also political and could shift rapidly as the decades progressed. In the United States, for example, State Department correspondence revealed the range of possible factors influencing whether or not the United States should vote against sanctions in respective debates about Rhodesia and South Africa – many of which had little to do with the prospect (or not) of regime change in either country. In discussing the 1963 UN resolution on Southern Rhodesia, the Secretary of African Affairs advised the Secretary of State that 'a negative vote would be understood in Africa to indicate that the US was less than sympathetic to African aspirations for majority rule. Further, he added, 'an anti-black African vote, and this is the way a negative vote here would inevitably be interpreted, will not ease our serious domestic civil rights situation'. For the United States, in other words, both the domestic politics of civil rights and the politics of the Cold War were crucial, and the tensions between them would continue to shape the American government's responses to the UN's efforts (see, for example, Mitchell 2016: 11–15). For neighbours of sanctioned states, the economic costs of adopting sanctions or other measures were potentially severe. Namibia, which remained under South African control, was particularly vulnerable to South African retaliation – a point raised by Algernon Rumbold in the discussion quoted earlier. The concentration of infrastructure investment in Southern Rhodesia during the Federation period also made it potentially costly for both Zambia and Malawi to impose sanctions, as they were dependent on Rhodesia for transport and the provision of power.

In her history of sanctions in South Africa, Bronwen Manby (1992: 193) notes that 'it is only in the twentieth century, with increasing interdependence of the world economy and the ever more costly nature of war, that economic sanctions have really come into their own as a serious alternative to the use of military force'. While this may be true, it does not mean that there was a straightforward method for coordinated international pressure, particularly in the UN's first decades as an organisation. Debates remained about the effectiveness of sanctions relative to the use of force in certain circumstances. Further, the flexibility adopted by the United Nations following the experience of the League of Nations generated prolonged debates about which sanctions should be imposed and when. As the next two sections show, these debates affected both the implementation of sanctions and the ability of sanctioned economies to adapt to the constraints imposed.

Implementation and Enforcement of Sanctions

The first coordinated sanctions against South Africa and Rhodesia were adopted in the 1960s. They expanded – and sometimes contracted – intermittently over the next several decades until they were abandoned after the end of white minority rule in 1979 (Rhodesia) and 1994 (South Africa). Over this period, a wide range of sanctions were adopted – only rarely rising to the level of comprehensive sanctions but including a variety of sectoral and informal sanctions which were enforced to varying degrees. The UN's focus was primarily on sectors thought to be crucial to elite enforcement of policies of racial discrimination, especially arms, energy, and financial transfers. They would often start as voluntary actions which UN members were encouraged to adopt, before later being made mandatory. The UN had limited enforcement mechanisms, however, so even mandatory sanctions could have mixed results depending on the follow-up of member states. This section draws on both primary and secondary sources to examine the drawn-out implementation of sanctions, while the following section examines their impacts on the South African and Rhodesian economies.

The transition from condemnation to action was quickest in Rhodesia, in large part due to pressure from the British government, which was trying to use sanctions to resist calls from African states to use force against the white minority regime. It imposed its own unilateral sanctions immediately after UDI – expelling Rhodesia from sterling area, freezing Rhodesian assets in the United Kingdom, banning investment and any trade in arms along with the imports of Rhodesian tobacco (Strack 1978; Doxey 1980; Mlambo 2019; Jentleson 2022). Prime Minister Harold Wilson reassured an audience of African leaders at the Commonwealth Summit in Lagos that these measures would bring about the collapse of the Rhodesian regime within weeks (Minter and Schmidt 1988: 207). This prediction proved not to be correct, owing both to the limited cooperation of other states with the British initiative and measures taken by Rhodesian actors, discussed in the next section. The UN's first major intervention came in 1966, when the Security Council passed Resolution 232 mandating member states to ban the import of a list of Rhodesian goods, the export of arms and motor vehicles, and the transfer of funds to Rhodesia. This was the first time in United Nations history that the Security Council had imposed mandatory sanctions (Losman 1979: 94). These more targeted sectoral sanctions became comprehensive sanctions in 1968, banning all trade and air transport with the exception of the export of medical or humanitarian items to Rhodesia.

Mlambo (2019: 372) speculates that 'had all the countries strictly lived up to their promises, the regime would, indeed, have collapsed in a matter of weeks'. In practice, this apparently forceful action had significant limits largely due to the uneven adoption and enforcement of sanctions by member states. From the start, several countries either refused to cooperate or were not bound by UN decrees. South Africa and Portugal, perhaps unsurprisingly, voted against and refused to cooperate. These two refusals alone provided a crucial channel between Rhodesia and the global economy that sanctions were supposed to isolate it from (Mlambo 2008). As early as April 1966, a statement by the chair of the UN Security Council's Sanctions Committee noted that a Greek tanker carrying oil had anchored in the port of Beira in Portuguese Mozambique – the oil presumably destined for Rhodesia.[1] West Germany and Japan were not yet members of the UN and also refused to participate. Switzerland, though a member, also failed to comply.

Some states that had initially supported the sanctions failed to enforce them rigorously in practice. The United States, for example, which had voted in favour of the Security Council sanctions for the political reasons outlined above, did not pass its own legislation enforcing them until

---

[1] Statement made by the Chairman and the 401st Meeting of the Special Committee, 6 April 1966, UN Archives S-0884-0020-04-0000. The British government later attempted to blockade the port of Beira, but this had little effect.

1968, nearly three years later. Three years after that, in 1971, Congress passed the Byrd Amendment – named after Virginia Senator Harry S. Byrd, Jr – which permitted the import of strategic minerals (particularly chrome) from Rhodesia despite the sanctions. Michel (2018) attributes this decision, which put the United States in open violation of the UN, to a shift in priorities under the Nixon administration. Nixon was less concerned about the implications for American civil rights campaigns, which had been one of the motivations for US support for the initial imposition of sanctions, than with access to strategic materials. Communist support for the African opposition in both Rhodesia and South Africa also softened American opposition to the Smith regime – part of the Nixon Doctrine adopted in 1969 advocated a strategy of influence through friendly governments, which could include 'unpalatable regimes provided they had distinctively anticommunist credentials'. The Byrd Amendment remained on the books until 1977, when it was overturned by the Carter administration (Jentleson 2022: 61).

In other countries, a refusal to implement and enforce the mandatory sanctions was not an act of political cynicism but rather necessity. As a result of the infrastructure investments made during the Federation period, Zambia was too dependent on Rhodesia to cut off economic relations, despite being, as Losman (1979: 14) puts it, Rhodesia's 'staunchest political adversary'. Infrastructure links between Zambia and Rhodesia included the railways, which were Zambia's only way of exporting its copper, and supplies of electricity from the Kariba Dam power plant. The only available replacement for electricity from Kariba Dam was coal, for which the largest source in the region was the Wankie Coal Mines in Rhodesia. In the first years of Zambian independence, expenditures related to the severing of economic relations with Rhodesia absorbed some two-thirds of annual revenue, generating large deficits. In 1968, Britain agreed to contribute to the cost of constructing alternative trade routes through Tanzania, after having spent some £10 million on the airlift of fuel into Zambia after Rhodesia blocked its exports (Gardner 2012: 236–237).

While enforcement of the Rhodesian sanctions was far from perfect, in the case of South Africa there appears to have been considerably greater reluctance among some member states – particularly but not limited to Britain and the United States – to impose the sanctions recommended (or even mandated) by the United Nations. Contemporary correspondence suggests that this reluctance was driven by both economic and strategic considerations linked to the Cold War. As one of the world's leading producers of gold and other strategic minerals such as uranium, South Africa cast a bigger shadow on the global economy than Rhodesia, and the costs to sanctioning states of cutting off relations were correspondingly higher. South Africa's experiments with the development of a nuclear weapon are one illustration of this (Liberman 2001). As the Cold War progressed, and African opposition turned increasingly to Russia for support, the apartheid state was increasingly seen in Washington and London as a reliable bulwark against Soviet expansion, however distasteful its domestic policy might be. However, support for white minority regimes, in particular, had to be balanced against the growing economic importance of other African countries – during the energy crisis that followed the 1973 oil embargo, for example, Andrew Young (a civil rights activist and former US Congressman who had been appointed ambassador to the United Nations by Jimmy Carter) observed that 'one out of every eight gallons of gasoline sold in this nation comes from Nigeria' (quoted in Mitchell 2016: 5). Beyond these considerations, several countries in Southern Africa were by this point highly dependent on trade with South Africa. This included Botswana, Lesotho, Swaziland, Mozambique, Zambia, and Malawi, in addition to Rhodesia. As in the case of Zambia and Rhodesia, political opposition to apartheid was often in conflict with the high economic costs of sanctioning South Africa (Becker 1987: 150).

While there were unilateral measures adopted by, for example, the Indian government, it took several decades for the condemnations of the 1940s and 1950s to translate into serious economic sanctions in the 1980s (Manby 1992). In 1959, African National Congress President Albert Luthuli first called for a boycott of South African goods. During the 1960s, particularly following the Sharpeville Massacre of 1960, the UN passed a series of resolutions imposing a voluntary embargo on the export of arms and oil.[2] The first mandatory sanctions were passed in 1963, but these were limited to embargoes on equipment for arms manufacture (Manby 1992). At the same time, member states were also asked to restrict other trade with South Africa, closing their ports to South African ships and refraining from investing in South Africa. The text of repeated resolutions passed by the UN makes clear the difficulty they faced in enforcing such action. Several resolutions were passed imploring states to comply and condemning those that had not yet done so, observing with frustration that trade with South Africa and its major trading partners had increased rather than decreased over the 1960s.

The earliest sanctions imposed were not against major sectors of the South African economy but rather targeted against cultural and sporting

---

[2] For a chronology of sanctions imposed on South Africa, see Mozia (1991a, 1991b).

events. South Africa was banned from the Olympics from 1964 and the World Cup in 1976. Cricket tours were also boycotted from the 1970s, and South Africa was barred from the first ever Rugby World Cup in 1977. A range of celebrities including Elton John, Tina Turner, and Bruce Springsteen refused to perform in South Africa. Private campaigns for the boycott of South African goods and goods produced by companies investing in South Africa expanded during the 1970s. The Organization of the Petroleum Exporting Countries (OPEC) imposed an oil embargo in 1973, though this was circumvented by Iran, which continued to supply South Africa with oil until 1979. In 1977, a private sector coalition led by Leon Sullivan adopted a code of conduct known as the Sullivan Principles for companies investing in South Africa (Manby 1992: 196–197; Jentleson 2022: 66–67).

The Soweto Uprising of 1976 prompted another wave of international outrage, and the first mandatory arms embargo passed by the UN in 1977. Still, it was not until the middle of the following decade that South Africa's largest trading partners, including the UK, the US, and many European countries, adopted more stringent economic measures against South Africa. It remained a fraught decision for several governments even at this point. Both the British and American governments abstained from a UN resolution in 1985 encouraging further sanctions (Nanda 1991). A year later, the US Congress passed the Comprehensive Anti-Apartheid Act in 1986, overriding President Reagan's veto to do so. The UK and European Union also imposed sanctions during this period. Private sanctions also became more stringent, perhaps the most impactful of which were withdrawals of credit by international banks. It is not always clear whether these withdrawals were because of public pressure against apartheid or because an increasingly unstable South Africa had ceased to look like a good investment (Jentleson 2022).

Impact of Sanctions

Losman (1979: 18) argues that 'the longer sanctions are in force, the more likely it is that import substitutes will be found'. The piecemeal imposition and enforcement of sanctions in Rhodesia and South Africa allowed both countries time to adapt to their constraints. Evasion through sympathetic states helped, but this was not enough and in both countries substantial domestic adaptations were used to cope with growing external isolation. In Rhodesia, these adaptations were largely made after sanctions were imposed. By contrast, in South Africa the long period in which sanctions had been recommended but not enforced meant that most changes were adopted in advance of enforcement.

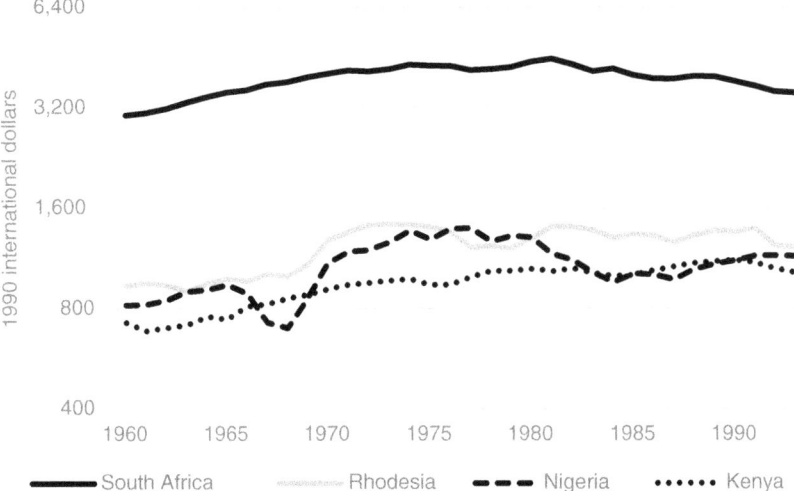

Figure 8.2 GDP per capita of four African economies, 1960–1995 (1990 international dollars)
Source: Broadberry and Gardner (2022).

One common feature, however, was the dramatic expansion of state intervention in the economy – which often survived long after sanctions were removed.

It remains empirically difficult to isolate the impact of sanctions from other developments at the time, such as the increasingly violent repression of domestic opposition. Both governments also tried mask their effects by withholding or manipulating official statistics on trade (Davis 1991: 75). Figure 8.2 shows GDP per capita in Rhodesia, South Africa, Nigeria, and Kenya. It shows that all three exhibited declines in per capita incomes from the middle of the 1970s, despite the fact that Rhodesia and South Africa were under sanctions and Nigeria and Kenya were not. Impacts are thus difficult to spot at a macro level. This is perhaps because impacts were mixed – sanctions weakened some sectors while strengthening others through the effective protection of domestic industries. Costs were disproportionately born by Africans while some white elites may have even gained.

In his study of the Rhodesian sanctions, Porter (1978) lists three criteria that impact the potential effectiveness of sanctions: dependence on imports and exports, the flexibility of production structures, and local preferences on consumption. As section two, on the rise of white minority regimes in Southern Africa, showed, both South Africa and Rhodesia were less dependent on imports and exports than other African economies owing to the growth in manufacturing which occurred in both the interwar and post-war periods. However, both relied on commodity exports as a source of foreign capital which created potential vulnerabilities.

Rhodesia's most important export was tobacco. When UDI was declared, tobacco was 10 per cent of GDP and contributed 34 per cent of export earnings (Rowe 2011: 63). Prior to sanctions, the tobacco sector was also the largest employer of African workers (Handford 1976: 69). Rhodesian tobacco is both of high quality and sufficiently distinctive to be recognisable by purchasers (Losman 1979: 98). Further, prior to UDI, tobacco sellers had extracted a commitment from the London tobacco market to take a significant portion of the crop. If London stopped buying, then demand would collapse. This was perhaps the British government's most important leverage over Ian Smith's government. However, Rhodesian tobacco farmers had two methods to counter this pressure. First, during the protracted dispute between the Rhodesian and British governments which preceded UDI, purchasers stockpiled as much tobacco as they could. Figure 8.3 gives data on Rhodesian tobacco exports under sanctions, and shows a boom year in 1965 as purchasers placed larger than usual orders. The next year, however, showed a steep decline and even at the end of the sanctions period had not yet recovered to half the boom year in 1965. Exports did not completely collapse, however, as there were some efforts to rebrand

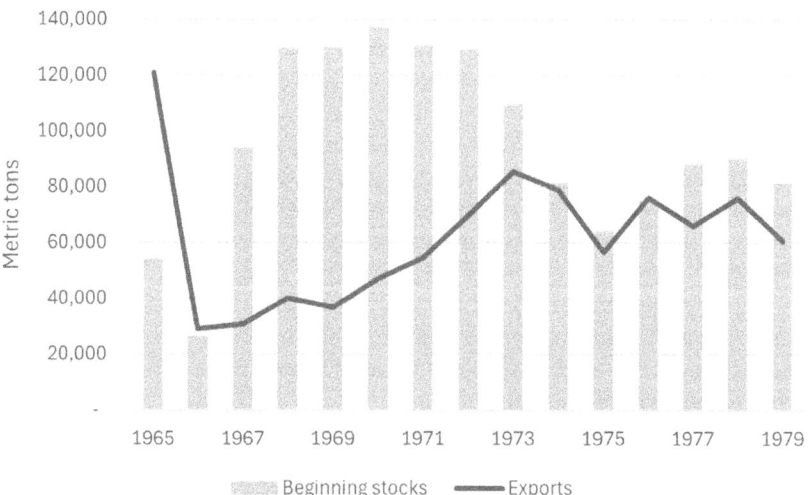

Figure 8.3 Rhodesia's tobacco exports and stocks under sanctions, 1965–1979 (metric tons)
Source: Rowe (2001: 77).

Rhodesian tobacco which could then go to the London market (Minter and Schmidt 1988: 221). Some continued to be exported through the port of Beira, and the Netherlands became an important destination (Mlambo 2019: 387).

None of these efforts made up for the overall decline, and advance purchases could only ever be a temporary measure. The next step involved government intervention, something that Rhodesian tobacco farmers had previously resisted even as government marketing schemes proliferated elsewhere in British colonial Africa. With the threat of sanctions cutting into their export market, however, they hoped that government support might be able to guarantee a minimum price that covered their costs. The Tobacco Corporation, established 1966, became the monopoly supplier and marketer of crops. From 1967, it imposed mandatory limits on production in an attempt to maintain prices. This system persisted through the rest of the 1960s and into the 1970s. Farmers were encouraged to diversify their production, but crops such as cotton, corn, and wheat were not enough to replace the income from a decline in tobacco exports (McKinnell 1969; Rowe 2011).

For South Africa, the main export which might be targeted was minerals. Gold exports – which for decades had been the vehicle of South African prosperity – had begun to decline in the 1970s before sanctions were imposed due to declining productivity of the mines (Feinstein 2005: 206). This is shown in Figure 8.4. Even with declining volumes, the value of gold exports rose as gold prices increased following the abandonment of Bretton Woods in 1971. After sanctions were imposed, it was possible to export gold in unminted form to new markets in East and South East Asia (Jenkins 1995: 114–115). Other minerals, such as uranium, were among the reasons why major trading partners like the US and the UK resisted the earlier imposition of sanctions (Crawford and Klotz 1999: 78).

For both countries, the export of commodities was important not only for the producers of those commodities (and those who worked for them) but also for the manufacturing sector. Commodity exports brought in vital foreign exchange which could then be used to purchase intermediate goods and capital investments for industry (Feinstein 2005: 214; Rowe 2011: 113–114). The decline in exports thus had wider implications which needed to be managed. In both cases, they were managed largely by the state. In Rhodesia, the government established a system for rationing access to foreign exchange through a set of emergency power laws which gave it, among other powers, the ability to nationalise any company it considered to be working against Rhodesia's interests and which also required that any profits, dividends, interest, or rents normally

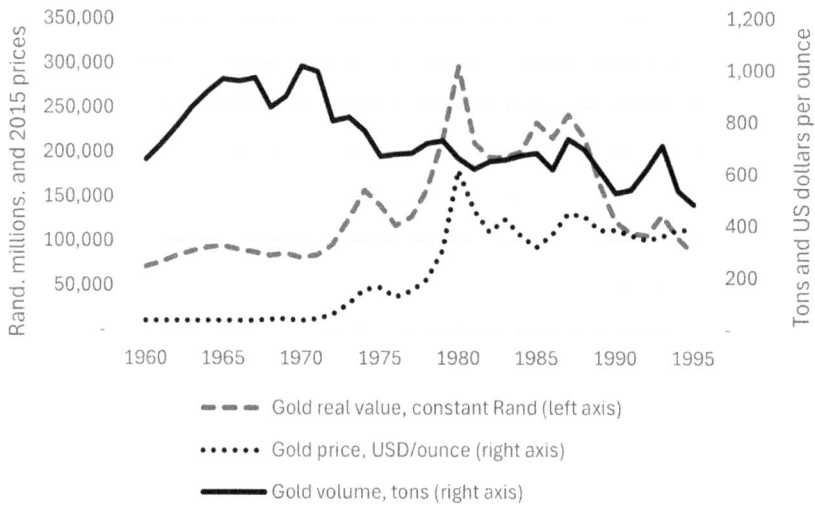

Figure 8.4 South Africa's gold exports, 1960–1995: volume, value, and gold price
Source: South African Reserve Bank (2018).

paid overseas would be paid to a government-administered Blocked Funds trust. These steps allowed the government to control the allocation of foreign exchange so that it could target the imports it considered most important. By early 1966, eight companies had been nationalised (Rowe 2011: 113–114). In South Africa, the slow implementation of sanctions meant this was less of a problem. During the 1960s, foreign direct investment increased, and only declined from the 1970s. However, the South African government also implemented controls on foreign capital to limit capital flight. The principal mechanism was re-establishing the financial Rand system that had first been used in the 1930s. Under this system, South Africa effectively had two exchange rates, the financial rand for non-residents and the standard exchange rate for residents, effectively devaluing capital exports and rewarding capital inflow. There were also blocked Rand accounts for non-residents which limited their ability to repatriate their earnings (Havemann 2014; Roussouw 2018). Efforts to manage the withdrawal of foreign capital often led to gains among the elite, as they could frequently acquire foreign assets at cut prices. They gained again with the return of multinational corporations after sanctions were lifted (Barnard and Luiz 2024).

Another key sector targeted by sanctions was energy, particularly oil. Many attributed the limited impact of League of Nations sanctions against Italy in the 1930s to the failure to impose an oil embargo. As a result, oil embargoes were imposed on both Rhodesia and South Africa. In neither case did this have a crippling impact on energy consumption, though both governments took steps to manage consumption and locate alternatives. In Rhodesia, the legacy of Federation helped mitigate the impact by providing alternative sources of energy through the Kariba Dam hydroelectric plant constructed in the 1950s. It also continued to import oil through the Mozambican ports of Beira and, after the British blockade, Lourenco Marques (Cohen 2011). It also expanded state control over the sector, imposing rations and creating a parastatal authority, Genta to facilitate imports (Losman 1979). South Africa imported oil freely from Iran until 1979, but in anticipation of more limited access to foreign energy sources also invested heavily in the conversion of coal to oil, the extraction of oil from shale and the production of ethanol from sugar cane (Jenkins 1995). This, likewise, was managed under a state-owned company (SASOL). These efforts were costly but prevented any serious shortages of energy.

Manufacturing grew in both countries, in part due to more limited access to imports. For Rhodesian manufacturers, the period of isolation was timely. During the Federation years there had been overinvestment in Rhodesia's manufacturing capacity. Under sanctions, this was put to use to substitute for imported goods. The number of products produced domestically rose from 602 before sanctions to 3,837, and the contribution of manufacturing to GNP increased from 17.9 per cent to 24.7 per cent (Rowe 2011: 126). However, these firms remained uncompetitive beyond the barriers of sanctions.

In some cases, sanctions stimulated the rise of new manufacturing industries. This was the case with the South African arms industry. The long period between first voluntary arms embargoes in the 1960s and the mandatory arms embargo in 1977 gave the South African government ample opportunity to import intermediate technology for the production of weapons. As in the case of the Tobacco Corporation, the development of the arms industry occurred under extensive state intervention. In 1964, the Armaments Act established the Armaments Production Board, later renamed the Armaments Development and Production Corporation of South Africa (ARMSCOR). This consisted of several companies owned by the state and others that were partially owned by the state. During the mid-1970s, in anticipation of a mandatory arms embargo, it accelerated the purchasing of imports so it could scale up production for both export and domestic use. By 1987, ARMSCOR was South Africa's largest exporter of manufactured goods (Jenkins 1995; Crawford and Klotz 1999).

Ironically, the expansion of manufacturing began to generate calls from at least some of the white elite to soften the policies of racial discrimination that the sanctions were at least partly intending to change. Colour bars and the restriction of Africans to unskilled jobs had been a feature of both South Africa and Rhodesia since at least the inter-war period. However, the expansion of manufacturing created demand for skilled labour that the comparatively small white population could not fill. By keeping majority incomes low, it also restricted local markets for manufactures that were generally uncompetitive in export markets (Nattrass 1991; Mariotti 2012).

There remains much work to be done to identify the precise distributional consequences of the changes made in response to sanctions. The expansion of manufacturing may have provided additional skilled jobs which might be taken up by Africans once discriminatory policies were abandoned. On the other hand, the comparatively high costs of import substitution and alternative energy supplies, for example, were likely to have had a greater impact on the poor than the wealthy, who might even have gained from the upheaval.

Lessons from Southern Africa

How big a role did sanctions play in the ultimate end of white minority rule in Southern Africa? In sum, both Rhodesia and South Africa were able to manage the effects due to a combination of evasion and internal adaptations. Rhodesia's continued trade with the outside world was facilitated by access to friendly ports in South Africa and Mozambique – at least until 1975, when the end of Portuguese rule made the management of sanctions much more difficult. The reluctance of South Africa's major trading partners to impose sanctions at all also limited the impact of the UN's efforts. Both were also helped by the fact that they were among the most diversified economies in the region prior to the imposition of sanctions. However, sanctions did prompt substantial sectoral shifts and the expansion of state intervention in both economies, suggesting that they were not entirely toothless.

This remains the subject of debate, not only for the case of Southern Africa but for the much wider range of sanctions adopted since then. In these and other cases, impacts are difficult to assess empirically owing to the interaction of sanctions with a range of other factors – both domestic and international – which also contributed. It is likely that there will never be a definitive answer. It may be more feasible to draw out lessons from the experience of these two countries which could be instructive in the implementation of future sanctions.

One key lesson is that timing matters. New export markets and domestic mitigation measures take time to develop – time afforded in these cases (and especially in South Africa) by the long delay between threats of sanctions and enforcement. Second is that globalisation cuts both ways – while it might make target countries more susceptible to bans on trade or investment, it also opens up new opportunities for evasion in a world where there is never perfect unity of purpose between governments. Third, the political and economic costs to sanctioning countries influence whether sanctions are likely to be imposed and, if so, what form they will take.

A final lesson is not so much about the effectiveness of sanctions in achieving their aims but on their legacies after they have been lifted. In Rhodesia and South Africa, the mitigation of sanctions required extensive state intervention in all sectors of the economy, from agriculture to finance. Many of the parastatals established during this period, from SASOL to ARMSCOR, remain to this day. What happened to the other powers appropriated by governments during the sanctions era after sanctions is beyond the scope of this chapter but remains a question for future research.

References

Adelman, S. 1993. 'The Politics of Research on Sanctions against South Africa', *Canadian Journal of African Studies* 27(1): 89–94.

Arrighi, G. 1967. *The Political Economy of Rhodesia*. Germany: Mouton.

Austin, G., and S. N. Broadberry. 2014. 'Introduction: The Renaissance of African Economic History', *Economic History Review* 67(4): 893–906.

Barnard, H., and J. M. Luiz. 2024. 'The South African Economic Elite and Ownership Changes in Foreign Multinationals' Assets during and after Apartheid-Era Sanctions', *Journal of World Business* 59: 101555.

Becker, C. M. 1987. 'Economic Sanctions against South Africa', *World Politics* 39(2): 147–173.

Broadberry, S. N., and L. A. Gardner. 2022. 'Economic Growth in Sub-Saharan Africa, 1885–2008: Evidence from Eight Countries', *Explorations in Economic History* 83: 101424.

Cohen, A. 2011. 'Lonrho and Oil Sanctions against Rhodesia in the 1960s', *Journal of Southern African Studies* 37(4): 715–730.

Cooper, F. 2019. *Africa since 1940: The Past of the Present*, 2nd ed. Cambridge: Cambridge University Press.

Crawford, N., and A. Klotz. 1999. *How Sanctions Work: Lessons from South Africa*. New York: St Martin's Press.

Davis, L. E., and S. Engerman. 2003. 'Sanctions: Neither War nor Peace', *Journal of Economic Perspectives* 17(2): 187–197.

Davis, S. P. 1991. 'Economic Pressure on South Africa: Does It Work?', in G. W. Shepherd (ed), *Effective Sanctions on South Africa: The Cutting Edge of Economic Intervention*, pp. 65–80. New York: Greenwood Press.

Doxey, M. P. 1980. *Economic Sanctions and International Enforcement*. London: Palgrave Macmillan.

Feingold, E., J. Fourie, and L. A. Gardner. 2021. 'A Tale of Paper and Gold: The Material History of Money in South Africa', *Economic History of Developing Regions* 36(2): 264–281.

Feinstein, C. 2005. *An Economic History of South Africa: Conquest, Discrimination and Development*. Cambridge: Cambridge University Press.

Fourie, J. 2016. 'The Data Revolution in African Economic History', *Journal of Interdisciplinary History* 47(2): 193–212.

Frankel, S. H. 1938. *Capital Investment in Africa: Its Course and Effects*. Oxford: Oxford University Press.

Frederick, K., D. Juif, and F. Meier zu Selhausen. 2024. 'The Revival of African Economic History in the 21st Century: A Bibliometric Analysis', *Industrial History Review* 33(92): 11–48.

Gardner, L. A. 2012. *Taxing Colonial Africa: The Political Economy of British Imperialism*. Oxford: Oxford University Press.

Guelke, L. 1985. 'The Making of Two Frontier Communities: Cape Colony in the Eighteenth Century', *Historical Reflections* 12(3): 419–448.

Gwande, V. M. 2019. 'Federation, Factories and Foreign Capital: Economic Growth in Southern Rhodesia, 1953–1956', *International Journal of African Historical Studies* 52(2): 231–253.

Handford, J. 1976. *Portrait of an Economy: Rhodesia under Sanctions*. Salisbury: Mercury Press.

Havemann, R. 2014. 'The Exchange Control System under Apartheid', *Economic History of Developing Regions* 29(2): 268–286.

Jenkins, C. 1995. 'Adjusting to Economic Sanctions in South Africa', in O. Morrissey and F. Stewart (eds.), *Economic and Political Reform in Developing Countries*, pp. 97–122. Basingstoke: Palgrave Macmillan.

Jentleson, B. W. 2022. *Sanctions: What Everyone Needs to Know*. Oxford: Oxford University Press.

Jones, L. 2015. *Societies under Siege: Exploring How International Economic Sanctions (Do Not) Work*. Oxford: Oxford University Press.

Liberman, P. 2001. 'The Rise and Fall of the South African Bomb', *International Security* 26(2): 45–86.

Losman, D. L. 1979. *International Economic Sanctions: The Cases of Cuba, Israel and Rhodesia*. Albuquerque: University of New Mexico Press.

Manby, B. 1992. 'South Africa: The Impact of Sanctions', *Journal of International Affairs* 46(1): 193–217.

Mariotti, M. 2012. 'Labour Markets during Apartheid', *Economic History Review* 65(3): 1100–1122.

Maylam, P. 2001. *South Africa's Racial Past: The History and Historiography of Racism, Segregation and Apartheid*. Aldershot: Ashgate.

McKay, V. 1963. *Africa in World Politics*. New York: Harper and Row.

McKinnell, R. 1969. 'Sanctions and the Rhodesian Economy', *Journal of Modern African Studies* 7(4): 559–581.

Michel, E. 2018. 'The Luster of Chrome: Nixon, Rhodesia, and the Defiance of UN Sanctions', *Diplomatic History* 42(1): 138–161.

Minter, W., and E. Schmidt. 1988. 'When Sanctions Worked: The Case of Rhodesia Reexamined', *African Affairs* 87(347): 559–581.

Mitchell, N. 2016. *Jimmy Carter in Africa: Race and the Cold War*. Washington, DC: Woodrow Wilson Center Press.

Mlambo, A. S. 2008. '"We Have Blood Relations over the Border": South Africa and Rhodesian Sanctions, 1965–1975', *African Historical Review* 40(1): 1–29.

2009. 'From the Second World War to UDI, 1940–1965', in B. Raftopoulos and A. S. Mlambo (eds.), *Becoming Zimbabwe: A History from the Pre-colonial Period to 2008*, pp. 75–114. Johannesburg: Jacanda Media.

(2019) '"Honoured More in the Breach than in the Observance": Economic Sanctions on Rhodesia and International Response, 1965–1979', *South African Historical Journal* 73(3): 371–393.

Mozia, T. U. 1991a. 'Chronology of Arms Embargoes against South Africa', in G. W. Shepherd (ed.), *Effective Sanctions on South Africa: The Cutting Edge of Economic Intervention*, pp. 97–108. New York: Greenwood Press.

1991b. 'Chronology of Economic Embargoes against South Africa', in G. W. Shepherd (ed.), *Effective Sanctions on South Africa: The Cutting Edge of Economic Intervention*, pp. 109–125. New York: Greenwood Press.

Mulder, N.. 2022. *The Economic Weapon: The Rise of Sanctions as a Tool of Modern War*. New Haven, CT: Yale University Press.

Nanda, V. P. 1991. 'Multilateral Sanctions against South Africa: A Legal Framework for Comprehensive Implementation', in G. W. Shepherd (ed.), *Effective Sanctions on South Africa: The Cutting Edge of Economic Intervention*, pp. 1–23. New York: Greenwood Press.

Nattrass, N. 1991. 'Controversies about Capitalism and Apartheid in South Africa: An Economic Perspective', *Journal of Southern African Studies* 17(4):, 654–677.

O'Meara, D. 1975. 'The 1946 African Mine Workers' Strike and the Political Economy of South Africa', *Journal of Commonwealth and Comparative Politics* 13(2): 146–173.

Phimister, I. R. 1988. *An Economic and Social History of Zimbabwe, 1890–1948: Capital Accumulation and Class Struggle*. London: Longman.

Porter, R. C. 1978. 'Economic Sanctions: The Theory and the Evidence from Rhodesia', *Journal of Peace Science* 3(2): 93–110.

Posel, D. 2011. 'The Apartheid Project, 1948–70', in R. Ross, A. K. Mager, and B. Nassin (eds.), *The Cambridge History of South Africa, Volume 2 1885–1994*, pp. 319–368. Cambridge: Cambridge University Press.

Rossouw, J. 2018. 'Politics and Policies: Determinants of South Africa's Monetary Policy Problems in the 1980s', *Economic History of Developing Regions* 33(1): 51–68.

Rowe, D. M. 2001. *Manipulating the Market: Understanding Economic Sanctions, Institutional Change, and the Political Unity of White Rhodesia*. Ann Arbor: University of Michigan Press.

Simons, H. J., and R. E. Simons. 1969. *Class and Colour in South Africa 1850–1950*, Harmondsworth: Penguin Books.

South African Reserve Bank (SARB). 2018. www.resbank.co.za/en/home/what-we-do/statistics/releases/online-statistical-query.

Stoneman, C. 1976. 'Foreign Capital and Prospects for Zimbabwe', *World Development* 4: 25–58.

Strack, H. R. 1978. *Sanctions: The Case of Rhodesia*. Syracuse, NY: Syracuse University Press.

Trapido, S. 1971. 'South Africa in a Comparative Study of Industrialization', *Journal of Development Studies* 7(3): 309–320.

United Nations. 1994. *The United Nations and Apartheid, 1948–1994*. New York: The United Nations.

Wood, A., and K. Jordan. 2000. 'Why Does Zimbabwe Export Manufactures and Uganda Not? Econometrics Meets History', *Journal of Development Studies* 37(2): 91–116.

Index

adaptation, 142, 166, 171, 256, 262
   cost of, 17–19, 25
   limits to, 176
Admiralty theory, 5
Adwa, Battle of, 115
African Mineworkers Strike, 245
agriculture
   incentives for farmers, 91
   policies, 82
Agriculture Act, 105
air power
   advent of, 3
   strategic, 22
Albania, 118, 120
American Civil War
   economic losses, 77
   effects of, 67–69, 75
   moral considerations, 70
   population losses, 77
   role of blockade, 72
American colonies, 34, 38
American Confederacy, 9, 13, 15, 22, 66–67
   arms purchases, 74
   economic losses, 62
   purchase of ships, 68
   recognition of, 71
   support from Manchester, 71
   surrender of, 20, 75
   trade with, 63
American Export Prohibition Act, 100
American Independence War, 41–42
American Neutrality Acts, 145
Americas, discovery of, 32
Amiens, Peace of, 42
Amsterdam
   bond market, 73
   financial markets, 34
Anaconda Plan, 59
Anglo-Swedish agreement, 181
apartheid, 12, 23, 240, 246
   condemnation of, 242
appeasement, 38, 42

Armaments Development and Production Corporation of South Africa, 261
armed forces, professionalisation of, 32
arms
   as contraband, 93
   manufacturing, 68
   purchase of, 74
   race, 116
   trade, 116, 118
Asiento, 35–37, 42
Asquith, Herbert Henry, 90
Aushungerung, legend of, 96
austerity, 121
Austerlitz, Battle of, 46
Australia, 70, 149
Austria, 42, 94
Austria–Hungary, 118
Austrian succession, 37
autarky, xvii, 17, 24, 67, 99, 105, 107, 109, 114–115, 120, 124, 137, 142, 149, 151, 153, 156, 170, 177, 211
authoritarian rule, 128
Axis powers, coordination of, 137, 177

B-17 Flying Fortress, 179
ball-bearing industry, 16, 180, 186, 197–198
Bank of England, 48, 69
barley, 105
Battle of Britain, 184
Battle of the Atlantic, 181, 190
Battle of the Ruhr, 187
BBC, 209
Beijing, 146
Belgium, 88, 103
Bethmann-Hollweg, Theobald von, 85
black market, 63, 96, 99, 205
blockade, 6, 9–10, 142, 176–177, 218
   adaptation to, 160
   Allied, 11, 21–22, 177, 180–181, 211. *See* blockade, British
   anticipation of, 18, 181

267

268   Index

blockade (cont.)
  Atlantic, 40
  belief in the power of, 105, 107, 109
  Berlin, 224, 228
  breaking, 101
  British, 93, 96, 107, 218, 261. *See* Allied blockade
  bypassing, 34
  counter-, 224
  of Cuba, 114
  economic, 150
  effectiveness of, 72
  effects of, 99, 106, 108
  evasion of, 72
  fear of, 196, 212
  food, 16
  German, 84, 181, 183
  gradual, 101
  myth, 107
  naval, 3, 15, 22, 34, 40–41, 43, 59
  of neutral ports, 93
  pacific, 4
  perception of, 117
  preparation for, 177, 194
  rules, 95
  running of, 43, 60
  self-, 45
  shortage inducing, 107
  siege, 28
  submarine, 82, 84, 102, 108–109
  surface, 82
  of technology, 216
  types of, 43
  unrestricted, 94
blue water policy, 33
Bolivia, 118
bomber planes, numbers, 185–186
bombing, 6, 22, 117, 148, 176–178
  Allied, 11, 16, 179
  American survey of, 209
  bombsight, 179
  daylight, 186
  effects of, 202
  indiscriminate, 179
  influence on strategy, 184
  intensity of, 199
  phases of, 202
  precision, 179, 184, 186, 211
  psychological effects, 179
  strategic, 13, 176
  targeting transportation, 180
  tonnage, 184, 187
bonds
  Erlanger, 72–74
  price of, 48

Boutros-Ghali, Boutros, 240–241
boycott, of South African goods, 255–256
boycotts, 147–148
brass, 104
bread, price of, 90
Bretton Woods, 259
Britain
  air defence, 189
  army, 41
  balance of payments, 47
  capital formation, 89
  cooperation with Allies, 177
  cotton textile manufacturing, 58
  diet, 190
  domestic production, 190
  economy, 10, 70
  exports, 48, 68, 89, 94
  financial system, 48, 69
  food consumption, 92
  food imports, 16, 190
  food supply, 84, 90
  imperialism, 96
  imports, 46, 66–67, 72, 83, 88, 90, 104–105, 107
  investment, 89, 108
  merchant fleet, 33, 44, 69
  merchant marine, 101
  military spending, 128–130
  mobilisation, 32
  navy, 22, 34, 38, 43, 211
  protectionism, 83
  public health, 191
  share of agriculture in economy, 105
  shipping capacity, 182
  stock of bullion, 48
  structural change, 91
  subsidies, 47
  trade, 42, 48–49
  War Cabinet, 90
British South Africa Company, 243
bronze, 104
Brussels, 147
Bulgaria, 94, 118
bullion, shortage of, 133
Byrd Amendment, 254
Byrd, Harry S., 254

Canada, 41, 71, 88
Cape Colony, 244
capital controls, 260
capital markets, 47
capital stock, 228, 235
capital–labour ratio, 231
Carter, Jimmy, 254
Casablanca Conference, 185

Index

ceasefire, Japan–China, 145
census, British, 58
Central African Federation, 246
  breakup of, 248
Chamberlain, Neville, 145, 147
charity, 67
China
  anti-Japanese boycotts, 144
  currency reforms, 145–146
  invasion of, 148
  Nationalist government of, 143
Churchill, Winston, 184
civilian
  affected by bombing, 208
  attacks on, 115
  consumption, 18
  deaths, 206
  drafting, 176
  exposure to war, 196
  health, 190, 206
  impact on, 212
  resistance, 209
  sacrifices, 176
  sector, 25
  sparing of, 74
  supplies, 191
  targeting of, 118
coal, 18, 64–65, 103, 117, 120, 126, 137, 154, 180
  shortage, 100, 104
Colbert, Jean-Baptiste, 28, 31, 33
Cold War, 216, 220, 235, 251, 254
collectivisation, 217
colonialism, 115, 247
  administration, 243–244
  collapse of, 241
  expansion of, 43
Columbia (South Carolina), 75
Committee for Imperial Defence, 101
commodities, 124
  colonial, 36
  essential, 17–18, 24
  as main exports, 258
commodity, essential, 20
Commonwealth, 246
  Summit, 253
communist
  economies, 217
  technological leader, 222
complementary force, 21–23, 25
Composite Index of National Capabilities, 131
Comprehensive Anti-Apartheid Act, 256
consumerism, mass, 231

containment, xviii
Continental Blockade, 31, 45, 47–48, 250
  failure of, 49
  interpretation of, 45–47, 50
Continuous Voyage, doctrine of, 41
contraband, 41, 93
convertibility of the British pound, 48
convoy system, 31, 38, 85, 108, 181
copper, 104, 247
Corn Laws, 82
  repeal of, 107
Corn Production Act, 91, 104
Corn Production Acts (Repeal) Act, 105
Correlates of War, 131
cotton, 56, 64, 93
  burning of, 60
  as an economic weapon, 56
  famine, 9, 59, 67, 70–71, 76
  famine roads, 67
  Indian, 70
  mills, 63–64, 67, 75
  price, 59, 62, 66–67, 69–70, 72
  production, 60, 72
  sales, 72
  sales, US, 76
  shortage of, 63–64
  substitutes, 63
  textile industry, 67, 70
  trade, 59
Cotton Supply Association, 70
Coventry, raid on, 189
Covid, 225
creative destruction, 219
Crimea, 114
Cuba, 23
  alliance with USSR, 15
  economic liberalisation, 232
  economy of, 217
  GDP per capita, 233
  life expectancy, 218
Cuban missile crisis, 23
currency, manipulation of, 120
Czechoslovakia, 226

debt
  default of, 4
  sovereign, 4, 32
decolonisation, 248
Denmark, 44, 46
deportations, forced, 103
deterrence, 178
diamonds, 243
diplomacy, 32, 144, 150, 180
disarmament, 23, 114, 116, 136
Disarmament Conference, 116

displacement effect, 19–20
Dolchstoss Legende. *See* stab in the back myth
doux commerce ideology, 39
Dreadnought, 130
Du Tot, Nicolas, 40
Dunkirk, 34
Dutch East India Company, 243
Dutch East Indies, 149, 155–157

Eastern Europe, 15, 104, 107, 194, 217, 227–230
 capital stock, 235
Eastern front, 184
economic cooperation
 among the Allies, 183
 between Italy and Germany, 127
economic planning, 217
economic warfare, 4–5, 31–32, 50
 abandonment of, 50
 adaptation to, 16
 as complement to military action, 82
 definition of, 250
 effect of, 4, 18, 20, 22–23, 49, 184, 203–204, 210
 with genocidal intent, 96
 irrelevance of, 7
 in maritime conflict, 32
 protracted, 21, 25, 211
 public discourse of, 2
 purpose of, 2
 success of, 43, 212
 types of, 28, 176, 240
economising, 18, 24, 85, 88, 108, 198
Eden, Treaty of, 42
Eden, Anthony, 147
Egypt, 67, 69–70, 72
emancipation, 77
Emancipation Proclamation, 65–66, 70
embargo, 125, 216
 arms, 11, 145, 256
 consequences of, 232
 Cuban, 218
 export, 5
 legal, 6
 list, 225
 moral, 148
 naval, 60
 oil, 117–119, 123, 126, 147, 170
 oil crisis of 1973, 255–256
 steel scrap, 170
 technology, 228
 trade, 4, 226
 voluntary, 255
energy crisis, 255

England. *See* Britain
Eritrea, 115
espionage
 economic importance of, 221
 effects of, 223
 industrial, 216, 235
 industrial, fear of, 220
 of military capabilities, 223
 Stasi, 227
Ethiopia, 115, 119
 annexation of, 116
 invasion of, 10, 23, 120, 250–251
 military, 115
European Union, 256
exhaustion, 19, 21, 25
explosives, 104

fascism, 114–115, 120, 133–136
 economic doctrine, 120
fertiliser, 21, 93, 99–100, 104
fighting power, 4–5
film, 133
financial crisis of 2008, 225
firearms, 68, 125
fiscal states, 32
food shortage, 63, 103, 107, 208
foreign direct investment, 260
foreign exchange, 119, 259
France
 army, 48
 bankruptcy, 35, 40, 42
 colonies, 41
 cooperation with Allies, 177
 debt, 35
 defeat of, 20, 30
 economy of, 36
 fall of, 180–182, 184, 190
 industrialisation, 45
 invasion of, 185
 military spending, 128–130
 naval tonnage, 131
 navy, 33–34, 39–42, 50
 policy, 47
 protective duties, 72
 shipping capacity, 182
 textile industry, 72
 textile trade, 49
 trade, 42, 44–45, 49
French Revolution, 31, 39, 42, 50
fuel, 148, 254
 shortage, 104

genocide, 96, 178
German High Seas Fleet. *See* Germany, navy

Index

Germany
  agriculture, 10, 98, 106–107
  air defence, 15, 186, 197
  air force, 179, 189, 197–198, 211
  balance of payments, 120
  bias, 8
  capital stock, 198
  conquest of the East, 178, 194
  cooperation with Italy, 184
  currency devaluation, 100
  defeat of, 19–20, 22
  domestic consumption, 195–196
  domestic investment, 195
  domestic production, 21, 99–101, 104, 108, 196, 199, 201
  Drang nach Osten, 15
  East, 222, 224, 226, 234
  economic policies, 114
  economy of, 10–11, 100–101, 180
  ersatz goods, 104, 108
  exploitation of occupied territories, 195–196
  exports, 98
  food consumption, 99, 105
  food production, 97
  food supply, 100, 102–103
  Gross National Product, 195
  housing stock, 198
  imports, 21, 93, 98–100, 107, 195
  industry, 179
  malnutrition, 177
  marriage of rye and iron, 83
  merchant fleet, 101–102
  metal mobilisation, 104
  military spending, 128
  mobilisation, 10, 19, 21, 100, 106, 108, 204
  naval policy, 102
  naval tonnage, 131
  navy, 85, 102, 108, 178
  pig massacre, 103
  public health, 205
  rearmament, 22
  reunification, 223
  trade with Soviet Union, 180
  unification, 82, 231, 234
Gettysburg
  Address, 64
  victory, 73
Ghana, 248–250
Gibraltar, 94
globalisation, 263
gold, 64, 243, 254
  as means of payment, 3
Gone with the Wind, 75

government controls, 90, 132, 153
grain
  battle for, 120
  invasion, 83
  prices, 83, 104
  production, 91, 109
  rationing, 90, 102
Great Depression, 116, 121, 123, 125
Great East Asia Co-Prosperity Sphere, 156–157, 170
Greece, 118, 190
greenbacks, 65
growth
  endogenous, 219
  post-war, 225
  Schumpeterian, 219, 226
  Smithian, 219, 231
growth theory, modern, 218

Haber–Bosch process, 104
Hague Convention, 84
Hammond, James Henry, 56
Hankey, Maurice, 144
Heckscher, Eli, 45
Hemingway, Ernest, 20
Hindenburg Programme, 100
Hitler, Adolf, 18, 178, 184
  alliance with Mussolini, 125
Hoover, Herbert, 143
human capital, 218, 220
hunger, 19

imperial preference, 105
indemnities, 47
India, 43, 67, 69–70, 72, 247, 255
  tax revenue, 70
Indian Rebellion, 70
Indochina, 149, 154–155, 160
industrial dispersal, 198
industrial espionage, 12
industrialisation, 219
infections, 193, 205
inflation, 121
  during the American Civil War, 65
infrastructure, 19, 101, 151, 224, 252, 254
institutions, 42, 217
  local, 243
interest rates, 69
iron, 18, 23, 64–65, 89, 103, 120, 149, 152, 154, 162, 177, 181, 212
Iron Curtain, 231
isolationism, 146
Italo-Ethiopian War
  Second, 114, 117, 123

Italy, 46, 114
  alignment with Germany, 128, 137, 184
  alignment with Germany and Japan, 126
  balance of payments, 120
  colonial empire, 15, 115, 120, 123
  colonial expenditures, 133
  economy of, 116, 120
  energy dependence, 126
  energy supply, 118–119
  entry into World War II, 180
  exports, 10, 115, 119, 121, 125
  fiscal policy, 123
  foreign policy, 120
  foreign trade, 136
  imports, 121, 124, 126
  military capacity, 131
  military spending, 128–130
  naval tonnage, 130
  navy, 130
  new towns, 120
  public spending, 123
  trade, 127

Japan
  army of, 150
  balance of payments, 153
  children's heights, 167
  colonial empire, 10, 15
  defeat of, 19–20, 22
  domestic production, 162, 167
  economic collapse of, 11
  economic policies, 114
  economy of, 23, 142, 147
  entry into World War II, 117
  Five Year Plan, 152
  food consumption, 167
  freezing of assets, 155
  imports, 155, 164
  industry of, 154, 160
  Issekikai, 150
  merchant fleet, 157–160, 166
  military spending, 128, 167
  mobilisation, 19, 23
  navy, 157
  production of aircraft, 152
  real gross national product, 166
  relations with Britain, 145, 147
  seizure of assets, 147
  ship building, 158–160, 166, 168
  textile industry, 145
Japan–Manchukuo Protocol, 151
Japan–United States Commerce and
    Navigation Treaty, 154
Jay Treaty, 44
Jefferson's Embargo, 76

Jews, 107
  expulsion of, 63
Jutland, Battle of, 15, 102

Kenya, GDP, 257
Keynes, John Maynard, 3

labour
  drain, 75
  forced, 196
  mobility, 216, 244
  movement, 70
  productivity, 226–227
  shortage, 104
  unskilled, 65
Lancashire, 67, 70, 145
land
  ownership in Africa, 244
  seizure of, 243
Laws of Naval War, 93
League of Armed Neutrality, 41
  Second, 44
League of Nations, 113–114, 123, 127,
    133, 143
  abandonment of sanctions, 23
  Article Sixteen, 113, 117–118, 144, 147,
    249
  Charter of, 2, 4
  decision making, 115, 126–127
  enforcement capabilities, 116
  establishment of, 117
  mandate territories, 241
  opposition to sanctions, 143
  public opinion of, 138
  raison d'etre, 136
  sanctions clause, 76
Leith-Ross, Frederick, 146
Lend–Lease Act, 148
Leontief, Wassily, 179
liberal international order, 50
liberalism, 30, 45
Libya, 120
licensing system, 63
Lincoln, Abraham, 59, 63–66, 70–71, 74
  letter to, 71
linen, Irish, 68, 72
Liverpool, 72
living standards
  Cuba, 218
  in Japan, 168
Lloyd George, David, 85, 90–91
Lloyd's list, 44
loans
  to China, 147–149
  international, 146

Index

lobbying, 145
London, 189
  bond market, 73
  capital market, 48
Ludendorff Offensive, 106
Luftwaffe. *See* Germany, air force
Lusitania, attack on, 84
Lytton Commission, 144–145

Maastricht Treaty, 5
Macon's Bill Number 2, 46
maize, 244
Malawi, 246, 252
Malaya, 156
malnutrition, 96
Malta, 45
Manchester, 71
Manchukuo, 144
  buffer regimes, 146
  Emperor of, 151
  legitimacy of, 145
Manchuria
  economic plan for, 151
  economy of, 151–152
  invasion of, 23, 142–143, 151
  investment in, 146
  Japanese aggression, 116
  response to invasion of, 143
Mandela, Nelson, 240, 242
March to the Sea. *See* Sherman, William Tecumseh
market controls, 177
Marshall Plan, 224
means of payment, 3
mercantilism, 3, 28, 30, 37, 45, 50
Metal Collection Act, 162
Mexico, 72, 77
microchips, 216
Midway Sea Battle, 158
military alliance, 113
military capacity, 131–133, 137
military revolution, 32
minerals, 243, 259
mining, 104, 108, 245, 247, 259
Ministry of Economic Warfare, 2
Mises, Ludwig von, 221
monopoly, 77
morale
  during the American Civil War, 63, 75
  breaking of, 179
  British, 190, 193
  civilian, 176
  German, 185, 203, 205, 208, 212
  during World War I, 107, 177
  during World War II, 184

morbidity, 208
mortality
  adult, 191
  of German civilians, 203
  infant, 191, 208, 218, 232
  World War I, 97
Mukden incident, 144
munitions, 93
  shortages, 60
Mussolini, Benito, 10, 115–116, 120, 250
  public support for, 133–137
  rallies, 133

Nagano, Shushin, 157
Namibia, 251
Nanjing, 143, 146, 153
Napoleon III, 72
Napoleon, Bonaparte, 31, 45–47, 50, 250
Napoleonic Milan Decree, 45
Napoleonic Wars, 3, 16, 53, 218
national income accounting, 3
nationalisation, 232, 258
navicert system, 94, 181
Navigation Acts, 82
Netherlands, The, 93, 149
neutral shipping, 38–39, 41, 44–45, 47, 85, 93
New History of Capitalism, 63, 76–77
newspapers, 134
Nigeria, 255
  GDP, 257
Nine Power Treaty, 147
Nine Years War, 34, 38
Nixon Doctrine, 254
Nixon, Richard, 221, 254
Non-Intercourse Act, 46
Normandy landings, 197, 211
North Africa, 180
North Sea, 84
Norway, 46
  shipping capacity, 182
nuclear
  bomb, 22, 223
  energy, 223
  technologies, 216
  weapons, 255
nutritional deprivation, 99
Nutter, Warren, 221

oats, 105
oil, 18, 23, 56, 103, 117–118, 120, 123, 126, 137, 147, 149, 155, 177, 212, 255–256, 260–261
  synthetic, 180, 186, 212
Olson, Mançur, 16–17, 77

Olympic Games, 256
OPEC, 256
Ottoman Empire, 36, 118

Pacific War, 143, 157, 164, 169
Pact of Steel, 126
Paraguay, 118
Paris
  banking firms, 73
  Treaty of, 41
peace, 31
  treaty, 30
Peace of Amiens, 45
Pearl Harbor, attack on, 11, 15, 157
petroleum, 154–155, 160
physiocracy, 40
Poland, 103
Poor Law, 67–68
Population Registration Act, 246
Portugal, 241, 247
price controls, 99, 102, 204
price guarantees, 105
prisoner exchanges, 40
prisoners of war, 45
privateering, 31, 33–34, 38, 43–44
productivity, catch-up, 231
productivity shocks, 228–229
propaganda, 96, 133–134, 232
protectionism, 45, 107, 145
Prussia, 42, 45–46, 82
public finance, 40, 49
public relief programmes, 67
Putin, Vladimir, 7
Puyi. *See* Manchukuo

Quesnay, Francois, 40

racial segregation, of schools, 243, 246
radio, 133
RAF Bomber Command, 185, 188
raiding, 6, 8–9, 13, 15, 21
railways, 60, 100, 143, 151, 180, 186, 190, 198, 201, 212, 254
  destruction of, 75
  hub, 74
rationing, 17, 95–96, 102, 108, 190, 204
  formal, 90
  grain, 102
  voluntary, 90
raw materials, 93
Reagan, Ronald, 256
rearmament, 129, 189
recycling, 104, 108
regime change, 232
repression, 5, 243, 257
Republican Party, 56
resistance
  against Japan, 146, 148
  against Nazis, 209
Rhodes, Cecil, 243
Rhodesia. *See* Southern Rhodesia
right of convoys, 41
Romania, 103
Roosevelt, Franklin, 146, 148, 150
rubber, 154, 177, 186, 212, 220
Ruhr campaign, 201
Russia, 44, 46, 112, 117, 127
  bias, 8
Russo-Japanese War, 151

sabotage, 6, 103
Saint-Domingue, declaration of independence, 46
Salazar, Antonio, 247
Saltier, Arthur, 117
sanctions
  affecting neighbour states, 251
  anti-apartheid, 242
  anticipation of, 18
  birth of, 7, 76, 112
  counter-, 15
  on cultural and sports events, 255
  economic, 115, 137, 142, 154
  effectiveness of, 5, 22, 113, 252, 257, 263
  effects of, 6–7, 12–13, 116, 119, 125, 133, 147
  enforcement of, 5, 253
  ethics of, 251
  evasion of, 262
  failure of, 10, 13, 22, 124, 127–128, 138
  Global Sanctions Database, 114
  informal, 249
  legal foundations of, 4
  mandatory, 255
  on neutrals, 180
  perception of, xvii, 107, 114, 117, 136, 144
  to promote regime change, 216
  secondary, 249
  super-, 4
  on trade and investment, 113
  types of, 114, 249, 251
  unintended consequences of, 125
  vulnerability to, 148
savings banks, 64
Scandinavia, 93–94
scorched-earth practices, 32
scurvy, 43

Index

sectoral shifts, 219, 262
sender and target, 8, 14, 24
Senegal, 250
Serbia, 118
Seven Years War, 38, 40–41
Seward, William, 56
sharecropping system, 72
Sharpeville Massacre, 255
Sherman, William Tecumseh, 74–76
ship
  building, 87, 108, 158
  capture, 34, 38, 40, 43
  copper coating, 43
shipping capacity, Allied, 87
siege, 64
silk, 42
silver, 64
  prices, 146
silver standard, 146
Sino-Japanese War, 146
  expansion of, 148
  Second, 143, 153
slavery, 56, 70–71, 74
  compensation of owners, 66
smuggling, 15, 49
social instability, 168, 190
socialism, 233
Somalia, 115, 120
South Africa
  agriculture, 245
  arms industry, 261
  British citizenship, 246
  cotton production, 70
  currency, 246
  domestic economy, 247
  elections, 244
  end of white minority rule, 252
  energy consumption, 261
  exports, 259
  GDP, 244, 257
  investment, 243
  manufacturing, 244, 257
  strikes, 245
  synthetic oil industry, 12
  trade with neighbours, 255
South African War, 243
South Sea Company, 37
Southern Rhodesia
  declaration of independence, 241, 246, 248, 252–253, 258
  domestic economy, 247, 251
  end of white minority rule, 252
  energy consumption, 261
  exports, 249
  freezing of assets, 253

GDP, 244, 257
infrastructure, 252
investment, 246
Kariba Dam, 246, 254, 261
manufacturing, 244, 247, 257, 261
self-governing status, 244
strikes, 245
Soviet Union
  aid from Britain, 183
  cooperation with Allies, 177
  economic growth, 221
  Five Year Plan, 152
  GDP per capita, 221
  industrial capacity, 221
  support for China, 149
Soweto Uprising, 256
Spain
  colonial empire, 33, 40
  navy, 37
Special Department for European War History, 157
speculation, 62, 73
Speer, Albert, 196, 208
stab in the back myth, 106
starvation, 21, 28, 34, 96
starving out. See *Aushungerung*
Stasi (Ministry for State Security in the German Democratic Republic), 222, 227
state intervention, 257, 262–263
steel, 89, 162, 212
stockpiling, 24
strike, 149, 177, 245
submarine
  attacks, 158, 170, 182
  blockade, 11, 13, 91
  blockade, failure of, 92
  German fleet, 10, 181
  offensive, 189
  role in world wars, 178
  warfare, 84–85, 88, 90, 95, 102, 157
subsidies, 105, 191
substitution, 17–20, 77, 92, 104, 108, 124, 166, 194, 210, 218
  import, 15, 18, 24, 85, 121, 128, 218–219, 225, 256, 262
  import, policies, 232
Suez, 94
sugar, 90
Sullivan Principles, 256
superpower status, 77
supply chain, 43
  disruptions, 77
Sweden, 44, 46, 181
Switzerland, 46, 95, 181

Index

Tanzania, 254
tariffs, 83, 105, 107
taxation, 33, 47
technology, obsolescence, 219, 228
telegraph, 75, 101–102
telephone, 101
Texas, annexation of, 76
Thirty Years War, 32
timber, 89
tobacco, 251, 258
Tobacco Corporation, 259, 261
total factor productivity (TFP), 222, 225, 228
   in Eastern Europe, 231
Trabant, 231
trade, 19
   agreements, 181
   Atlantic, 32, 40
   ban, 34
   collapse of, 124
   colonial, 46
   diversion, 226
   entrepot, 49
   flows, 124
   free, 82
   imbalances, 69
   neutral, 180
   policy, 45, 107
   restrictions, 148–149
   surplus, 33
   talks, 30
   theory, 45
   treaties, 42
Trafalgar, Battle of, 46
transportation
   costs, 243
   improvements, 83
Treasury theory, 5, 119
treaty, 9
   commercial, 30
   trade, 45
Tripartite Pact, 148, 154
Turkey, 94
Tyler, John, 76

US Export Control Act, 224
Uganda, 245
Ukraine, 181
   Russian invasion of, xviii, 7, 112
unemployment, 67, 70
uniforms, during the American Civil War, 63
United Kingdom. *See* Britain
United Nations
   Article 16, failure of, 250
   Charter, 2, 5, 113
   discrimination in South Africa, 247
   enforcement mechanisms, 252
   General Assembly, 242
   limits of, 248
   stance against Rhodesia, 253
United States Neutrality Act, 146
United States of America, 94
   air force, 179, 186
   civil rights, 251, 254
   cooperation with Allies, 177
   debt, 73
   domestic production, 60
   entry into World War I, 95, 102
   exports, 58, 60, 76, 95, 149, 160
   financial system, 76
   infrastructure, 63, 67
   merchant fleet, 69
   navy, 157–158, 166, 170
   shipbuilding, 182
   shipping capacity, 182
   shipping earnings, 47
   superpower, 44
uranium, 254
urbanisation, 245
Utrecht, Treaty of, 31, 35

Vauban, Sébastien Le Prestre, 33
Versailles, Treaty of, 106
Vienna
   Congress of, 50
   Treaty of, 30
V-weapon, 179, 210

wages, real, 65
war
   of attrition, 4, 9, 11, 32, 176, 197, 211
   financing, 3, 35, 38, 100
   materials, 90
   nuclear, 6
   readiness for, 22–23, 25
   short, 18
   support for, 56
   total, 74, 112, 150
   trade, 28, 50
war crimes, 115
War of American Independence, 38
War of Austrian Succession, 38
War of Jenkin's Ear, 37
War of Spanish Succession, 36
War of the Quadruple Alliance, 38
War of the Spanish Succession, 33–34
warfare
   anti-submarine, 15, 157, 183
   gas, 117

Index 277

industrialisation of, 3
psychological, 6
Washington Conference, 185
weapons, 123, 125–126
  chemical, 115
  imports of, 137
  of mass destruction, 117, 223
West Indies, 34, 39, 49
wheat, 105
white supremacy, 12
Wilson, Harold, 253
Wilson, Woodrow, 76, 118
wood, 89
wool, 63–64, 72
  textiles, 68
World Cup, 256

World War I, 10–11, 13, 15, 21–22, 82, 89, 107, 116, 150, 178
  armistice, 106
World War II, 11, 13, 15, 22–23, 105, 176
  attrition, 4
  Eastern front, 212
  lead-up to, 116
  outbreak of, 154

Yorktown, Battle of, 41
Young, Andrew, 255
Yugoslavia, 118

Zambia, 246, 252, 254
  independence, 254
Zollverein, 82